ARCHITECTURE
INSIDE + OUT

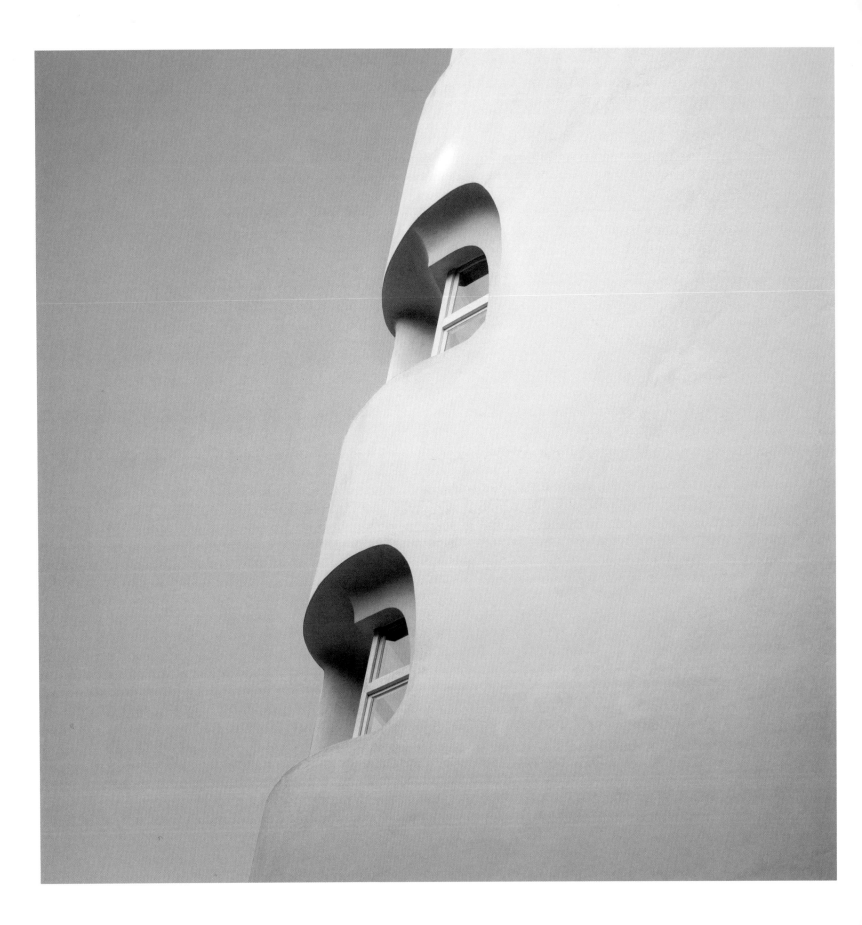

ARCHITECTURE INSIDE + OUT

50 Iconic Buildings In Detail

John Zukowsky & Robbie Polley

Thames & Hudson

Contents

Arts and Education 112

Living 180

Worship 234

Introduction

Author

John Zukowsky

If you were to glance only at this book's table of contents, you might question whether another volume about the greatest landmarks of the world is really needed. What more can be said about fifty great buildings like the Parthenon, Colosseum, Hagia Sophia or Chartres Cathedral? Indeed, this book includes internationally recognized monuments such as those and more – world-class constructions that are recognized by UNESCO (the United Nations Educational, Scientific and Cultural Organization) and appropriately placed on their World Heritage List. This book, however, also includes some more recent buildings whose distinctive appearance and design solutions may well make them international landmarks beyond our own era. Any of the buildings in this book are equivalent to significant works of fine art – masterpieces if you will. They deserve more than just a few glances. As with all great works of art, revisiting them often reveals aspects hitherto unnoticed. They can constantly educate us about the accomplishments of their creators and the values of the societies within which they were built.

This book intends to provide some of the historic and socio-cultural context for the creation of the buildings described within. The selections include some of the 'usual suspects' as well as a few buildings that might surprise you. If your favourite is missing, we apologize and can only state that narrowing down the world's monuments to fifty examples is indeed a daunting task. There was much debate over the course of our team-based selection, as is perhaps inevitable with survey books of this nature. But whatever our final choice and the means of getting there, all of the featured buildings are visually interpreted through the cutaway sketches of accomplished architectural illustrator Robbie Polley. His compelling studies offer you pictorial insights into those constructions, as seen through the analytical eyes of an architectural renderer today. Polley's drawings also serve as a reminder that architecture starts with an idea, and usually one expressed on paper. This has been the case at least since the Middle Ages, and possibly even antiquity. Perhaps the earliest extant drawing is the schematic monastic Plan of St Gall (c. 817–23) assembled on five pieces of sewn parchment, housed within the Stiftsbibliothek Sankt Gallen (Abbey library of Saint Gall) in Switzerland. Some 500 other medieval architectural drawings on parchment from the thirteenth to the sixteenth centuries survive in a variety of European archives, many of them within the Academy of Fine Arts in Vienna.

The process of going from drawing to building is an established one. A napkin sketch with a somewhat spontaneous preliminary design might develop into a more believable perspective rendering for a client, who might then use it as a sales and marketing tool for the project. If the project moves ahead, a variety of design development and then more detailed, scaled working drawings, with building material indications and specifications, are all created to physically construct the building. The latter often include what are called shop drawings, which are initiated by the contractor and contain even greater detail. Nowadays the sequence might start with an idea that a designer develops on a laptop into a 3D spatial model using one of more than seventy programs. When the project gets the go-ahead, those data are used by another program, or an expansion of the initially selected program, to create the relevant documents used to build it. Beyond that, BIM (Building Information Modelling) programs are utilized to coordinate design, construction and even maintenance plans in a virtually paperless process. Whether through old-fashioned pencil or pen drawings on paper or via computer programs, architecture starts with a structural and spatial concept – an idea made into reality through the design process and its documents, whether in electronic or hard copy form.

After a building is constructed, recording drawings are sometimes created. These can include personalized travel sketches, which can be visually akin to initial conceptual sketches. They might also include finished presentation renderings, like those used in nineteenth-century publications as a promotional record of completed buildings. More importantly, they may include clinical, measured drawings that serve as important historic documents – and that might one day help to restore and even reconstruct a building, especially if the working drawings no longer survive. The illustrations published here are essentially Robbie Polley's recording drawings of these world landmarks. As with a travel sketch, they are his interpretation of the building. But they are much more than that; they are also analytical. His perspective cutaways and sections reveal spatial and structural relationships within each of the sites. The places are further illuminated through striking colour photographs and fascinating discussions chronicling important historical facts and little-known details.

The book is organized into thematic chapters. In some cases you might think an entry could have been included within another chapter, and that may well be true. But you might also acknowledge that those entries are multifaceted in their functions, as are many buildings. Indeed, functions can also change over time. Temples and cathedrals often served urban functions beyond their intended religious purpose. Religious buildings may also sometimes serve multiple faiths over time. The structuring of the chapters attempts to balance out the inclusion of buildings within five categories: Public Life, Monuments, Arts and Education, Living and Worship.

The first chapter on Public Life spans examples from antiquity to the present. It includes a palace planned as a military camp that was later subsumed by a city. Also featured are sports complexes, a skyscraper at the centre of urban development and legislative buildings, as well as air and rail transportation structures. The second chapter on Monuments has established favourites from antiquity through to the twentieth century. These encompass a temple, funerary monuments, a private home and estate, a palace complex, and a tiny observatory. The third chapter on Arts and Education highlights cultural buildings from the nineteenth century through to today, including structures for the visual and performing arts as well as those that record historic events. Overall, it is museums that come to the forefront of this chapter. These buildings chronicle our struggles and accomplishments, having become today's secular temples to human history. The fourth chapter on Living looks at examples of shelter, the primal function of architecture, though here existing in forms that extend well beyond the basics. Examples range from a fifteenth-century almshouse to spectacular private homes built over five centuries to creatively conceived high-rises. The fifth and final chapter on Worship focuses on a range of churches, mosques and temples that have been built over the past 1,500 years. Among the most interesting are the ones that have served multiple religions, having been adapted from one to another according to the historic situation. Many demonstrate the power of faith and the dedication of the faithful over decades and longer to complete tangible expressions of their beliefs.

This volume's uniqueness lies in its illustrative approach, taking you behind the facades and finishes to understand how some of the most important buildings in the world were constructed. Describing each structure both literally and visually, it aims to simulate the experience of spending time with the architects themselves, providing a deeper understanding of the thinking and expertise behind their designs. It is a chronicle of humanity's architectural achievements over two millennia – achievements that will continue to wow observers for centuries to come, even as future architects add to the list of the world's great monuments.

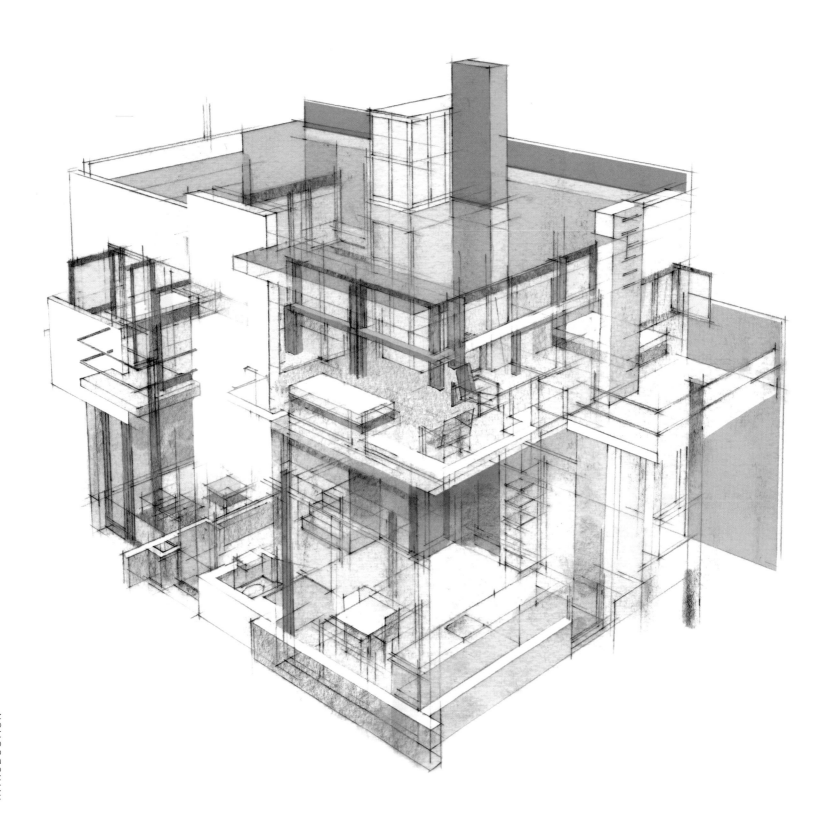

Artist
Robbie Polley

My passion for drawing architecture manifested itself during my first years of living in London, when I started drawing and painting West End theatre facades 'plein air'. Their combination of ornate stonework and garish illuminated lettering was irresistible to this trained graphic designer with an enthusiasm for drawing. I am sure the 1960s boys' comics of my childhood – with their wonderfully detailed exploded views of skyscrapers, ocean liners and jet planes – must have contributed to my early obsession with technical images. Whatever it was that ignited the spark, I love drawing buildings.

Sketching or painting any object makes you focus, look harder and therefore better understand it. While drawing a building is in a sense no different from drawing a plate of pears or a wooden chair, the complexity of the task can seem overwhelming at first. After analyzing a seemingly complicated design, it should be possible to reduce it to a set of simple visual ideas. In studying a building through drawing, the aim is to get closer to its architectural truth. On that journey it is also possible to become better acquainted with the architect's original vision.

My architectural drawings are usually visualized through my mind's eye. We each perceive spaces in a highly individual and personal manner, but using the mind's eye is the only way to really get inside a building when trying to understand it, especially when using a combination of plans and photos as reference. How we perceive and communicate this interaction is then reflected in a sketch. Though quite tightly bound by a building's form, the sketching style can still be loose – choosing from a range of techniques and scale, and varying amounts of detail. Everyone will have a different response to an architectural space and how to visually interpret it.

I have a theory that drawing an object that doesn't exist frees up the drawing style. When drawing from the mind's eye, we're liberated from the act of trying to recreate what's in front of us. We are free to express the imagined image. This lack of inhibition is important. The drawing itself becomes the object; the drawing visualizes the image in the mind's eye.

In this way I have often found sculptors' drawings more interesting than the solid, finished sculpture. They can convey an immediacy, a spontaneity that's more revealing, compelling – perhaps even more honest – than a hardened, lifeless bronze or stone statue.

My workflow usually consists of drawing a series of sketches to build up a view, then fine-tuning them for the final drawing. I like to use different papers – whatever suits the particular illustration – but always start with a base image made using the computer, from plans and/or sections. This base image can be in perspective or in axonometric, angled projection. I then draw over this, on a light box, creating the different three-dimensional elements needed to make the building simple to understand.

I have a great admiration for 'draughtsmanship', although the term is a rather traditional one and is sometimes used to deride a drawing that is felt to be stiff or unemotional. It speaks of drawing as a craft rather than as an art. But it is possible for a drawing to be precise and still be expressive: precision is a form of expression, too. And why be narrow-minded when drawing can be so liberating? After all, rulers (especially plastic ones) are there to be broken.

The visualization of each architectural space should be approached in a style that best suits the individual structure. Some buildings have an important feature that must be emphasized, like a domed roof or amazing concert space. A simple roof-off drawing can work in those cases, especially for a single-storey building. But you still must find the angle of view or projection type that presents the whole building at its best while showing off those key features. In contrast, how do you start to explain a multi-level building?

Some buildings are almost impossible to explain in a single view. The more you explode the architecture, the more the original (and sometimes simple) concept can be lost. The best exploded views are therefore those that simplify the architecture, exposing only areas of the building that clarify the original design.

What is removed from a building when drawing it must also be carefully considered. I find it best to visualize the building as a wooden model that can be sliced apart. Slice with care, with straight cuts or curved, and you can usefully reveal the innards of the building. Take too much and you are left with a pile of unsupported walls and fictional structures.

In the end, the drawing must be strong enough to be appreciated in its own right. It can be an accurate interpretation of the building as well as an aesthetically pleasing image. An expressive drawing can reveal something new that would be lost in an overly technical architectural illustration.

Although computers are now commonly used to design and visualize buildings, a good handmade drawing has something special that cannot be replicated by a digital image. As viewers, we respond to drawings or paintings differently from the way we respond to mechanized, realistic computer-rendered images. We look not just at the architecture, but also at the way the drawing and maker have interpreted the building. A computer-generated image has less humanity. Perhaps it is just too real.

The pencil, which I have used exclusively for the drawings in this book, is arguably the purest of mark-making tools. It is still the first thing to my hand when devising an original sketch. And although I do incorporate some computer imaging, nothing can really beat the feel of paper and pencil. The pencil can tease or tap-dance across a paper's knotty surface, leaving any variety of graphite trails. It is fun to consider which quality of line will best describe an ancient stone edge or a modern glass balustrade. A pencil mark can describe anything, with unique individuality.

All artists have their favourite pencils. Mine is the Blackwing 602, apparently the kind used by Jack Kerouac. Though better known as a novelist and poet than as an artist, Kerouac did sketch and might have appreciated the lead's oily, inky quality. Choosing when to draw freehand and when to use a ruler or set square for a straight edge line is crucial, but combining a 'fast' pencil line with a 'slow' one can be used to great effect. Every drawing needs a variety of tones.

However, perhaps the most important decision when setting up a drawing is scale. Drawing a massive building on a sheet that is too small will limit the message, defining only the overall space while missing its tactile qualities; the building's details and materials will be lost.

The plans created by architects of the pre-computer age are often beautiful things. I am thinking in particular of Frank Lloyd Wright's watercolour plans or Christopher Wren's ornate ink drawings. I find beauty in the way that a form that is mechanized, engineered and logically structured can be represented through a handmade image that is human and tactile. Such works are an elegant reminder that every building intended to last for hundreds of years has to start with just a single, simple, hand-drawn line.

In the drawings for this book I have tried to humanize complicated buildings and three-dimensional architectural concepts that can be quite hard to fully understand. My hope is that I have achieved this aim by creating drawings that are tactile, technically factual and intriguing, but most importantly pleasing to the eye.

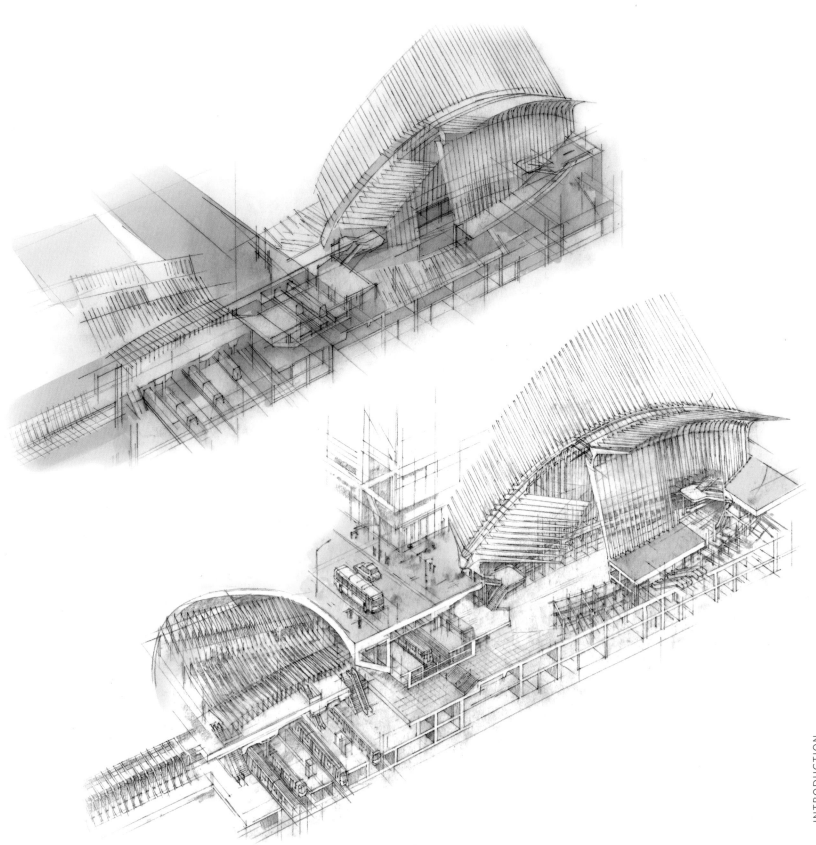

Public Life

DOGE'S PALACE (SEE P. 28)

When people see the word 'public' associated with architecture they immediately think of civic buildings – structures built by governments, often financed by taxes paid by that public, to provide citizens with essential services. These might include post offices, police and fire stations, refuse facilities, transportation structures, city halls and various legislative structures, governmental office buildings and courthouses, among many other architectural types. The most predictably prominent are legislative structures built to house the law-making bodies whose representatives are chosen by the public. These bodies derive from medieval councils or parliaments, and are sometimes divided into two (or more) separate assemblies. The two-chamber system developed in England from the thirteenth to the eighteenth centuries has been the model for numerous other parliamentary systems. In many ways, then, England is the mother of such democratic assemblies throughout the world today, with the famed Houses of Parliament, the Palace of Westminster (1840–70) designed by Charles Barry (1795–1860) and Augustus Pugin (1812–52), as the centrepiece of its two-chamber assembly. Its Gothic Revival style pays homage to the creation of England's parliament that can trace its heritage back to the thirteenth century and the signing of the Magna Carta in 1215, which established basic freedoms of noblemen from arbitrary royal punishment. Other legislative assemblies are equally prominent, though in different styles. In this volume they span six centuries, with examples from Bangladesh, Germany, India, Italy and the United States.

Of those five examples, four project an image that relates in some ways to the classical tradition of centrally planned, often domical structures. Architects have long considered the governmental assembly buildings in Chandigarh, India (1952–61), by Le Corbusier (1887–1965), and those in Dhaka in Bangladesh (1962–82) by Louis Kahn (1901–74) to be among the great twentieth-century

architectural pilgrimage sites in the world. Berlin's Reichstag (1884–94) has more recently joined that club because of the addition of a spectacular steel and glass dome (1999) designed by Norman Foster (b. 1935). The Capitol building (1792–1891) in Washington, D.C., perhaps because of its architectural changes over two centuries, is not in the same league in terms of governmental design. Yet it is an internationally recognized symbol of the United States, a major tourist attraction that eclipses its governmental function far beyond those three twentieth-century landmarks. All four buildings, erected during the nineteenth and twentieth centuries, were essentially specialized to focus on the legislative functions of government. A fifth example, the Doge's Palace in Venice (1340–1614 and later), also incorporated a legislative role with a Grand Council Chamber, but it was a multifunctional government structure in terms of having ducal residential quarters along with judicial and prison spaces that expanded over some three centuries.

This chapter also includes internationally significant recreational and transportation structures. The recreational buildings analyzed here span millennia, from antiquity through to the present – Rome's Colosseum (c. 72–80 CE) and the London Aquatics Centre (2012). Both were designed as major sports and entertainment venues, and both were intended to serve their urban communities. The Colosseum, with tiered stadium seating accommodating spectators in the tens of thousands, has served as the conceptual model for major sports facilities since antiquity. Though smaller, the London Aquatics Centre was planned to accommodate Olympic spectator crowds with temporary stands that were removed afterwards, when the building continued service as a community recreation centre.

Transportation sites in this chapter include two US examples – a mid-century modern classic as well as a high-profile newcomer: Washington Dulles International Airport (1958–62) and the World Trade Center Transit Hub (2004–16) in New York. Designed with

swooping curved forms by Eero Saarinen (1910–61) in an era
long before such imagery was made commonplace by today's
computer-design programs, Dulles made its mark as arguably
the first purpose-built airport to accommodate new jet-powered
airliners of the 1960s. The location in farmland and open
woodland kept such aircraft engine noise far from the city
of Washington, D.C. The World Trade Center Transit Hub
created by Santiago Calatrava (b. 1951) springs from the ground
as a giant symbol of peace – a dove. Its spacious commercial
atrium connects to suburban rail and urban subway systems,
as part of the revitalization of this site after the terrorist attacks
of 11 September 2001, destroyed nearby buildings. Over the past
five decades, Dulles has had a great impact on the ex-urban
growth of its site, with plans being implemented to connect
it to the city through an extension of the Metro rail system.
Likewise, the World Trade Center Transit Hub was built to
accommodate increased commuter traffic as new commercial
high-rise buildings are erected nearby.

Those examples of transportation buildings that relate to,
and even catalyze, adjacent economic growth bring to mind
the remaining two examples within this chapter that are integral
to the story of urban development – the Palace of Diocletian in
Split, Croatia (c. 295–305) and the Chrysler Building (1929–30)
in New York. The former was created as an imperial retirement
villa, whereas the latter is one of the world's great examples of a
commercial Art Deco skyscraper. Diocletian's palace was initially
arranged on the rectilinear, cross-axial plan of a Roman military
encampment. Built on the site of an earlier Greek settlement of the
second or third century BCE called Aspálathos, Diocletian's palace
and its 10,000 or so occupants grew into a Byzantine, Venetian and
then Austrian-Habsburg city through World War I (1914–18). Today
the population of Split is approximately 170,000, with more than
340,000 in the metropolitan area.

The Chrysler Building's location in midtown Manhattan,
within New York City, was one of several sites on 42nd Street that
witnessed the construction of similar tall commercial buildings.
The most important of these are the comparably detailed Chanin
Building (1929) by Irwin Chanin (1891–1988) and Sloan and
Robertson; the formidably arched Bowery Savings Bank, now
Cipriani's (1921–33), by York and Sawyer; and the Commodore
Hotel, now Grand Hyatt (1920), by Warren and Wetmore. This last
was rebuilt in 1980 by Der Scutt for Donald J. Trump, being that
real-estate entrepreneur's first major project. As with those other
buildings, the Chrysler owes its location to the development of
Grand Central Station (1913) by Reed and Stem, and the subsequent
replanning of Park Avenue into a grand boulevard. Post-1930s
Great Depression and post-World War II (1939–45) high-rises
boomed nearby, especially just north on Park Avenue. They also
filled in the blanks along 42nd Street because of the rail terminal's
role as a transportation hub. Today the terminal feeds the high-rises
nearby with more than 750,000 commuters daily, certainly making
the much-loved Chrysler an integral part of public life for a host
of pedestrians.

WORLD TRADE CENTER TRANSIT HUB (SEE P. 70)

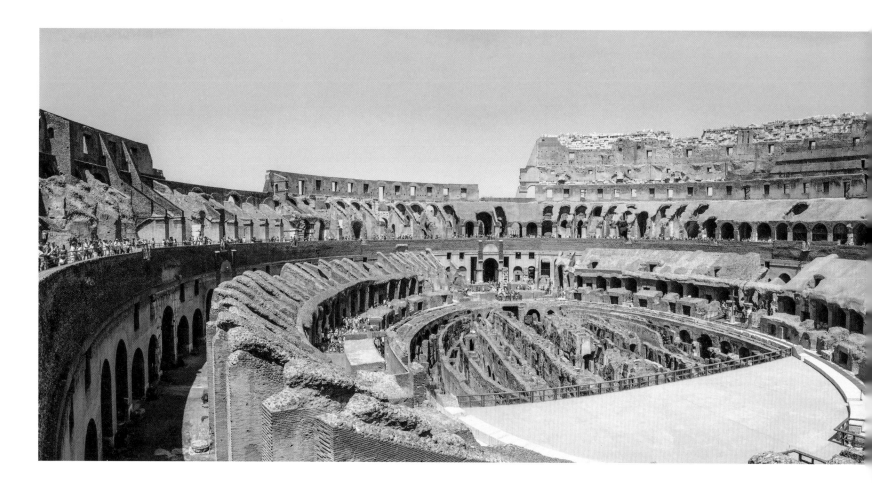

Colosseum

LOCATION   Rome, Italy
ARCHITECT   Unknown

STYLE   Roman Classicism
BUILT   c. 72–80 CE

Of historic ruins, the Colosseum is arguably the one that most captivates the public's imagination about the Roman Empire. It was the largest of such arenas, begun under Emperor Vespasian and finished between c. 72 and 80 CE under Emperor Titus, and measures 189 m (615 ft) long, 156 m (510 ft) wide and 48 m (157 ft) high. It is constructed of brick and concrete faced with travertine marble. Created as an amphitheatre – the main floor of which (above) could be flooded for mock naval battles – the complex underwent several modifications under Emperor Domitian that included enlargements to what would be its ultimate seating capacity for more than 80,000 spectators.

Vespasian chose this site on what was part of Emperor Nero's private grounds and villa, created after the Great Fire of Rome in 64 CE. The Colosseum's construction was funded by the sack of the temple in Jerusalem in 70 CE, which included booty as well as 100,000 Jewish slaves as part of the workforce. Its use during the empire ranged from gladiatorial conflicts and wild animal spectacles to classical dramas. These made it the centre of large-scale urban entertainment, much as stadia are used today for sporting events and rock concerts. The phrase 'bread and circuses', coined within decades of the building's completion, refers to the popularity of events there as well as the imperial tradition of giving the masses free grain to win public support. Even though the structure was originally called Amphitheatrum Flavium, the more popular term 'Colosseum', used since the Middle Ages, may have derived from the sculpture of Nero nearby, which was said to have been modelled on the Colossus of Rhodes.

After the various sacks of Rome and natural disasters in the fifth and sixth centuries, the building was still used but eventually fell into a partially ruined state. Medieval usage included as a cemetery as well as work and shop space, fortress and monastery, though a massive earthquake in 1349 sealed its fate as a ruin and, essentially, stone quarry. Papal officials lobbied for its reuse from the sixteenth through to the nineteenth centuries. Although it was used briefly for bullfights, its survival may, in part, be due to possible papal recognition of it as being sacred ground where Christians were martyred. In any case, the papacy helped initiate structural stabilization through the nineteenth century, prompting further national stabilization plans in the twentieth century, including under Benito Mussolini. Repairs and restoration work were conducted between 2013 and 2016. Because of its scale and history, the Colosseum remains one of the most visited attractions in Rome, receiving some 4 million visitors annually. The massive structure has served as a conceptual model for equally large sports arenas, from the Los Angeles Memorial Coliseum (1923) by John and Donald Parkinson, to the Olympic Stadium in Berlin (1936) by Werner March (1894–1976), to Houston's Astrodome (1965) by Lloyd and Morgan.

HISTORY PAINTING

History paintings that showed important people and events were akin to feature films such as *Gladiator* (2000), capturing what sports combat was like within the Colosseum. French artist Jean-Léon Gérôme's painting *Pollice Verso* (1872) was a comparable vision of that spectacle for nineteenth-century viewers. The artwork's title means 'Turned Thumb' or 'Thumbs Down', and it popularized the legend of imperial and aristocratic spectators in the lower levels determining the fate of defeated contestants.

LEFT Lower-level passages were created and floored over to house animals and gladiators in the Colosseum's often brutal spectacles. The top seating levels were likely ringed with a fabric awning called a *velarium*.

ABOVE Arcades of the Colosseum provide a formal expression of the tiers within. The travertine was quarried near Tivoli about 20 km (12 miles) from Rome. A road was said to have been built to transport the stones to Rome.

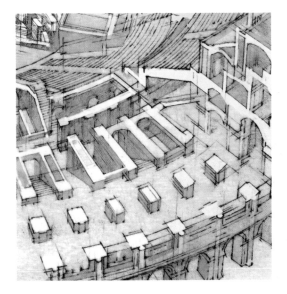

DESIGN

Like any stadium, circulation is foremost. The 80,000 spectators arrived through more than seventy-six entrances. There is tiered seating according to rank, starting with marble-covered senatorial seats furnished with portable cushions, then tiers of benches, and standing room only at the top for slaves and women.

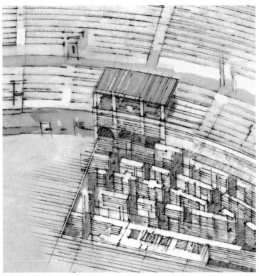

IMPERIAL BOX

The Imperial Box was where the Roman emperor sat, with VIP seats for the nobility and tribunes nearby. Here gladiators could most easily see the thumbs-up and thumbs-down hand signals. Which of the gestures meant life and which meant death is still to be accurately interpreted.

ARENA ACCESS PORTAL

Participants in the deadly entertainment that transpired here passed through portals that connected in part to the underground maze below the arena stage. The portal of death is a reminder of the brutality of entertainment in imperial Rome.

TRAVERTINE STONE

The arcades, main supports and flooring used travertine, but most of the structure was built of brick, volcanic stone and concrete. Roman concrete has been found to be more durable than the type used today, which derives from nineteenth-century Portland cement.

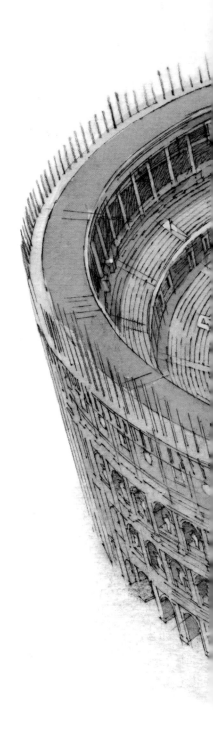

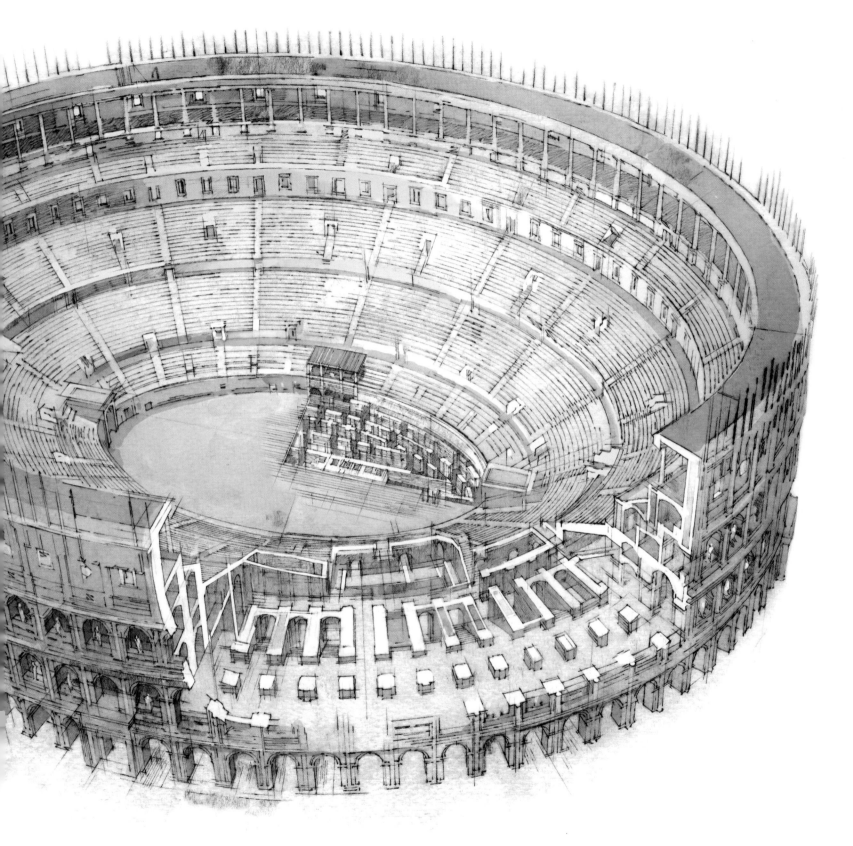

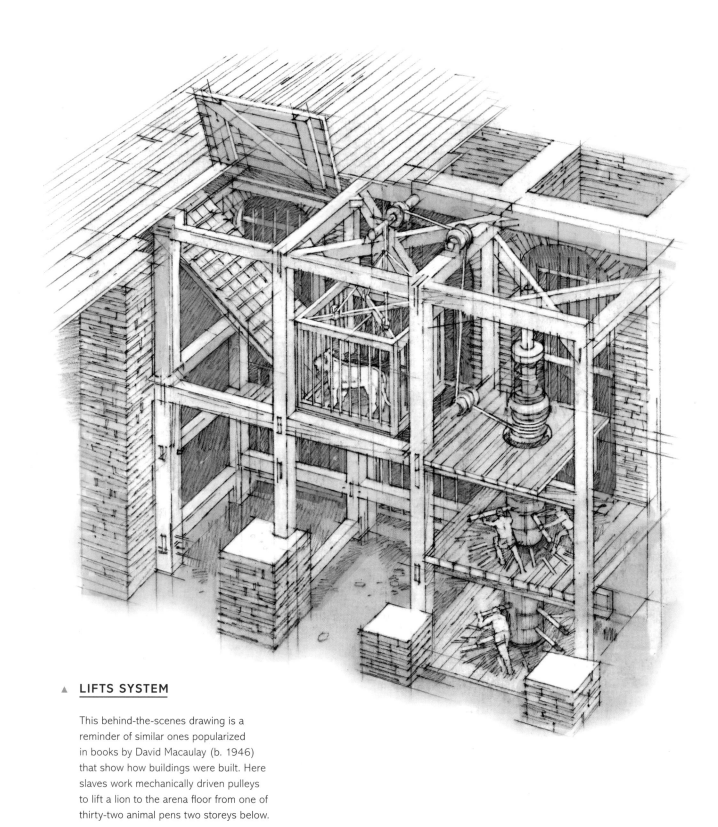

▲ LIFTS SYSTEM

This behind-the-scenes drawing is a
reminder of similar ones popularized
in books by David Macaulay (b. 1946)
that show how buildings were built. Here
slaves work mechanically driven pulleys
to lift a lion to the arena floor from one of
thirty-two animal pens two storeys below.

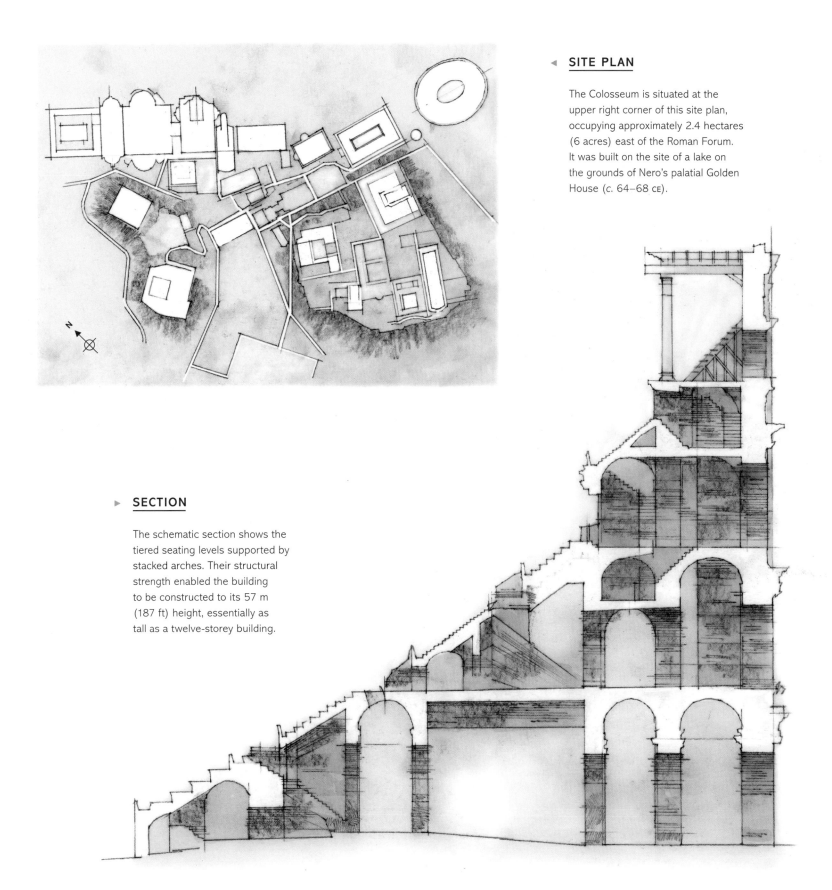

The Colosseum is situated at the upper right corner of this site plan, occupying approximately 2.4 hectares (6 acres) east of the Roman Forum. It was built on the site of a lake on the grounds of Nero's palatial Golden House (*c.* 64–68 CE).

▶ **SECTION**

The schematic section shows the tiered seating levels supported by stacked arches. Their structural strength enabled the building to be constructed to its 57 m (187 ft) height, essentially as tall as a twelve-storey building.

Palace of Diocletian

LOCATION   Split, Croatia
ARCHITECT   Unknown
STYLE   Late Roman Classicism
BUILT   c. 295–305

It was common for Roman emperors to build elaborate palaces, but few survive today. Tiberius built his on the Isle of Capri. Hadrian built his in Tivoli beginning in the first decades of the second century CE, with more than thirty buildings on more than 1 sq km (250 acres). Archaeologists in 2006 discovered what may well be the ruins of Villa Magna southeast of Rome in the Lazio region, the long lost estate of Antoninus Pius. Great imperial villas such as these are the context for the palace of Emperor Diocletian. Gaius Aurelius Valerius Diocletianus, or Diocletian, was likely born near Split,

now in Croatia and the site of his palace built from around 295 to 305 CE. Born of a poor family, he rose in status through military service, eventually becoming commander of the Imperial Guard in 283 CE.

Historians suggest that he had a role in the deaths of emperors Carus and Numerian, in 283 and 284 CE. He essentially became emperor, and was confirmed as such in 285 CE after the defeat of rivals related to Numerian. Diocletian continued soldiering on the Danube and farther east as far as Syria in 290 CE, and appointed Maximian as Augustus in Rome, a junior partner to

administer the western parts of the empire. Diocletian made a radical step in 293 CE by dividing the empire into a tetrarchy of four parts, each with a different ruler, adding two more junior emperors, Constantius and Galerius. He further subdivided the empire into thirteen smaller provinces to reduce the likelihood of their governors to revolt. He reintroduced compulsory military service, the Roman army then growing to over 500,000. A more controversial feature of his reign was the systematic persecution of cults, particularly Christians from 297 to 304 CE. As he had a mostly military background that drove his ambition, the palace built in his native Split is no surprise in being both a planned retirement villa and imperial headquarters.

The palace now subsumed within the city of Split (opposite) was planned according to the Roman *castrum*, a rectangular or square fortress with cross axes connecting to gates on each side. It was essentially a walled city, with three elaborate main gates on the land side and a simple smaller gate on the south facing the Adriatic Sea. The plan was approximately 160 by 190 m (525 × 623 ft). The southern half contained most of the imperial villa with its living and religious quarters. The

oft-photographed and drawn peristyle, its architectural details influenced by Diocletian's service in the eastern part of the empire, served as a monumental access to the imperial quarters, as well as Diocletian's mausoleum (now the Cathedral of St Domnius founded in the seventh century and visible in both the photograph opposite and reconstruction below) and the Temple of Jupiter (now a baptistery). The northern half contained the military garrison, housing and related services. The palace's total population at the time was about 9,000.

The entire construction is mostly brick and limestone, sometimes clad with marble that was

quarried from the island of Brač opposite Split in the Adriatic Sea. The palace fell into disrepair after the dissolution of the Roman and Byzantine empires, and the city surrounding it as Split or Spalato was later ruled by a variety of kings and countries.

The ruins were virtually unexplored until British architect Robert Adam (1728–92) published *The Ruins of the Palace of the Emperor Diocletian at Spalatro in Dalmatia* (1764). The palace's slender columns, Corinthian capitals and arcades, as in the peristyle, all influenced Adam's own work in the late eighteenth century.

RIGHT This reconstructed aerial view of the palace bears comparison with the photograph of Split opposite. The typical Roman *castrum* plan is clearly indicated in the reconstruction.

BELOW The peristyle of the central square or main entry into the emperor's quarters is among the most recognizable of the ruins within the former palace.

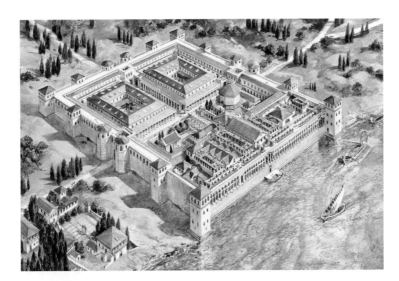

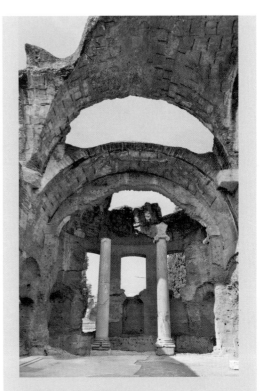

HADRIAN'S PALACE

Emperor Hadrian built his country villa in Tibur, now Tivoli. Hadrian designed much of it himself, with more than thirty buildings based on styles he saw across the empire. These include the Serapeum grotto and Canopus pool, which were influenced by the Greek temple of Serapis in the Egyptian city of Canopus. A Greek-styled Maritime Theatre sits within a lake. Domed Roman baths exist there as well. The fourth-century chronicle *Historia Augusta* (Augustan History) describes the villa as 'marvellously constructed' with 'names of provinces and places of the greatest renown'.

1 TEMPLE OF JUPITER

This reconstruction is of the Temple of Jupiter, later
Diocletian's Mausoleum, to the east of the peristyle.
The building dates from *c*. 305, and is constructed
of marble and limestone with porphyry columns
inside. No trace of Diocletian's porphyry tomb remains
today. The building became a church dedicated to
the Virgin Mary and was consecrated as part of the
Cathedral of St Domnius in the early seventh century.
St Domnius was martyred in 304 as part of Diocletian's
persecutions of religious cults, including Christianity.
The saint's relics are enshrined within. The large
bell-tower adjacent was built in 1100, though
renovated in 1908 with the removal of original
Romanesque sculptures.

Z

2 PALACE VESTIBULE

The *vestibulum* at the centre of the drawing (see peristyle photograph, p. 23) has an arched lintel and Egyptian granite columns, though it is not certain if it was domed or pyramidally roofed. It is likely that a statue of an imperial quadriga was situated atop the pediment. This was the entrance to Diocletian's private quarters. An arched entry at the base leads to the basement level. The arcuated entry porch is said to have derived from Syria, its forms often later repeated in drawings by Italian Mannerist architect Sebastiano Serlio (1475–c. 1564) and Palladian-style windows of the sixteenth to the early nineteenth centuries.

3 TEMPLE OF AESCULAPIUS

The rectilinear temple at the east end was most likely dedicated to Aesculapius, the god of medicine. There were smaller temples nearby likely dedicated to Venus and Cybele, goddess of love and goddess of Rome, respectively. This temple was one of the last to be built in the Roman Empire. The section shows its columned entry portico before the *cella*. With conversion to Christian worship the temple became the church's baptistery, with a stone baptismal font in the centre, and the crypt space was consecrated to St Thomas.

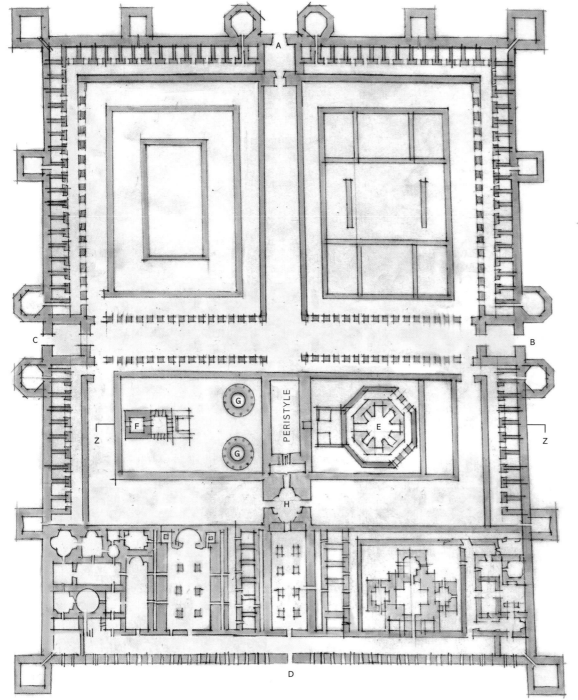

SITE PLAN: THEN AND NOW

The comparative site plans show the palace as it was originally constructed (left) compared with the remains today, which have been subsumed by subsequent alterations (opposite). The cut line (z) indicates the sectional view (previous page).

KEY

A Golden Gate
B Silver Gate
C Iron Gate
D Southern wall with small gates to sea
E Jupiter's Temple (Diocletian's Mausoleum)
F Temple of Aesculapius
G Small round temples
H Vestibule

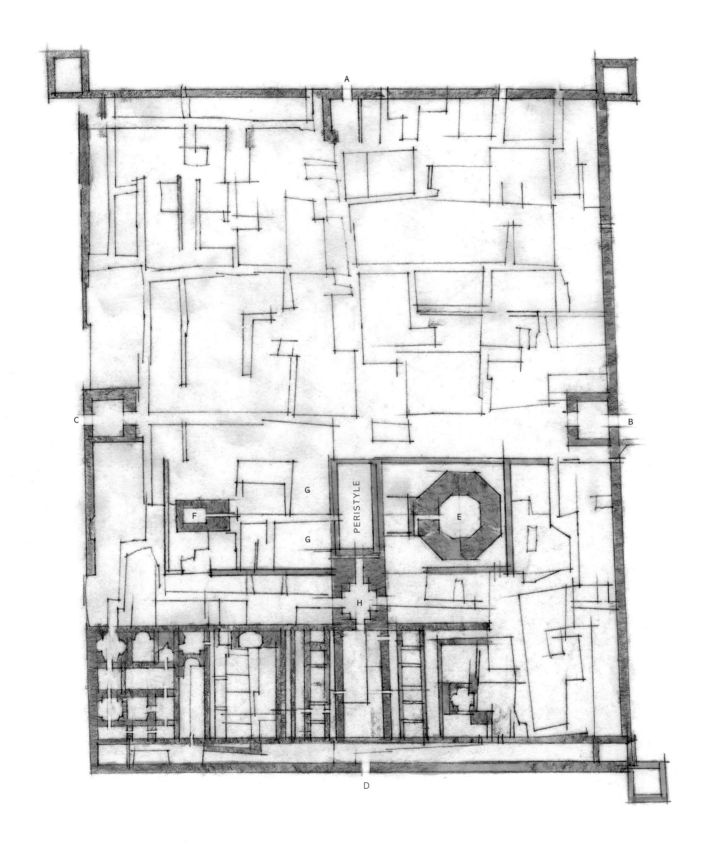

PERISTYLE

A

B

C

D

E

F

G

G

H

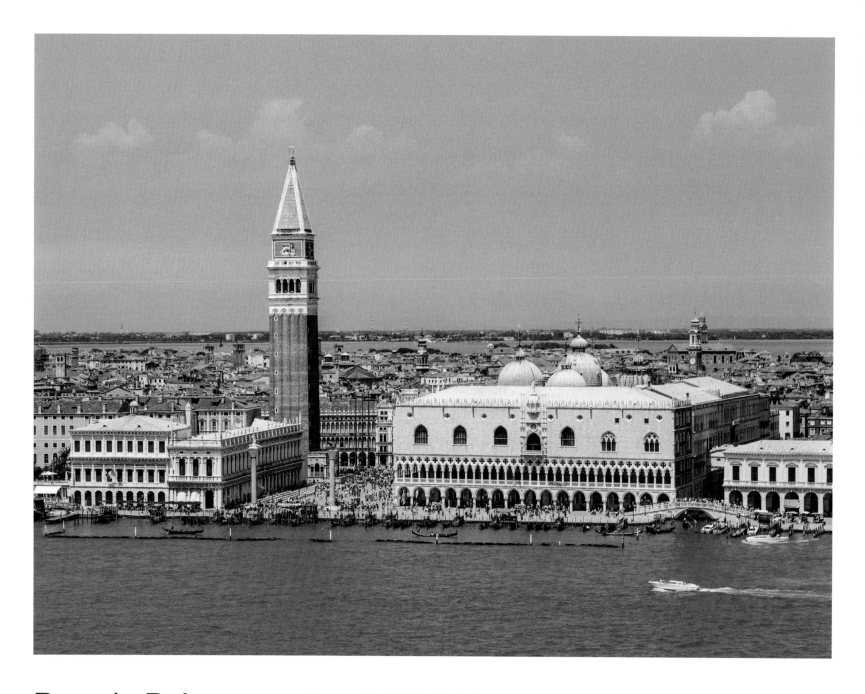

Doge's Palace

LOCATION   Venice, Italy
ARCHITECT   Pietro Baseggio, Filippo Calendario and others
STYLE   Venetian Gothic
BUILT   1340–1614 and later

Florence and the Medici banking family epitomize the power, influence and artistic creativity of Italian city-states of the Renaissance. Venice, however, can claim to rival that legendary financial and artistic capital. The Republic of Venice was an offshoot of the Byzantine Empire whose consular leaders were elected, including their head, the Doge. The city became a great naval and maritime trading power in the Middle Ages and Renaissance era. Its territory stretched across the Adriatic, Ionian and Mediterranean seas as far as Cyprus and, at points, bordered the Ottoman Empire.

In many ways it was a major gateway to the east, compared with other Italian cities.

With this background in mind, and the scarcity of building space in this seemingly floating city, the Doge's Palace was a multifunctional residential, administrative, legislative, judicial and penal complex sited immediately adjacent to the Basilica of San Marco. In fact, it adjoined the church walls on the courtyard's north side, in a demonstration of the power of church and state. There are remains of earlier residential buildings on the site that date to the twelfth century, but the current multicoloured masonry complex was built from the fourteenth to the sixteenth centuries. It was begun in 1340 on the south facade facing the lagoon (left), under the design direction of Pietro Baseggio (d. *c.* 1354) and Filippo Calendario (1315–55), and continued after 1424 on the west facade along the narrow Piazzetta. The elaborate main portal, or Porta dell Carta, wedged between the basilica and palace, was created in 1442 by architect Giovanni Bon (1355–1443) and his son Bartolomeo (*c.* 1400–1464). It contains the likeness of the Doge Francesco Foscari and sculptures of Venice's Lion, Justice, and the virtues of Charity, Prudence, Fortitude and Temperance, all as one might find on a cathedral facade. Additionally, a distinctive

balcony of the Sala della Scrutinio from after 1536 was added above the arcades on the west. The arcades needed restoration after the fires of 1574 and 1577, as well as in the nineteenth century. The overall image of Venetian Gothic arcades on the facade is the one that often inspired nineteenth-century Gothic copies, popularized after writings by John Ruskin, such as his *The Stones of Venice* (1851–53).

Beyond the famed Gothic facades, the complex expanded to include the Doge's apartments and government offices on the canal and east sides from the late 1480s through the mid-sixteenth century, much of it designed by Antonio Rizzo (1430–99). Of these additions Rizzo's Staircase of Giants (c. 1485–91) within

the courtyard is the most important architecturally and was used for state ceremonies. Interior spaces within the palace complex changed elaborate decorative schemes with the times and include paintings by Tintoretto and Paolo Veronese. The most famous of these spaces is the Grand Council Chamber by Andrea Palladio (1508–80), said to be one of the largest rooms in Europe at 53 by 25 m (174 × 82 ft). As the government expanded further, a new building south of the older complex across the canal was constructed to house the municipal prison and magistrates' offices, along with the Bridge of Sighs, which connected both structures after 1614. The complex has been a museum since 1923.

ABOVE LEFT The courtyard, with the Staircase of Giants shown at the lower centre. Visible atop the stairs are two oversized statues of Mars and Neptune from 1567 by Italian sculptor and architect Jacopo Sansovino (1486–1570).

ABOVE RIGHT The ceiling in the Senate Chamber, one of several decorated halls within the palace. The sixteenth-century Venetian artist Tintoretto executed the palace's interior paintings, which include the world's largest oil painting, *Il Paradiso*.

VENETIAN GOTHIC

The National Academy of Design in New York (1865; demolished) by Peter B. Wight (1838–1925) was one of the earliest nineteenth-century buildings to look to the patterned masonry of the Venetian Gothic for its design inspiration. Wight created it after he had seen similar stonework used in the nearby Italian Romanesque All Souls Church (1855) by Jacob Wrey Mould (1825–86), which earned the nickname 'Church of the Holy Zebra'. Wight's building used alternating grey and white marble. By 1900 the academy had outlived its quarters at 23rd Street and what is now Park Avenue South and sold the building, which was then demolished.

KEY
A Staircase of Giants
B Bridge of Sighs
C Adam and Eve sculpture
D Ponte della Paglia
E Porta della Carta
F Cortile dei Senatori
G Well
H *Drunkenness of Noah* by Filippo Calendario

COURTYARD

This detail shows the palace's courtyard towards the north, where the Basilica of San Marco adjoins the palace. At the upper right is the Staircase of Giants. A door from the basilica's nave led to the palace courtyard, which is symbolic of the power of church and state intertwined.

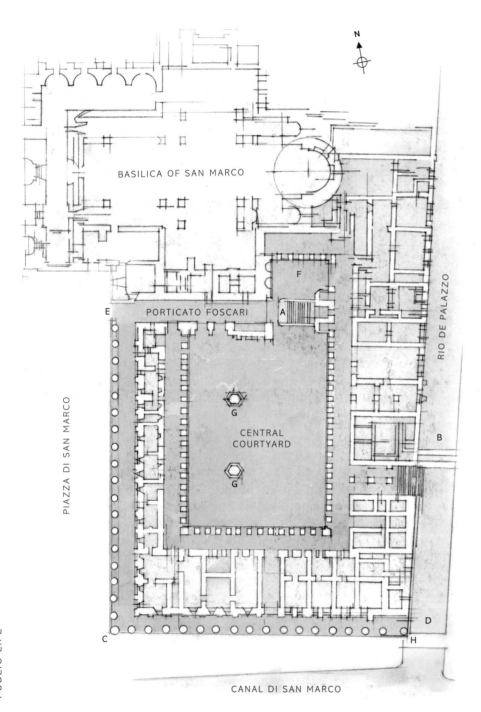

N

BASILICA OF SAN MARCO

PORTICATO FOSCARI

F

A

E

PIAZZA DI SAN MARCO

RIO DE PALAZZO

G

CENTRAL
COURTYARD

G

B

D

C

H

CANAL DI SAN MARCO

SITE PLAN

This plan shows the palace's location in relation to the canal and the Basilica of San Marco. The Adam and Eve sculpture above the capital at the southwest corner of the piazza arcade (C), possibly the work of Calendario, is considered one of the masterpieces of fourteenth-century Italian sculpture. The southeast corner of the building on the opposite end has a comparably placed sculpture of an inebriated Noah and his sons (H), each with a different reaction.

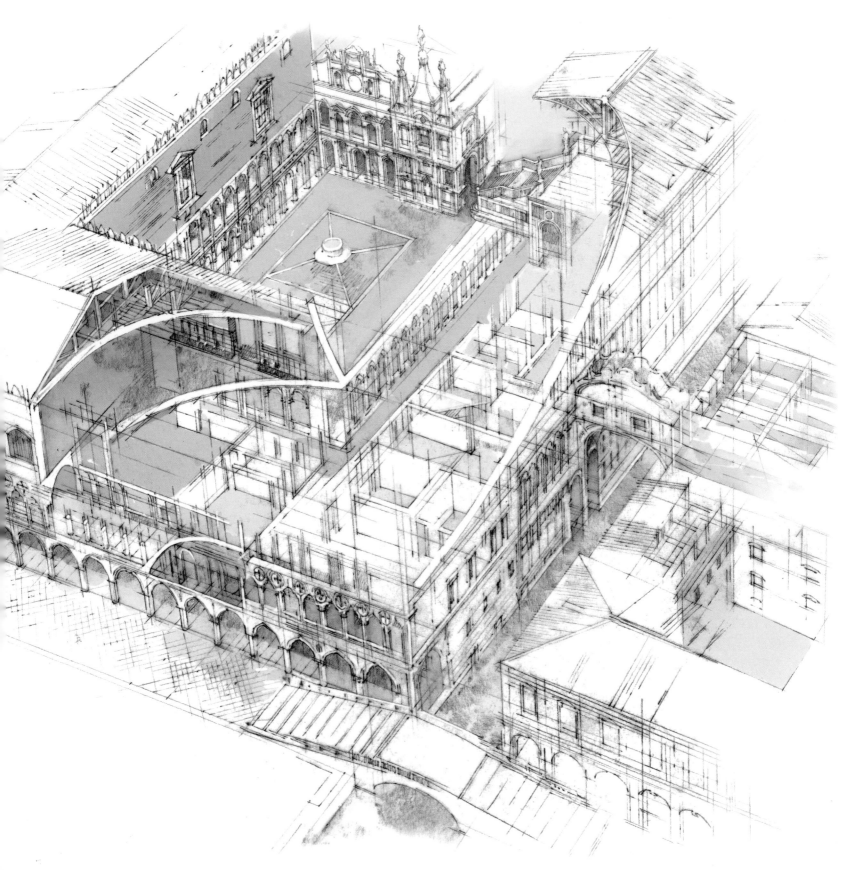

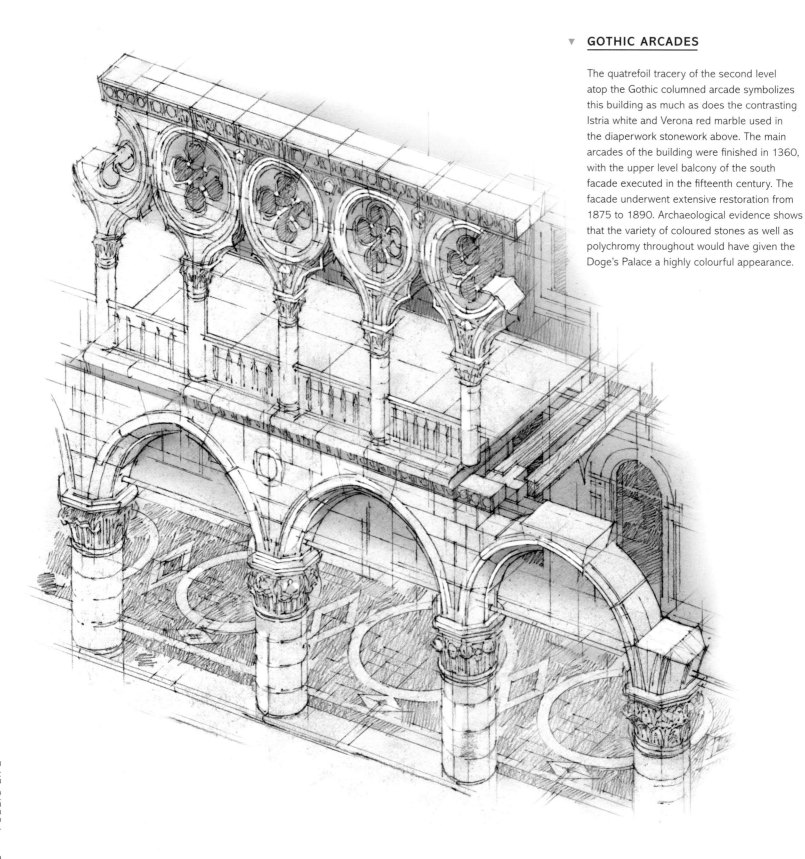

GOTHIC ARCADES

The quatrefoil tracery of the second level atop the Gothic columned arcade symbolizes this building as much as does the contrasting Istria white and Verona red marble used in the diaperwork stonework above. The main arcades of the building were finished in 1360, with the upper level balcony of the south facade executed in the fifteenth century. The facade underwent extensive restoration from 1875 to 1890. Archaeological evidence shows that the variety of coloured stones as well as polychromy throughout would have given the Doge's Palace a highly colourful appearance.

▲ BRIDGE OF SIGHS

Antonio Contino (1566–1600) built this limestone bridge from 1595 to 1600, connecting the Doge's Palace and its judicial courts with the prison across the canal. The bridge's association with the prison lends a poignancy to its name, referring to the 'sighs' of the prisoners who passed over it. The film *A Little Romance* (1979) suggested that lovers kissing under the bridge at sunset, simultaneously with the ringing of San Marco's bells, will be granted endless love.

Capitol Building

LOCATION   Washington, D.C.,
United States of America
ARCHITECT   William Thornton (initial design) and
others, including Thomas Ustick Walter
STYLE   Classical Revival
BUILT   1792–1891 and later

On 20 January 2017, Donald J. Trump was sworn in as forty-fifth President of the United States on the steps of the Capitol. This is a ceremony that, with only one exception, has taken place either in or just outside this building since the inauguration of President Andrew Jackson in 1833. Despite the contentious election of 2016 and aftermath in 2017, the mostly marble and sandstone Capitol building stands as a tangible reminder of US democracy back to its original competition design of 1792–93 by British émigré and architect William Thornton (1759–1828). His design combined aspects of the Louvre palace in Paris (see p. 162) and the central dome of the Pantheon in Rome. It was sited within the capital city plan designed by French-born Pierre Charles L'Enfant (1754–1825).

Construction began on this mostly sandstone and marble building using paid labour and enslaved workers from local plantations.

Thornton's design was initially executed by Étienne Sulpice Hallet (1755–1825) and James Hoban (*c.* 1762–1831), the latter best known as the architect of the presidential home, the White House (1792–1800). During the War of 1812 (1812–15), fought between the United States and Great Britain, the White House and partly completed Capitol were greatly damaged when British troops set fire to the city on 24 August 1814. Alterations to the Capitol before then, and repair and reconstruction after, included the work of one of the United States' most important architects of the early nineteenth century – British-born Benjamin Henry

Latrobe (1764–1820). His contributions to the building include the half-domed National Statuary Hall south of the main rotunda. Prominent Boston architect Charles Bulfinch (1763–1844) succeeded Latrobe as Architect of the Capitol, completing the originally conceived building in 1824 by finishing the rotunda and temporary wooden dome to his own design, thus connecting both working wings for the legislature.

By the 1840s the existing building was considered cramped as the new nation expanded. Moreover, the temporary dome called out for a more permanent solution. Robert Mills (1781–1855), architect of the Washington Monument (1848–88), made suggestions to Congress, which prompted members to set up a competition that was won by Philadelphian Thomas Ustick Walter (1804–87). His proposals for new, expanded marble wings were approved in 1851 and a cast-iron-supported dome was begun in 1855 and finished in 1866, based in part on that of the Pantheon (1758–90) in Paris. Walter's 87.5-m (287-ft) high dome was designed to accommodate the 5.9-m (19-ft-6-in.) tall *Statue of Freedom* by sculptor Thomas Crawford. Dome construction was suspended for a year at the beginning of the American Civil War (1861–65). Walter's design office was supervised by the Department of the Interior, under US Army civil engineer Captain Montgomery C. Meigs, who organized the logistics, engineered the system for erecting the dome's iron trusses and hired artists who created the sculptural and decorative works.

The dome construction (restored 2016) and legislature building expansions (the Senate is in the north wing and the House of Representatives is in the south wing) are essentially what is there today. The building occupies about 1.6 hectares (4 acres), with a facade approximately 229 m (751 ft) long. Terraces with extensive staircases that link to the landscaped Mall were added between 1884 and 1891, designed by Frederick Law Olmsted (1822–1903). These visually connect the building to the Washington Monument and subsequent Lincoln Memorial (1922), as part of the McMillan Plan of 1902 that created this large east–west landscaped axis. Beyond this ensemble, the Capitol grounds have expanded to include nearby Senate and House Office buildings from the 1930s through to the 1960s, linked by an underground subway for legislators and their staff, as well as buildings for the Library of Congress (1897–1980) and a new Visitor Center (2009).

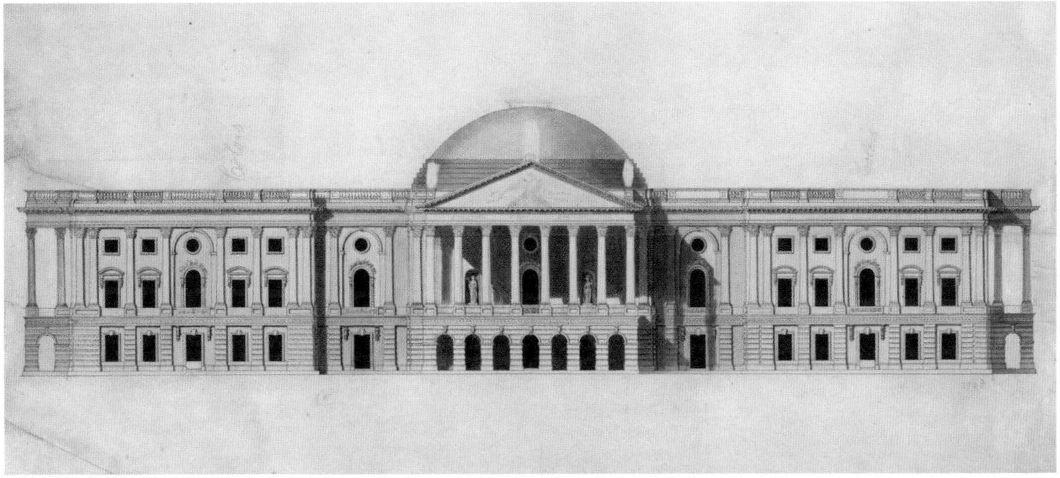

ABOVE This watercolour elevation (*c.* 1796) in the Library of Congress documents Thornton's design for the Capitol, one praised by President George Washington.

RIGHT Walter's dome shows the fresco painted by Constantino Brumidi in 1865. It depicts the Apotheosis of Washington. His ascent into heaven is joined by figures of Liberty and Victory, thirteen maidens symbolizing the original states, and representations of science, maritime activity, commerce, mechanics and agriculture.

ARCHITECT OF THE CAPITOL

Thomas Ustick Walter, the son of a Philadelphia mason, was a teenage apprentice with Greek Revivalist William Strickland (1788–1854) and began his own practice in 1830. Walter's works were equally classicist, such as the First Presbyterian Church (1832) and the Bank of Chester County (1836), both in West Chester, Pennsylvania, and Girard College (1833–48) in Philadelphia. The appointment of a lifetime came as Architect of the Capitol in 1851, a position that he held until his retirement in 1865.

STATUE OF FREEDOM

Crawford sculpted the bronze statue at the top of the drum, which was placed there in 1863. It is 5.9 m (19 ft 6 in.) tall and weighs 16,800 kg (5,000 pounds). The statue brings the height of the Capitol to 88 m (288 ft) above the East Front Plaza. The female figure wears a toga and a helmet adorned with an eagle's head and feathers, her right hand rests on a sheathed sword, and her left holds a laurel victory wreath and shield. Platinum-tipped bronze points on the head and shoulders protect the statue from lightning strikes. The work was cast in Clark Mills's nearby foundry.

ROTUNDA

The space is 29 m (96 ft) in diameter, built between 1818 and 1824 and modelled on Rome's Pantheon. In the Capitol, curved sandstone walls 15 m (48 ft) high have carvings of Doric pilasters and olive branch wreaths that create eight niches for paintings documenting historic events. Over the rotunda floor is the top of the dome with Brumidi's fresco, but he also began the frescoed frieze at the base of Walter's work surrounding the rotunda. Statues throughout the rotunda include those of presidents and prominent Americans.

DOME STRUCTURE

The sandstone rotunda drum, with classicist Renaissance-style details, supports the dome of the Capitol. The dome has a structure within that is industrial-age cast iron, including the white painted coffers. The dome alone contains 4,041,145 kg (8,909,200 pounds) of bolted cast iron. It is arguably one of the oldest such structures in the world, contemporary with the comparably styled St Isaac's Cathedral (1858) in St Petersburg, Russia. Walter's cast-iron structure required restoration in 2015 and 2016.

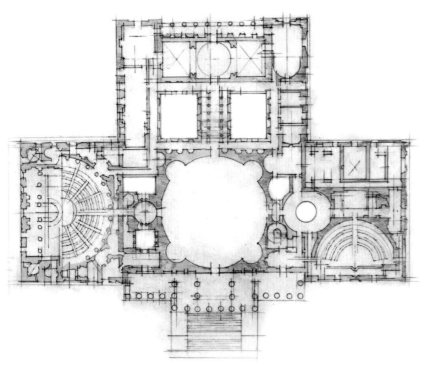

EXPANSIVE PLAN

Although the Capitol includes spaces from
the originally executed building of 1824, Walters
was commissioned to greatly expand the building
to house Senate and House of Representatives
chambers that would accommodate increased
numbers representing the expanded territory
of the United States. The footprint is over 229 by
107 m (751 × 350 ft) and contains approximately
540 rooms in 6,250 sq m (175,000 sq ft). The
total estimated cost of the building as seen today
was approximately $133 million.

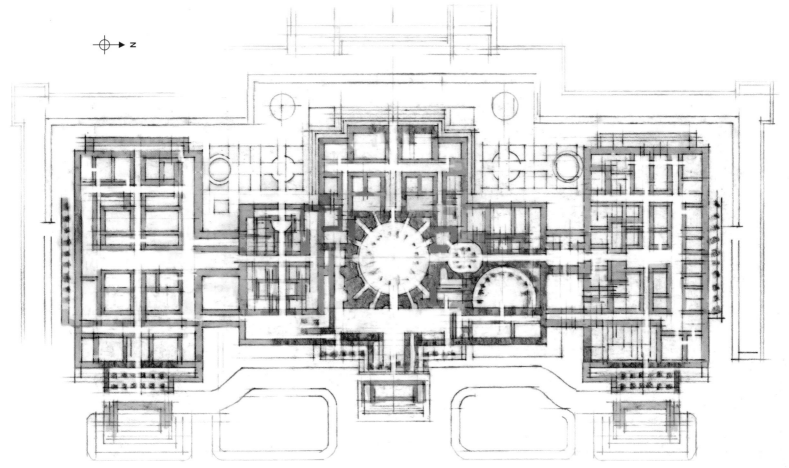

Chrysler Building

LOCATION   New York, New York,
United States of America

ARCHITECT   William Van Alen

STYLE   Art Deco

BUILT   1929–30

In a 2007 American Institute of Architects poll, the Chrysler Building ranked within the top ten of America's favourite buildings. This is no surprise. If you were to ask tourists and residents of New York, they would concur, perhaps even putting it in the top two or three. Even noted architect Le Corbusier called it 'hot jazz in stone and steel'. The design was the work of William Van Alen (1883–1954), a native New Yorker who attended Pratt Institute and who travelled to Paris under a 1908 fellowship to study at the École nationale supérieure des Beaux-Arts. After his return in 1910, he partnered with Harold Craig Severance (1879–1941) and they created buildings such as 1107 Broadway (1915) and 724 Fifth Avenue (1923). In the mid-1920s these partners became competitors, with Severance designing skyscrapers such as 40 Wall Street (1929–30) and 400 Madison Avenue (1929), and Van Alen shaping mostly smaller spaces such as the Childs restaurant at 604 Fifth Avenue (1924; greatly altered) and the Delman shoe store, 558 Madison Avenue (1927; demolished). But Van Alen's star rose again with the commission for a 246-m (807-ft) high skyscraper whose complex crown was redesigned after automotive industry executive Walter P. Chrysler obtained rights to the site lease and design.

In an eighteen-month construction race with other Manhattan buildings, the two men ensured that their brick-and-steel structure was the tallest by tweaking its giant stainless-steel radiator cap and hood ornaments, and its Art Deco crown. With its 38-m (125-ft) stainless-steel-clad spire, the Chrysler Building soared to 319 m (1,046 ft). When finished in 1930 it was the world's tallest structure – the first to surpass 305 m (1,000 ft) in height.

BELOW The building's foyer and lifts use exotic combinations of ash and walnut, with Moroccan marble for vertical surfaces, floors of Siena marble and a ceiling mural by Edward Trumbull. Evergreene Architectural Arts with Beyer Blinder Belle Architects restored the area in 2001.

EMPIRE STATE BUILDING

The Empire State Building by Shreve, Lamb and Harmon (1931) beat the Chrysler as the world's tallest structure when it topped out at 381 m (1,250 ft) high. It soon made its populist mark within the final scenes of the film *King Kong* (1933). The building was the tallest skyscraper in the world for more than four decades, being surpassed by the North Tower of the World Trade Center (1972) at 417 m (1,368 ft) and then the Sears Tower (1974) in Chicago at 443 m (1,454 ft). Today the Sears (now Willis) and Empire State are far from being record holders.

In addition, the building had distinctive design features that were a tangible expression of its client and his own flamboyant image. Chrysler was self-taught in mechanical engineering through mail-order courses. He began his automotive career after 1911 as an executive with Buick at General Motors where, within a decade, his stock payouts had made him a millionaire. He acquired the Maxwell Motor Company in 1925, the basis for his new Chrysler Corporation. Being named *Time* magazine's Man of the Year in 1928 and financing the world's tallest office building, he had reached the apex of his fortune and fame. In 1928 his corporation had total sales of $315,304,817, selling 360,399 cars and trucks and yielding profits of $30,991,795. His extravagant hand, perhaps even more than Van Alen's, can be seen in his building.

The office spaces were all air-conditioned, which was a first. Public areas such as the foyer have floors of Siena travertine, walls of Moroccan marble, with lifts and panelling of inlaid woods. Chrysler automobiles were showcased in an adjacent showroom. Another public space was on the seventy-first floor, featuring planetary sculptures within the Celestial observatory. The exclusive Cloud Club on the sixty-sixth to sixty-eighth floors held an English pub as well as a barber shop, gym and what were reputedly the best lavatories in the city. Also in the club was Chrysler's private dining room, which was adorned with relief murals of automobile workers. His own Tudor-style office and duplex apartment on the fifty-sixth floor were frequented by so-called five-o'clock girls – showgirls and starlets who visited for cocktails after office hours.

Chrysler's family sold the building in 1953; it went through a variety of owners and was later restored. After the completion of his masterpiece, Van Alen appeared in a Chrysler Building costume at the Beaux-Arts Ball of 1931, but his fame was short-lived. He successfully sued Chrysler for unpaid fees but never realized another building equal to what he created here.

▶ UPPER FLOORS

This cutaway shows that the highest occupied space was on the seventy-first floor. This was the Celestial Observatory, complete with planetary sculptures hanging from the ceiling, reproduced in this view. On the floor immediately below is a lift machinery room followed by the exclusive Cloud Club on the sixty-sixth to sixty-eighth floors, which hosted 300 members. This included Chrysler's own private dining room. Outside this view on the lower floors were Chrysler's corporate offices and private apartment. All those specially furnished spaces are no longer there, having been renovated in the 1970s.

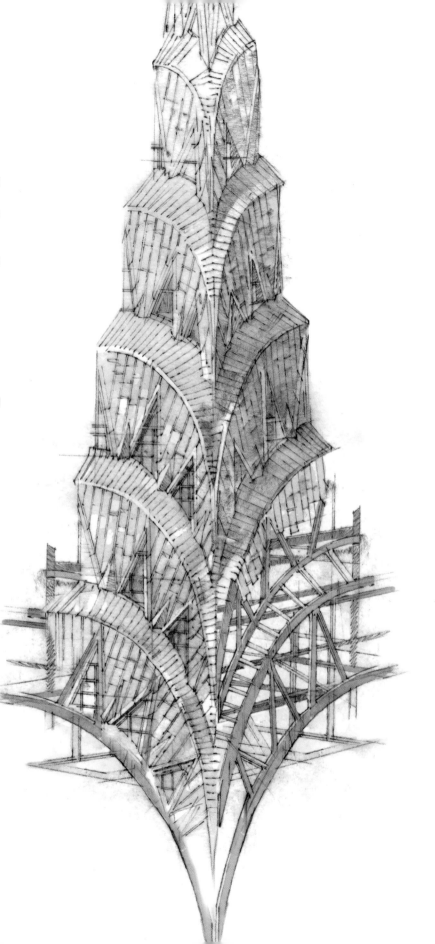

▶ STEEL EXTERIOR

Van Alen wanted a crystal top but Chrysler, being an automobile entrepreneur, demanded metal. Steel was used for the framework, and more particularly Nirosta steel – a contraction of *Nichtrostende Stähle* (non-rusting steel) licenced by the German company Krupp – which was employed for much of the external siding of decorative details as well as the spire's dynamic termination. The type of steel chosen was called 18-8 steel, named for its composition of 18 per cent chromium and 8 per cent nickel steel. The decorative steel spire appears to spring from the building's brickwork as if it were a 1930s spacecraft. Its triangular windows create a distinctive silhouette for the building and provide framed views for the occupants of the upper levels.

▶ GARGOYLES

The distinctive stainless-steel gargoyles
are made of riveted sheet metal that, as with
the spire, seems to spring organically from
the brickwork-clad steel structure. Chrysler's
labs provided research on a variety of metal
building materials. The chosen 18-8 stainless
steel was strong yet easily worked for details.
Here the stylized eagle gargoyles are joined
by hubcaps and hood ornaments, all made of
stainless steel, as befits an automotive tycoon.
Thornton Tomasetti restored the spire and
decorative details such as this in 2001.

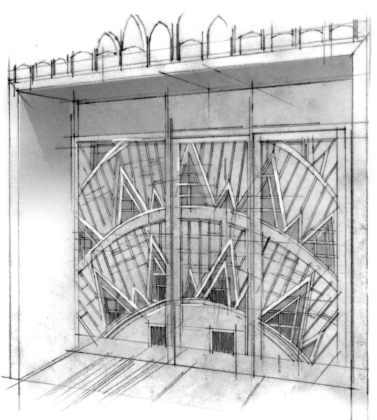

◀ ART DECO ELEMENTS

The stainless-steel doorways (opposite, left) on 42nd
Street and the smaller doors within the foyer (left)
are tangible expressions of the Art Deco style found
throughout in the building. The term derives from the
Exposition internationale des arts décoratifs et industriels
modernes (International Exhibition of Modern Decorative
and Industrial Arts) held in Paris in 1925. French pavilions
for some of the country's department stores, such as the
Galeries Lafayette, featured angular decorative schemes
similar in spirit to those of the Chrysler Building. The
exhibition greatly influenced design for the next decade.

Dulles International Airport

LOCATION   Chantilly, Virginia, United States of America
ARCHITECT   Eero Saarinen
STYLE   Organic Modern
BUILT   1958–62

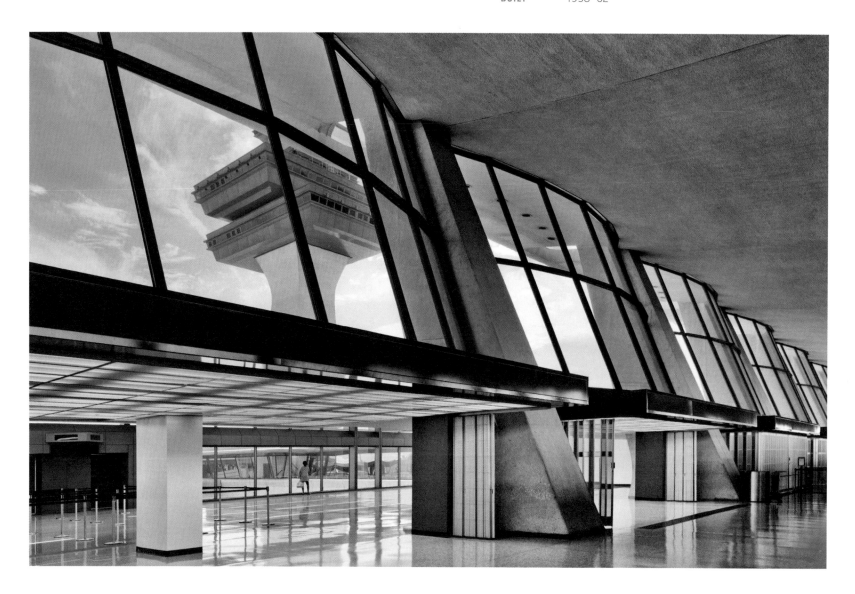

With the dawn of the jet age in commercial aviation during the mid-1950s and early 1960s, airlines and airport authorities scrambled to update their image and build modern facilities that reflected the times. Often these airport terminals were steel and glass rectilinear Modernist constructions, as witnessed in Chicago O'Hare, London Gatwick, New York Idlewild (later John F. Kennedy International) and Paris Orly. Other architects of the era used more expressive forms that imply travel and transport. The thin-shell concrete vaults at Lambert International Airport in St Louis (1956)

by Minoru Yamasaki (1912–86) evoke the grand railroad terminals of a previous era. But the work of Eero Saarinen (1910–61) in this building type went a step farther: his dynamically arching and curving shapes suggested the drama of air transportation in a jet-powered age. Two such buildings from 1962 are his TWA terminal at John F. Kennedy International Airport in New York, a landmark converted into a hotel, and Dulles International Airport in Virginia, outside Washington, D.C. The latter's plan and form arguably had an even greater impact on air travel.

If the swooping concrete curves of Saarinen's architecture epitomized the drama of air transport, then the creativity of Charles (1907–78) and Ray (1912–88) Eames (see p. 220) impacted the furnishings and interior design of the airport. Eames airport seating, designed in the early 1960s for Dulles, became the standard for public spaces. The couple's cartoon film *The Expanding Airport* (1958), readily seen on various internet sites such as YouTube, promoted the planning of Dulles Airport's decentralized gates on midfield terminals, connected to the main terminal by mobile lounges. Ideas proposed there were implemented by the team commissioned in 1958 to build Dulles with Saarinen: bridge and civil engineers Ammann and Whitney, who constructed the airport; industrial and transportation facility engineers Burns and McDonnell, who specialized in the mechanical engineering; and Ellery Husted, master-planning consultant (1901–67). Together, they created a jet-age airport where jet noise was far from the city, on a 4,000-hectare (10,000-acre) site in Virginia farmland 42 km (26 miles) from Washington, D.C. The airport first occupied 1,200 hectares (3,000 acres) for the terminal, related midfield structures, and three runways, two of which were each

3,500 m (11,500 ft) long to accommodate larger, faster aircraft. Saarinen's terminal was originally 183 m (600 ft) long, though it was expanded 91 m (300 ft) in the same style by Skidmore, Owings and Merrill (1997).

The airport was officially dedicated on 17 November 1962 by President John F. Kennedy. It was originally named after Secretary of State John Foster Dulles, though in 1984 the name was changed to Washington Dulles International Airport. During the remainder of 1962 it handled more than 52,000 passengers, hitting 1 million annually in 1966. Today it has witnessed several midfield additions and renovations, its passenger capacity reaching 21.6 million people in 2015. Its

impact in airport design, especially the main terminal serviced by buses or underground people movers from midfield terminals or hardstands, cannot be overestimated. Its location within ex-urban Washington catalyzed suburban growth in neighbouring corporate offices and residential subdivisions. One of the major projects nearby was the 2003 opening of the Steven F. Udvar-Hazy Center of the National Air and Space Museum, which contains 14,970 sq m (161,145 sq ft) of exhibition space. This suburban growth also includes infrastructure improvements in surface transportation, which incorporates Metrorail service to the District of Columbia.

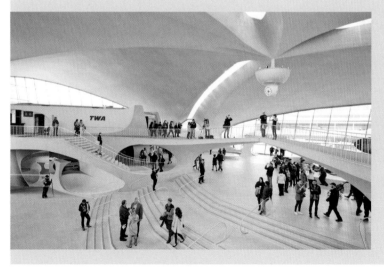

ABOVE LEFT The mobile lounges or motorized gates that shuttled passengers between gates and aircraft were created by the Chrysler Corporation and the Budd Company. Each was capable of carrying 102 people.

ABOVE RIGHT Passengers walked only approximately 61 m (200 ft) from the curb, through the terminal space and to the mobile lounge gate.

TWA TERMINAL

After Saarinen's TWA Terminal opened in 1962 at Idlewild Airport (now John F. Kennedy International Airport) in New York, a taxi driver was quoted as saying: 'This is not just a building, Mac. It's a feeling. You get inside and you feel like you're floating.' The space was intended to be a theatrical, emotional experience about journeys and the excitement of air travel. Saarinen intended it to be 'non-static' and about 'movement'. The poured-in-place concrete masterpiece preceded what is done through computer-aided design by more than half a century, making it even more exceptional. In 2012 Beyer Blinder Belle completed a ten-year restoration of the building in preparation for its reuse as a hotel.

TOWER

The airport's distinctive tower precedes the standardization of air traffic control facilities by the Federal Aviation Administration (FAA) just a few years after Dulles opened. I. M. Pei designed a pentagonal concrete shaft (1965) that curved up to the tower platform on top, which was adopted by the FAA. This design can be seen at a number of airports such as Chicago O'Hare, Indianapolis International, Lambert St Louis and Bush Intercontinental in Houston.

ENTRY

The curb-to-gate experience began with a short walk after check-in to the mobile lounge gate, where passengers were transported to midfield aircraft locations. Multiple entries targeted people towards specific airline check-in counters. Today the spatial experience has changed, as it has in many older airports, where security interventions and checkpoints have slowed passenger traffic flow. Nevertheless, spacious volumes such as these hark back to a golden age of early jet travel.

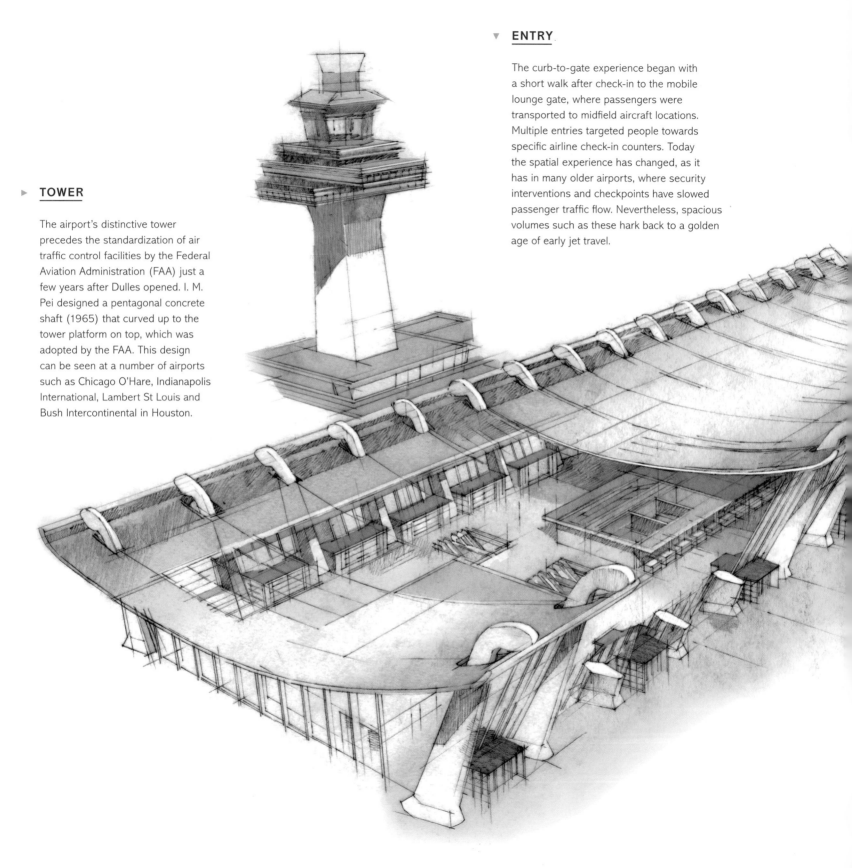

▼ ROOF

The sweeping roofline is akin to the curved ramps and walkways at Saarinen's TWA Terminal, which project the image of journey to the passenger. The graceful curve combines with the rounded, angled entry columns, which suggest that the roof is more fabric than concrete, floating above the traveller. Saarinen described the roof as 'a huge, continuous hammock suspended between concrete trees'.

▼ COLUMNS

The curved columns help to define the entrances and are the hanging points for the roof, which is secured with steel suspension-bridge cables within the concrete cladding. Moreover, their placement along the building's perimeter frees up the space within, creating that swooping or (as Saarinen said) 'soaring' look of the interior volume inside the shedlike building.

Palace of Assembly

LOCATION   Chandigarh, India
ARCHITECT   Le Corbusier
STYLE   Organic Modern
BUILT   1952–61

With the official independence of India on 15 August 1947, the new nation, though still part of the British Commonwealth, continued to use New Delhi as its capital city. The twenty-eight states within the nation have regional capitals: Chandigarh is the capital of the states of Haryana and Punjab, its languages being Hindi and Punjabi, respectively. Chandigarh is one of the new cities created after India's independence. Polish architect Matthew Nowicki (1910–50), who worked on the post–World War II (1939–45) reconstruction of Warsaw, developed an initial master plan for the city with US architect Albert Mayer (1897–1981). Mayer worked on a variety of Indian planning projects and was supported by India's first prime minister, Jawaharlal Nehru, who stated: 'Let this be a new town, symbolic of

the freedom of India unfettered by the traditions of the past . . . an expression of the nation's faith in the future.'

With Nowicki's death, Mayer left his position in Chandigarh, their plan then becoming the starting point in 1951 for Charles-Edouard Jeanneret (1887–1965), known as Le Corbusier. He made his modifications and eventual building developments with the assistance of English architects Maxwell Fry (1899–1987) and Fry's wife, Jane B. Drew (1911–96). They were joined by a team of Indian architects and planners, including M. N. Sharma (1923–2016), Eulie Chowdhary (1923–95) and Aditya Prakash (1924–2008). Post-Corbusian planning and selected buildings were executed by Pierre Jeanneret (1896–1967), Le Corbusier's cousin.

This 1951 commission came to Le Corbusier while he was gaining international prominence for such post–World War II buildings as the United Nations building in New York (1947–52), the Unité d'Habitation (1947–52) in Marseille and the chapel of Notre-Dame-du-Haut (1950–55; see p. 282) in Ronchamp. His plan for what was originally conceived as a city of 150,000 (now over 1 million) placed the government buildings within the centre of Chandigarh. In addition to the Palace of Assembly (1952–61), his buildings here included the High Court of Justice (1951–56); the enormous Secretariat (1952–58) with government offices, its facade some 250 m (820 ft) long; and an unexecuted design for the governor's palace. All

three buildings were constructed of *béton brut*, poured-in-place reinforced concrete whose wooden formwork left its patterns upon the finished structure. The Palace of Assembly, however, was the most prominent, being at the centre of his plan.

The Palace of Assembly houses two assembly halls, for the Punjab and Haryana legislative bodies, which are the main features of this building. These interior spaces are distinctly shown on the exterior by the cooling-tower-like form of the former and the pyramidal roof of the latter. The larger Punjab assembly's hyperboloid tower has a thin shell of just under 15 cm (6 in.) thick. It is 39 m (128 ft) in diameter at its base and 38 m (124 ft) high, creating space for 117

elected officials. The Haryana legislature is smaller, at ninety elected members. Unlike the stark concrete of most of the building, these spaces are highly decorated with enamelled murals. Additional interior areas include grand vertical circulation courts with related legislative offices. Thick concrete perforations on the exterior provide a sunscreen, and the giant curved roof atop an arcade facing the reflecting pool further distinguishes the exterior, in contrast to the more rectilinear Justice and Secretariat buildings. Of the Palace of Assembly, Le Corbusier said: 'A palace magnificent in its effect, from the new art of raw concrete. It is magnificent and terrible; terrible meaning that there is nothing cold about it to the eyes.'

ABOVE One of two assembly halls at Chandigarh, this highly coloured space enlivens the grey-toned concrete of the building. The hues of red, yellow and green are also used in the chamber's entry door, with an enamelled finish, created by Le Corbusier. The Haryana assembly chamber is likewise polychromed, with large tapestries of Le Corbusier's design.

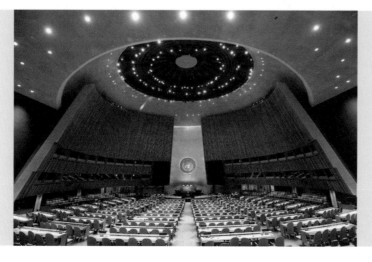

UN GENERAL ASSEMBLY

Le Corbusier was part of the team that created the United Nations headquarters in New York. The committee consisted of ten other international architects under the planning chairmanship of Wallace K. Harrison (1895–1981) of New York's Harrison and Abramowitz. Le Corbusier and Oscar Niemeyer (1907–2012) are often credited with the overall final plan, and Harrison with its execution. It is interesting to note that the General Assembly, in some ways, became a conceptual model for the assembly spaces within Chandigarh.

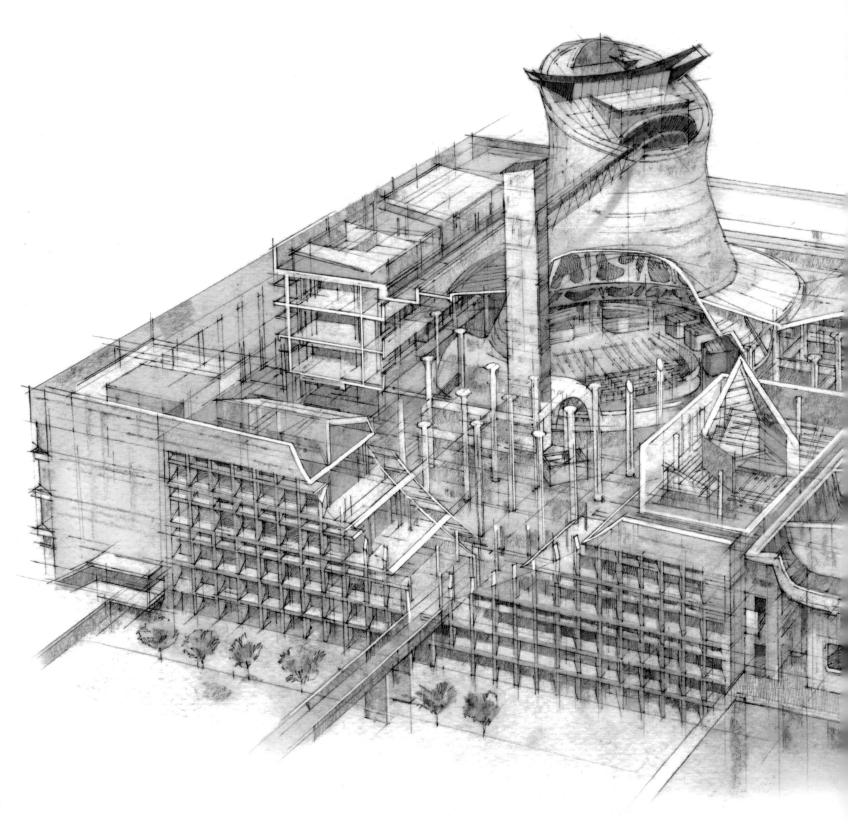

ABSTRACT SCULPTURE

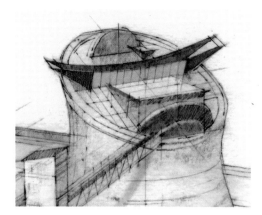

Le Corbusier is known for his architecture but he was also a sculptor; his 26-m (85-ft) tall Open Hand Monument, installed in 1985, stands to the northeast of the Palace of Assembly. His drawings for the building include sketches for this sculpture atop the Punjab assembly hall. Le Corbusier's sculptures are an extension of his organic approach to architecture.

PUNJAB ASSEMBLY TOWER

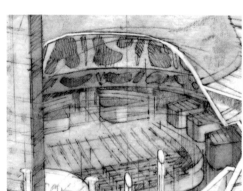
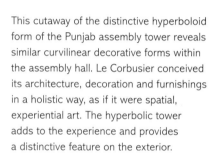

This cutaway of the distinctive hyperboloid form of the Punjab assembly tower reveals similar curvilinear decorative forms within the assembly hall. Le Corbusier conceived its architecture, decoration and furnishings in a holistic way, as if it were spatial, experiential art. The hyperbolic tower adds to the experience and provides a distinctive feature on the exterior.

STRUCTURAL GRID

Typical of many of Le Corbusier's building facades is a deep structural grid that also, in hot climates such as this, acts as a brise-soleil or sunscreen. The sun-shading along the offices provides a frame for the people inside to view the surrounding site. The grid is lifted above the floorplate by pilotis (see below) that extend through, and are integrated within, the facade.

PILOTIS

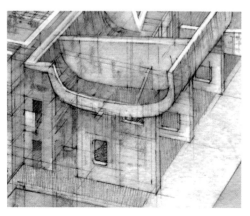

In modern buildings, pilotis are piers or columns that support structures above. Here giant vertical piers support a dramatically curved roof, providing another distinguishing design element. The pilotis allow the structure to express a grand expanse of space, as Le Corbusier intended. From that landing the pilotis also frame views of the Shivalik Hills mountain range of the outer Himalayas in the distance.

▼ HARYANA ASSEMBLY TOWER

The irregular, angled pyramidal shape
of the Haryana assembly tower is visible
on the exterior, identifying it as such and
contrasting with the hyperbolic shape of
the Punjab assembly tower. The angular
planes admit north light into the chamber.
The interior layout reflects its shape and
contrasts with the interior of the Punjab
assembly space. There are multiple
galleries above the legislators' floor
for men, women and the press.

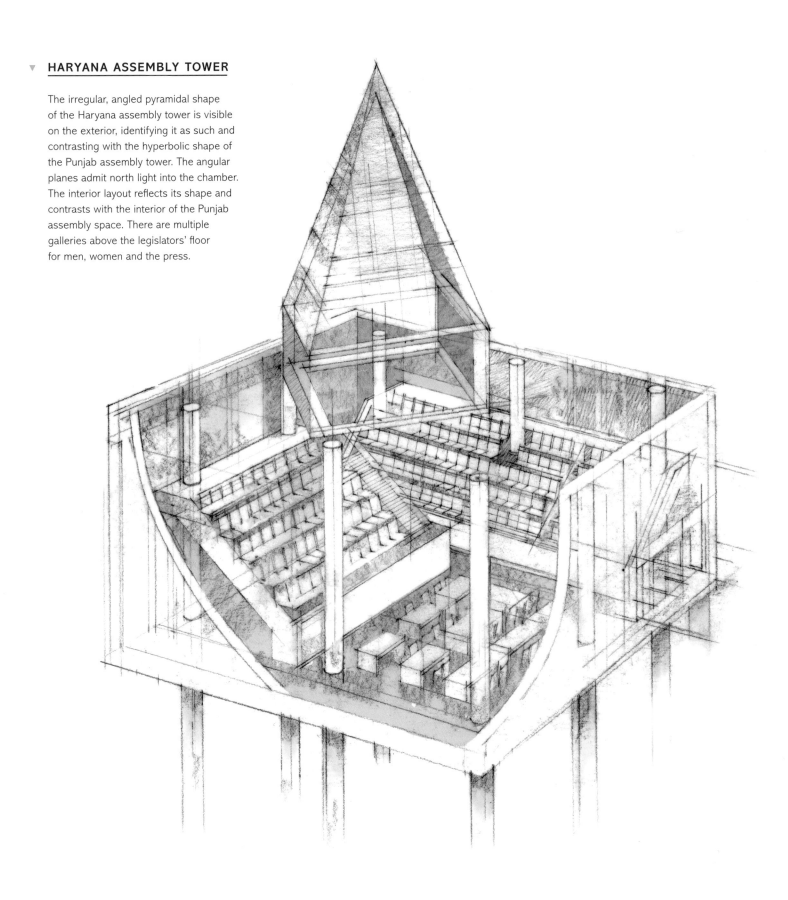

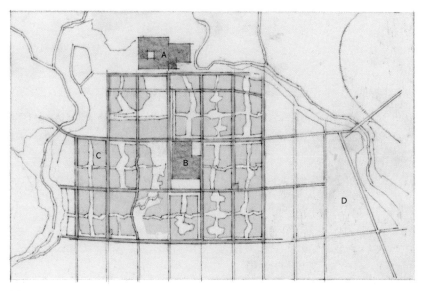

CITY PLAN

PLANNED CITY

Although originally intended as an administrative city for 150,000, Chandigarh today has over 1 million residents. The plan incorporated expansion in two phases, the first for a population of 500,000 and the second for high-density sectors accommodating an eventual growth to 3.5 million. Each sector is a planned neighbourhood that measures 800 by 1,200 m (2,624 × 3,937 ft) with a population density that ranges from 3,000 to 20,000.

KEY
A Capitol
B City centre
C University area
D Industrial area
E Secretariat
F Palace of Assembly
G Governor's Palace (unbuilt)
H Palace of Justice

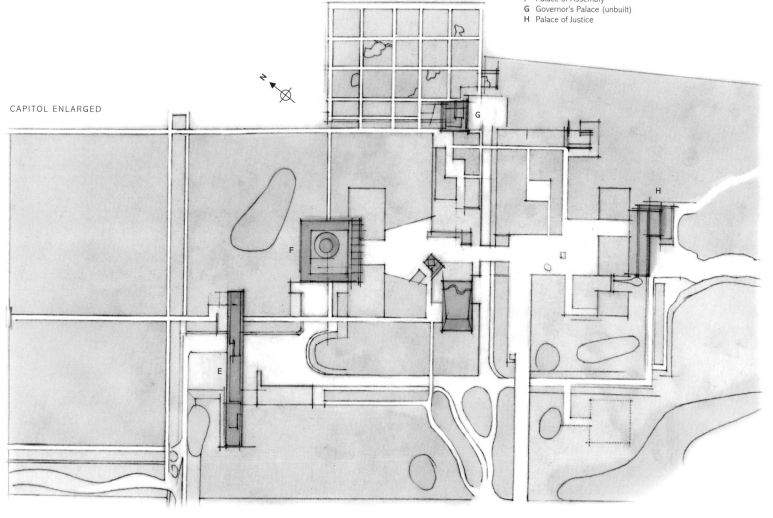

CAPITOL ENLARGED

National Assembly Building of Bangladesh

LOCATION	Dhaka, Bangladesh
ARCHITECT	Louis Kahn
STYLE	Organic Modern
BUILT	1962–82

The Bangladesh War of Independence (1971) and the establishment of Bangladesh (formerly East Pakistan) as an independent state on 26 March 1971 partly led to the greater Indo-Pakistani War. India supported Bangladeshi secession, which led to Pakistan's defeat on 16 December 1971. As a new nation, Bangladesh built its new capital building, the National Assembly or Parliament, officially called Jatiyo Sangsad Bhaban, at Sher-e-Bangla Nagar, Dhaka. The building was conceived from 1959 to 1962 while the area was still East Pakistan. Its purpose was to be a second seat for the parliament of Pakistan, which was headquartered

in West Pakistan at Islamabad. After the creation of Bangladesh in 1971, the building's function changed to accommodate a national parliament.

US architect Louis Kahn (1901–74) was its designer, and he was selected due to the efforts of Muzharul Islam (1923–2012), who was a leader in bringing modern architectural design to the region. Islam trained in architecture and engineering in Calcutta, graduating in 1942 and 1946, respectively. He then studied architecture in the United States and England at various times between 1950 and 1961, becoming friends with Kahn and other architects such as Paul Rudolph (1918–97)

and Stanley Tigerman (b. 1930) through his study at Yale in 1961. Islam's early works include the Dhaka University Library and the College of Arts and Crafts, as well as the Bangladesh National Archives (all 1954– 55). Islam was Senior Architect for East Pakistan from 1958 to 1964. He brought in Kahn to work with him on the Assembly and capital from 1962 to 1963, until Kahn's death, and was instrumental in having Rudolph and Tigerman design buildings in Bangladesh.

The National Assembly Building sits within a moat-like lake, as the centre of an 81-hectare (200-acre) complex that includes gardens, support structures, housing and parking. Its was Kahn's masterpiece, completed in 1982 after his death at a cost of $32 million. This fortresslike structure, often termed the Citadel building, is built of concrete with inlaid marble; the central octagon is 47 m (155 ft) high. The parliament chamber at the centre seats 354 and is surrounded by eight blocky forms, each 33.5 m (110 ft) high. These are separated from the central assembly by a nine-storey space that serves as a dramatic entry and circulation area. Geometric penetrations in the blocky masses manipulate the natural light, something that obsessed Kahn (see p. 146). Light filters into the assembly space from above its canopy, augmented by minimalist artificial light sources that pepper the space above. The building's centralized planning on a monumental scale has been compared to Mughal masterpieces such as the Taj Mahal (see p. 92), but its plan and the giant geometric shapes on the walls relate to Kahn's other buildings from the same era, such as the Phillips Exeter Academy Library (1965–72) in New Hampshire.

The structure contains lounges for the parliament members, a library, meeting rooms, offices and a prayer hall. This last was conceived as a free-standing mosque but was integrated into the building. Its plan is off-axis to face Mecca directly. Writers have said that Kahn devoted a considerable number of drawings to its development. Its turreted exterior form and appearance have been likened to medieval town gates as well as Mughal architecture and Bengali Sultanate mosques.

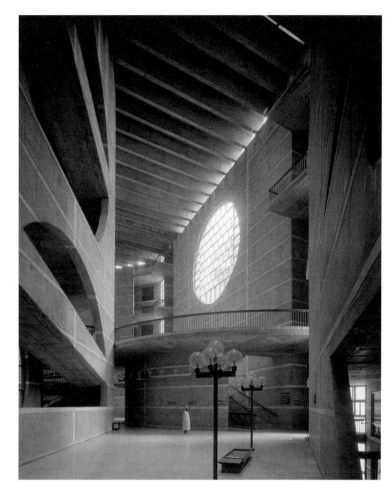

LEFT Kahn's interiors here, as elsewhere, use simple, bold geometric forms whose interaction with natural light shapes the spatial experience. In this building their grand scale is evident in relation to the human figure. The geometric piercing of the wall planes permits light to enter and provides spectacular frames for views of the landscape.

BELOW By 2017 the assembly at the building's core had seated ten elected parliaments. Members number 350, but maximum seating is 354, with VIP galleries above. The total height of the chamber is 36 m (117 ft).

SALK INSTITUTE FOR BIOLOGICAL STUDIES

Kahn (left) is shown here with US virologist Jonas Salk at the Salk Institute for Biological Studies (1965) in La Jolla, California, in 1966. Designed by Kahn, the building's simple geometric forms shaped by light are characteristic of a number of the architect's works, including the First Unitarian Church (1962, 1969) in Rochester, New York.

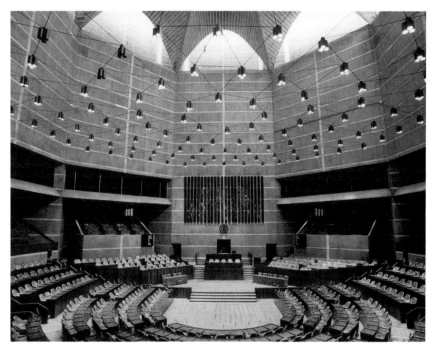

THE BIG PICTURE

This cutaway provides a unique view of the assembly building. The legislative chamber is at the heart. The curved spaces in the right foreground represent services including the cafeteria, whereas the rectilinear structures to the left and right of the cafeteria contain offices.

▼ NATIONAL ASSEMBLY

The real reason for the building is at the core, lit by the skylight and oculi above. There are 350 members in the assembly chamber, 300 of whom are elected. Fifty seats are allocated to women, who are appointed according to parliamentary representation of political parties. Members serve five-year terms.

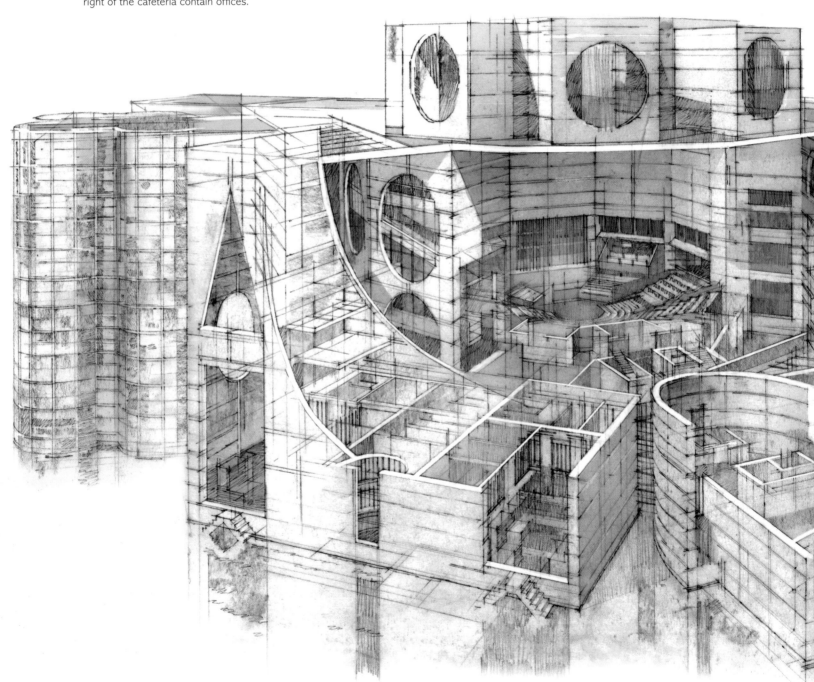

MASSIVE GEOMETRY

Large dramatic cutouts provide light to modulate the structure and its wall planes around the central core. Also surrounding the centre are secondary spaces for offices, lounges and circulation corridors. Kahn's philosophy of design encompassed the idea of 'served' and 'servant' areas, or primary spaces fed or supported by secondary ones.

MONUMENTAL PLAN

The plan shown here has the entry point at the upper right (D), the turreted prayer hall and court of ablutions diagonally opposite at the lower left (B), and the assembly hall (E) between. Rectangular buildings surrounding the core are office spaces. The centre is ringed with circulation and secondary spaces. The monumental scale of the plan and its architectural forms have led to its comparison as a masterpiece to the Taj Mahal.

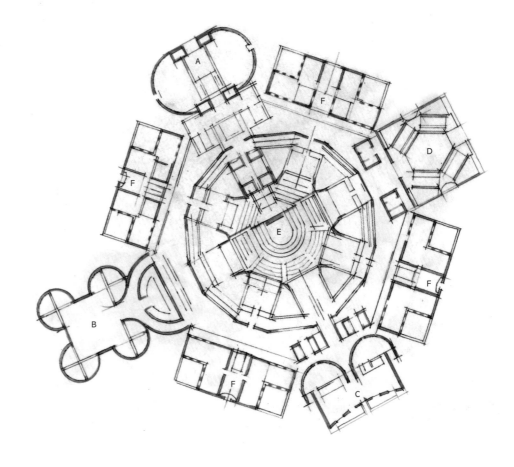

KEY
A Ministers' lounge
B Prayer hall
C Cafeteria and recreation
D Entry hall
E National Assembly chamber
F Offices

Reichstag

LOCATION   Berlin, Germany
ARCHITECT   Paul Wallot; Norman Foster
STYLE   Renaissance Revival; Contemporary
BUILT   1884–94; 1999 renovation and additions

The unification of various German provinces by Otto von Bismarck in 1867 resulted in the establishment of the German Empire in 1871, with Bismarck as its first Chancellor from 1871 to 1890 and Wilhelm I as Kaiser or Emperor. Berlin – a regional or Prussian capital since the early 1700s – became capital of the empire. The city's population then hovered around 500,000 to 700,000 residents. After 1871 it quickly jumped to more than 800,000 and soared to well over 1.3 million by the mid-1880s. This rapid growth warranted new transit systems, housing and offices, especially for commercial and governmental agencies.

Late nineteenth- and early twentieth-century examples tended, more often than not, to be grand classicist buildings appropriate to a world-class capital. They include the Reichsversicherungsamt or Imperial Insurance Offices (1894) at Reichpietschufer 50–54 by August Busse (1839–96), the Berliner Dom (Berlin Cathedral, 1894–1905) on the Museumsinsel by Julius Carl Raschdorff (1823–1914) and his son Otto (1854–1915), and the Reichsmarineamt (Imperial Naval Office, 1911–14) on Reichpietschufer 72–76 by Reinhardt and Sussenguth. The Reichstag or Imperial Diet, the parliament building (1884–94), was one of those great classicist structures, designed by Paul Wallot (1841–1912) and selected in a competition in 1882. His building was constructed on the Königsplatz (now Platz der Republik), specifically on the former grounds of the Raczyński Palace, which the government purchased and demolished. Wallot's winning design was based

on the overall massing and glazed steel cupola of Philadelphia's Memorial Hall (now the Please Touch Museum), erected for the 1876 Centennial Exhibition in Fairmount Park by German American architect Herman J. Schwarzmann (1846–91). When finished, Wallot's building was 75 m (246 ft) high.

After World War I (1914–18), the building continued to serve as the parliament for the Weimar Republic (1919–33) until soon after the accession of Adolf Hitler as Chancellor of Germany. On 27 February 1933, a fire that the Nazis blamed on Communists led to the arrest, trial and execution of Marinus van der Lubbe, who was caught within the building after the fire was started. This act of vandalism provided a catalyst for Hitler to suspend rights within the Weimar constitution and

abolish the current parliament. When reinstated the puppet Nazi parliament, or Reichstag, met in the nearby Kroll Opera House (demolished 1951) between 1933 and 1942. Throughout World War II (1939–45) Wallot's Reichstag remained a partial ruin, and it was damaged further in Allied bombing raids as well as during the Russian liberation of Berlin.

During the Cold War (1948–89) and the division of Germany into two countries with their parliaments meeting elsewhere, the building sat mostly vacant in West Berlin near the infamous Berlin Wall of 1961. Architect Paul Baumgarten (1900–84) repaired and renovated the building to a more Modernist look, but it remained limited to ceremonial use. After the fall of the Berlin Wall in 1989, subsequent reunification

of Germany in 1990 and move of the capital from Bonn back to Berlin, Norman Foster won the competition to restore and revitalize the building for a new, united German democracy. He approached the project by restoring and uncovering the historic elements of the structure as well as creating a new dome atop, totalling 47 m (154 ft) in height. The steel-and-glass structure (opposite) provides a landmark image for both the city and the country, a symbol of the transparency of democracy. The hall seats 669 in an area of 1,200 sq m (12,900 sq ft). Typical in Foster's work is an environmental concern, and here the revitalized Reichstag uses renewable vegetable bio-fuel burned in a co-generation plant to produce electricity, along with hot water stored below to help heat the building.

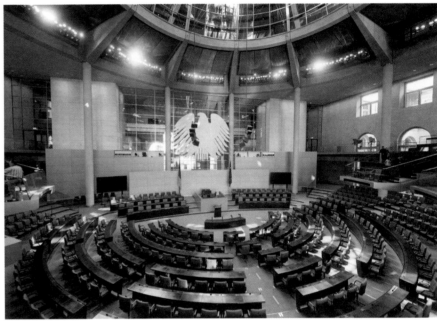

ABOVE LEFT The east foyer at the Reichstag. Foster's design utilizes natural light as an architectural feature. Careful attention was paid to the sun's movement around the building and how it could be used to bring light into the space.

ABOVE RIGHT Foster created a new space for the German parliament. The Bundestag (assembly of representatives) met there for the first time under the new dome on 19 April 1999.

WORLD WAR II RUINS

In a famous photograph, Red Army soldiers planted a Soviet flag atop the Reichstag on 2 May 1945, at the end of the Battle of Berlin, when the city and the Reichstag were in ruins. Ironically, the Soviets saw the building as a symbol of Nazi Germany – despite the fact that the Nazis closed it in 1933. The building still existed after the war but was a shell of its former self, complete with skeletal dome and pock-marked masonry. Postwar West German renovations simplified its appearance without a dome until German reunification in 1990 led to its rebirth.

FOSTER'S DOME

The dome is 47 m (154 ft) high and more than 40 m (131 ft) in diameter. This cutaway shows the mirror-glazed light cone of 360 pieces weighing 300 tonnes (330 tons), which brings natural light to the Bundestag's parliament below. The Bundestag of elected representatives shares legislative responsibility with the Bundesrat, or council, which represents the sixteen states across Germany. The total of 630 seats within the Bundestag consists of 502 directly elected representatives, the remainder being allocated via proportional representation of the political parties.

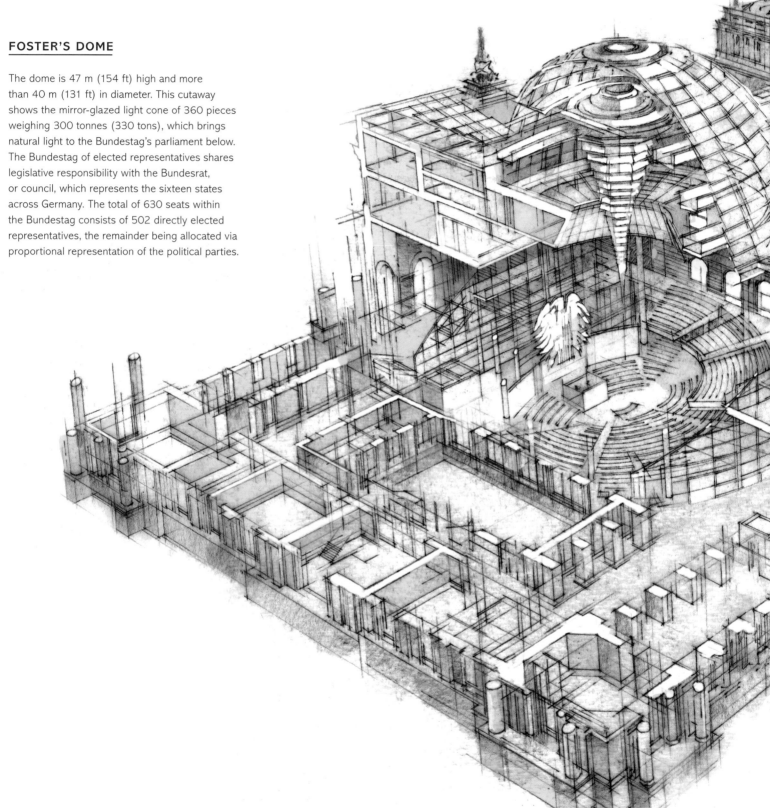

◄ CORNER TURRET

The four square turrets delineate the corners
and also two courtyards that flank the domed
space. A rooftop terrace surrounds the courts
and gives visitors access to a restaurant as well as
a closer look at those turrets and solar photovoltaic
panels on roofs that cover the courtyard wings.
Unfortunately the turret details have generally all
been simplified compared with the extravagant
originals. Sculptures originally atop the building's
turrets were war-damaged and removed during
renovation and stabilization in the 1960s.
The building, dome and rooftop restaurant
are accessible to the public. Over 2.7 million
people visit the building annually.

◄ PEDIMENTED ENTRY

The classical west portico was restored in 1999.
It contains the inscription *Dem Deutschen Volke*
('To the German People'), placed on the pediment's
lintel in 1916. Equestrian statues atop the facade
were removed and destroyed after World War II,
but are shown in vintage photographs. The crowning
glory of these was the *Germania* group (*c.* 1892–93)
by Reinhold Begas, atop the portico. The pediment
still bears a sandstone relief by Fritz Schafer from
that era. The eagle sculpture within the parliament
is Foster's reinterpretation of the one by Ludwig
Gies used in West Germany's Reichstag in Bonn
from 1953 until 1999.

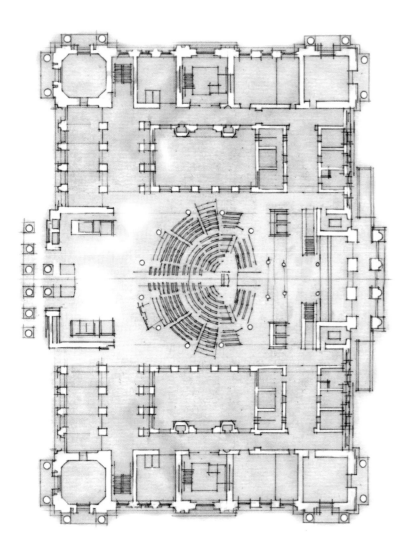

PERSPECTIVE CROSS SECTION

This cutaway peeling back the building's elevation gives a good idea of the relationship between the new dome and Bundestag space below. The reflectively glazed cone provides light to the meeting space, yet energizes the new dome above as if it were a tornado in glass. The dome also provides an amazing beacon at night for all to see – essentially a symbol of democracy representing a united Germany.

FLOOR PLAN

The plan is oriented with the facade at the top facing north and the grand west portico facing left. Many of the rectilinear office and service spaces within have been restored, though the central chamber, defined by columns on the plan, is new, as is the dynamic dome above. The plan's colours indicate the original structure (grey) and the 1999 changes (pink), which are mostly in the centre.

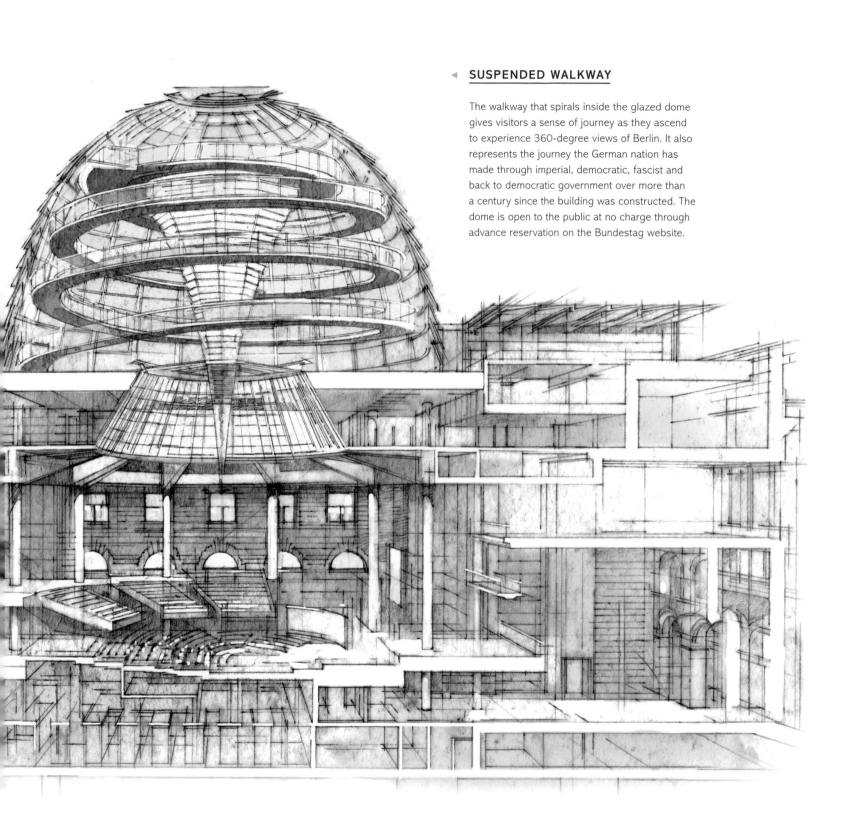

◄ SUSPENDED WALKWAY

The walkway that spirals inside the glazed dome gives visitors a sense of journey as they ascend to experience 360-degree views of Berlin. It also represents the journey the German nation has made through imperial, democratic, fascist and back to democratic government over more than a century since the building was constructed. The dome is open to the public at no charge through advance reservation on the Bundestag website.

London Aquatics Centre

LOCATION London, United Kingdom
ARCHITECT Zaha Hadid
STYLE Contemporary Organic
BUILT 2008–12

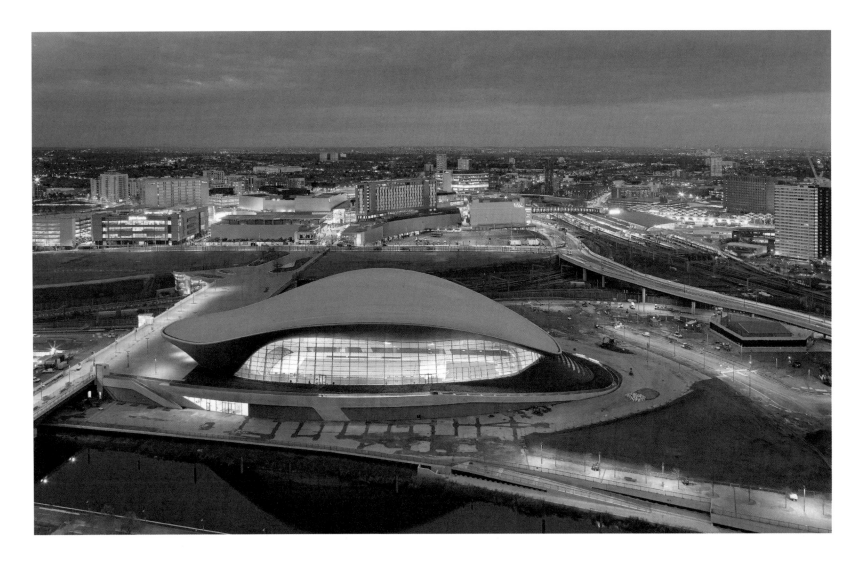

Olympics, like World's Fairs, provide a reason for cities and countries to increase tourism but also improve their infrastructure with new transportation, residential and sports facilities. The 2012 Olympics in London were no exception. Over 9 million people attended those activities and helped boost the city's economy by their related spending. In terms of construction impact, it was calculated that 75 per cent of every pound spent on the project contributed to the regeneration of East London. The government spent £300 million on the Queen Elizabeth Olympic Park for not only sports facilities but also construction for housing, schools and health care. London Transport invested £6.5 billion

in infrastructure improvements. The Olympic Village (East Village) was converted into 2,800 residential units and an additional 11,000 residences are planned for the area, with more than a third being classified as affordable housing. As part of this large-scale project, the London Aquatics Centre built for the Olympics remains as a community recreational facility. This swimming facility was the work of one of the world's great architects, Zaha Hadid (1950–2016).

In 2004 Hadid became the first woman to win the prestigious Pritzker Architecture Prize, and in 2015 she was the first woman to receive the Royal Institute of British Architects' Gold Medal. Born in Baghdad, Iraq,

she studied at the American University of Beirut and the Architectural Association in London in the 1970s. She started her own practice in London in 1980, and her multifaceted design work first became known to the world at the New York Museum of Modern Art's *Deconstructivist Architecture* exhibition in 1988, as well as through her Vitra Fire Station (1993) in Weil am Rhein, Germany. Her work took off afterwards, moving from angular forms to anthropomorphic ones, her vision and talent for daring design aided by various 3D computer programs. Some examples are the Phaeno Science Center (2005) in Wolfsburg, Germany; MAXXI National Museum of the 21st Century Arts (2010) in

Rome, Italy; and the Heydar Aliyev Cultural Center (2012) in Baku, Azerbaijan. The London Aquatics Centre, like other examples, earned her the nickname 'Queen of the Curve'.

Designed for swimming competitions during the 2012 summer Olympics, the London Aquatics Centre underwent its main phase of constructions between 2008 and 2011 at a cost of £269 million, some £196 million over the initial budget. Its seemingly floating shape was inspired by the fluidity of water in motion and responds to the waterside environment of the Queen Elizabeth Olympic Park. Its curved roof –

the image of a gigantic wave – encompasses the interior space. The undulating roof 46 m (150 ft) high covers 1,000 sq m (11,200 sq ft). Constructed of steel, its top exterior is clad in ribbed aluminium and its interiors are faced with grey-stained Brazilian hardwood.

Hadid designed the building with two projecting temporary steel grandstands clad in PVC, 43 by 79 m (140 × 260 ft), for 17,500 viewers, which were removed after the international event. Then, for its 'legacy' mode, the wall plane was glazed and seating scaled back to 2,500 capacity. The building and three pools are aligned on axis with the Stratford City Bridge. The training

pool is 50 m (164 ft) long, connected to the bridge on a plinth, and the diving and competition pools are 25 m (82 ft) and 50 m (164 ft) inside the building's volume. The pools were reconfigured after the Olympics for neighbourhood use, and the curved diving platforms of reinforced concrete add another element of graceful drama within the organic space.

When opened, critics praised the structure as 'liquid volume' and nicknamed it the 'stingray'. But, more importantly, children who use it now as their neighbourhood pool have described swimming under the roof as 'like swimming in a spaceship'.

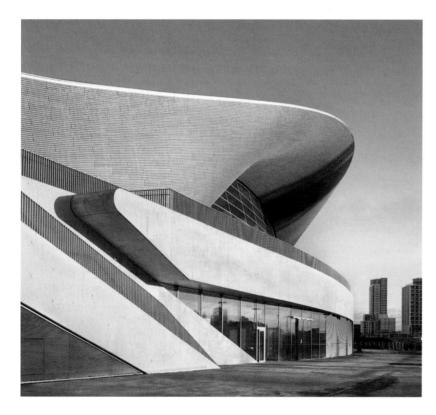

ABOVE LEFT The Aquatics Centre exterior gently curves along the embankment, its shape responding visually to the River Lea nearby.

ABOVE RIGHT The Aquatics Centre pool and related facilities are important neighbourhood amenities that have remained after the 2012 Olympics.

OLYMPIC LEGACY

A key legacy of the 2012 Olympics is the Queen Elizabeth Olympic Park. Adapted after the games at a cost of £300 million, it covers 2.5 sq km (1 square mile) and is the largest new park constructed in Europe for the past 150 years. Retaining a handful of the sporting venues, it is also home to forests, wetlands, lawns and meadows. The South Park Plaza was designed by James Corner, the landscape architect behind New York's High Line park.

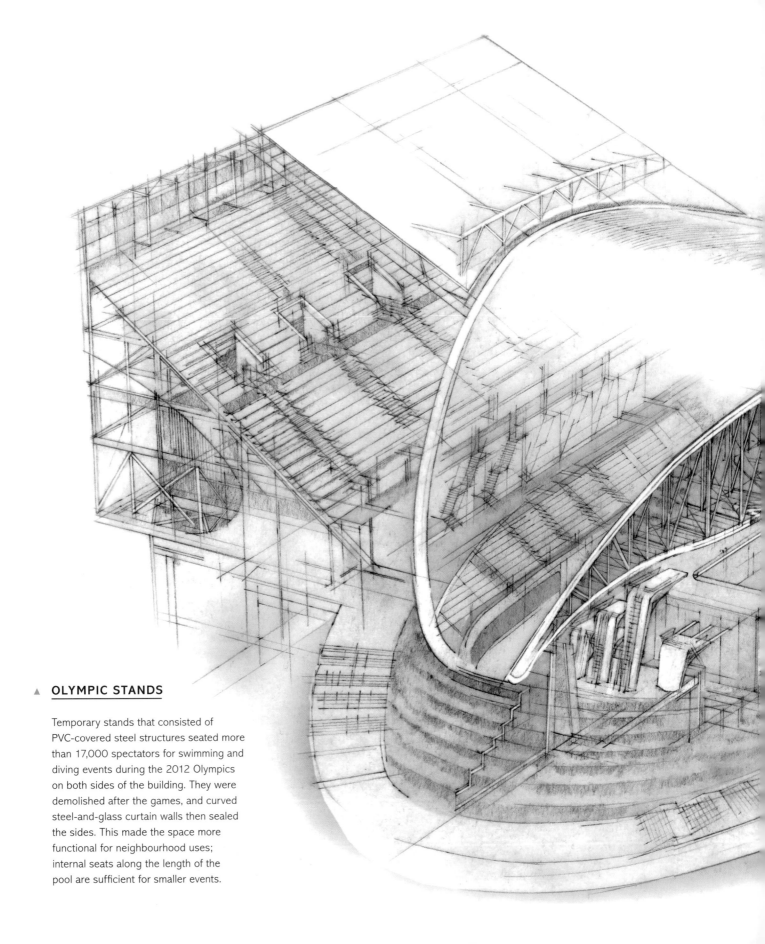

▲ OLYMPIC STANDS

Temporary stands that consisted of
PVC-covered steel structures seated more
than 17,000 spectators for swimming and
diving events during the 2012 Olympics
on both sides of the building. They were
demolished after the games, and curved
steel-and-glass curtain walls then sealed
the sides. This made the space more
functional for neighbourhood uses;
internal seats along the length of the
pool are sufficient for smaller events.

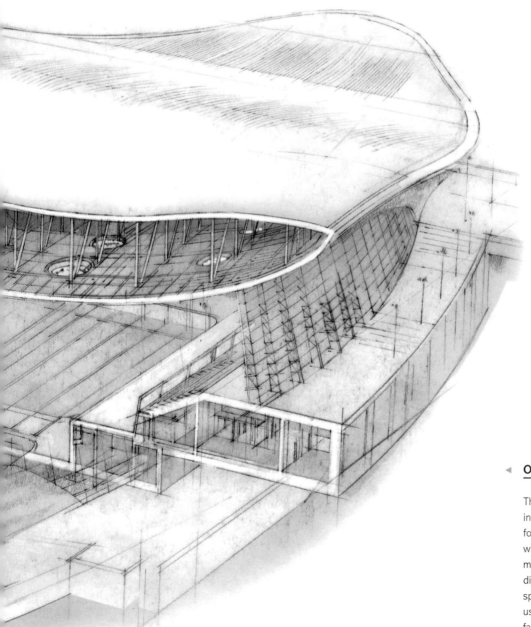

◁ DYNAMIC ROOFLINE

Zaha Hadid Architects, like many architects today, uses computer software to help create its dynamic designs. It reportedly used a variant of CATIA design software developed by Frank Gehry (b. 1929; see p. 168) as well as other programs such as Autodesk Maya. The wavelike roofline reflects the water-based events within and relates to the River Lea nearby. Its visual mass disguises the fact that it is hollow, being constructed of steel and roofed in aluminium.

◁ OLYMPIC POOL

The interior roof over the pool is covered in moisture-resistant hardwood. Its wave form also responds to the fluidity of motion within the pools below. The large pool measures 50 m (164 ft). Curved concrete diving platforms provide ample space for special events as well as for community use, including swimming lessons and family entertainment.

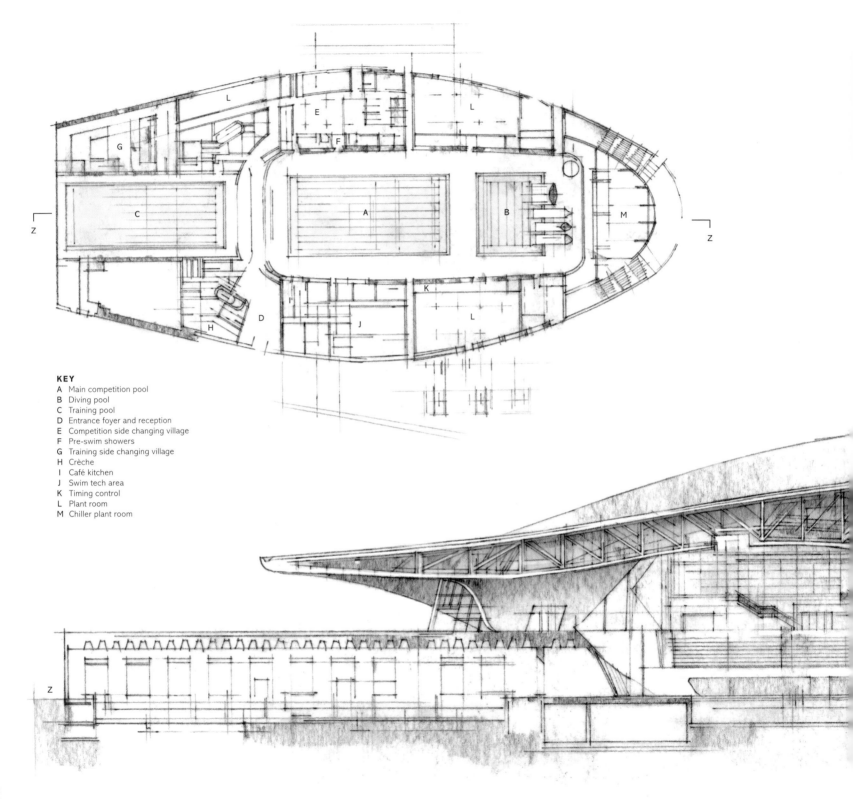

KEY

A Main competition pool
B Diving pool
C Training pool
D Entrance foyer and reception
E Competition side changing village
F Pre-swim showers
G Training side changing village
H Crèche
I Café kitchen
J Swim tech area
K Timing control
L Plant room
M Chiller plant room

FLOOR PLAN

The overall curved shape of the plan suggests a variant of an aerodynamically designed starship from a science-fiction film. The spaces within are, however, mostly rectilinear. This is especially important as regards the need for officially standardized pools. The starship experience is further intensified by the volume, as seen in the section below.

LONGITUDINAL SECTION

This section (marked as z on the plan opposite) shows the varying pool depths for the two large 50-m (164-ft) long pools and smaller diving pool. The steel trusses within the roof span the length of the building, north to south. Some of the larger ones are more than 40 m (131 ft) long and weigh 70 tonnes (77 tons).

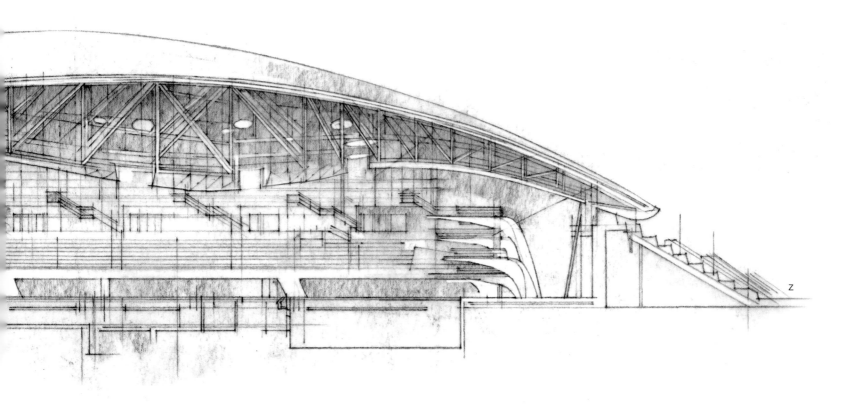

World Trade Center Transit Hub

LOCATION   New York, New York, United States of America
ARCHITECT   Santiago Calatrava

STYLE   Contemporary Expressionist
BUILT   2004–16

The day of 11 September 2001 had an enormous impact on the world, the United States and the site of the World Trade Center (1972) designed by Minoru Yamasaki (1912–86). The terrorist hijacking of two airliners, being piloted into the twin towers of the complex, caused the collapse of those skyscrapers, killed over 2,600 people, injured thousands more and caused extensive damage to buildings nearby. Subsequent rebuilding of the 5.9-hectare (14.6-acre) Ground Zero site in Lower Manhattan sparked a

variety of controversies, many of which centred on the skyscraper to replace Yamasaki's towers. After an international competition in 2002 won by a team headed by Daniel Libeskind (b. 1946), the proposal to create the centrepiece Freedom Tower morphed into One World Trade Center by Libeskind and David Childs (b. 1941) of Skidmore, Owings and Merrill. Built between 2006 and 2014, the 541-m (1,776-ft) high tower went through several redesigns that incorporated greater security features. Additional

buildings on neighbouring sites include 7 World Trade Center (2006) by Childs; 4 World Trade Center (2013) by Fumihiko Maki (b.1928); the National September 11 Memorial (2011) on the site of the twin towers by Michael Arad (b. 1969) and Peter Walker (b. 1932); the memorial museum (2014) designed by Snøhetta and Davis Brody Bond; and the World Trade Center Transit Hub (2016) by Santiago Calatrava (b. 1951).

Born in Spain, Calatrava studied architecture at the Polytechnic University in Valencia, graduating in 1974, and also studied engineering at the Federal Institute of Technology (ETH) in Zurich, graduating there in 1979. His Zurich practice specialized in striking, boldly arched bridges such as the Bac de Roda Bridge in Barcelona (1987) and the Puente del Alamillo, Seville (1992). Later works included transportation structures such as the Stadelhofen Railway Station in Zurich (1990), the Gare do Oriente in Lisbon (1998) and Bilbao International Airport (2000). Later works became even more sculptural and visually dynamic, such as the Milwaukee Art Museum addition (2001), the Turning Torso skyscraper (2004) in Malmö and the Museum of Tomorrow in Rio de Janeiro (2015). This

context helps to explain Calatrava's design, which he unveiled in 2004 for the Port Authority Trans-Hudson (PATH) service between New York City and New Jersey.

Calatrava's design adjacent to the memorial gardens replaces a PATH rail station structure from 1966 to 1971 that was destroyed on 11 September 2001. Underground lines to the subways and PATH trains to New Jersey still existed, and were repaired and renovated. The central elliptical Oculus is 48 m (160 ft) above the marble floor, though 29 m (96 ft) above grade outside, and approximately 122 m (400 ft) long. To Calatrava, its steel arches with glazed panels represent a bird being released by a child – a dove of peace. He intended

his building to rival Freedom Tower as the defining structure on the reborn site, stating: 'We wanted to give the sense that it is not the tower that makes the place, but the station.' The double-level area around this open hall is a shopping mall of 33,900 sq m (365,000 sq ft) and that wow-factor space was also conceived for special events to generate additional income. Pundits have compared the structure to a dinosaur's carcass and criticized that the funds are needed so that the Port Authority can recoup some of the $4 billion spent on the project – twice the originally estimated cost – and to pay for maintaining its pristine whiteness.

ABOVE LEFT Calatrava calls the atrium the 'Oculus'. The space serves as a retail mall as well as a grand hub that seeks to surpass those in transportation landmarks of the past.

ABOVE RIGHT The white-painted structural ribs appearing as stylized bird's wings create a distinctive exterior and define the dramatic interior space.

NATURAL INSPIRATION

Calatrava's works sometimes relate to his sculptures, but they also refer to the underpinnings of natural forms. He created a sketch of a child releasing a dove – a symbol of peace appropriate to this site – to explain the source of inspiration for the terminal and his vision that it should evoke a bird taking flight. His interest in the movement of natural structures found expression in the Milwaukee Art Museum pavilion (left), where ribs that resemble the wings of a bird or a sailboat act as a moving sculpture and brise-soleil, pivoting in relation to the sun. He wanted to do something comparable at the terminal, but financial considerations prevented it.

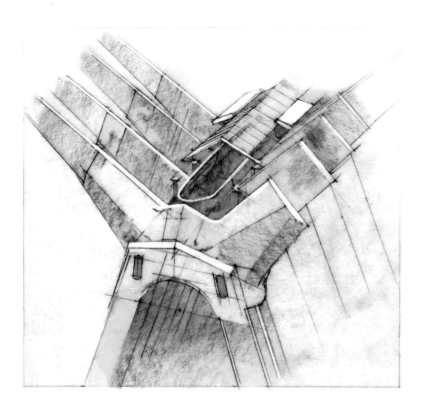

STRUCTURAL DETAIL

The ribs are white-painted steel like many of Calatrava's similar structures such as those at the Gare do Oriente in Lisbon, the Guillemins TGV Railway Station (2009) in Liège, Belgium, and the Reggio Emilia AV Mediopadana Railway Station (2013) in Italy. Although he does not use painted steel exclusively, it is a material familiar to Calatrava since his early career as a bridge designer.

TRANSIT

Being a surface and underground mass-transit hub for the area is the primary function of this elaborate design, and particularly important is its direct connection to the New Jersey suburban PATH trains shown in this drawing. Secondarily, underground connections can also be made to New York's subway system.

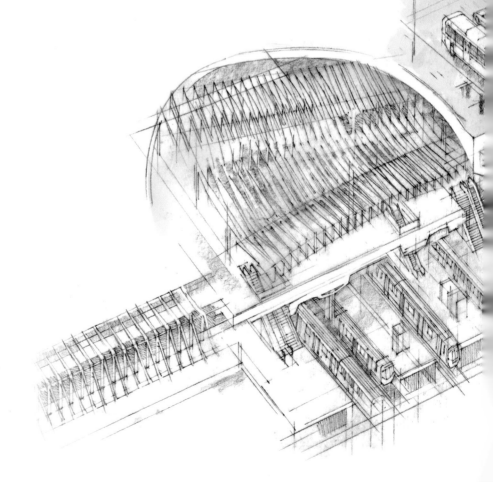

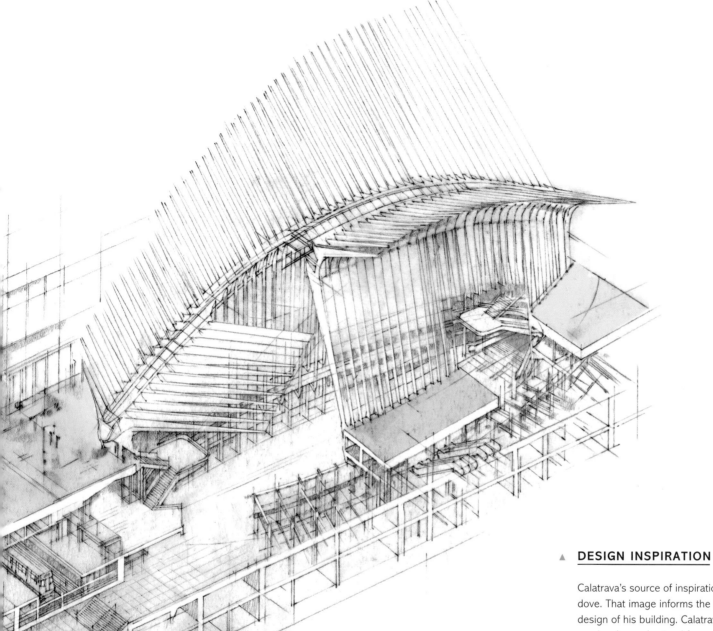

MALL

The shopping hall within the Oculus provides additional income for the Port Authority client as well as services for the thousands of commuters who pass through the area daily. The dramatic volume projects a contemporary version of the grand spaces that once existed within railroad terminals of the nineteenth century.

DESIGN INSPIRATION

Calatrava's source of inspiration was a dove. That image informs the winglike design of his building. Calatrava has previously used natural forms as the inspiration for his work. Other engineers and architects have done so, too – scientists at the National Aeronautics and Space Administration are using birds and flying insects as the basis for some of their designs.

CROSS SECTION

Based on Calatrava's drawing, this sketch shows a subsequent design development of his bird concept, here delineating the circulation spaces through, under and around his Oculus atrium. This sectional sketch gives a good idea of the atrium's size, rising 48 m (160 ft) above the main floor.

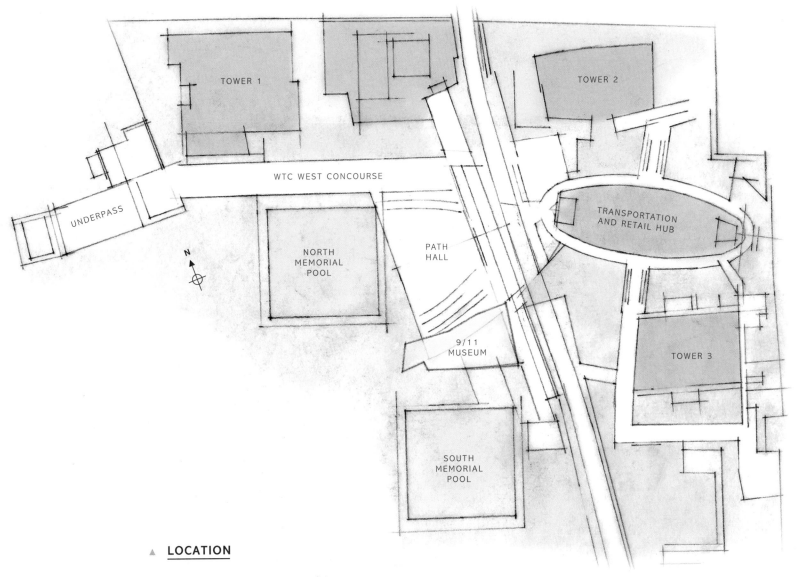

TOWER 1

TOWER 2

WTC WEST CONCOURSE

UNDERPASS

N

NORTH
MEMORIAL
POOL

PATH
HALL

TRANSPORTATION
AND RETAIL HUB

9/11
MUSEUM

TOWER 3

SOUTH
MEMORIAL
POOL

▲ LOCATION

The site plan provides an idea of the
location of the Oculus (here labelled
'Transportation and Retail Hub') in relation
to the other buildings constructed or
planned on this 5.9-hectare (15.6-acre)
site, as well as to the underground
passages of the transit hub that connect
to the rail station. As a point of reference,
the North and South Pools of the 9/11
Memorial Garden represent the footprints
of the twin towers of the World Trade
Center that were destroyed.

Monuments

ANGKOR WAT (SEE P. 86)

When people think of monuments, they invariably think of commemorative structures and sculptures dedicated to important events or people. Indeed, the word itself derives from the Latin *monumentum* (memorial), which is intended to remind people of past accomplishments and personalities. Now the word also connotes buildings that are great symbols or cultural icons of their own time.

Historic preservation efforts for many of these major buildings began in Europe mostly in the nineteenth and early twentieth centuries: in France after the Revolution of 1789 with the establishment of an inspector general of historic sites in 1840, leading to today's *monuments historiques* (historic monuments); in Britain after passage of the Ancient Monuments Protection Acts in 1882, the establishment of the National Trust in 1894 and the Royal Commission on the Historical Monuments of England in 1908, up through today's National Heritage List for England launched in 2011; and in Germany with the initial establishment of the *Denkmalschutz* (monument protection laws) in Hesse in 1902 and then Saxony in 1908. Efforts such as those eventually led to the creation of the Athens Charter for the Restoration of Historic Monuments at the first International Congress of Architects in 1931.

In the United States, individual preservation efforts at George Washington's Headquarters in Newburgh, New York, in 1850, and his home at Mt Vernon in 1858 were followed by state and national efforts such as the Historic American Buildings Survey.

This was established in 1933 during the Great Depression to employ architects, researchers and writers who created measured drawings, photographs and narratives on deposit in the Library of Congress. The creation of the National Trust for Historic Preservation in 1949 also added to recognition of the problem. Further agencies, organizations and institutions grew internationally during the twentieth century, particularly so when the post–World War II building boom of the 1950s and 1960s threatened the existence of historic buildings worldwide. In the United States this led to the National Historic Preservation Act of 1966.

It is the norm for most nations and cities to have landmark protection laws. The United Nations Educational, Scientific and Cultural Organization (UNESCO) was formed in 1945. Together with the United Nations (UN), UNESCO has created and maintained a World Heritage List since 1972. It monitors especially endangered sites and maintains a fund of mandatory contributions from UN member states as well as voluntary commitments. The list has more than 1,000 sites across the globe that are culturally or naturally significant on an international scale. Of the fifty buildings within this volume, twenty-four are included on that list or within city historic districts of the list, such as Cordoba, Istanbul, Kyoto and Rome. Many of the other older sites are on national or regional lists. In this chapter alone, every site is on UNESCO's list except the Einstein Tower (1919–21). This distinctive local structure is monumental in design, despite its being minuscule in scale compared with other buildings featured here.

But what links these sites beyond their recognition as monuments? The Parthenon (*c.* 447–432 BCE), Angkor Wat (*c.* 1113–50) and the Taj Mahal (1632–48) might well be placed in the chapter on Worship, since their functions relate to religious beliefs. The Parthenon and Angkor Wat would also fit within the Public Life chapter, since they were an integral part of urban development for their respective sites. Versailles' massive royal palace complex (1624–1770) and, by contrast, the modest villa of Monticello (1796–1809) belonging to Thomas Jefferson (1743–1826) could have easily made their way into the Living chapter. The tiny Einstein Tower could have fit within the chapter on Arts and Education, since it sits within a centre for astrophysics research. It may seem arbitrary, then, that they are here while other sites within the book are placed in chapters related to building typology. This is particularly true when it comes to major architectural sites such as the Roman Colosseum (see p. 16), New York's Chrysler Building (see p. 38) and Sydney's Opera House (1957–73; see p. 150), which are internationally recognized as 'monuments'. Indeed, this chapter is the shortest compared with the others. So, what links the six sites within this chapter is their instant recognition by masses of people regardless of their cultural contexts as monuments – sparking memories and awareness of the personalities and historic events related to those sites.

For example, the temple at Angkor Wat, the Taj Mahal mausoleum and gardens and the Palace of Versailles and its gardens are monuments built on an enormous scale by royalty who intended their greatness to be recognized by their peers and remembered or memorialized by later generations through those massive expressions in stone. Beyond that, they have taken on popular associations of, respectively, an exotic empire in the jungle in the case of Angkor Wat, eternal spousal love at the Taj Mahal, and pre-revolution, pre-democratic extravagance and court intrigue at Versailles. The Parthenon, and its hilltop Acropolis site, is a beacon of western democracy regarding ancient Greece through today. Monticello, a home of one of the United States' early presidents, brings to mind the classical tastes of a sophisticated Anglo-American gentleman farmer as well as his own inventive quirkiness in the English tradition of the talented gentleman amateur. But do not forget the Einstein Tower, significant both architecturally and historically. Its dynamically curved form foreshadowed an Expressionist architecture movement during the interwar years of the 1920s and 1930s, and its name links it to one of the most important scientists of its era: physicist Albert Einstein. UNESCO's World Heritage List already includes the Palaces and Parks of Potsdam, whose 500 buildings were constructed between 1730 and 1916, mostly for Prussian royalty. Perhaps one day this little observatory and its scientific cousins from the early 1900s at the Leibnitz Institute for Astrophysics in nearby Potsdam–Babelsberg will merit inclusion in that list as an addendum. Regardless, every building in this chapter qualifies as monumental, or *monumentum*, by reminding people of some of humanity's most important personalities and major historic events.

PALACE OF VERSAILLES (SEE P. 96)

Parthenon

LOCATION Athens, Greece
ARCHITECT Ictinus and Callicrates, with Phidias
STYLE Greek Doric Classicism, with Ionic details
BUILT c. 447–432 BCE

Little did Thomas Bruce, 7th Earl of Elgin, suspect that his removal of some of the Parthenon's sculptures between 1801 and 1805 – with the blessing of the Ottoman Empire, which then controlled Athens – would cause a firestorm between Greece and the United Kingdom more than two centuries later, with each nation having arguably valid claims to curated ownership. The so-called Elgin Marbles – housed in the British Museum in London since their sale by Lord Elgin in 1816 – comprise about half of the sculptures still extant when originally acquired. Additional sculptures today are protected within the Acropolis Museum near the Parthenon.

Beyond the significance of those contested artworks, no one would dispute that the Parthenon (c. 447–432 BCE)

atop Athens' Acropolis is one of the most important works of architecture in the world, along with the nearby Erechtheum (421–405 BCE), Propylaeum (437 BCE) and Temple of Athena Nike (c. 420 BCE). The Parthenon sculptures, including the long-lost colossal statue of the goddess Athena Parthenos within, were the work of artist Phidias, whereas the temple was constructed by architects Ictinus and Callicrates, and – according to the Roman author Vitruvius – Karpion. The statue of Athena was likely polychrome, gold and ivory, installed adjacent to a reflecting pool. Sculptures on the frieze within the blank metopes above the colonnade that surrounded the temple's exterior depicted various mythic battles, and were also likely polychrome. Sculptures within the west pediment depicted the rivalry between Poseidon and Athena to be patron of the city, whereas those on the east pediment depicted the birth of Athena. An internal frieze around the *cella* depicted the Panathenaic procession.

The Parthenon is built of marble on a limestone foundation. It measures 69.5 by 30.9 m (228 × 101 ft). The *cella* is divided into the *naos*, the larger worship space, and the *opisthodomos*, the smaller treasury. It covers approximately 29.8 by 19.2 m (98 × 63 ft) and is 13.7 m (45 ft) high. Simple Doric columns surrounded the exterior of the temple, eight on each short facade and seventeen on each longer one. Columns within the temple supported the roof and divided space related to the large statue of Athena. A smaller space for the treasury at the rear of the temple incorporated four Ionic columns.

The building, constructed near the site of two earlier, smaller temples to Athena, represents Athens at the height of its influence as a Greek city-state and naval power under fifth-century BCE general and statesman Pericles, whose leadership helped create the Athenian Empire. The temple's cost of 469 silver talents was roughly equal to that of constructing over 400 trireme or triple-decked warships. To place this in context, Athens then had a fleet of some 200 vessels and the Athenian treasury had 6,000 talents in reserve, with an annual gross income of 1,000 talents.

Despite its location on the Acropolis at 150 m (490 ft) above sea level, Athens and its citadel witnessed invading armies before and after the Parthenon's construction. Later Hellenistic and Roman occupants often repaired older temples such as this and made their own temple additions nearby. During the Byzantine Christian era, the Parthenon became a church dedicated to the Virgin Mary in the sixth century, after Emperor Theodosius II decreed in 435 CE that all pagan temples be closed. The great statue of Athena was said to have been taken to Constantinople (now Istanbul) at a later date and destroyed in 1204 during the Crusades. With the Siege of Athens by Turkish armies in 1456 and the city's surrender in 1458, the Parthenon and Athens became part of the Ottoman Empire until 1832, when Greece became an independent nation. During this era the Parthenon was used as a garrison and then mosque, and was heavily damaged in 1687 during the Venetian invasion.

The Greek government has been restoring the building and related structures on the Acropolis since 1975, and in 2009 a new archaeological museum, the Acropolis Museum, of some 21,000 sq m (226,000 sq ft), was opened nearby.

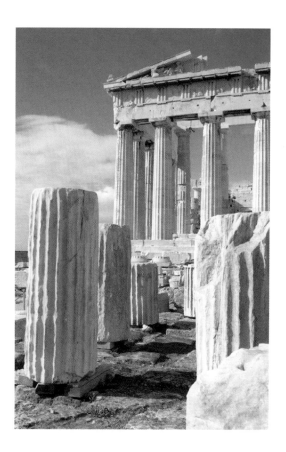

RIGHT This reconstruction drawing shows polychromed temple details as well as the oversize statue of the goddess Athena Parthenos, long since destroyed.

ABOVE RIGHT Ruined marble columns in front of the Parthenon. The marble used was extracted from a quarry 16 km (10 miles) northeast of central Athens.

NASHVILLE PARTHENON

There are copies of the temples on the Acropolis worldwide. Among them is the reconstruction of the Parthenon built in Nashville for the Tennessee Centennial Exposition in 1897. It refers to that city's tagline as the 'Athens of the South' and its interior houses a reconstruction of the Athena Parthenos statue (1990) by US artist Alan LeQuire.

1 PEDIMENT SCULPTURES

What remains of the pediment sculptures within the tympanum are contested fragments that are mostly in the British Museum, with others in the Acropolis Museum and selected European institutions. They were damaged in 1687 when Venetian artillery bombarded the Acropolis. This reconstruction shows the east facade and pediment, which held the story of Athena's birth, marking the entry to the *naos* devoted to her. Three points of the pediment were ornamented with floral or palmette finials called *acroteria*.

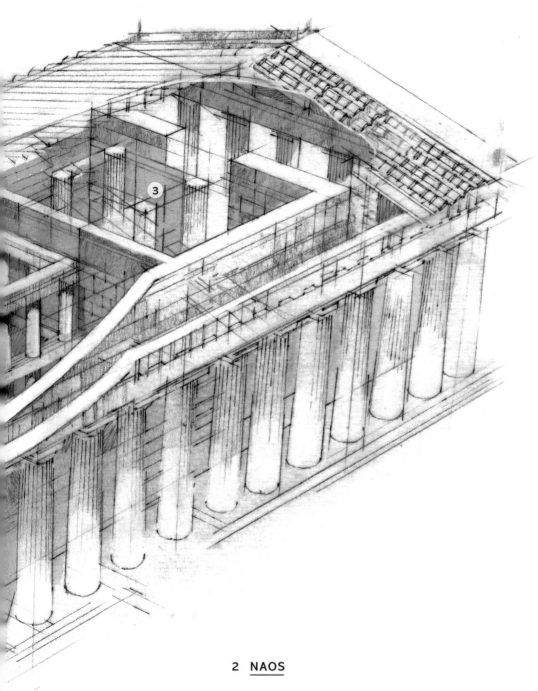

3 OPISTHODOMOS

Opisthodomos translates as 'back room'. This
smaller space acted as a vestibule in the Parthenon
and provided access to the small part of the *cella*
on the west end of the temple that housed the
treasury. The *opisthodomos* is the equivalent
of the *pronaos* vestibule on the eastern end
just outside the *naos*, past the columned entry.
The treasury had four Ionic columns whose
scroll-like capitals were more elaborate than
the severe-looking Doric ones throughout.

2 NAOS

Naos derives from the Greek for 'dwelling'. The
larger *cella*, or *naos*, devoted to the worship of Athena
housed the statue of the goddess at its western end,
with a small reflective pool likely positioned before
it. Two rows of smaller stacked Doric columns made
the space look even larger. *Naos* spaces were used
for votive offerings to deities. Variants of this type
of central worship space are seen in later Roman
temples, and could have housed dedicated spaces
for priests and temple guards.

FLOOR PLAN AND LONGITUDINAL SECTION

The temple plan and section, read left to right or east to west, show the *naos* votive space to the left and the treasury at the right, as well as the location of the reconstructed statue of Athena Parthenos. The Parthenon and its sculptures were all created from Pentelic marble quarried from Mt Pentelicus approximately 16 km (10 miles) northeast of Athens. The section shows Phidias' giant statue upon a pedestal, making it approximately 12 m (40 ft) high.

▶ ROOF TILING

The Parthenon's roof structure used cedar beams with Pentelic marble tiles, as opposed to ceramic ones. As with many Greek temples, the roof's corners also had carved lion-head drain spouts to discharge rain water. Sculpted gargoyle heads of comparable medieval water spouts can trace their origins back to these fanciful Greek lion's heads.

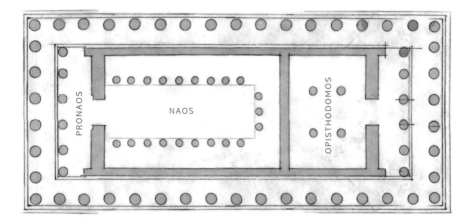

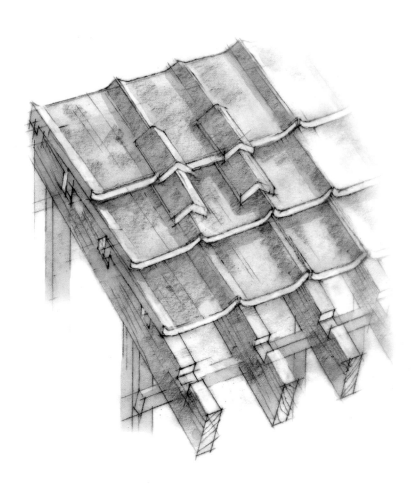

COLUMNS

Most of the columns used on the Parthenon are Doric, with the exception of those in the treasury of the *opisthodomos*, which are Ionic. Greek temples featured those and elaborate Corinthian columns, all of which informed the variants used in many classicist buildings that followed (see Glossary, p. 298). These classical orders are part of a 'post-and-lintel' system, in which vertical columns support horizontal beams. The large Doric columns on the temple's exterior are characterized by entasis, meaning that each column curves towards the middle slightly as it rises. At the Parthenon the corner columns are slightly larger in diameter than the others, and so they frame the colonnade on all sides. Each of the Parthenon's exterior Doric columns is more than 1.9 m (6 ft) in diameter and 10.4 m (34 ft) high.

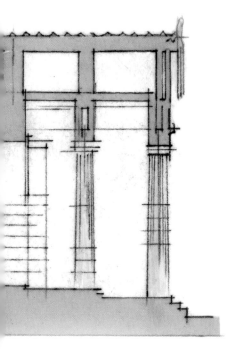

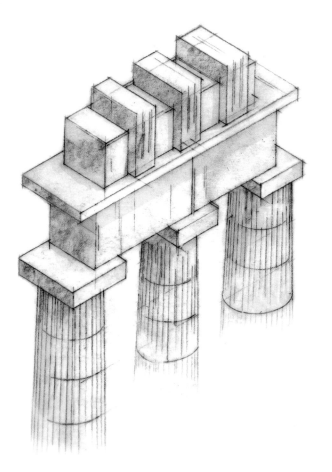

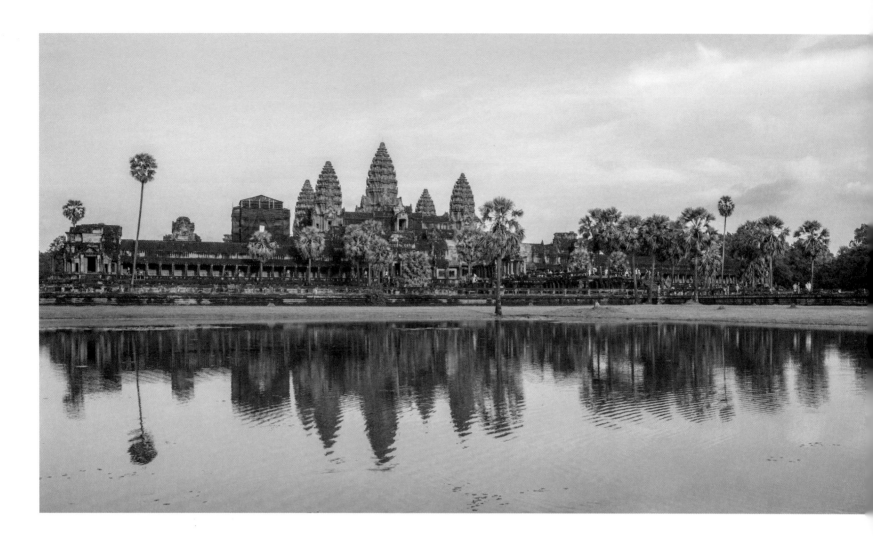

Angkor Wat

LOCATION   Krong Siem Reap, Cambodia
ARCHITECT   Unknown

STYLE   Khmer Imperial Hindu
BUILT   c. 1113–50

When the temple of Angkor Wat was built in the first half of the twelfth century, it was the largest religious complex in the world. It covered 163 hectares (402 acres), its central tower sitting upon raised levels, 213 m (699 ft) above the ground outside the complex. It is taller than the Great Pyramid (c. 2580–2560 BCE) at Giza, which is 138.8 m (455 ft) high. The temple was situated in the city of Angkor in modern Cambodia, when the city's residents numbered from 700,000 to 1 million. In overall population, Angkor rivalled ancient cities such as Rome, let alone any Western European capital in the Middle Ages.

Today, visitors to the highly accessible Notre Dame Cathedral (1163–1345) in the heart of Paris number more than 13 million per year, whereas Angkor Wat sees about 2 million annually in its more isolated location. Such statistics from the distant past and present serve as a reminder that the wonders of the world recognized by scholars and the general public alike go well beyond pyramids, palaces and cathedrals.

The great temple complex of Angkor Wat was built c. 1113 to 1150 in the Khmer Empire's capital by King Suryavarman II, whose reign from 1113 to 1150 was considered the empire's golden age. This gigantic temple to the Hindu god Vishnu is thought to have been the state temple and funerary complex for the king, in part because of its unorthodox orientation to the west, or setting sun, rather than the east. Its design is meant to represent the cosmos, and its five towers the peaks of the mythic Mt Meru, the universe's centre. The towers are of lotus-bud design, and archaeologists posit that their roofs were gilt and both outer and inner walls whitewashed. The structure is built of mostly dry laid sandstone, with the outer walls and foundations of laterite. Approximately 5 to 10 million sandstone blocks were used, quarried about 40 km (25 miles) to the northeast. The blocks were often dovetail or mortise and tenon jointed, almost as if they were wood cabinetry. Galleries within the concentric surrounding walls often contain elaborate bas-reliefs; the space between the outer walls and second level is thought by some to have been flooded to represent the ocean around Mt Meru. The 5-km (3.1-mile) long and 220-m (656-ft) wide moat outside the complex controlled the rising water table during the monsoon season, thereby preventing flooding within the temple complex.

Internal rivalries in the Khmer Empire, natural disasters, disease and conversion to Buddhism all led to the sack of Angkor in 1431, followed by the deterioration of numerous temples near that previous Khmer capital. While natural vegetation slowly engulfed the temple ruins, European visitors – missionaries, explorers, tourists and then archaeologists – first experienced its scale and architectural wonders from the sixteenth through to the early twentieth century. From 1907 to 1970 the École Française d'Extrême-Orient (French School of Asian Studies) spearheaded its stabilization and initial restoration. Work continues by multinational efforts after minor damage in the Cambodian Civil War (1967–75), and today Angkor Wat is recognized as one of the architectural wonders of the world.

BOTTOM LEFT This aerial view of Angkor Wat shows the site, surrounded by an apron of open ground and the moat that collects runoff from the temple site during monsoon rains.

BOTTOM RIGHT The construction of the Ta Prohm temple complex at Angkor was initiated by the Khmer monarch Jayavarman VII. It was built in the Bayon style during the late twelfth and early thirteenth centuries.

SURYAVARMAN II

Suryavarman II was the first Khmer king to be depicted in art in a sculpted relief at Angkor Wat. He expanded the Khmer Empire via successful military campaigns. The empire stretched over 2.5 million sq km (965,000 square miles). It included much of modern Cambodia, Thailand, Laos, and parts of Myanmar, Vietnam and even India. He changed religious orientation in the region from Buddhism to Hindu cults of Shiva and Vishnu. His massive temple of Angkor Wat was the centrepiece symbol of his power, before and after his death.

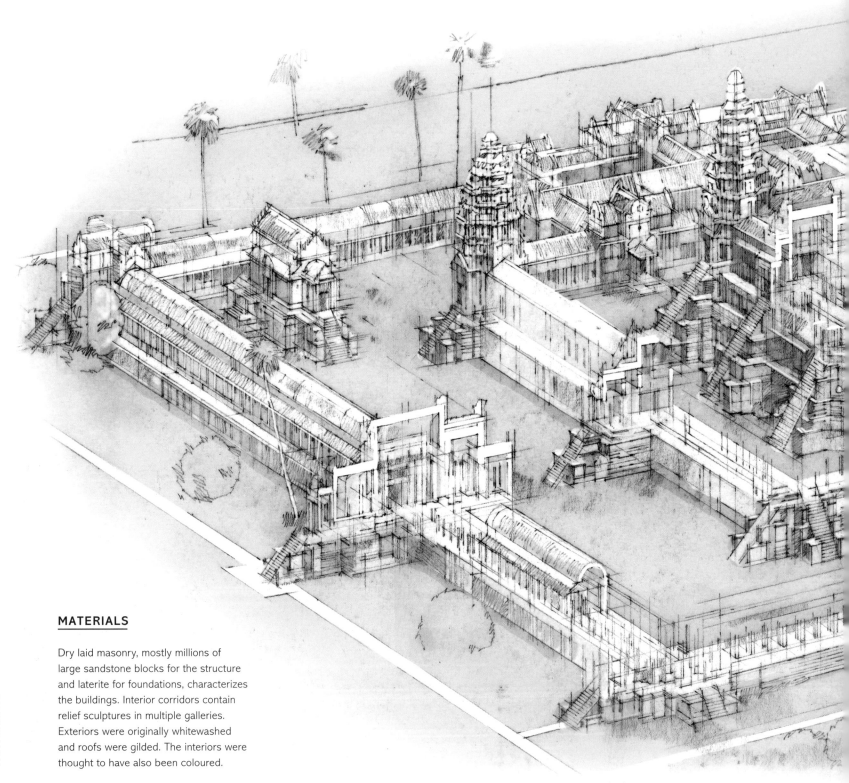

MATERIALS

Dry laid masonry, mostly millions of large sandstone blocks for the structure and laterite for foundations, characterizes the buildings. Interior corridors contain relief sculptures in multiple galleries. Exteriors were originally whitewashed and roofs were gilded. The interiors were thought to have also been coloured.

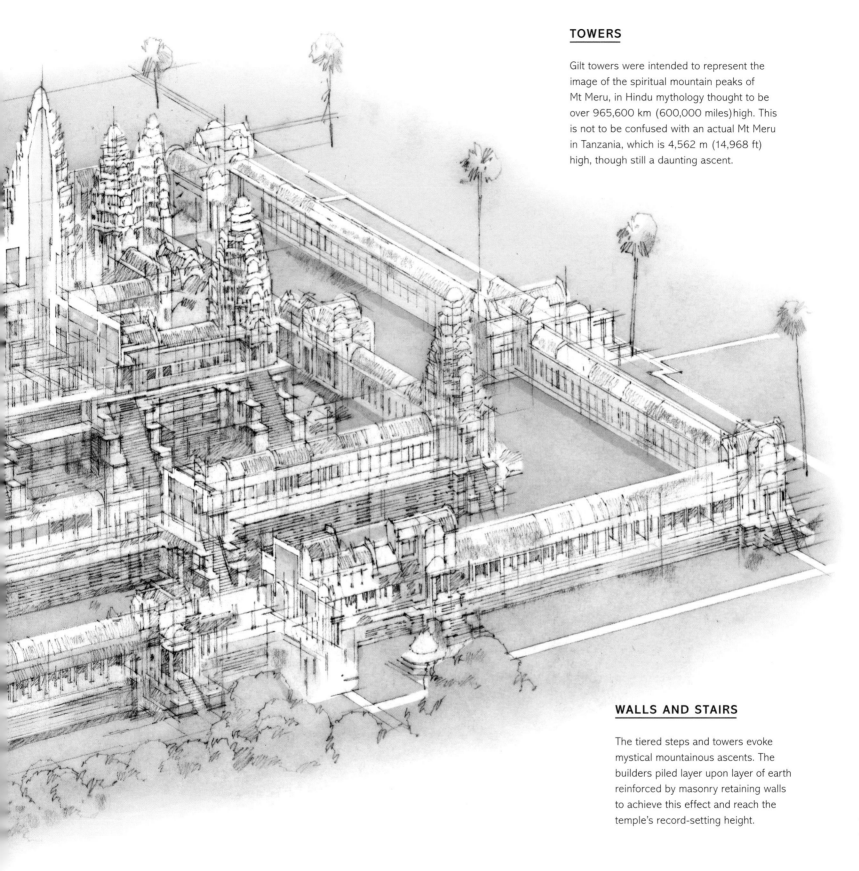

TOWERS

Gilt towers were intended to represent the image of the spiritual mountain peaks of Mt Meru, in Hindu mythology thought to be over 965,600 km (600,000 miles) high. This is not to be confused with an actual Mt Meru in Tanzania, which is 4,562 m (14,968 ft) high, though still a daunting ascent.

WALLS AND STAIRS

The tiered steps and towers evoke mystical mountainous ascents. The builders piled layer upon layer of earth reinforced by masonry retaining walls to achieve this effect and reach the temple's record-setting height.

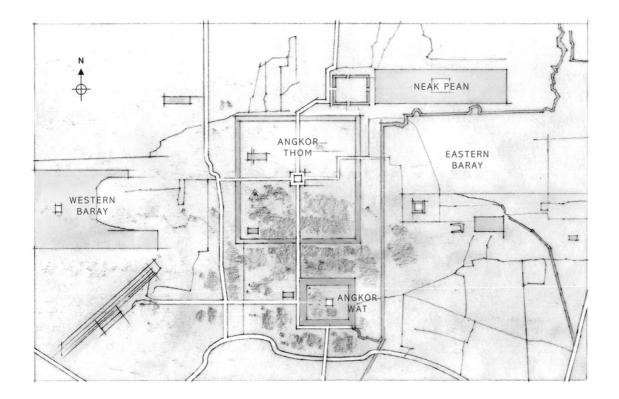

▲ SITE PLAN

The plan shows Angkor Thom at the centre of the image. This was the capital of the Khmer Empire ruled from 1181 to 1218 by Jayavarman VII, one of the successors to Suryavarman II. Jayavarman VII reinstated Buddhism as the state religion. His capital overlapped earlier Khmer Empire capitals such as the one built by Suryavarman II. These cities, with Angkor at the core, lasted until sacked in 1431. The barays shown were large bodies of water created by Khmer kings, possibly to control the water table. The west one is still extant, whereas the east one is farmland today. They were part of Angkor's infrastructure, which spread over 1,000 sq km (390 square miles).

▶ STATE AND FUNERARY TEMPLE

The temple was thought to be not only Suryavarman II's state temple but also his funerary one. Whatever was in the cryptlike space at the bottom of the shaft well below the central tower was long ago looted, though excavations show traces of gold and crystal. Likewise, the sculptural image of Vishnu atop the main tower has long since been destroyed. Recent discoveries include several hundred paintings throughout the temple complex and in the main tower.

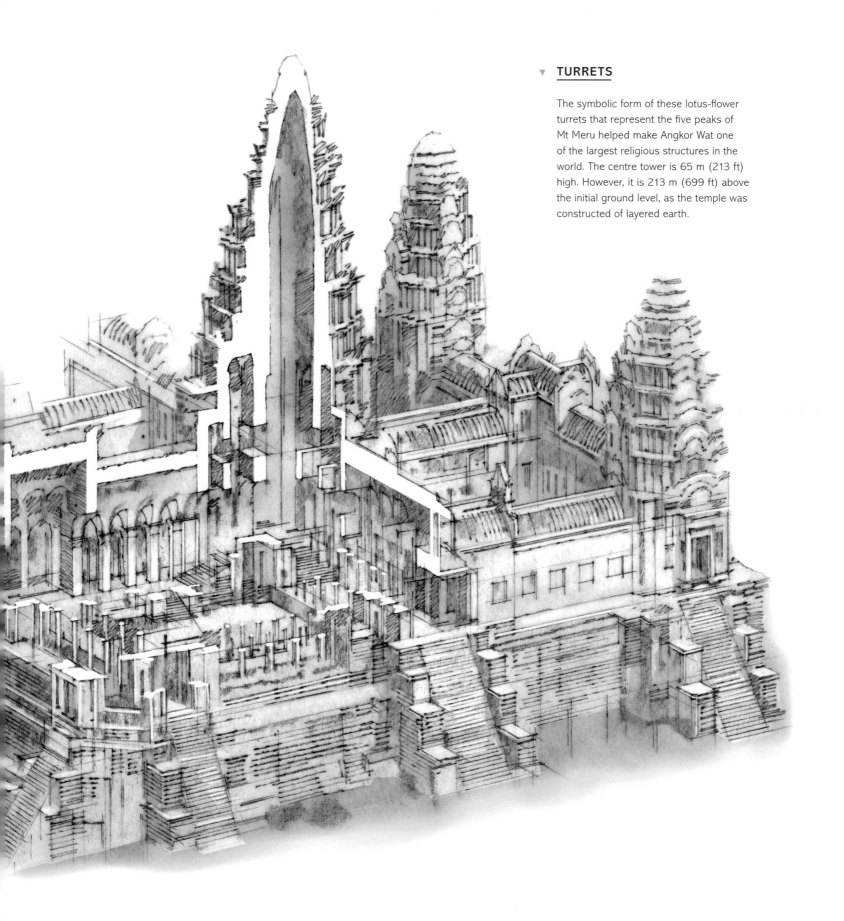

▼ TURRETS

The symbolic form of these lotus-flower turrets that represent the five peaks of Mt Meru helped make Angkor Wat one of the largest religious structures in the world. The centre tower is 65 m (213 ft) high. However, it is 213 m (699 ft) above the initial ground level, as the temple was constructed of layered earth.

Taj Mahal

LOCATION   Agra, India
ARCHITECT   Ustad Ahmad Lahauri, Ustad Isa Shirazi and others
STYLE   Mughal Indian
BUILT   1632–48

When people think of the Taj Mahal, many recall the photograph of Diana, Princess of Wales, sitting on a bench in front of it in 1992, or the visit of her son Prince William, Duke of Cambridge, with his wife Catherine, Duchess of Cambridge, in 2016 and their photograph on the same bench. Many associate this site with romance – associations prompted by the story of this building constructed by a king for his queen.

The seventeenth-century Mughal emperor Shah Jahan built this structure for his favourite wife, Mumtaz Mahal, who died in childbirth, to serve as her palace-scaled, marble mausoleum (1632–48). The emperor is considered to have brought a golden age of Mughal art and architecture to India, of which the Taj Mahal is the epitome. But it is more than a single building; it is the centrepiece of a walled complex of more than 17 hectares (42 acres) containing elaborate gates, smaller mausoleums, gardens and a mosque. Historians posit that the complex was planned in a modular way. It sits on the Yamuna River at the edge of the walled city of Agra. The Taj Mahal mausoleum is built of white marble cladding over brick, set on a foundation of brick and rubble, which contrasts with the red sandstone of the gates, wall and mosque. Mughal poets often likened this great white building to a cloud.

The smaller mausoleums in the complex were built for the emperor's other wives as well as one of Mumtaz's favourite servants. The four-part gardens derive in plan from Persian 'paradise gardens' and included trees that signified life (fruit-bearing) and death (cypress). The mausoleum within the Taj Mahal consists of a multilevel vaulted space that houses the emperor's and empress's sculptural sarcophagi and their tombs below

on the lowest level. The exterior and some surfaces have highly decorated inlaid abstract and calligraphic patterns representative of much of Islamic architecture. The Taj Mahal has an enormous dome 44 m (144 ft) high with a finial, now bronze, that was originally gold. The finial is the symbolic *tamga*, or seal of the Mughal Empire. Emperor Shah Jahan had a team of architects working on the complex, and no single design architect is identified. However, some believe Ustad Ahmad Lahauri (1580–1649) and Ustad Isa Shirazi to be the primary architects, with additional supervision of

the 20,000 construction workers by others such as Mir Abd-ul Karim and Makramat Khan. The total cost of the work is estimated at 32 million rupees – the equivalent of $827 million today.

Emperor Shah Jahan's son deposed him, and when the emperor died he was buried alongside his favourite wife. During invasions in the eighteenth century the mausoleum experienced some damage through plundering. The nineteenth century witnessed further deterioration, as did the twentieth, though repairs and maintenance were implemented during the

British Indian period. More recent damage includes increased discoloration of the marble by pollution, and a decreasing water table that threatens the foundations. It is a UNESCO World Heritage Site that is recognized by the Indian government for its historic and touristic importance. For the 800,000 or so tourists who visit the Taj Mahal each year, and the millions more who see its image elsewhere, from souvenirs to theme park and casino replicas, its importance lives on in popular culture as an exotic architectural monument from the distant past.

ABOVE LEFT Inlaid inscriptions and abstract floral patterns found on the exterior and interior of the Taj Mahal.

ABOVE RIGHT The elaborate polygonal arcades beneath the dome surround the decoratively sculpted cenotaphs for the emperor and empress, though their actual tombs are located within the crypt below.

ISLAMIC INDIA

India has a variety of faiths including Hinduism, Islam, Buddhism and Christianity. Islamic traditions along the coast date to Arab trading routes and subsequent successful military operations of the seventh and eighth centuries, particularly in Pakistan and Afghanistan. However, many think that the golden age of Islamic influence came with the sixteenth-century Mughal emperor Babur, a descendant of the Turkic conqueror Tamerlane and the Mongol ruler Genghis Khan. The Mughal dynasty controlled much of India from 1526 until its influence waned in the eighteenth century.

1 DOME

The Taj Mahal's double-shelled dome soars 65 m (213 ft) above ground level. It derives from Timurid domes of the fourteenth and fifteenth centuries. Among the earliest of these is Tamerlane's tomb, Gur-e Amir (1408) in Samarkand, Uzbekistan. The first double dome in India may be at the tomb of Sikandar Lodi (1518) in Lodi Gardens, New Delhi.

2 MINARETS

Islamic architectural forms were introduced in the region after 1206. One such masterpiece is the 73-m (240-ft) high minaret Qutub Minar of the Qutb complex in Delhi (1192–1220 and later). The four towers at the corners of the Taj Mahal are more typical of those in Islamic architecture. Minarets function as stations from which *muezzin* call to prayer. The earliest likely date from stair towers at each corner of a mosque built in Fostat, later Old Cairo (*c.* 658).

3 PISHTAQS

A *pishtaq* is a recessed arch. *Pishtaq*s are shown as cutaways on two facades here. Each measures 33 m (108 ft) high and provides a wall plane for decorations and Koranic inscriptions. The one on the main entry reads: 'O Soul, thou art at rest. Return to the Lord at peace with Him, and He at peace with you.'

4 CHHATRIS

Chhatris are the four smaller pavilion-like domed structures that flank the main dome of the Taj Mahal. *Chhatri* derives from the word for canopy, and these structures were adapted from Hindu architecture by the Mughals. They were originally used as freestanding memorial pavilions in Hindu culture.

SECTION

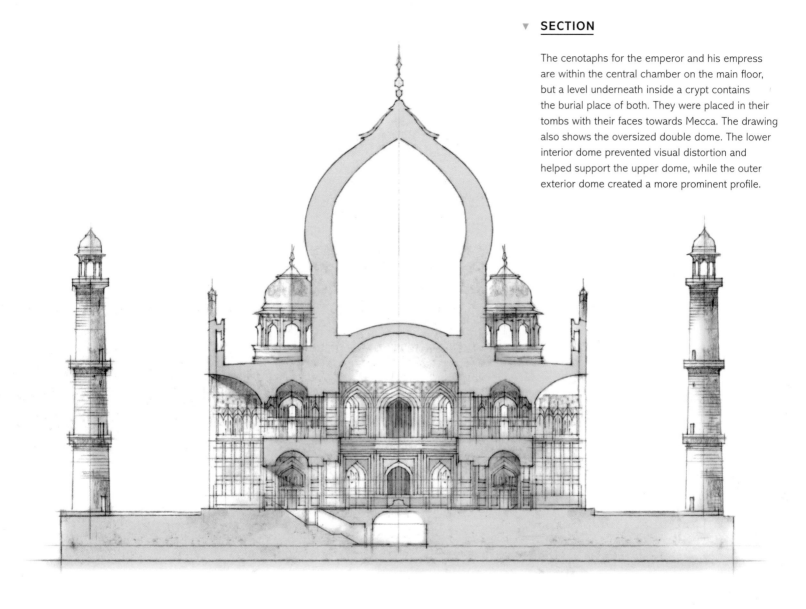

The cenotaphs for the emperor and his empress are within the central chamber on the main floor, but a level underneath inside a crypt contains the burial place of both. They were placed in their tombs with their faces towards Mecca. The drawing also shows the oversized double dome. The lower interior dome prevented visual distortion and helped support the upper dome, while the outer exterior dome created a more prominent profile.

▶ SITE PLAN

The 17-hectare (42-acre) walled site has gardens that derive from Persian iconographic sources, additional mosques and burial sites, and gatehouses guarding the royal mausoleum. More than 20,000 workers built the Taj Mahal and structures throughout the funerary complex. The walled garden across the river was the Mahtab Bagh, or Imperial Moonlight Garden, the last of eleven Mughal gardens here.

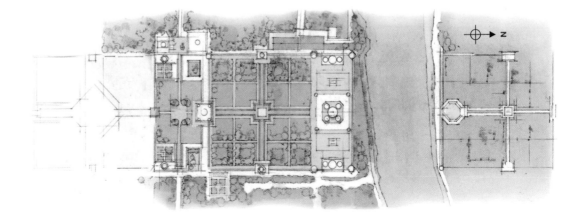

Palace of Versailles

LOCATION   Versailles, France
ARCHITECT   Louis Le Vau, Jules Hardouin-Mansart and others
STYLE   French Baroque
BUILT   1624–1770

People get a taste of the extravagance and decadence of the Palace of Versailles in the seventeenth and eighteenth centuries from films such as *Marie Antoinette* (1938; 2006) and television shows such as *Versailles: The Dream of a King* (2008) and *Versailles* (2015–). The massive, mostly marble palace, gardens and various outbuildings occupy an area of approximately 800 hectares (2,000 acres). They serve as a reminder of the French monarchy's glory and opulence before the Revolution of 1789.

Today the town of Versailles is a commuter suburb southwest of Paris, but in the early seventeenth century it was rural woodland where King Louis XIII built a chateau–hunting lodge in 1624. His son, King Louis XIV, expanded the hunting lodge into a palace between 1661 and 1680. Architect Louis Le Vau (1612–70) began the design, and work continued under his second in charge, François d'Orbay (1634–97). Artist Charles Le Brun worked on the elaborate decorative schemes and landscape architect André Le Nôtre created the

extensive gardens. Versailles' construction took the hunting lodge as its centre and expanded it into a U-shaped courtyard plan, creating accommodation for the royal family, the king's suite being on the north side and the queen's on the south, each having a sequence of seven rooms. When it was completed, Louis XIV moved the royal court from Paris to Versailles in 1682 and continued to plan expansions. The next campaign of works took place from 1699 to 1710 and concentrated on building the Royal Chapel

designed by Jules Hardouin-Mansart (1646–1708). Mansart created the north and south wings and the 73-m (239-ft) long Galerie des Glaces, or Hall of Mirrors, in the terrace between the two royal apartments. Mansart also designed the Grand Trianon (1688) on the palace grounds for the king's mistress, Françoise-Athénaïs de Rochechouart, Marquise de Montespan.

The death of Louis XIV in 1715 saw the accession to the throne by the boy king Louis XV, followed by the move of the court back to Paris. Louis XV returned

to the palace in 1722 to complete construction and implement new projects. Renovations on the upper floors continued for the royal family apartments, and the Royal Opera (1770) theatre and opera house was completed as a counterbalance to the chapel in the same wing. This work was done by architect Ange-Jacques Gabriel (1698–1782), who also designed the Château of the Petit Trianon (1762–68) on the grounds for the king's mistress, Jeanne Antoinette Poisson, Marquise de Pompadour.

The next ruler, King Louis XVI, focused on garden replanting and some redesign by landscapist and painter Hubert Robert, as well as interior redesign. This included the apartment for Queen Marie Antoinette designed by Richard Mique (1728–94), who also worked on the garden near the Petit Trianon. After the French Revolution the château at Versailles served various purposes; it was made a museum in 1837 and has been used for a variety of state functions. Today 7.5 million people annually tour the site.

ABOVE LEFT The scale and decorative grandeur of the Royal Chapel at Versailles rival even its famed Gothic predecessor, the Sainte-Chapelle in Paris (1248), commissioned by King Louis IX.

ABOVE RIGHT Royal architect Ange-Jacques Gabriel used the Petit Trianon as a manifesto for the Neoclassical movement – the Greco-Roman style that was spreading across Europe in the eighteenth century.

HALL OF MIRRORS

The Hall of Mirrors is on the second floor of the palace, overlooking the gardens. The room measures 73 m (239 ft) long and contains 357 panes of mirrored glass. Its elaborate ceiling decorations include thirty murals painted c. 1680 by Charles Le Brun that depict accomplishments and military victories from the life of Louis XIV. The capitals atop the pilasters are a variant of Composite (Corinthian and Ionic) capitals that was called a new French order. The room has national symbols of roosters, the fleur-de-lis and the royal sun of Louis XIV, all designed by Le Brun.

AERIAL VIEW

This impressionistic view indicates
the expanse of the palace grounds that
cover nearly 809 hectares (2,000 acres).
By contrast, the United States Capitol
(1792–1891; see p. 34) sits within
landscaped grounds just under 24 hectares
(59 acres), and the original Disneyland
in California covers only 35 hectares
(85 acres). The palace shown at
the lower right covers 67,000 sq m
(712,000 sq ft) and is one of the
largest in the world.

1   GRAND CANAL

Numerous water features on the grounds
include eleven fountains and the Grand Canal.
The main portion of this waterway runs almost
1.6 km (1 mile) long on an east–west axis
with the palace. It is more than 61 m (200 ft)
wide and has cross canals that connect to the
Trianon grounds to the north. During Louis
XIV's tenure, the king took gondola rides on
the canal. Today visitors can emulate past
royalty by rowing in small boats kept moored
within the eastern basin.

2   LATONA FOUNTAIN

The centrepiece of the formal gardens created by
Le Nôtre just west of the palace is the Latona Fountain.
The fountain tells the story in sculptures of Apollo the
sun god, whose emblem Louis XIV adopted as Sun
King. Sculptural additions were made by the brothers
Gaspard and Balthazar Marsy beginning in 1667, here
and throughout the gardens. Figures such as turtles
and lizards gave this water feature its initial name of
Frogs' Fountain. But the story of Apollo's childhood
held sway and in 1668 a sculpture was introduced
representing Latona, mother of Apollo and Diana,
who punished some people who had insulted her by
changing them into frogs. Jules Hardouin-Mansart and
artist Claude Bertin modified the composition further.

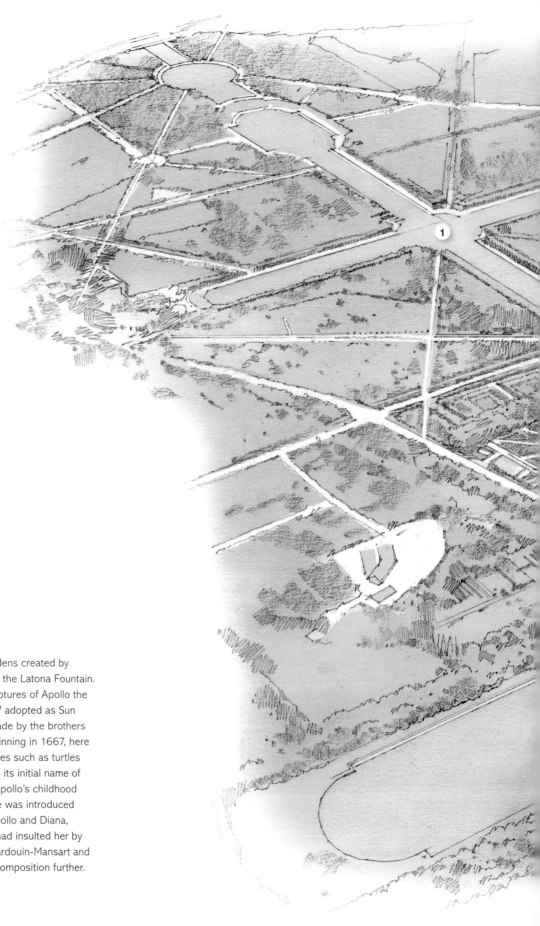

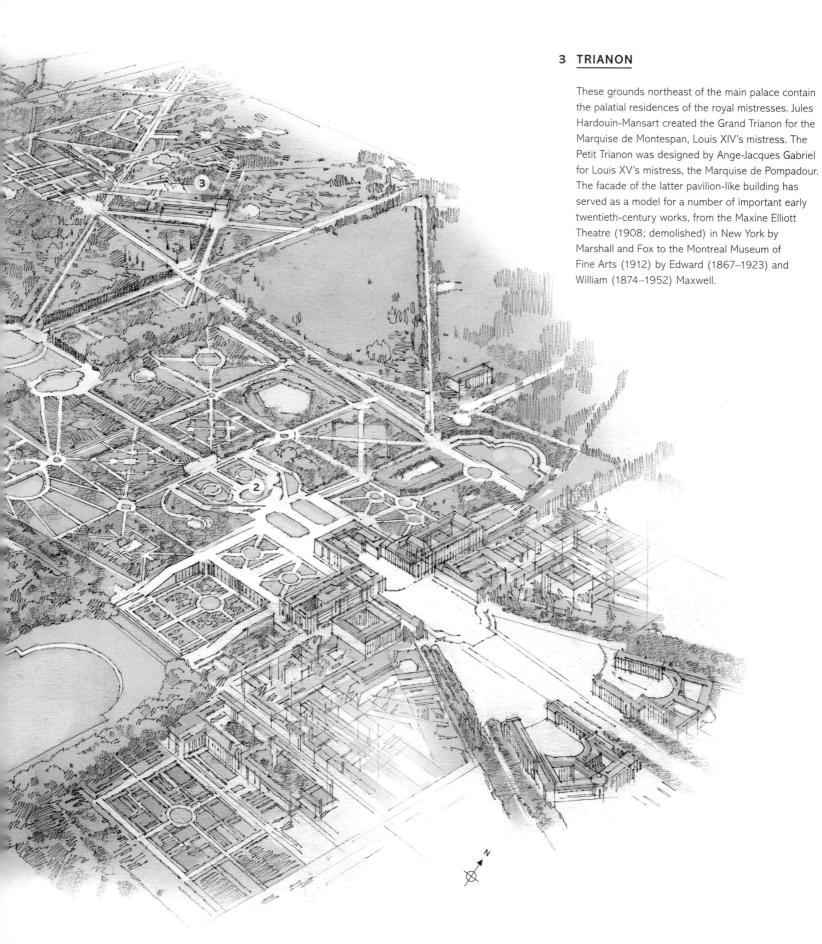

3 TRIANON

These grounds northeast of the main palace contain the palatial residences of the royal mistresses. Jules Hardouin-Mansart created the Grand Trianon for the Marquise de Montespan, Louis XIV's mistress. The Petit Trianon was designed by Ange-Jacques Gabriel for Louis XV's mistress, the Marquise de Pompadour. The facade of the latter pavilion-like building has served as a model for a number of important early twentieth-century works, from the Maxine Elliott Theatre (1908; demolished) in New York by Marshall and Fox to the Montreal Museum of Fine Arts (1912) by Edward (1867–1923) and William (1874–1952) Maxwell.

▶ FLOOR PLAN

The core of the palace complex plan shows the Hall of Mirrors (A) at the top and the Marble Court (B) just below at the very centre. The wider Royal Court (C) is immediately below that, its space expanding from the plan's setbacks. The king's chambers (D) were to the right, in the north side, and the queen's (E) to the left, or south. The curved space on the right side is the Royal Chapel (1710; F) and the Royal Opera (1720; G) theatre is located farther down the north wing.

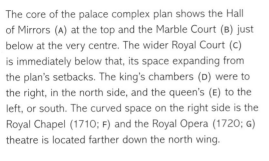

▼ HALL OF MIRRORS

The Hall of Mirrors connected to Halls of War and Peace on either side, which then led to the royal apartments. The space below the Hall of Mirrors is a gallery.

▲ ROYAL APARTMENT

The king's private quarters were adjacent to the Marble
Court on the second floor, north side, and the spaces
nearby were for state apartments. His private quarters
from 1701 also included dining and guards rooms,
a council chamber and various other chambers and
antechambers, as well as internal courtyards. The queen
had a comparable expanse of rooms accessible via the
Hall of Mirrors on the other side of the Marble Court.

▲ MANSARD ROOF

This is a schematic depiction of the facade from the Marble
Court, on the east side of the palace, so called for its patterned
marble floor. Atop this structure immediately adjacent to the
court are elaborately detailed mansard roofs, named after
Baroque architect François Mansart (1598–1666). He often
utilized these gambrel-style hip roofs, which created extra
space within. François's grandnephew Jules designed the
Hall of Mirrors and made additional changes to the palace.

Monticello

LOCATION   Charlottesville, Virginia, United States of America
ARCHITECT   Thomas Jefferson
STYLE   Neoclassical
BUILT   1796–1809

Few US presidents' homes have received as much attention as that of Thomas Jefferson (1743–1826). Virginia born, Jefferson was educated at the College of William and Mary. He was the principal author of the Declaration of Independence in 1776 and served as the United States' Minister to France from 1785 to 1789, as well as the first Secretary of State from 1790 to 1793. He was elected vice president in 1797 and then third president of the new nation in 1801. Perhaps his biggest contribution to the future of the United States was to acquire territory from France in 1803 through

the Louisiana Purchase. For $15 million Jefferson added 2,144,480 sq km (827,987 square miles) of territory to the south and west. This act laid the groundwork for the subsequent belief in 'manifest destiny', which promoted expansion to the Pacific Ocean and the Gulf of Mexico. Upon his retirement to Monticello in 1809 after two terms as president, Jefferson stated that he was now 'a prisoner released from his chains'.

Jefferson began building his dream home in 1768 of locally moulded brick, timber and stone on his 2,000-hectare (5,000-acre) plantation, constructed by

local tradesmen and his enslaved workers. The main house that we see today was built between 1796 and 1809 and contains thirty-three rooms over 990 sq m (10,660 sq ft). The house is 33.5 m long by 26.8 m wide (110 × 88 ft) and almost 13.7 m (45 ft) high to the oculus of the dome.

The architectural result was inspired by Jefferson's experiences as Minister to France. There he came in contact with the latest ideas about French architecture, as well as with Roman ruins, particularly the Maison Carrée (2–7 CE) in Nîmes. This building served as

the model for the Virginia State Capitol (1788) in Richmond, which he designed with French architect Charles-Louis Clérisseau (1721–1820). Jefferson's architecture is also informed by the designs of Italian architect Andrea Palladio (1508–80; see p. 188). Jefferson's design for the Rotunda (1822–26) at the University of Virginia was inspired by the Roman Pantheon (118–128 CE) as published by Palladio. For Monticello, Jefferson had consulted an English translation *The Architecture of A. Palladio* (1721). *Jefferson's Memorandum Book*s (1767–1826) refer to Palladio's book as well as that of Palladio-influenced Englishman James Gibbs (1682–1754), *A Book of Architecture* (1728). Jefferson's drawings document his efforts to create a Palladian country villa at Monticello. Indeed, many compare this work with the similarly styled Chiswick House (1729) in London, designed by William Kent (*c*. 1685–1748). Jefferson was buried on the grounds now part of the Monticello graveyard.

Beyond architecture, Jefferson's quirkiness was reflected in his inventions. He was noted for being the creator of the first swivel chair, a cipher wheel for coded secret messages, an award-winning plough and a spherical sundial. Monticello had other practical innovations, such as a clothes carousel in Jefferson's bedroom closet, dumbwaiters on pulleys to bring wine from the cellar into the dining room, a revolving service door with shelves for dishes to be easily transferred from the kitchen, double doors in the parlour that, when one is opened the other automatically follows, and a revolving bookstand in his office. The site has been open to the public since 1923.

ABOVE An alcove bed, open on two sides, joins Jefferson's bedroom with his office. A hinged, double-door screen separated the two rooms when shut.

RIGHT Two sets of window sashes insulate the dining room, which was inspired by Palladio. The room also features one of Monticello's thirteen skylights.

UNIVERSITY OF VIRGINIA

Jefferson's other architectural statements include the Virginia State Capitol in Richmond as well as the University of Virginia at Charlottesville, the latter approximately 5 miles (8 km) northwest of Monticello. His style is evident in the Palladian-influenced Rotunda, which served as the library, measuring 77 ft (23.5 m) in height and diameter. It is the centerpiece of a U-shaped campus of classicist brick buildings connected by colonnades. Jefferson designed it in 1817 with the advice of architects such as William Thornton and Benjamin Henry Latrobe, who were designers for the United States Capitol (1792–1891; see p. 34).

DOME

The building is visually marked by its dome, especially on the west or garden side. The domical space above is punctuated by oculi that ventilate the room above the portico and draw air through the entire building. The space below was Jefferson's parlour, shaded by the garden-side portico. The domed space was infrequently used. It has been restored with yellow and white walls and a painted green floor – colours from Jefferson's era.

PORTICO

The western portico helps provide shade on the garden side. A similarly scaled eastern portico highlights the main entry on the opposite side of the building. The home appears initially to be a bilaterally symmetrical rectilinear design, but closer inspection reveals that the north and south ends have polygonal corner rooms (see p. 106). The north and south sides have porches and are framed by piazzas. The classical porticoes at Monticello project the image of an Italian country villa.

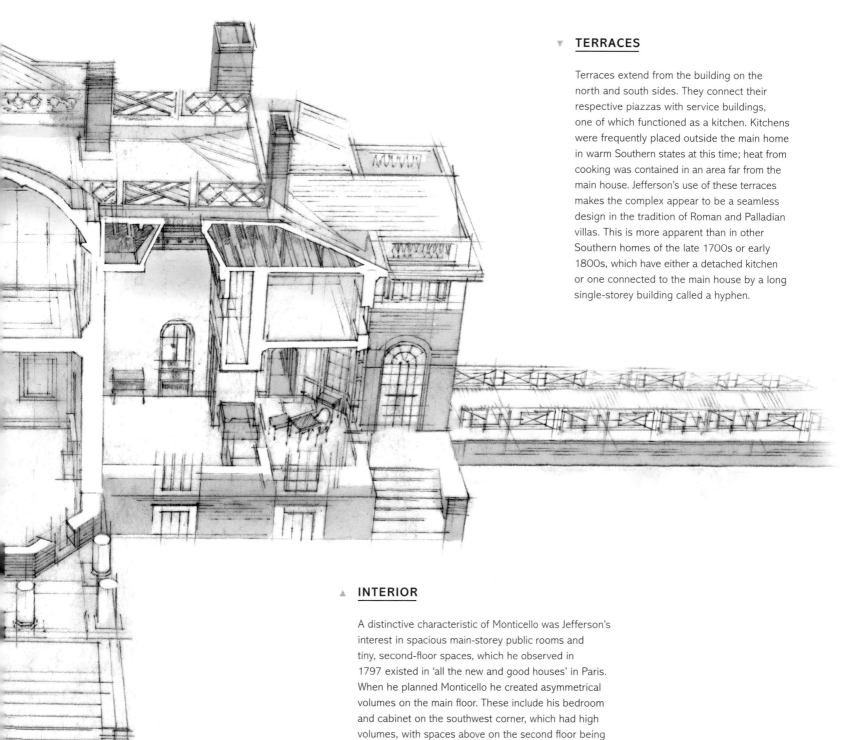

▼ TERRACES

Terraces extend from the building on the
north and south sides. They connect their
respective piazzas with service buildings,
one of which functioned as a kitchen. Kitchens
were frequently placed outside the main home
in warm Southern states at this time; heat from
cooking was contained in an area far from the
main house. Jefferson's use of these terraces
makes the complex appear to be a seamless
design in the tradition of Roman and Palladian
villas. This is more apparent than in other
Southern homes of the late 1700s or early
1800s, which have either a detached kitchen
or one connected to the main house by a long
single-storey building called a hyphen.

▲ INTERIOR

A distinctive characteristic of Monticello was Jefferson's
interest in spacious main-storey public rooms and
tiny, second-floor spaces, which he observed in
1797 existed in 'all the new and good houses' in Paris.
When he planned Monticello he created asymmetrical
volumes on the main floor. These include his bedroom
and cabinet on the southwest corner, which had high
volumes, with spaces above on the second floor being
greatly compressed in size. Oculi within the walls
of his bedroom also facilitated airflow.

▼ FLOOR PLAN

The plan includes generic guest rooms such as the North Octagonal Room, which was informally dedicated to President James Madison and his wife, Dolley, who frequently visited the home. The square room near Jefferson's library was used by his daughter Martha Randolph as a family sitting room in which to educate her children.

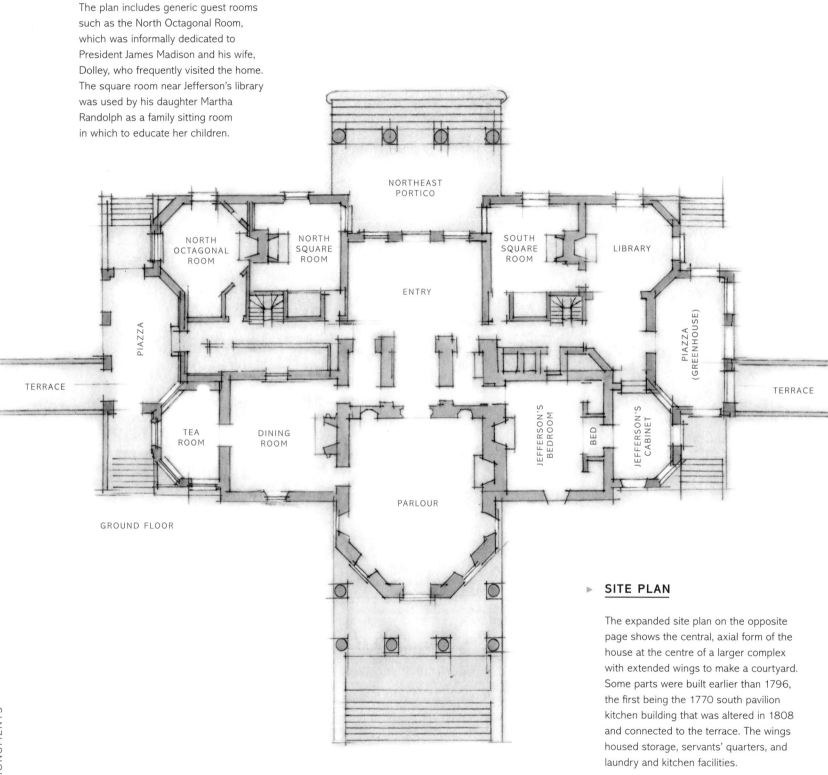

NORTHEAST PORTICO

NORTH OCTAGONAL ROOM

NORTH SQUARE ROOM

SOUTH SQUARE ROOM

LIBRARY

ENTRY

PIAZZA

PIAZZA (GREENHOUSE)

TERRACE

TERRACE

TEA ROOM

DINING ROOM

JEFFERSON'S BEDROOM

BED

JEFFERSON'S CABINET

PARLOUR

GROUND FLOOR

► SITE PLAN

The expanded site plan on the opposite page shows the central, axial form of the house at the centre of a larger complex with extended wings to make a courtyard. Some parts were built earlier than 1796, the first being the 1770 south pavilion kitchen building that was altered in 1808 and connected to the terrace. The wings housed storage, servants' quarters, and laundry and kitchen facilities.

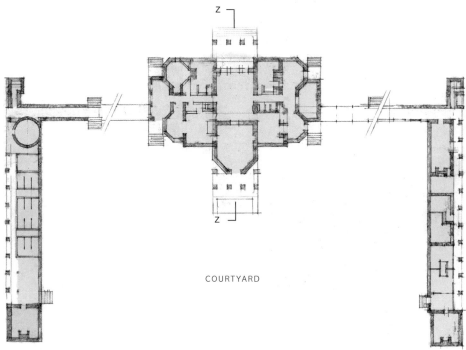

COURTYARD

The section (marked as z on the plan left) gives a good idea of the space between the entry and garden porticoes. The dome atop its octagonal drum is illuminated by large oculi, including one within the apex. The spacious parlour is below. The basement had a wine and beer cellar serviced by dumbwaiters on either side of the dining-room mantel above. Beer and cider were made here, with Jefferson's wife, Martha, in charge of the operation.
In 1813, long after Martha's death in 1782, Jefferson arranged for British captain Joseph Miller, stranded in the United States during the War of 1812, to teach one of his staff the fine art of brewing.

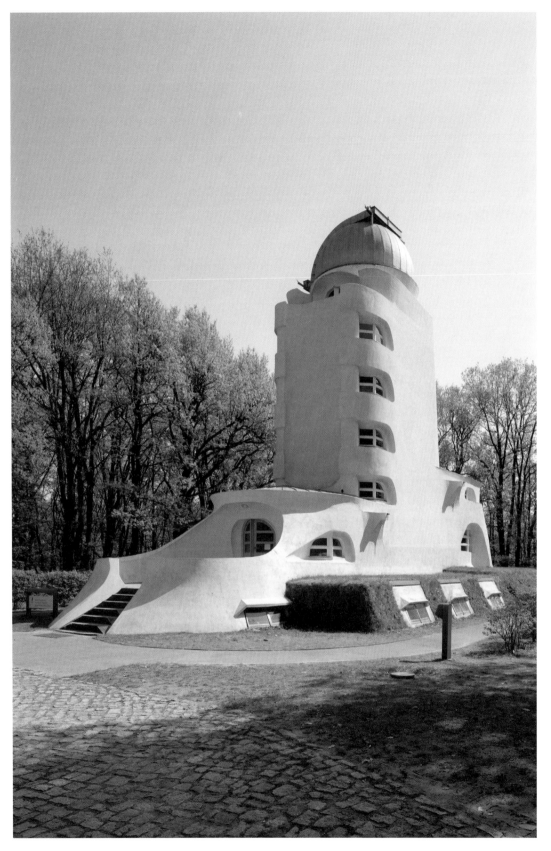

Einstein Tower

LOCATION	Babelsberg, Germany
ARCHITECT	Erich Mendelsohn
STYLE	Expressionist
BUILT	1919–21

What does $E=mc^2$ – the Theory of Relativity developed by physicist Albert Einstein – have to do with this building? Many say it was meant to represent a tangible, architectural expression of that theory. The equation expresses the fact that mass and energy are the same and can be changed into each other. So, the building is meant to visually convey mass and energy dynamically coexisting in one structure. The tower's client, astronomer Erwin Finlay-Freundlich, was an associate of Einstein who also tested this theory through astronomical experiments. Nevertheless, the story is a little more complex and derives from the early visions of the tower's architect, Erich Mendelsohn (1887–1953).

Mendelsohn was one of the most prominent German architects of the interwar years. Born in East Prussia, he studied under architect Theodor Fischer (1862–1938) at the Technical University in Munich, graduating in 1912. After his service in World War I (1914–18), his dramatic design for the Einstein Tower, and particularly the more visible renovation of the Mossehaus (1923) in Berlin, launched him on a career over the next decade creating dynamically expressive, mostly curvilinear designs for various buildings, especially department stores. Examples include the Schocken Department Stores in Nuremberg (1926), Stuttgart (1928) and Chemnitz (1930), all later adapted for other functions.

As a prominent Jewish architect, with the rise of National Socialism Mendelsohn chose to flee to England in 1933, where he designed several homes, as well as the De La Warr Pavilion in Bexhill-on-Sea, East Sussex (1935), with Russian-born architect Serge Chermayeff (1900–96). He also worked in Palestine (now Israel) on a variety of projects. He moved to the United States in 1941. During World War II (1939–45) he was one of several modernists who advised the US Army and Standard Oil Company in creating the German Village at the Dugway Proving Ground in Utah – traditional German housing blocks tested with incendiary and high-explosive munitions. After the war he designed a variety of Jewish-sponsored buildings: his last works included Park Synagogue in Cleveland Heights, Ohio, and Maimonides Hospital in San Francisco (both 1950).

The *Einsteinturm* (Einstein Tower; 1921) in Babelsberg near Potsdam was developed by Mendelsohn from his architectural visions sketched from 1917 to 1918, during World War I, and additional sketches from 1919, with plaster models made soon after. The tower is a diminutive one, only six storeys or 20 m (65.6 ft) high. The building has a larger footprint than shown above ground; underground spaces exist for laboratories as well as a spectrograph room. A workroom and an overnight room at the eastern curved end contain furnishings designed by Mendelsohn, but the remainder is principally a tower structure with a curved staircase that holds the heliostat under the observatory dome.

Mendelsohn met Finlay-Freundlich through his wife, Luise Maas. She and the astrophysicist were cellists. Finlay-Freundlich was employed at the Berlin Observatory in 1910, moving to new facilities in suburban Babelsberg in 1913. After being interned in Russia in World War I, Finlay-Freundlich returned to Berlin to work for the Einstein Institute, becoming their astronomer at the observatory in Potsdam from 1920 to 1924. With their friendship and Mendelsohn's dynamic design, the interpretation of Einstein's Theory of Relativity in architectural form makes sense. Soon after the structure was completed Mendelsohn described it as 'organic' and said it was related to Einstein's ideas. Mendelsohn wanted to build this solar observatory in concrete for its plasticity, but instead he made a sculptural tour de force from brick and stucco, with some concrete, though these materials have needed consistent maintenance since 1927. The tower was restored in 1999 and functions as a solar observatory as part of the Leibniz Institute for Astrophysics.

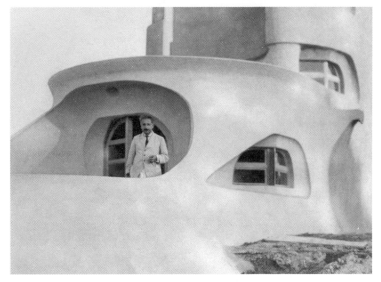

ABOVE The workroom in the 1920s. Mendelsohn even designed the office furniture and fixtures. Angled windows are located in streamlined niches, which are moulded into the round corners of the building.

LEFT Albert Einstein at the Einstein Tower in 1921.

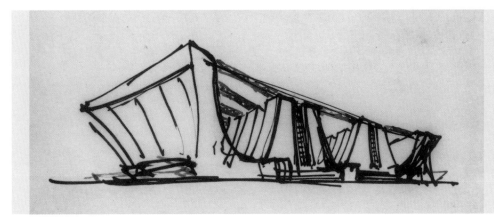

MENDELSOHN AND WORLD WAR I

While in military service during World War I, young Mendelsohn dreamed of a new architecture that reflected the dynamism of a new century, and his drawings acted as a psychological escape as he dreamed of the future. After the war he exhibited and published them in books such as *Das Gesamtschaffen des Architekten* (*The overall creation of the architect*, 1930). His wartime architectural dreams led to postwar realizations. Mendelsohn's expressive designs spoke of movement and modernity and were akin to what others theorized at the time, notably Italian Futurists such as Antonio Sant'Elia (1888–1916).

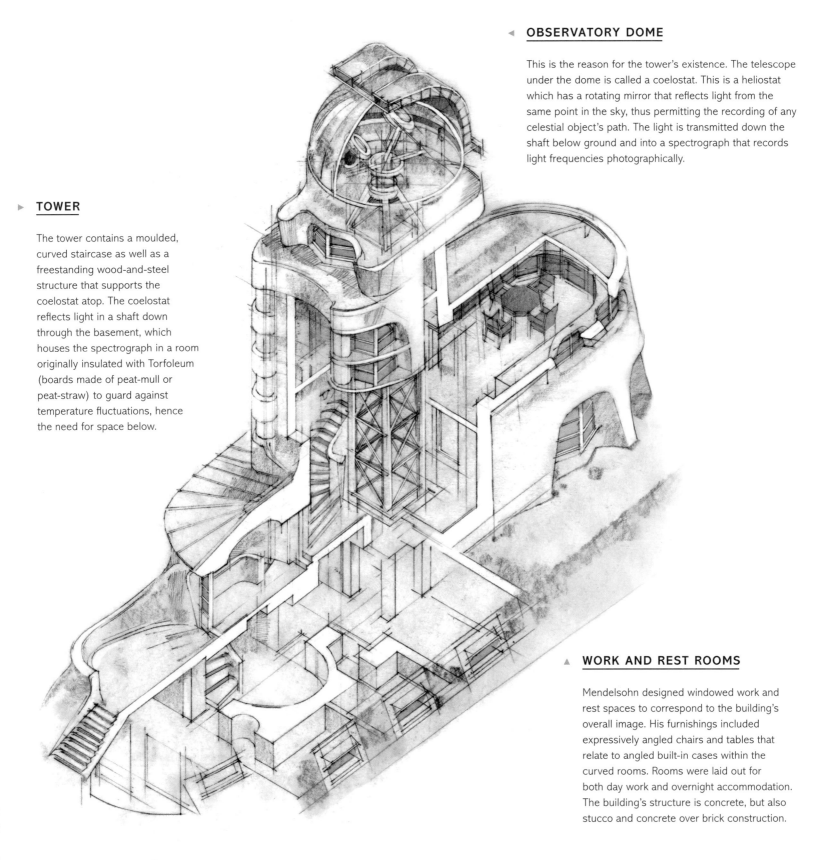

OBSERVATORY DOME

This is the reason for the tower's existence. The telescope under the dome is called a coelostat. This is a heliostat which has a rotating mirror that reflects light from the same point in the sky, thus permitting the recording of any celestial object's path. The light is transmitted down the shaft below ground and into a spectrograph that records light frequencies photographically.

TOWER

The tower contains a moulded, curved staircase as well as a freestanding wood-and-steel structure that supports the coelostat atop. The coelostat reflects light in a shaft down through the basement, which houses the spectrograph in a room originally insulated with Torfoleum (boards made of peat-mull or peat-straw) to guard against temperature fluctuations, hence the need for space below.

WORK AND REST ROOMS

Mendelsohn designed windowed work and rest spaces to correspond to the building's overall image. His furnishings included expressively angled chairs and tables that relate to angled built-in cases within the curved rooms. Rooms were laid out for both day work and overnight accommodation. The building's structure is concrete, but also stucco and concrete over brick construction.

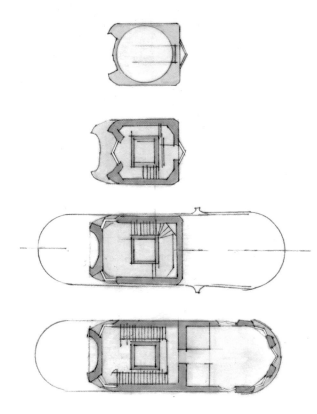

▲ SITE PLAN

This site plan of Albert Einstein Science Park shows the oblong-like tower situated on Telegraphenberg Hill (A). The hill has housed astronomical observatories since the 1870s. The original triple-domed Michelsonhaus (1879; c) is nearby, as is the large domed Grosser Refraktor (1899; B). The latter is one of the largest telescopes of its kind in the world. Various other buildings shown here house scientific organizations dedicated to climate, polar and marine studies.

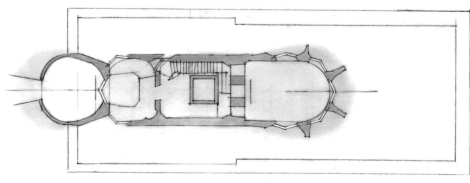

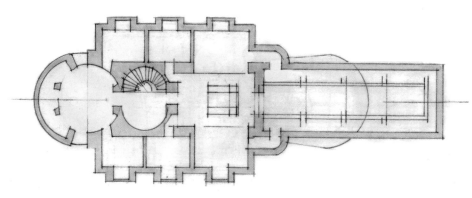

◀ FLOOR PLANS

The varying plans show the progression of the building from its subterranean level up to the round observatory dome. The building is deceptive in terms of the space needed for scientific purposes below ground, in relation to the smaller, more visible structure.

Arts and Education

The theme of arts and education throws a wide net. It encompasses art schools and museums, but also performing arts structures. In fact a host more could have been included within this category, including libraries, universities, schools, polytechnics and just about anything that involves formal and informal education. In reality, people are perpetual students and there is always something new to learn.

Both formal and informal education can be traced to antiquity if not further. Some related building types of today have a long pedigree. One can think of open-air Greek theatres, such as the one at Epidaurus (fourth century BCE), or European medieval universities, particularly the Late Gothic examples at Cambridge University in England such as King's College Chapel (1446–1515) or the First Court of St John's College (1511–20). The first museums – the etymology of the term deriving from the Greek *mouseion* denoting the muses – can likely be traced back to Plato's museum and library. They were initially cabinets of curiosities. The earliest extant building is likely the Ashmolean Museum (1683) at the University of Oxford. Public museums followed in the eighteenth and especially nineteenth centuries.

Today museums have an important influence in terms of providing educational opportunities as well as entertainment. Various national and regional museum associations exist, as well as the International Council of Museums (ICOM) established in 1946. ICOM represents more than 20,000 museums worldwide. Moreover, museums have an enormous economic impact. The American Alliance of Museums calculates that in the United States they employ more than 400,000 people and directly contribute $21 billion to the nation's economy each year. These statistics do not even include cultural tourism. Likewise, similar British organizations estimate that £1 in every £1,000 in the United

Kingdom's economy can be directly related to the museum and gallery sector, and that museums there employ more than 38,000 people and directly contribute £2.64 billion per year to the British economy. Of the twelve buildings in this chapter there are two art schools and two performing arts centres, but eight are museums.

Examples of museums designed by prominent architects can be found throughout the recent past, such as the Kimbell Art Museum (1966–72; see p. 146) in Fort Worth, Texas, by Louis Kahn (1901–74). However, that building type was launched into the foreground in the late twentieth and early twenty-first centuries. They have become secular, cultural cathedrals with so-called starchitects designing them. This is especially so for art museums, a phenomenon fuelled by the international media attention and popularity of two buildings in particular. The first is the Centre Georges Pompidou (1971–77; see p. 156) in Paris and the other is the Guggenheim Museum Bilbao (1991–97; see p. 168). Waves of art museums followed across the globe. Later prominent examples include the Neues Museum (2009) and Forum Museumsinsel (2016), both in Berlin and by David Chipperfield (b. 1953); the Modern Wing of the Art Institute of Chicago (2009) and the addition to the Kimbell Art Museum (2013), both by Renzo Piano (b.1937); the Museum of Fine Arts, Boston (2010) by Foster and Partners; the Aspen Art Museum (2014) by Shigeru Ban (b. 1957); and The Broad (2015) in Los Angeles by Diller Scofidio + Renfro.

Beyond art museums, history museums and science centres have also attempted to upgrade their facilities using A-list architects to create distinctive designs. Like the Bilbao effect, designs for these new buildings in the late twentieth century allowed them to compete for media attention and audience popularity, particularly after the creation of such facilities as the Cité des sciences et de l'industrie (Cultural Centre of Science, Technology

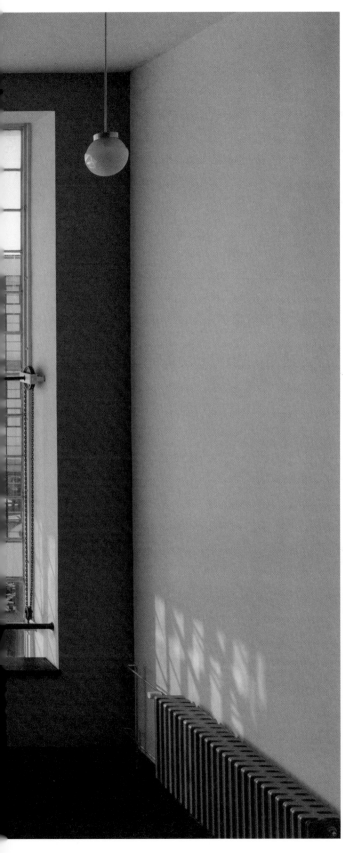

BAUHAUS (SEE P. 126)

and Industry; 1986) in Paris, designed by Adrien Fainsilber (b. 1932); the American Air Museum of the Imperial War Museum at Duxford (1998) in Cambridgeshire, England, by Foster and Partners; the Center for Science and Industry (1999) in Columbus, Ohio, by Arata Isozaki (b. 1931); and the Jewish Museum (2001) in Berlin by Daniel Libeskind (b. 1946). The major history museum came into its own in terms of cutting-edge design and is represented here by the National Museum of African American History and Culture (2016; see p. 174) in Washington, D.C., by David Adjaye (b. 1966).

In addition to those large institutions, the humbler house museum has come into its own recently, becoming a focal point for a number of organizations such as the American Association for State and Local History in the United States, founded in 1940. These small museums, many of which are hundreds of years old, are among the most difficult to preserve in terms of self-sufficiency (that is, acquiring enough funds for regular maintenance and repairs). Unless the building is special in terms of design, such as some of the 1930s to 1940s homes featured in the Living chapter (see p. 206), or the home's resident was famous, as with Monticello (1796–1809; see p. 102) in Virginia, it is a difficult task at best. After all, think of what it takes to keep a home in good condition and then imagine that task compounded by having several thousand relatives visit each year. As with their larger cousins, these institutions continue to think of ways such as creative rentals, special events and tours to generate sufficient earned and donated income. Of the museums within this chapter, two fall into this category: Sir John Soane's Museum (1792–1824; see p. 116), formerly the architect's London home, and the Barcelona Pavilion (1929; see p. 130) designed by Ludwig Mies van der Rohe (1886–1969). Akin to these are historic structures designed as schools: the Glasgow School of Art (1897–1909; see p. 122) and the Bauhaus (1925–26; see p. 126) in Dessau, Germany. Both are essentially utilitarian structures of their time, having studio lofts and workshop spaces within. Such historic schools may see some of the same enthusiastic external visitors as historic houses, but it is primarily their own student populations that cause the most wear and tear on the building fabric, some of which might be offset by tuition, along with donations and endowments established by alumni, at least in the case of the Glasgow example. Both buildings have interesting survival stories to tell, the Glasgow School of Art in terms of its surviving a fire in 2014 and the Bauhaus in terms of restoration after bomb damage from World War II (1939–45).

Finally, two concert facilities round out this chapter: the Berliner Philharmonie (1956–63; see p. 140) and the Sydney Opera House (1957–73; see p. 150). Both structures feature dynamically designed expressionist spaces from the postwar era, and both have a substantial following, much as large museums do. As with their fine-art counterparts, they make a massive contribution to their national and regional economies and cultural environments. But their individualistic architecture has put them at the forefront of their own locales, making them iconic performing-arts buildings, perhaps even more so than many art museums of the postwar era.

Sir John Soane's Museum

LOCATION	London, United Kingdom
ARCHITECT	John Soane
STYLE	Classical Revival
BUILT	1792–1824

British architects such as Nicholas Hawksmoor (*c.* 1661–1736), John Soane (1753–1837), Edwin Lutyens (1869–1944) and Quinlan Terry (b. 1937) are sometimes considered to be eccentrics and mavericks, bringing their own particular vision and proportional sensibilities to the classical language of architecture. In Soane's case, one might cite additional quirks that contributed to his creation of one of the earliest and most interesting architectural collections in history, installed throughout his home, which many consider to be the beginnings of the architectural museum.

Soane came from a builder's family and studied at the Royal Academy, London, from 1771 to 1778. He wrote his first book, *Designs in Architecture*, in 1778, and won a scholarship to travel abroad from 1778 to 1780. He toured France and Italy, visiting great architectural sites, from Versailles (1624–1770; see p. 96) to the Colosseum (*c.* 72–80 CE; see p. 16), continuing on to Austria, Belgium, Germany and Switzerland.

Upon his return to England, he had difficulty establishing a successful architectural practice until the mid- to late 1780s, when he received commissions for homes and was appointed architect of the Bank of England in 1788. His work for the bank through 1827 included what is likely his most famous buildings, which were demolished in the 1920s. With the bank as his primary client, he went on to secure important commissions such as the Dulwich Picture Gallery (1817) and the New Law Courts (1825; demolished), as well as positions such as Clerk of Works for royal buildings in 1791. Extant works include his home Pitzhanger Manor (1800–10) in Ealing, London; renovations at Moggerhanger House (1790–1812) in Bedfordshire; and St John on Bethnal Green Church (1826–28) in London.

Following Soane's appointment at the Bank of England he bought his first home at 12 Lincoln's Inn Fields, Holborn, London, in 1792. After being appointed to teach at the Royal Academy in 1806, he bought the adjacent property, 13 Lincoln's Inn Fields, in 1807, and renovated both into his design experiment. In 1824 he acquired the adjacent building, number 14, a rental property that had an extension from number 13 at the rear, which he used for his picture gallery. Today the entire complex is part of Sir John Soane's Museum, centred on number 13, whose facade Soane redesigned in white Norfolk brick. He intended the combined spaces to be home, atelier and educational institution featuring his extensive collection of drawings, architectural models and building fragments from antiquity. Although historians have often looked at this jumble of rooms and the pile of artefacts within each as examples of his eccentricity, his innovative tinkering extended to designing moving panels within the Picture Room and solving heating and plumbing issues, the latter including pumping enough running water to service bathrooms, a kitchen and toilets.

In 1833 Soane negotiated an Act of Parliament to preserve his house and collection exactly as it would be at the time of his death, and keep it open for education and inspiration. Today it houses 45,000 artefacts and 30,000 drawings and has more than 100,000 visitors annually. There is also access to the restored private bedrooms on the upper floors. This is where Soane converted his wife's bedroom, after her death, into a model display room and used the bathtub for storage of personal artefacts. This restoration caps off his quirky creation so that all can experience his approach to making an architectural education centre.

RIGHT The Picture Room is among the most ingenious of spaces, being created in 1824 out of mostly a stable when Soane bought the property next door. Here paintings are displayed on the equivalent of cabinet doors that maximize storage and viewing space, much like museum art-storage rooms with their movable steel racks.

BELOW RIGHT The domed Sepulchral Chamber features architectural antiquities, including a plaster cast of the Apollo Belvedere sculpture in the Vatican's collections, acquired by Soane in 1811. Soane obsessively collected and rearranged his artifacts throughout his life.

ARCHITECTURE MUSEUMS

The International Confederation of Architectural Museums was founded in 1979 and hosts conferences where dozens of such institutions are represented. The genre can trace its heritage to the collections of nineteenth-century architects like Soane, as well as art and educational exhibitions that displayed plaster casts of European sculptures and building fragments. Few such casts still exist, though some are on view at the Cast Court in London's Victoria and Albert Museum (left), opened in 1873. The collection is divided into casts of Northern European and Spanish sculpture and Italian monuments.

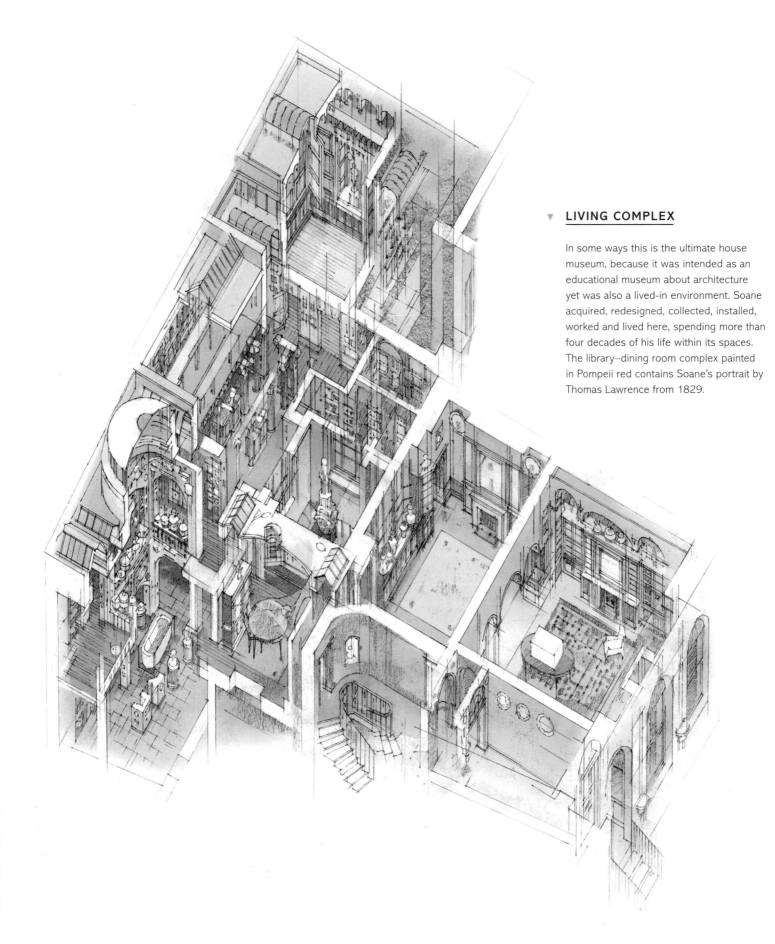

LIVING COMPLEX

In some ways this is the ultimate house museum, because it was intended as an educational museum about architecture yet was also a lived-in environment. Soane acquired, redesigned, collected, installed, worked and lived here, spending more than four decades of his life within its spaces. The library–dining room complex painted in Pompeii red contains Soane's portrait by Thomas Lawrence from 1829.

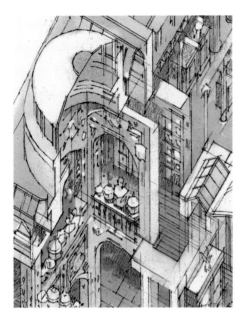

MUSEUM SPACES

Some of the more prominent museum spaces are arranged on a north–south axis at the back of the complex. Seen from above, these are the skylighted spaces that connect the domed, multistorey Sepulchral Chamber shown lower left on the opposite page to the Picture Room shown upper right. These rooms are somewhat distinct from the less museumlike living areas at the east/southeast front of the building, facing the green square of Lincoln's Inn Fields.

BREAKFAST PARLOUR

Soane's breakfast parlour at the centre of the complex in number 13 Lincoln's Inn Fields is distinct from the larger breakfast room in number 12. Both are on the ground floor, as are the living and dining rooms. The breakfast parlour is perhaps better known because of its tentlike yellow dome with mirrors throughout that seems to float lightly below the lantern skylight. The dome was a design prototype for like-styled versions at the Bank of England.

▶ FLOOR PLAN

This toned plan shows the three properties that Soane acquired throughout the course of his life: numbers 12, 13 and 14 Lincoln's Inn Fields. The various main-floor rooms are labelled. The plan is oriented with the main entry at the bottom, or south elevation.

KEY

A Entrance hall
B Library
C Dining room
D Sepulchral Chamber (basement)
E Breakfast parlour
F Anteroom
G New Court
H New Picture Room
I Central dome
J Colonnade
K Dressing room
L Small study
M Monk's Parlour
N Recessed room
O Picture Room
P Stairs to basement
Q Breakfast room

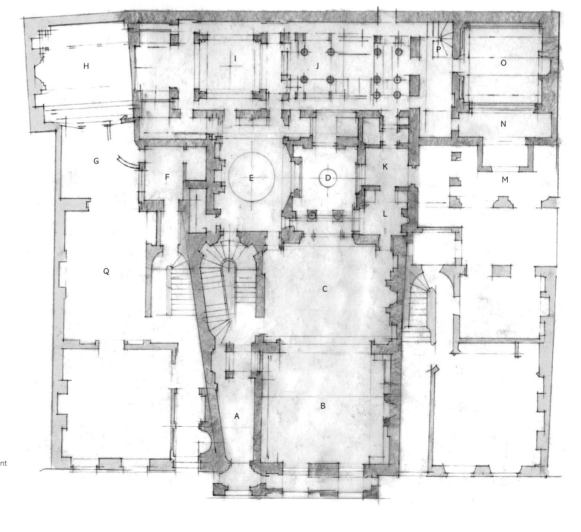

CROSS SECTION

This cross section is a variant of many such drawings dating back to Soane's time. It brings visual logic to what may appear initially as a mixture of overly decorated rooms. Shown here is a selection of some of the more important rooms in the museum.

1 SEPULCHRAL CHAMBER

The space within the dome is packed with antique architectural fragments. The centrepiece is the alabaster sarcophagus of the Egyptian pharaoh Seti I, who died c. 1279 BCE, which Soane acquired in 1824. He rearranged the sculptural fragments that are seen throughout this multistorey space constantly, as well as those ancient fragments in the so-called catacombs that connect to it.

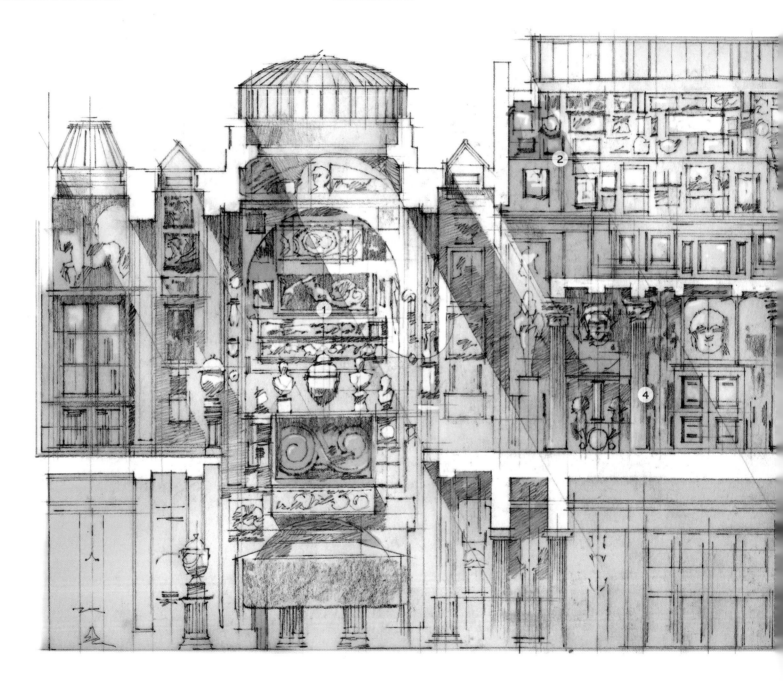

2　DRAFTING ROOM

A multistorey skylit drafting room atop the gallery colonnade was Soane's work space and the area used by apprentices in his studio. The top level of the drawing shows a number of skylights above the dome as well as the Picture Room.

3　PICTURE ROOM

Constructed in 1824 within number 14 Lincoln's Inn Fields from a converted stable, and then expanded into the space of number 13, the Picture Room contains works such as *A Rake's Progress* (1732–33), a series of eight paintings by William Hogarth. Those and other paintings are installed in built-in cabinetry whose multiple overlapping doors organize them more efficiently than if they were displayed on flat walls.

4　COLONNADE

The gallery colonnade's eight columns have Corinthian capitals. The hallway connects the Picture Room with the domed Sepulchral Chamber on the main, or ground, floor. A staircase adjacent serves the catacombs as well as the Monk's Parlour below and the drafting room above.

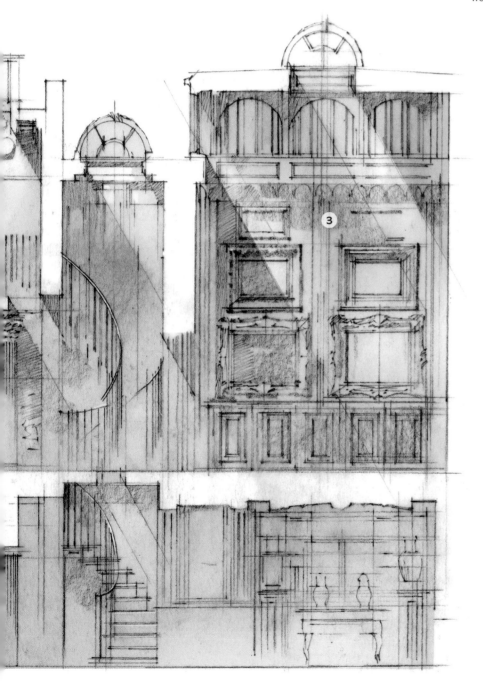

Glasgow School of Art

LOCATION   Glasgow, United Kingdom
ARCHITECT Charles Rennie Mackintosh
STYLE   Scottish Early Modern, Art Nouveau
BUILT   1897–1909

The works of Charles Rennie Mackintosh (1868–1928) are inextricably linked with Glasgow, as much as Louis H. Sullivan (1856–1924) is associated with Chicago and Otto Wagner (1841–1918) with Vienna. Any architectural enthusiast visiting Glasgow would certainly make the pilgrimage to see his Glasgow School of Art (1897–1909). Born and raised in that industrial city, Mackintosh studied at the Allan Glen's Institution, which then was similar to a polytechnic.

He was awarded a travelling scholarship in 1890, returning to a position he had in 1889 at architects Honeyman and Keppie, where he worked his way up the ladder to become a partner in 1904. When that firm closed in 1913, he continued work in his own practice, but found greater satisfaction in painting.

In his design work, Mackintosh strove to create a simplified, almost industrial modern masonry architecture with local decorative detailing and a touch of Japanese elegant simplicity. The latter was popular as an extension of 'Japonisme' in the last quarter of the nineteenth century and beyond. Some of his most famous buildings while at Honeyman and Keppie range from small to large scale, from the Willow Tearooms (1903) in Glasgow to the Scottish Baronial style Hill House (1902–04) in Helensburgh and the commercial Daily Record Printing Works (1904) in Glasgow. Like many of his contemporaries, including Frank Lloyd

Wright (1867–1959), Mackintosh was as renowned for his furniture and furnishings as he was for his buildings. His organic Argyle Chair (1897), designed for the Luncheon Room of the Argyle Street Tea Rooms (1898) in Glasgow and used in the Willow Tearooms, and the gridded Ladderback Chair (1902), made for Hill House, are classics that are still manufactured today. He and his wife, Margaret MacDonald, her sister Frances, and fellow architect from Honeyman and Keppie and Frances's husband, Herbert MacNair (1868–1955), became known as The Four, exhibiting their paintings in that city as well as London and Vienna. They met in art classes at the Glasgow School of Art, from 1888 to 1895, before Mackintosh won the competition in 1896 to design the new school.

Mackintosh's winning design was supported by the school's director, artist Francis Henry Newbery, though apparently the board desired a 'plain building'. Mackintosh's design supplied them with this, its ornament being confined to selected design detailing outside and within that combines Scottish regional with Japanese sensibilities. The five-storey building of rough-hewn sandstone quarried from Giffnock, south of Glasgow, was constructed in two phases. The first included the east wing and central space, from 1897 to 1899. The second, from 1907 to 1909, finished the west wing and library. According to the job books, the construction cost was £47,416. The final building is 74.7 m (245 ft) long and 28.3 m (93 ft) deep. Its highest point is 24.4 m (80 ft). The Renfrew Street main facade

has large windows that illuminate the classrooms and studios. The double-storey library was one of the interior's most discussed and illustrated spaces, with stained oak throughout.

In 2014 the school expanded directly opposite the historic building in a new glazed construction of 11,250 sq m (121,000 sq ft) designed by Steven Holl (b.1947). As pictured below, a disastrous fire on 23 May 2014 damaged much of the building and destroyed the library, but a £35 million reconstruction began in late 2016. The Glasgow campus will be the home of a larger school network that ranges from a redesigned former Stow College building four blocks away from the main building to a design campus in faraway Singapore.

ABOVE LEFT The striking double-storey library was the design centrepiece of this building, complete with the architect's distinctive furnishings. The original was destroyed in the fire of 2014.

ABOVE RIGHT The Seona Reid Building (2014) designed by Holl is a much-needed addition to the school campus that centres on Renfrew Street, opposite Mackintosh's landmark building. The student population numbers 1,900 and the school also has a campus in Singapore for polytechnic school students there.

GREAT FIRE OF 2014

A projector that exploded in the basement of this iconic school may well have been the cause of a disastrous fire in 2014 that quickly spread through the building, causing extensive damage up through the roof of this landmark structure. Fortunately no one perished in the blaze, but some parts of the building were completely destroyed, including the library. Restoration work on the building completes the school complex expanded with the Seona Reid Building.

CROSS SECTION

This sectional drawing shows the western addition (right) to complete the building in 1909. The basement contained the lecture hall and above it on the main floor were architecture studios. The second floor in the same tier contained the library. Pegged wooden roof trusses reflect Scottish Baronial origins. The large windows of the studios on the left face north, ideal for artists' spaces.

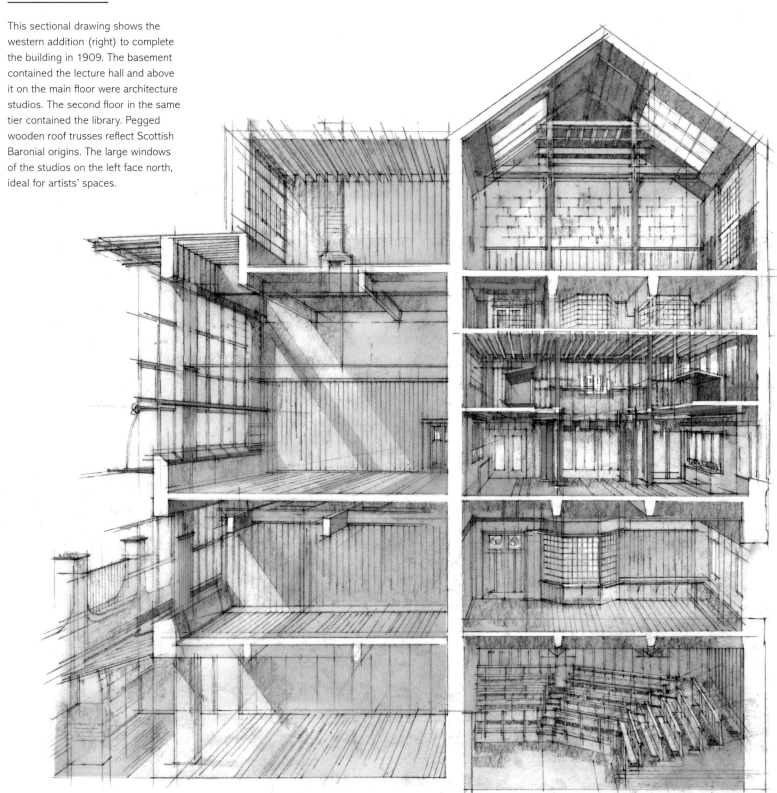

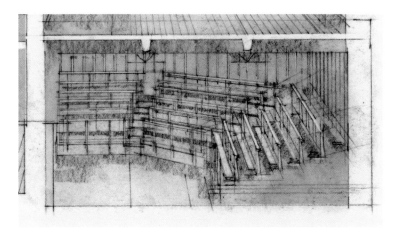

LECTURE HALL

The basement lecture hall, sometimes called the lecture theatre, at the southwest corner was accessed by a separate basement door so that public lectures might also be accommodated. Its raked, tiered bench seating in the windowless panelled room focused on a large curved lectern for object displays during presentations. It has been augmented by the new lecture hall in the Seona Reid Building nearby. Not shown here is a sub-basement below the lecture hall for storage and mechanical use with related ductwork.

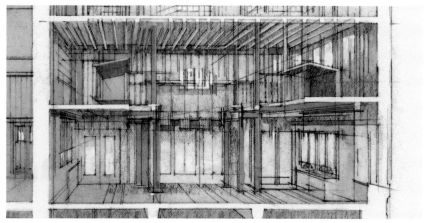

LIBRARY

The spectacular double-storey library had more studio space with large skylights above. It was completely destroyed in the fire of 2014, though the overall structure was preserved mostly intact. The reconstruction of the library has used pieces salvaged there, as well as replacement parts. One material that was imported for the job is Tulipwood, which was lightly stained to reveal the texture of the wood grain. The colour of the new wood is considerably lighter than what was there before, since the original wood had darkened greatly over the past century and more.

► **IRONWORK DETAIL**

The heavy masonry facade projects an almost industrial appearance, punctuated by large skylights and windows. Stone ornamentation is confined to the main entry. However, there is a profusion of Art Nouveau curved ironwork at the base of the large studio windows, indicating that the creation of art rather than industrial products happens within.

Bauhaus

LOCATION Dessau, Germany
ARCHITECT Walter Gropius
STYLE Functionalist Modern, European Modern
BUILT 1925–26

The Bauhaus building (1925–26) in Dessau was restored by the German Democratic Republic to commemorate the fiftieth anniversary of what is an important Modernist landmark. As impressive as the reconstruction work was, Western onlookers would have been even more surprised by the fact that the structure was in the middle of Soviet Army housing. This situation changed with the fall of the Berlin Wall in 1989, the reunification of Germany and the return of those soldiers to Russia. The Bauhaus Dessau Foundation spearheaded another restoration from 1996 to 2006 that focused on a comprehensive approach to infrastructure repair and facility restoration.

The architect of the Bauhaus was Walter Gropius (1883–1969). He came from a family of architects and studied in Munich and Berlin. Beginning in 1907, he worked with Peter Behrens (1888–1940) before establishing his own firm with Adolf Meyer (1881–1929) in 1910. Together they made history as designers of the Fagus Factory (1910) in Alfeld an der Leine, Lower Saxony, an early example of European Functionalist Modernism. After decorated service in World War I (1914–18), Gropius was invited to head the School of Arts and Crafts in Weimar in 1919, which he reshaped into the Bauhaus. He was instrumental in moving the school to Dessau after Weimar authorities closed it for funding reasons in 1924.

Dessau, the home of the Junkers aircraft company, had a larger industrial base that could accommodate the potential mass production of designs created at the

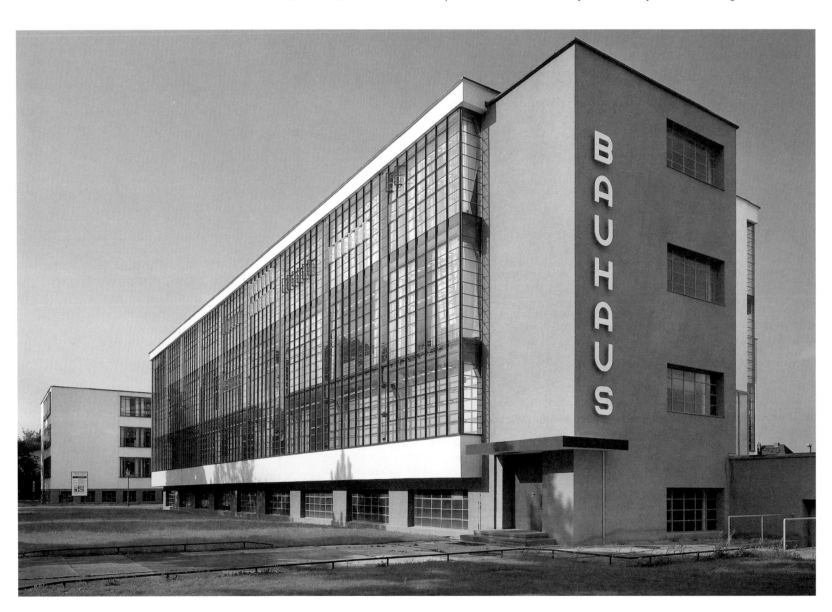

school. Gropius designed the new, minimalist facility of 1925 to 1926, along with the Masters' Houses (1925) for Bauhaus teachers and a number of other buildings, from affordable housing in the Törten Estate (1926–28) to the employment office or Arbeitsamt (1929).

The Bauhaus covers some 23,300 sq m (250,600 sq ft). Gropius planned the Bauhaus in three main wings related to three functions: the three-storey workshop wing with loft spaces and factory glazing; a three-storey vocational school block; and a five-storey wing for twenty-eight student and faculty dormitories, each less than 23 sq m (250 sq ft), with balconies. A two-storey bridge with administrative offices connects the vocational school with the workshops, and a central smaller building between the workshops and studios

houses an auditorium and canteen. Interiors had lightly toned walls, created by the director of the school's wall-painting workshop, Hinnerk Scheper, to visually reinforce the planar structural elements.

Gropius was director of the school until 1928, when he was replaced by Hannes Meyer (1889–1954). Meyer served only a year, his Communist leanings providing an excuse to replace him. Ludwig Mies van der Rohe (1886–1969) was the next and final director, from 1930 to 1932. The rise of National Socialism in the city government forced Mies to relocate the school to Berlin, though he operated it for only a year before the Nazis came to national power. In 1934 Gropius moved to England and then, in 1937, to Massachusetts, where he was head of Harvard University's Graduate

School of Design. In 1938 Mies left Germany for Chicago, where he became head of the architecture school at Armour Institute, later the Illinois Institute of Technology. Meyer left Germany before the rise of the Nazis, moving first to the Soviet Union in 1930, then to his native Switzerland in 1936, followed by Mexico City in 1939, before returning to Switzerland in 1949. The moves of those masters reflect the relocations of many Bauhaus teachers who fled Europe at this time, relocating to the United States, Great Britain and Australia. Under the Third Reich, the Bauhaus served as a school for girls, an office for administrators and a Junkers facility. The workshop wing was damaged in a bombing raid on 7 March 1945. It was stabilized after the war and was restored in 1975–76.

ABOVE LEFT The wide double-loaded main staircase presents a visually disciplined yet dramatically spacious promenade that accesses main-floor services like the auditorium as well as the spaces above. The stair is the subject of the painting *Bauhaus Stairway* (1932) by Oskar Schlemmer, which shows students ascending it.

ABOVE RIGHT The auditorium is off the main stairway and vestibule. The banks of folding seats attached to the floor are made of canvas-covered tubular steel. The original fabric was not canvas but a material with metallic flecks. Gropius hoped the Bauhaus would become a think tank of design for German industry.

DESSAU AND MODERNISM

The Bauhaus is famously associated with the Modern movement, but Dessau has several examples of such structures from the interwar years. They include the curved corridors of Gropius's Arbeitsamt (left), the Kornhaus (1930) restaurant overlooking the Elbe River by Carl Fieger (1893–1960), housing in Dessau-Törten by Gropius and Meyer, and Gropius's Konsum Building (1928) within the Törten complex. Because of the Bauhaus and other Modernist projects, Dessau has been declared a UNESCO World Heritage Site.

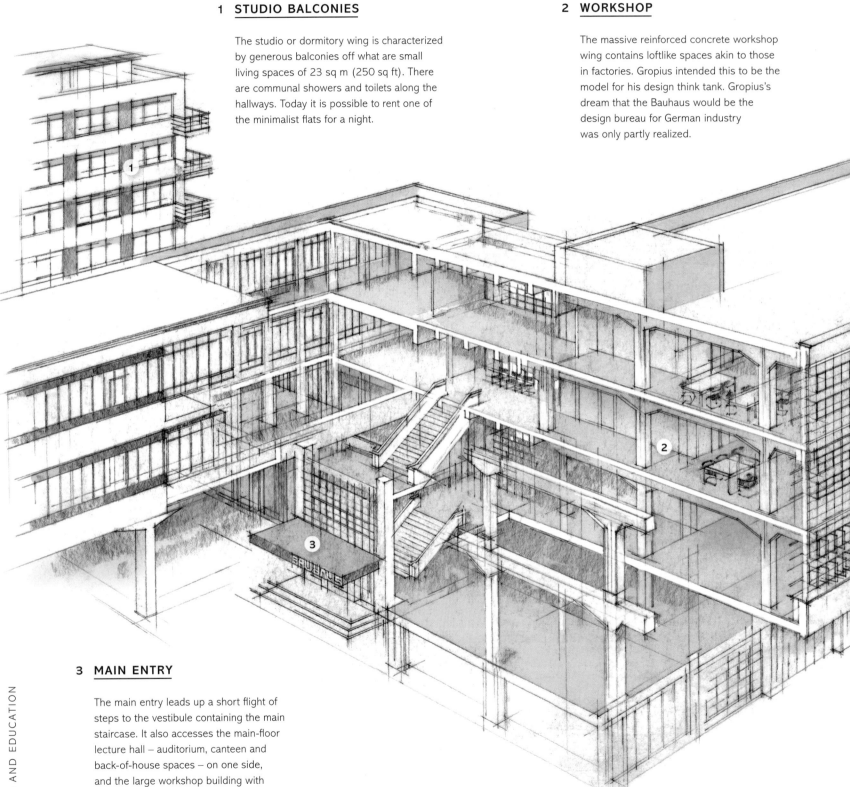

1 STUDIO BALCONIES

The studio or dormitory wing is characterized by generous balconies off what are small living spaces of 23 sq m (250 sq ft). There are communal showers and toilets along the hallways. Today it is possible to rent one of the minimalist flats for a night.

2 WORKSHOP

The massive reinforced concrete workshop wing contains loftlike spaces akin to those in factories. Gropius intended this to be the model for his design think tank. Gropius's dream that the Bauhaus would be the design bureau for German industry was only partly realized.

3 MAIN ENTRY

The main entry leads up a short flight of steps to the vestibule containing the main staircase. It also accesses the main-floor lecture hall – auditorium, canteen and back-of-house spaces – on one side, and the large workshop building with its factorylike curtain wall on the other.

▶ WINDOW DETAIL

The factorylike curtain wall of the workshop wing has steel-and-glass windows that pivot on a chain-and-pulley system. This system opened banks of windows to equal dimensions, creating a visually disciplined image for the fenestration.

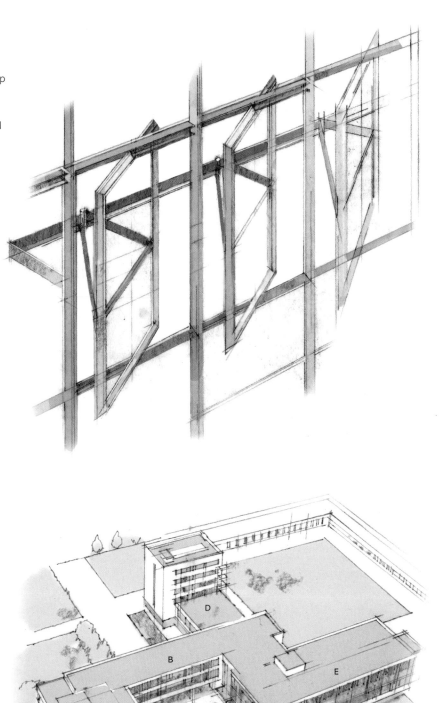

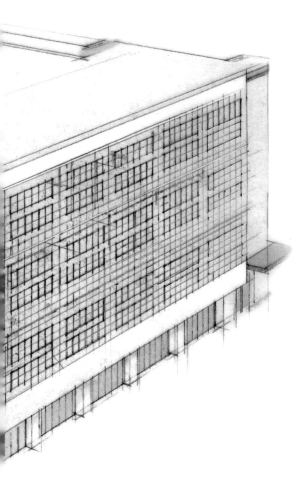

▶ SITE PLAN

This plan shows the five buildings of the complex. From left to right are the vocational school (A) on the near side of the road, the administrative office bridge (B) across the roadway, the main entry (C) and student-faculty services, the studio wing (D) to the upper left and the workshop wing (E) to the lower right.

Barcelona Pavilion

LOCATION   Barcelona, Spain
ARCHITECT   Ludwig Mies van der Rohe,
                 reconstruction by others
STYLE   European Modern, International Style
BUILT   1929, rebuilt 1986

'Build, don't talk', 'less is more', and 'God is in the details' are some of the maxims associated with Ludwig Mies van der Rohe (1886–1969) that have become common architectural taglines. Mies was one of the most important architects of his era, not only for landmark buildings such as 860–880 Lake Shore Drive (1951) in Chicago and the Seagram Building (1958) in New York, but also for his reshaping of the architecture school at Armour Institute of Technology into Illinois Institute of Technology, after he moved there from Germany in 1938. When he designed the German Pavilion for the 1929 International Exposition in Barcelona, he was one of his country's most progressive architects. His pavilion was intended to be a tangible representation of that nation's modern culture during the Weimar Republic (1919–33) as it distanced its government from the classicism of imperial Germany, an empire associated with the horrors of World War I (1914–18). Mies designed the building to be a ceremonial space for King Alfonso XIII of Spain and German officials at the fair, with the wide steel-and-leather 'Barcelona' chairs designed by Mies (below) being the equivalent of Modernist thrones.

The building is situated on a travertine plinth, with two reflecting pools, its design being related to the shifting wall planes similar to other Modern architectural styles, such as Dutch De Stijl (see p. 196). Only here they are massive shifting offset marble

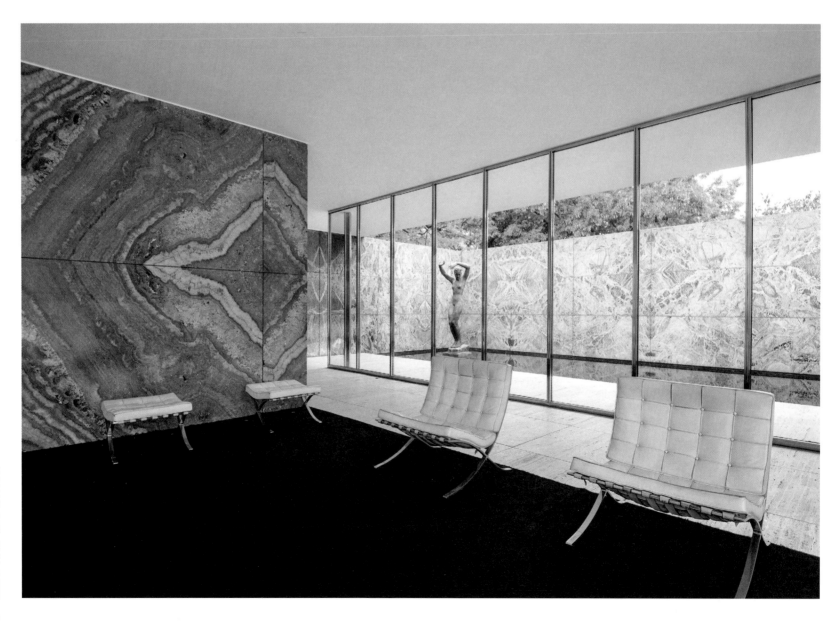

walls. Eight slender, minimal steel and reflective chrome columns make the roof appear to float above. This bold yet tranquil building demonstrates Mies's great talent for creating beautifully detailed and proportioned spaces.

Since it was intended to be a temporary exhibition pavilion, to be dismantled in 1930 after the fair, it was also an experiment for Mies. Its openness contrasts with his more closed stucco or brick houses of the era, whose walls featured large glazed panels, such as the Lange and Esters houses (1928–30) in Krefeld and the Lemke House (1933) in Berlin. Even his Tugendhat House (1930) in Brno, built just after the Barcelona Pavilion, is open on the garden side to the point of having operable floor-to-ceiling glass panes, but is more closed on the street facade. Writers have posited that Mies's architecture became much more open with large glazed walls after he left Nazi Germany for the United States in 1937, offering as evidence the Farnsworth House (1951) in Plano, and the McCormick House (1952), now part of the Elmhurst Art Museum, both in Illinois. In some ways, the Barcelona Pavilion along with unexecuted projects such as the Glass Skyscraper (1922) and numerous courthouse designs of the 1930s, often roughly sketched with an isolated modern figural sculpture as if it was a scale figure, were part of this transition to what Mies called *beinahe nichts* ('almost nothing').

Because it was a seminal building for Mies as well as for the twentieth century, his admirers lobbied for its reconstruction. Leading the movement were Barcelona city officials and architects such as Cristian Cirici (b. 1941), working alongside the Mies archive at New York's Museum of Modern Art and Mies's grandson Chicago architect Dirk Lohan (b. 1938) in 1986. The pavilion is open to the public and managed by the Fundació Mies van der Rohe.

LUDWIG MIES VAN DER ROHE

Mies trained as a stonemason, which explains his love of detail, but he also had a great eye for proportion. After working for Peter Behrens and Bruno Paul (1874–1968), he started his own firm designing comparable traditional homes. After World War I he began more open-plan, Modernist work and became a high-profile practitioner, mostly with private residences. His move to the United States secured an academic post, followers and larger commissions.

TOP The north side of the pavilion features a pond with a bronze reproduction of *Der Morgen* (*Morning*, 1925) by Georg Kolbe. An original of the sculpture stands with its counterpart *Der Abend* (*Evening*, 1925) in the Ceciliengärten in Berlin-Friedenau.

ABOVE The spacious travertine plaza contains a large pool, a feature replicated on a smaller scale on the opposite side of the building where the *Morning* sculpture is placed. Such water features help animate the building's windows with reflections, and vice versa. Mies often used them in later designs as well.

BARCELONA CHAIR

Perhaps the most recognized result of this pavilion is the spaciously proportioned steel-and-leather chair known as the Barcelona Chair, designed like a ceremonial throne for VIPs such as Spain's King Alfonso XIII for the exposition's opening. The view also suggests the richness of materials used here to elevate the building's image: Roman travertine, African onyx, and Grecian and Alpine marble.

FREESTANDING WALL PLANES

Mixing a variety of materials in freestanding walls that are often asymmetrically placed is typical of much Modernist architecture of the 1920s. These simple wall planes in Mies's work may have precedents in the early work of Frank Lloyd Wright, which was exhibited in Berlin in 1910 upon the publication of the portfolio of Wright's drawings and the book of plans and photographs by the firm of E. Wasmuth.

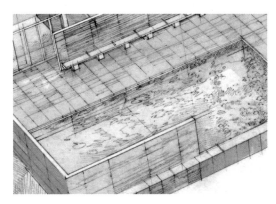

WATER FEATURE

Here a travertine plinth planned on a grid supports walls and a reflecting pool. The pool and comparable open spaces, often with a stylized sculpture, found their way into many courthouse designs of the 1930s that remained unexecuted because of the Great Depression. At that time, more of Mies's income came from furniture patents than from architectural designs.

FLOATING ROOF

The large roof appears to float above the walls. Its apparent weightlessness is created through the use of very slender cruciform columns made of reflective stainless steel. Germany was a leader in developing such products in the 1920s, with German stainless steel being used in the Chrysler Building (1929–30; see p. 38) in New York.

ARTS AND EDUCATION

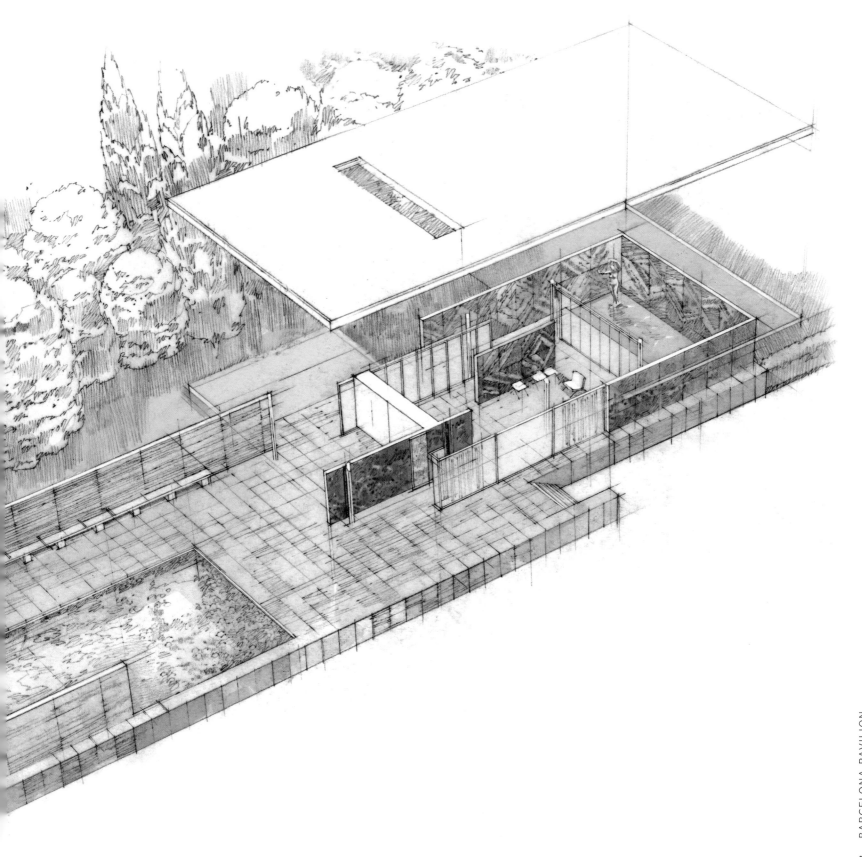

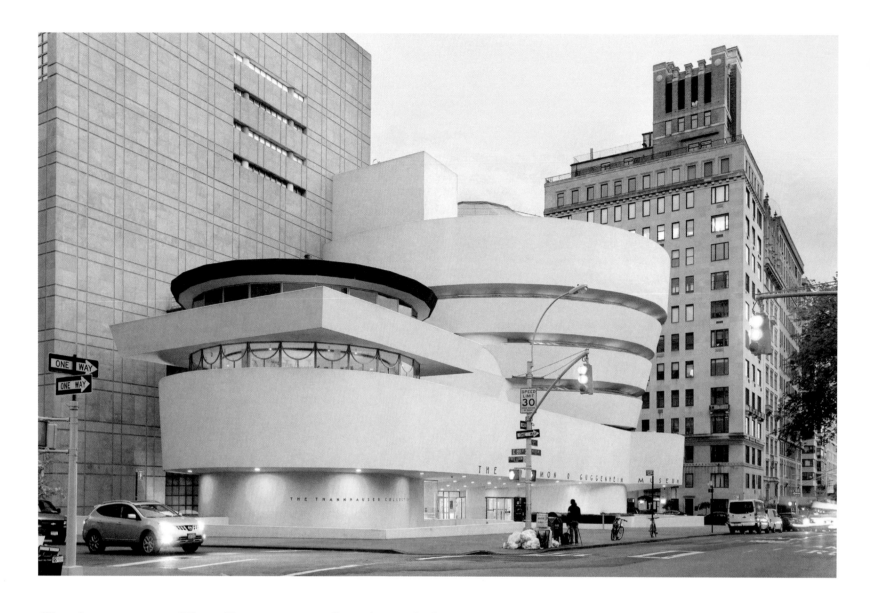

Solomon R. Guggenheim Museum

ARTS AND EDUCATION

LOCATION New York, New York,
United States of America
ARCHITECT Frank Lloyd Wright
STYLE Organic Modern
BUILT 1956–59

In a way, the Solomon R. Guggenheim Museum
in New York is the headquarters of international
contemporary art museums that bear the Guggenheim
name, from Berlin in Germany, Bilbao in Spain (see
p. 168) and Abu Dhabi in the United Arab Emirates to
Venice, Italy, as well as a planned expansion to Helsinki,
rejected by that city in 2017 for funding commitment
reasons. The seed for this successful operation began
with mining executive and art collector Solomon R.
Guggenheim, who wished to create a major foundation
and museum supporting contemporary art. He
established his foundation in 1937 and opened his

first museum two years later as the Museum of
Non-Objective Painting, a small storefront operation
in a renovated automobile showroom at 24 East 54th
Street in midtown Manhattan. They amassed such
an important collection that in 1943 Guggenheim
and his advisor Hilla von Rebay commissioned
Frank Lloyd Wright (1867–1959) to design a larger,
more permanent facility. After numerous redesigns
and site changes before and after Guggenheim's death
in 1949, Wright's vision became reality on Fifth Avenue
opposite Central Park on the Upper East Side of
Manhattan in 1959, despite objections by a variety

of civic groups – a response to his radical design but also related to the context of building on or near Fifth Avenue.

Wright's spiral design in concrete derives from his unexecuted concept for the Gordon Strong Automobile Objective (1924) planned for Sugarloaf Mountain, Maryland, and bears a comparative precedent in the spiral-ramp renovation he did for a store at 140 Maiden Lane in San Francisco (1948). For the Guggenheim, he initially wanted stone construction but, for budgetary reasons, chose concrete and lauded it for its plasticity and ability to represent the creative 'imagination'. Wright intended the space to be fluid, where walls, floors and ceiling blend together to create a dynamic exhibition experience for artist and museumgoer alike. He intended it to be a seamless experience that many resisted because it overshadowed the art on display and did not conform to the white neutral rectangular boxes often used as the spaces for exhibiting fine art.

Wright's Guggenheim of approximately 7,500 sq m (80,000 sq ft) broke ground in 1956 and opened three years later. Although the spectacular atrium has been used for large-scale sculptural installations along with special events, that signature space is limited for the display of paintings. The original building design included a fountain in the space that would have inhibited art installation, but Wright also included a more practical auditorium, bookshop and café space within. He had planned a ten-storey vertical slab adjacent for offices and gallery expansion but this idea was not implemented until 1991–92, when Gwathmey Siegel and Associates built a sixteen-storey addition with 4,700 sq m (51,000 sq ft) of new and renovated galleries and 1,400 sq m (15,000 sq ft) of office space. In 2008 the museum's atrium and skylight were restored by WASA Studio and other specialists. Additional renovations included The Wright restaurant (2009) and Café 3 (2007), both designed by Andre Kikoski (b. 1967). These restorations and expansions support more than 1 million visitors annually, making the Guggenheim the fourth most visited museum in New York.

ABOVE LEFT The sweeping curves of the museum's atrium ramps are a distinctive feature of the entry space, as is the angled skylight. The space has accommodated large-scale installations.

ABOVE RIGHT Fine dining within museums is an essential feature today, and the spaces often reflect that. Restaurant and retail designer Andre Kikoski created two such spaces at the Guggenheim. The Wright restaurant shown earned him the 2010 James Beard Foundation Award for Outstanding Restaurant Design.

140 MAIDEN LANE, SAN FRANCISCO

Wright designed several buildings with circular or semicircular forms, including one with an internal curved ramp, before he created the Guggenheim Museum. Most were designed after World War II in his mid-century modern phase, long after the rectilinear Prairie Schools of the early twentieth century. The most obvious extant precedent is the renovation Wright did in 1948 for the V. C. Morris Gift Shop at 140 Maiden Lane in San Francisco. The interior is lit from above through a large roof skylight that diffuses sunshine through a ceiling of domed white Plexiglas circles (left). The space was restored in the early twenty-first century.

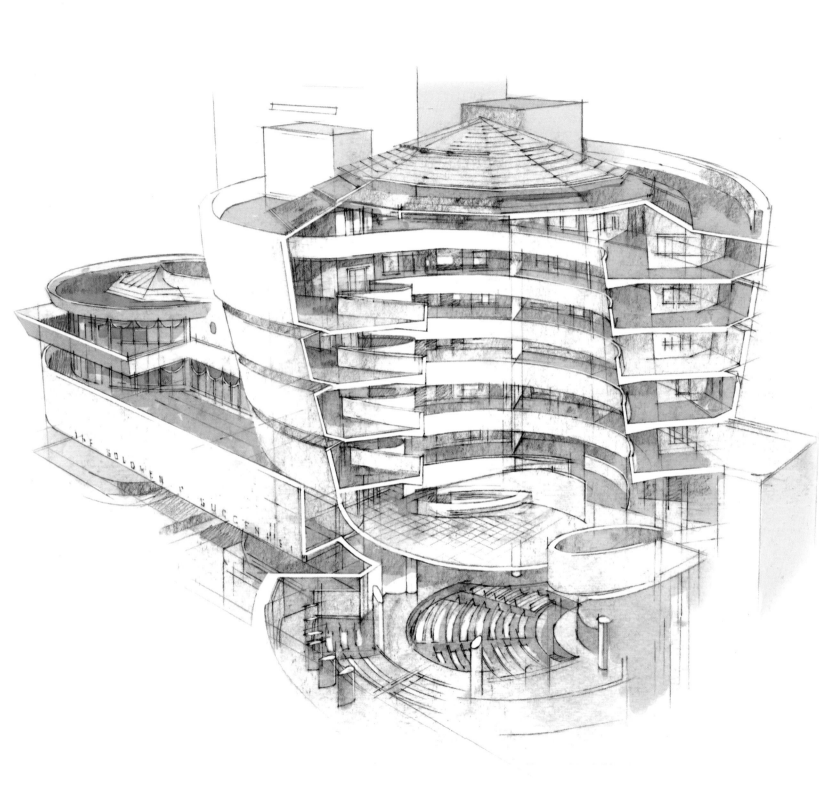

MUSEUM RETAIL

The double-storey rotunda off the terrace houses Café 3, a snack bar covering 80 sq m (850 sq ft) with the capacity to seat forty people. It was designed by Andre Kikoski, who also designed The Wright, a restaurant of fifty-eight seats and a communal table in 150 sq m (1,600 sq ft) of space at the other end of the museum.

ROTUNDA

The Ronald O. Perelman Rotunda off the entry is a grand 28-m (92-ft) high space akin to those created within domed Beaux-Arts museums half a century before. Wright originally designed a fountain for the space to bring nature inside, but this feature would have been impractical in an art museum.

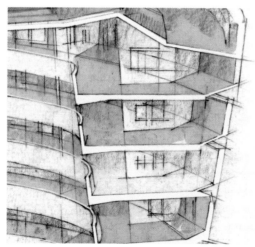

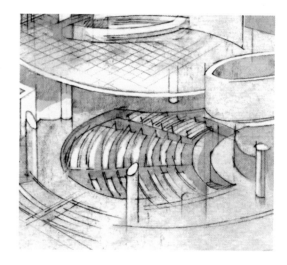

SERVICE CORE

As in just about every multistorey building, this concrete service core tower contains circulation such as lifts and access to toilets and is accessible to floors within the main building. Wright originally envisioned a glazed dome atop that would mirror the atrium skylight.

CONCENTRIC GALLERIES

The spiral-ramped atrium is the signature space of the museum. It provides a dynamic experience for visitors, though artists and curators might assert that it diverts attention away from the art objects and curved walls make it difficult to hang large rectilinear paintings.

THEATRE

The Peter B. Lewis Theater was designed by Wright. The auditorium seats 290 visitors. Concentric rows of sloped seating are intended to provide optimal views for the occupants. Its semicircular forms recall the the atrium space above.

▶ FLOOR PLAN

The three main floors of the original Wright-designed museum and the basement contain 4,700 sq m (80,000 sq ft) of space, most of which went through two major renovations in 1992 and from 2008 to 2009.

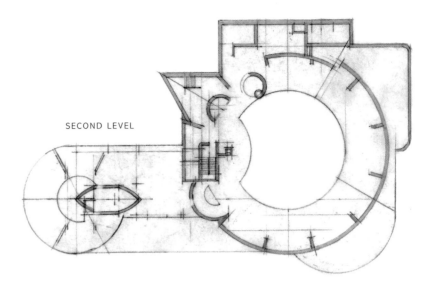

SECOND LEVEL

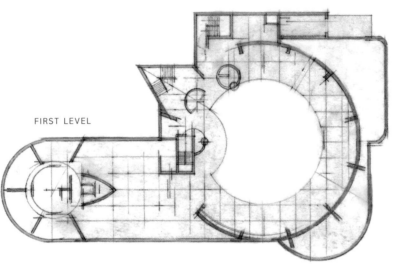

FIRST LEVEL

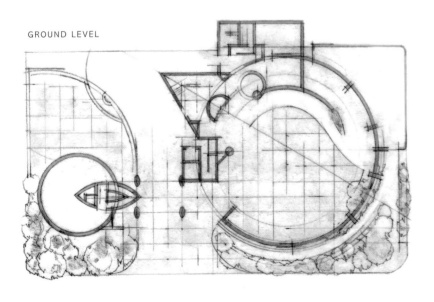

GROUND LEVEL

▶ MUSEUM OFFICE TOWER

Gwathmey Siegel and Associates (now Gwathmey Siegel Kaufman Architects) designed the eight-storey tower adjacent to the museum. The building provides new office space as well as expanded gallery and service spaces. It connects to the original building via a steel-and-glass infill, but is limestone clad.

▼ ANGLED AND CURVED GALLERIES

The Gwathmey Siegel expansion and renovation
permitted the museum to move offices and
services into the new tower, thereby freeing
up more space within the original building for
galleries. In this section the dilemma caused by
curving concentric walls is visible. Initially, artists
felt the curved design inhibited appreciation and
installation of their works.

Berliner Philharmonie

LOCATION   Berlin, Germany
ARCHITECT   Hans Scharoun
STYLE   Expressionist Modern
BUILT   1956–63

When the Berliner Philharmonie was officially opened on 15 October 1963, it proclaimed to all that it was a beacon of freedom for a modern Germany in a reborn West Berlin, just steps from the infamous Berlin Wall erected by the German Democratic Republic in 1961. The orchestra's conductor, Herbert von Karajan, whose opening-day concert featured Ludwig van Beethoven's *Ninth Symphony* (1824), actively supported the radical design of this symphony hall and he laid the cornerstone on 19 September 1960. The building was created by one of Germany's more expressive architects, Hans Scharoun (1893–1972).

Architect Scharoun and conductor von Karajan both lived through the horrors of World War II (1939–45). Von Karajan's career was as controversial as Scharoun's, but in different ways. The Austrian conductor was a member of the Nazi Party and an up-and-coming symphonic star during the war. He was able to distance his association with the party afterwards, becoming internationally known as principal conductor of the Berlin Philharmonic from 1955 until his death in 1989. Bremen-born Scharoun studied architecture at the predecessor to today's Technical University in Berlin from 1912 to 1914 before entering military service in World War I (1914–18). After the war he became one of Germany's avant garde, being associated with the artists of Die Brücke (The Bridge) and radical architectural groups such as Der Ring (The Ring) and Die Gläserne Kette (The Glass Chain). He is best known for Berlin housing blocks during the early 1930s that

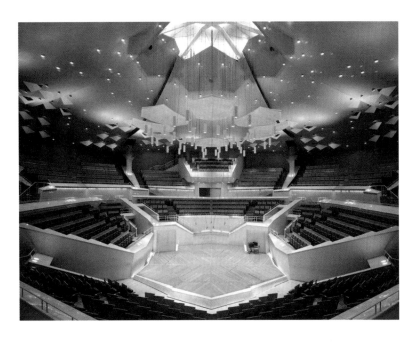

LEFT The design of the smaller chamber hall also puts the orchestra and conductor at the centre, with unobstructed views either way, from the stage to the audience and from audience to performers.

KULTURFORUM, BERLIN

The Kulturforum was planned to be a symbol of West Berlin's postwar modernity sited near the infamous Berlin Wall. Important Cold War–era buildings there included the two largest by Scharoun, the Philharmonie (upper right) and the State Library (lower left), Mies's New National Gallery, and the WZB Berlin Social Science Centre (1988) by Michael Wilford (b. 1938) and James Stirling (1926–92).

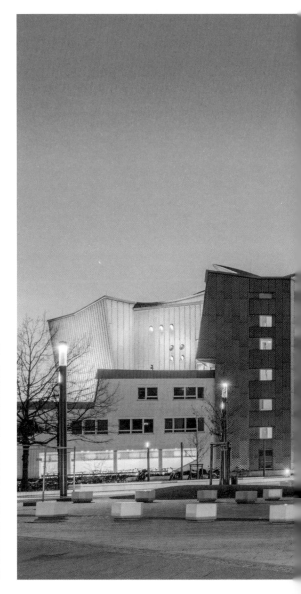

often have a dynamically curved component, and the spectacularly organic yet streamlined Schminke House (1930–33) in Löbau.

Under the Third Reich Scharoun designed only a few private homes and helped with reconstruction from bomb damage. After hostilities, he taught at his alma mater in Berlin and received major commissions such as the Romeo and Juliet apartment towers (1959) in Stuttgart, the German Embassy in Brasilia (1969) and several structures that had to be finished after his death, notably the Theatre Wolfsburg (1965–73) and Berlin State Library (1967–78). His postwar masterpieces, however, are the Berlin Philharmonie and the adjacent Chamber Music Hall (1987), conceived by him but built by his design partner Edgar Wisniewski (b. 1930).

The mostly concrete and steel Philharmonie, designed for a competition in 1956, was the sculptural centrepiece of the Kulturforum arts district conceived from 1959 to 1964, with the next important addition being the New National Gallery (1968) by Ludwig Mies van der Rohe (1886–1969). The Philharmonie's gold-toned, anodized aluminium skin, installed later between 1978 and 1981, and the phoenixlike sculpture by Hans Uhlmann on its roof, are reminders of the resurrection of West Berlin after the devastation of the war. The building's angular forms have been likened to conceptual Stadtkrone (City Crown) Expressionist designs from the early twentieth century. The entry foyer floor combines natural stone with mosaics designed by artist Erich F. Reuter. The spatial coup

de grâce, however, is the concert hall, centrally planned with the orchestra in the middle surrounded by 2,250 seats. The roof is 22 m (72 ft) above the performers to create the auditory experience planned by noted acoustician Lothar Cremer, as is the tentlike ceiling with its three convex shapes. The like-styled and planned Chamber Music Hall nearby seats 1,136 people.

As director Wim Wenders told *The Independent* newspaper when interviewed about the film *Cathedrals of Culture* (2014): 'Without von Karajan this building would not have been made. Its very concept of putting the orchestra (and the conductor!) into the centre of the room was revolutionary . . . He understood Scharoun's vision, and I guess he also understood how much it was putting him into the centre of attention.'

ENTRY HALL AND STAIRCASES

Visitors begin at the multistoreyed entry and take a journey up angled steel stairs and landings, past angled piers and cylindrical concrete columns, to their assigned concert-hall seating. The foyer contains original features such as a colourful mosaic pattern inset in the natural stone floor by Reuter that was inspired by the works of Johann Sebastian Bach, a large stained-glass window on the second level created by Alexander Camaro, and polygonal light globes designed by Günther Ssymmank. Kahlfeldt Architekten created a gift and book shop for the foyer in 2002.

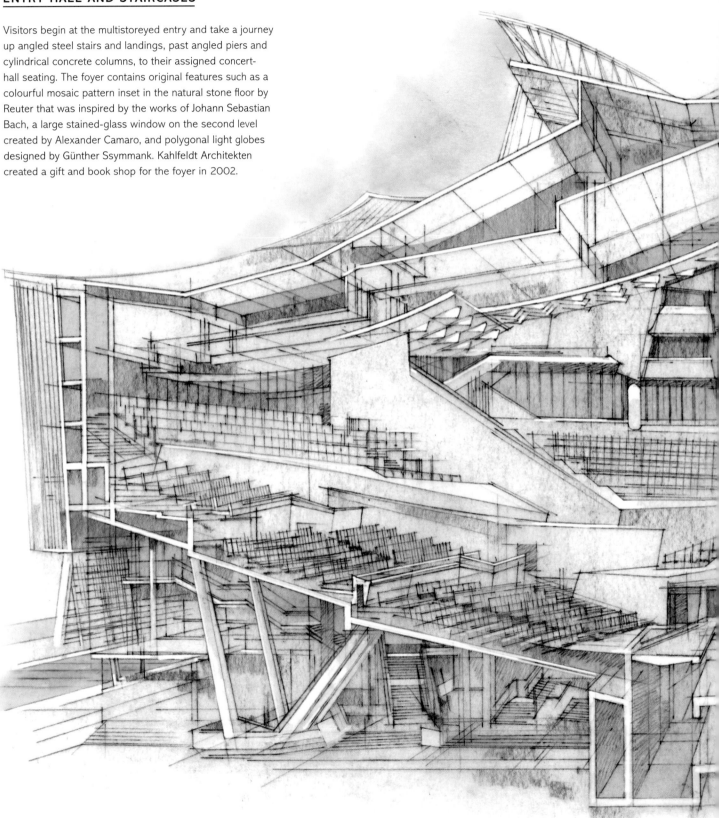

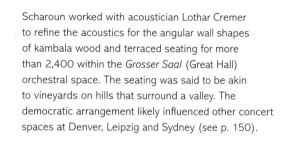

▼ GREAT HALL

Scharoun worked with acoustician Lothar Cremer
to refine the acoustics for the angular wall shapes
of kambala wood and terraced seating for more
than 2,400 within the *Grosser Saal* (Great Hall)
orchestral space. The seating was said to be akin
to vineyards on hills that surround a valley. The
democratic arrangement likely influenced other concert
spaces at Denver, Leipzig and Sydney (see p. 150).

◄ ANGULAR ROOF AND WALLS

The angular walls covered in anodized
gold-toned aluminium are an expression
of the spaces within. They project to
onlookers the appearance of a modern
temple of culture. Visitors have a preview
of the dramatically angled concert space
from the like-designed exterior. Being
inside gives the impression that Scharoun
started with the design here and worked
outwards. A fire in May 2008 caused
damage particularly to the roof, but
repairs brought the hall back into
use the following month.

These two half plans show an overall angular shape of both the entry and concert floors, whose interiors are expressed on the exterior. Today a passage connects the Philharmonie with the later, smaller Chamber Music Hall. The central plan of both buildings puts performers at the centre with the audience ringed around them as an image of democracy, unlike traditional concert halls.

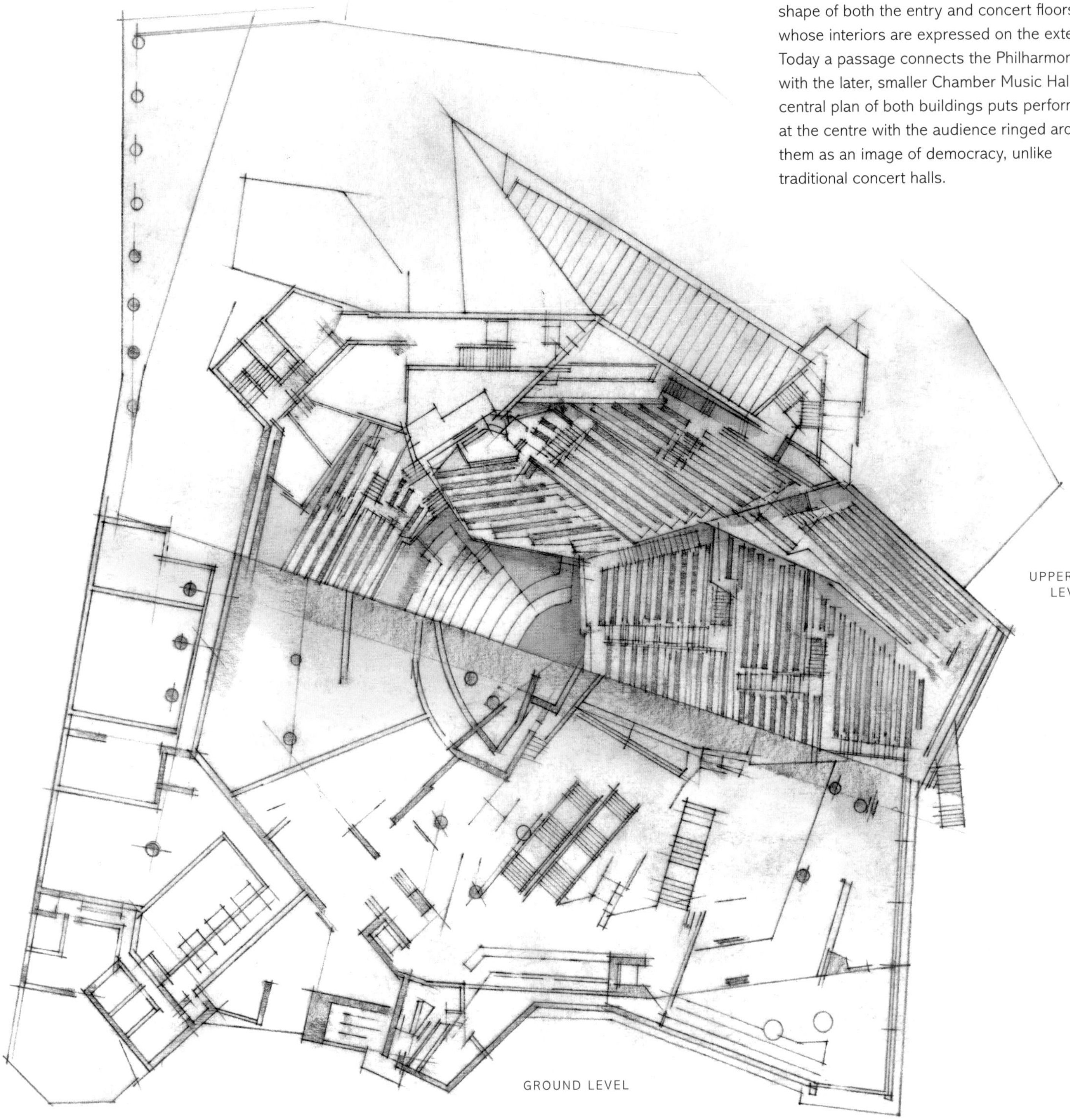

UPPER LEVEL/
LEVEL 4

GROUND LEVEL

This plan of the Kulturforum includes the Scharoun-designed Philharmonie to the right and the later Chamber Music Hall and his State Library to the left. Above the latter is Mies's New National Gallery. These mostly 1960s buildings were bastions of West German culture during the Cold War, when just right of the Philharmonie was a no-man's land defined by the double-layered concrete Berlin Wall. Today, few vestiges of that historic division between East and West Berlin remain, as the city was reunified in 1990; the Potsdamer Platz public square and traffic intersection that lies just to the east were redeveloped shortly after.

KEY
A   Philharmonie
B   Chamber Music Hall
C   New National Gallery
D   Berlin State Library
E   Kunstgewerbemuseum (Museum of
      Decorative Arts)
F   St Matthäus-Kirche (St Matthew's Church)
G   Kunstbibliothek (Art Library)
H   Kulturforum
I   Staatliches Institut für Musikforschung
      and Musikinstrumenten-Museum
J   Tiergarten
K   Ibero-American Institute Library
L   Spielbank Berlin Performing Arts Theatre

Kimbell Art Museum

LOCATION Fort Worth, Texas, United States of America
ARCHITECT Louis Kahn
STYLE Organic Modern
BUILT 1966–72

ARTS AND EDUCATION

Louis Kahn (1901–74) is remembered for his ideas about how natural light can illuminate space and aid the experience of architecture. Kahn's near obsession with the quality of natural light helped him secure commissions for a number of important art museums. Born in Estonia, Kahn graduated from the University of Pennsylvania in 1924. He worked for conservative modern architects such as Paul Philippe Cret (1876–1945) in the late 1920s, as well as with Modernists George Howe (1886–1955) and Oscar Stonorov (1905–70) during the Great Depression of the 1930s

and wartime years of the 1940s. He came into his own in the late 1950s and is best known for buildings from this era such as the First Unitarian Church (1959–69) in Rochester, New York, and the Salk Institute (1959–65) in La Jolla, California. Both are characterized by simple, clean, monumental masonry forms whose spaces are penetrated to permit dramatic natural illumination.

The Kimbell Art Museum (1966–72) in Fort Worth, Texas, was the first museum Kahn designed. Wealthy industrialist Velma Kimbell and his art collector wife,

Kay, left their fortune to the Kimbell Art Foundation, whose mission was to build an art museum. The foundation hired Richard Fargo Brown, former director of the Los Angeles County Museum of Art, to be its first museum director. Brown wanted the museum to be a major art statement as much as the paintings and sculpture within. The new building was to be situated on a 3.8-hectare (9.5-acre) site in the city's cultural district, near the Fort Worth Community Arts Center (1954) by Herbert Bayer (1900–85) and the Amon Carter Museum of American Art (1961), designed by

Philip Johnson (1906–2005). With the prominence of those designers in mind, an equally important architect had to be hired for the Kimbell. After several interviews with designers such as Marcel Breuer (1902–81) and Ludwig Mies van der Rohe (1886–1969), Kahn was selected, perhaps because of his prominent buildings such as the Salk Institute as well as having been recently chosen to design the National Assembly Building of Bangladesh (1962–82; see p. 54) in Dhaka. Even more relevant was Brown's interest in natural light within the new building, something that likely drew him to Kahn.

Kahn and consulting engineer August Komendant (1906–92) created a modest building of beautifully detailed, reinforced concrete. The design featured sixteen thin-shelled, barrel-vaulted tubes, each 30.4 m (100 ft) long and 6 m (20 ft) high and wide. The vaulted galleries on the second floor (opposite) are lit by skylight channels with reflective screens of perforated aluminium that dissipate the natural light; the end spaces have travertine-clad walls and the exterior of the vaults are covered with lead roofing. Occasional courts relieve this sequence of arched galleries.

A landscape plan by landscape architect Harriet Pattison is credited with the open arched porches here. The floor below houses the main entry as well as offices and workrooms.

Today Kahn's Kimbell Art Museum houses 350 artworks from the permanent collection. A new building (2007–13) lies west of the Kahn building's main entry. Designed by Renzo Piano (b. 1937), it provides 8,000 sq m (85,000 sq ft) for the museum's special events, large-scale auditorium programs, temporary exhibitions, and underground parking.

ABOVE The barrel vaults of Kahn's original museum building are visible in the upper half of this image. Renzo Piano's expansion is seen to the lower right. Piano, who early in his career once worked for Kahn, created a restrained Modernist design. He intended it to have a respectful visual dialogue with Kahn's landmark, its 91-m (300-ft) long symmetrical facade being comparable to that by Kahn.

KAHN'S ART MUSEUMS

Winning the Kimbell commission led Kahn to obtain other museum jobs, perhaps the most prominent being the Yale University Art Gallery (1953) and the Yale Center for British Art (1974). The gridlike structure of the latter's interior (left) is also expressed on its exterior. Galleries are planned as naturally lit courts. The museum went through a comprehensive restoration from 2008 to 2013. Exterior materials are matt steel and glass with interior finishes of travertine, oak and linen.

AUDITORIUM

The original auditorium designed by Kahn
has seating for under 200 people. It has been
supplemented by a larger one seating 299 in the
addition designed by Renzo Piano. The auditorium
descends below the second floor to accommodate
the sloped seating and stage design.

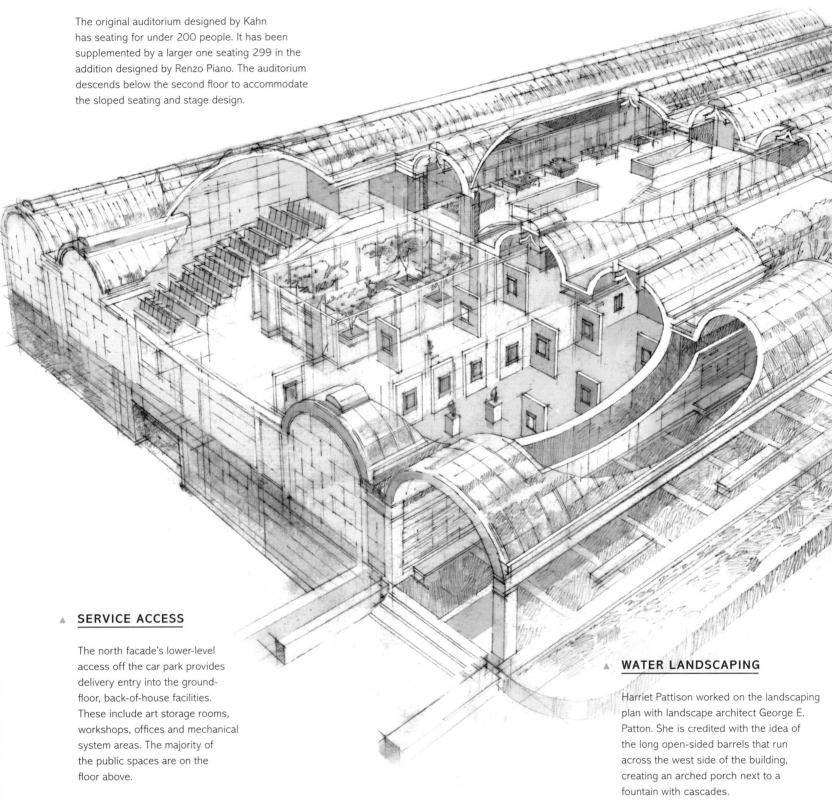

SERVICE ACCESS

The north facade's lower-level
access off the car park provides
delivery entry into the ground-
floor, back-of-house facilities.
These include art storage rooms,
workshops, offices and mechanical
system areas. The majority of
the public spaces are on the
floor above.

WATER LANDSCAPING

Harriet Pattison worked on the landscaping
plan with landscape architect George E.
Patton. She is credited with the idea of
the long open-sided barrels that run
across the west side of the building,
creating an arched porch next to a
fountain with cascades.

GALLERY WALLS

The interior features fixed walls of beautifully detailed concrete for gallery display, along with movable partitions for specific installations. The interiors are concrete with travertine and oak detailing throughout, something that Kahn carried over in later museums.

COURTYARD SPACES

The concrete cycloids are punctuated by glazed courtyards. These provide oases of natural light within the long barrel shapes. Courtyards appear in Kahn's subsequent museums, most notably the Yale Center for British Art. At the Kimbell, at times they serve as sculpture display spaces.

▶ CYCLOID BARRELS

There are sixteen parallel cycloid barrel vaults of poured-in-place concrete, each 30.4 m long by 6 m high by 6 m wide (100 × 20 × 20 ft). They are roofed in lead and were designed with a glazed slit down the centre to admit light below to the galleries. Within that space Kahn created aluminium diffusers to wash the walls with natural light.

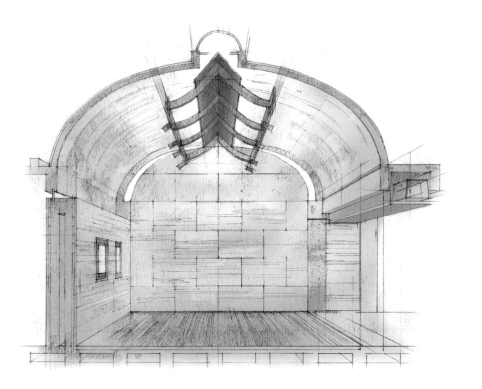

Sydney Opera House

LOCATION   Sydney, Australia
ARCHITECT   Jørn Utzon; Peter Hall
STYLE   Organic Modern
BUILT   1957–73

Controversies exist in many building types, but the prominence of public buildings, often funded through government appropriations and ultimately taxpayers, makes them an easy target for contention. One such structure is the Opera House in Sydney (1973) by Danish architect Jørn Utzon (1918–2008). He won this project in a competition in 1957, and moved to Australia in 1959 to begin work on it. His original design of concentric elliptical shells was praised by the competition jury, but replaced with more practically constructed spherical sections that some compare to the process of peeling an orange. Each is almost 75.2 m (247 ft) in radius. Structural engineers Ove Arup and Partners worked with Utzon to make these shells a reality in precast concrete clad with over 1 million white and cream coloured tiles, all equal to a height of a twenty-two-storey building. The remaining complex occupies 1.8 hectares (4.4 acres); its plinth is made of pink granite cladding, while interiors are of white birch plywood. There are seven performance spaces within, the largest of which is the Concert Hall seating 2,679 people, and one of the smaller being the Playhouse which seats 398. More than 1.2 million people attend performances and events at this complex each year.

During the construction phase Utzon and government officials disagreed on reporting structure, schedule, roof design and plywood material interior changes, as well as budget and related large cost overruns, which led to Utzon's resignation as architect in 1966. Local architect Peter Hall (1931–95) succeeded Utzon, completing the curtain wall and interior design somewhat differently, especially the two dedicated spaces for symphonic concerts and opera. When finished in 1973, the building cost was A$102 million, compared with the original projected completion date of 1963 and estimated A$7 million cost.

Although Utzon did not attend the official dedication on 20 October 1973, he and the Sydney Opera House Trust resumed communications three decades after his departure so that guidelines for future additions and renovations could be established. The first of these was the Utzon Room (2004), a multifunctional entertainment or event space. It is really the only completely Utzon-designed space within the complex. Other changes were implemented in 2006 to increase access for patrons with physical disabilities and to create theatre foyer views of the harbour. Utzon was awarded the prestigious Pritzker Architecture Prize in

2003 while he was undertaking these alterations, finally receiving official recognition for his contributions to architecture and his masterpiece of design in Sydney, only a few years before his death. While Utzon was developing the design guidelines for the Opera, he said: 'My job is to articulate the overall vision and detailed design principles for the site and for the form of the building and its interior. I like to think the Sydney Opera House is like a musical instrument, and like any fine instrument, it needs a little maintenance and fine tuning, from time to time, if it is to keep on performing at the highest level.'

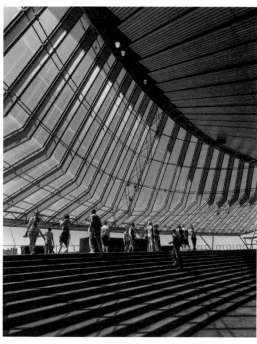

UTZON BUILDINGS

Jørn Utzon would have been catapulted to international stardom with the Sydney Opera House were it not for its rocky road to implementation. The other buildings that he designed remained in the background, ranging from the Bagsvaerd Church (1976) in Copenhagen, Denmark, to the National Assembly (1985) in Kuwait City. A lesser-known gem is the Ahm House (1962; right) in Harpenden, Hertfordshire, England. Utzon designed it for fellow Dane Povl Ahm, who was then associate partner – and later chairman – of Ove Arup, the firm that engineered Sydney Opera House.

ABOVE LEFT The Joan Sutherland Theatre proscenium theatre is the secondary performing space in the complex, having more than 1,500 seats. The orchestra pit can accommodate seventy musicians.

ABOVE RIGHT After Utzon's departure, Peter Hall was responsible for much of the interior. The bow-front terraces provide excellent views of the harbour.

CONCRETE SHELL

The competition's jury liked Utzon's high-arched parabolic and elliptical concrete shell design, which was then altered to the current one based on spherical sections, analogous to a peeled orange. The cantilevered roofs evoke Sydney's cliffs and harbour sailboats. The tallest of these arches reaches a height equivalent to a twenty-two-storey building. The detail shown here is from the roofline of the smaller building that houses the Joan Sutherland Theatre.

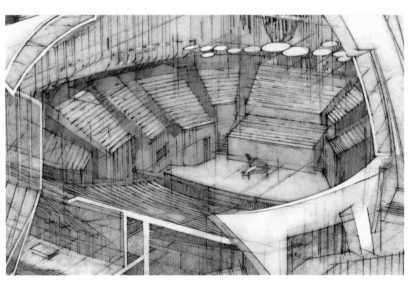

MAIN CONCERT HALL

The main concert hall can accommodate well over 2,000 people. Its centrally planned tiered design is said to have been influenced by similar design features at the Berliner Philharmonie (1956–63; see p. 140). It is home to the Sydney Symphony Orchestra and the Australian Chamber Orchestra. The interiors are Australian birch. Rehearsal rooms and a 544-seat drama theatre are below the main hall.

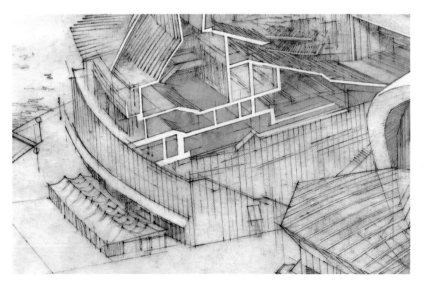

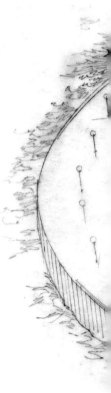

BOW-FRONT BASE

This view shows the glazed base of the main building that houses administrative offices and provides spectacular harbour views beyond. Comparable views can be had from the adjacent structure, which contains a gallery restaurant at the base of the Joan Sutherland Theatre. Both glazed structures sit atop a podium. The podium is a massive concrete base set upon a foundation secured by 700 steel-cased concrete shafts.

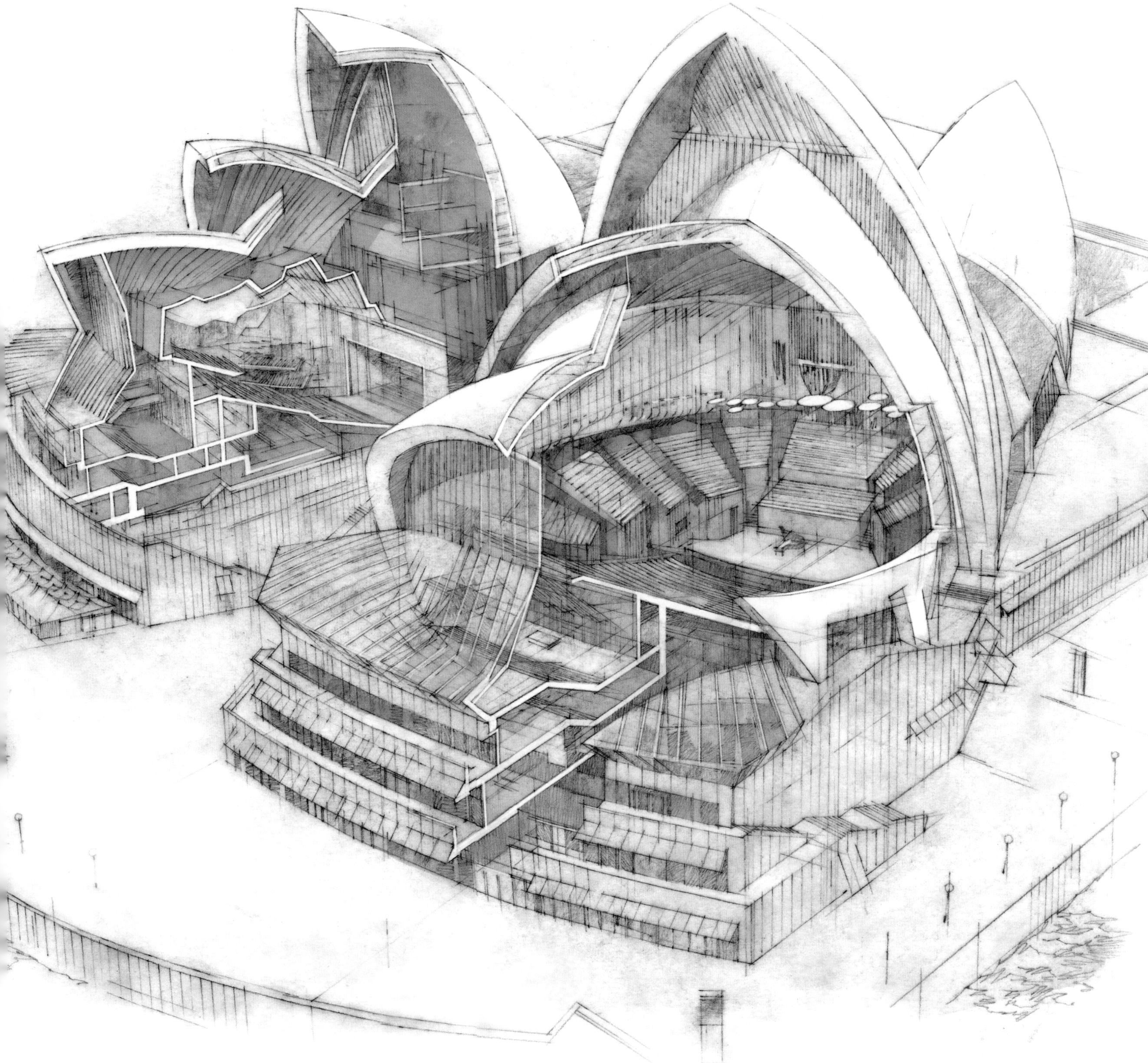

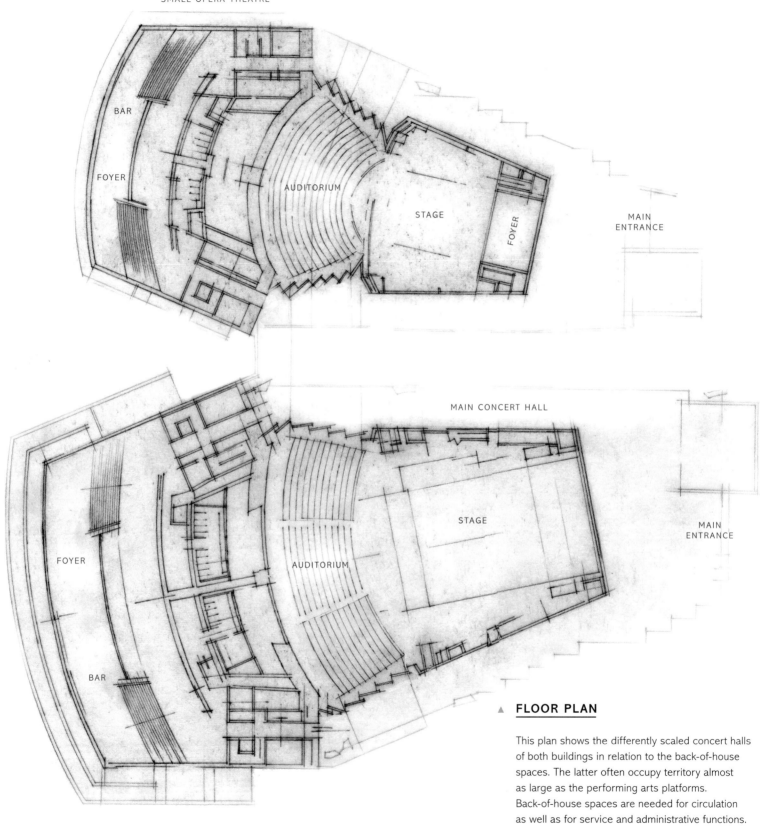

SMALL OPERA THEATRE

BAR

FOYER

AUDITORIUM

STAGE

FOYER

MAIN
ENTRANCE

MAIN CONCERT HALL

FOYER

BAR

AUDITORIUM

STAGE

MAIN
ENTRANCE

▲ **FLOOR PLAN**

This plan shows the differently scaled concert halls
of both buildings in relation to the back-of-house
spaces. The latter often occupy territory almost
as large as the performing arts platforms.
Back-of-house spaces are needed for circulation
as well as for service and administrative functions.

TILED ROOF FRAME

The concrete roof structure contains 2,194 precast concrete panels inserted into ribs 65 m (213 ft) high at their tallest. The roof is covered with more than 1 million cream-coloured, interlocking ceramic tiles. Produced in Sweden, each tile is approximately 120 mm (4.7 in.) square. Utzon said that the roof 'catches and mirrors the sky with all its varied lights dawn to dusk, day to day, throughout the year'. Architect Louis Kahn remarked: 'The sun did not know how beautiful its light was, until it was reflected off this building.'

Centre Georges Pompidou

LOCATION   Paris, France
ARCHITECT   Renzo Piano and Richard Rogers
STYLE   High-tech
BUILT   1971–77

When it opened in 1977 the Centre Georges Pompidou created a splash in the art and architectural worlds, not only in Paris but across the globe. The successful competitive design of Renzo Piano (b. 1937) with Gianfranco Franchini (1938–2009) and Richard Rogers (b. 1933) from 1971 essentially launched Piano and Rogers on their careers. Its instant success in terms of urban revitalization prefigured the nearby renovations of Les Halles market and transit district with the Forum des Halles shopping centre (1986) by Claude Vasconi

(1940–2009) and Jean Willerval (1924–96). Beyond its own district, its success prefigured the Grands Projets (Grand Projects) of French President François Mitterrand, beginning in 1982 with the construction of eight landmark contemporary buildings by leading architects that changed the face of Paris in the 1980s and 1990s (see p. 157). Beyond the boundaries of Paris, the Centre Pompidou had an effect on High-tech architecture of the 1970s and 1980s as well as museum and cultural edifice design of that era.

The Centre Pompidou's creation dates to the late 1960s when Minister of Culture André Malraux, President Charles de Gaulle and others began to work with planners and city officials to create a cultural centre, public library and arts complex near the historic food markets of Les Halles that were being moved from their central location. The result after an international competition was the Centre Pompidou, whose distinctive High-tech design vocabulary showcased the mechanical circulation elements on the outside of

the building in colour codes: green for plumbing; blue for heating ventilation and air conditioning (HVAC); yellow for electrical; and red for hazard control. Most of these are on the roof and east side of the building; their placement on the exterior enabled the opening of interior gallery spaces. The west side or entry facade facing the plaza features the public's processional escalator entry diagonally up the facade, making the visitor a part of the dynamic architectural experience as much as the plaza occupants below. The building, constructed mostly of steel and glass with concrete floors, is seven storeys, or 45.5 m (149 ft), high on the

plaza facade. It is a rectangle approximately 166 m (545 ft) long and 60 m (197 ft) wide. When it was officially dedicated on 31 January 1977, and opened to the public on 2 February, it was named after Georges Pompidou, who was president of France from 1969 to 1974 while it was being constructed.

Achieving world renown and publicity after its opening, the museum hosted major international exhibitions in its first years of operation that placed Paris art and architecture of the 1900s to 1930s in comparative context of cities such as Berlin, Moscow and New York. Exhibits such as these led to spectacular

attendance statistics, and over the next two decades the Centre Pompidou had more than 150 million visitors. The heavily trafficked facility was in need of extensive repair and renovation, which occurred from 1997 to 1999. It reopened in 2000 to over 16,000 people a day during that year, and has averaged more than 3.5 million visitors annually since. When first constructed, the building expenses totalled 993 million francs, whereas the renovation in 2000 cost 576 million francs. Centre Pompidou's Musée National d'Art Moderne has subsequently opened branches outside Paris, in Metz, France, and in Málaga, Spain.

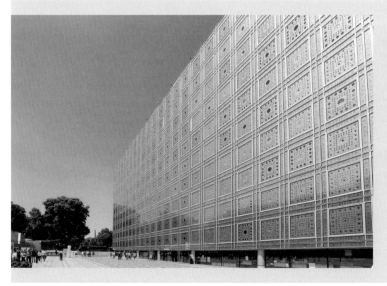

ABOVE LEFT External glazed escalators on the plaza side take visitors up to the main entry, providing dynamic spectacular views during their ascent.

ABOVE RIGHT Putting most structural, circulation and mechanical elements at the perimeter created large exhibition volumes within, though these spaces are not neutral boxes.

GRAND PROJECTS

After the success of the Centre Pompidou, the Grands Projets were instituted by President Mitterrand to commemorate the bicentennial of the French Revolution in 1989. Major cultural buildings, often by A-list architects, were constructed in Paris. They include the conversion of the Gare d'Orsay train station into the Musée d'Orsay (1986) by Gae Aulenti (1927–2012), the Grand Louvre (1984–89; see p. 162) by I. M. Pei (b. 1917), and the Grande Arche de La Défense (1989) by Johan Otto von Spreckelsen (1929–87) and Paul Andreu (b. 1938). One of the earlier projects was the Arab World Institute (1987; left) by Jean Nouvel (b. 1945). The steel-and-glass facade includes a photomechanical brise-soleil to control sunlight entering the building.

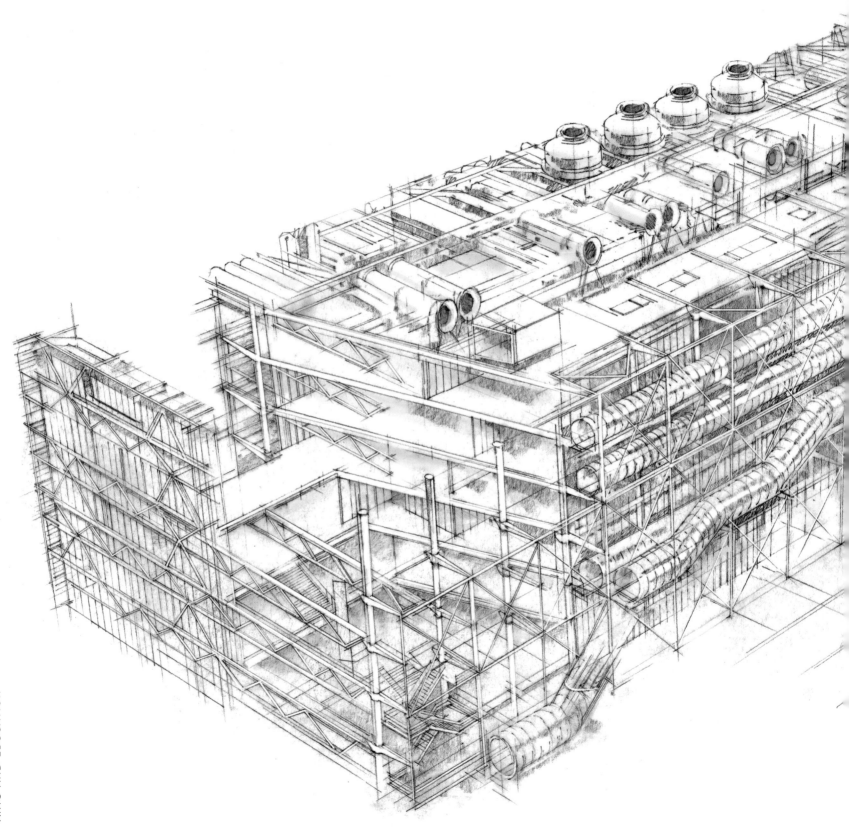

EXPOSED ELEMENTS

The building is considered a High-tech masterpiece because of its exposed structural and mechanical systems. Rogers became closely associated with this stylistic appelation, especially with the construction of the Lloyd's building (1986) in London, with distinct service towers, toilet modules and external lifts. The Centre Pompidou's appearance influenced other buildings of the era around the world. All those efforts might be traced back to 1950s and 1960s movements such as Brutalism in England, Metabolism in Japan (see p. 224), and the theoretical works of the English avant-garde architectural group Archigram.

MECHANICAL SYSTEMS

Mechanical systems are placed outside the building, thereby creating larger loft spaces inside. Piping on the roof as well as cascading down the east facade on the Rue du Renard is colour-coded, even when seen in the interiors. Green is used for plumbing, blue for climate control, yellow for electrical conduits and red for circulation as well as emergency functions, such as fire safety. Placing most of these systems on the street side freed up the west, or plaza facade, for the sculpturally dynamic escalators.

ESCALATOR EXPERIENCE

The glazed escalators provide visitors with changing views of the cityscape west of the building, as well as any animated activities on the plaza below, as they ascend to the upper entry. The tubed escalators ramp up the building approximately 45 m (150 ft) above the plaza. This people mover and the centre's systems were designed to accommodate 8,000 visitors daily, but they have handled five times that load as the structure and exhibits within proved popular.

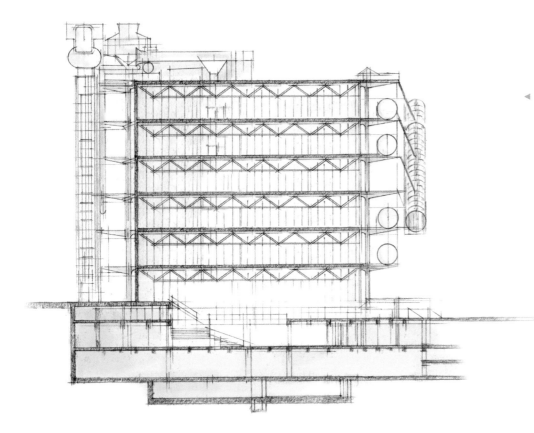

◄ CROSS SECTION

This section from the north side gives a good idea of the large spaces within each of the floors because the service elements are on the Rue du Renard to the left and plaza side on the right. The building is truly a tangible machine for art, in the spirit of 1920s Modernists such as Le Corbusier, who advocated his buildings as machines for living.

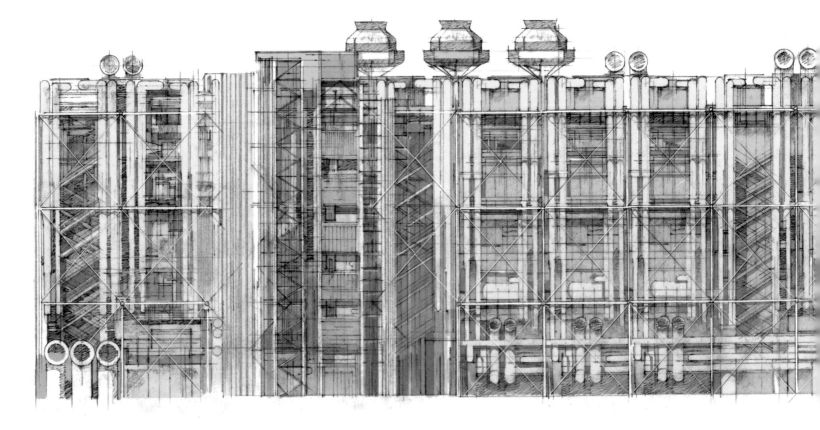

GERBERETTES

A *gerberette* is the point where a pole meets a beam, particularly at a building's entry. The *gerberettes* here refer to the exterior structure just beyond the glazed curtain wall. It holds the tiered escalator tubes that also connect to the structural trusses within the building.

◀ **STREET ELEVATION**

The east facade on the Rue du Renard contains the highly coloured pattern of the building's service piping. It projects the image of a mechanical overgrowth on the steel structure immediately behind. The system services clearly delineated on the exterior permitted expansive exhibition floors.

Grand Louvre

LOCATION   Paris, France
ARCHITECT   I. M. Pei

STYLE   Late Modern
BUILT   1984–89

Ieoh Ming Pei (b. 1917) has a reputation for designing some of the most striking museums that, like many of his buildings, have a strong sense of geometry. Examples include the Everson Museum of Art (1968) in Syracuse, New York; the Herbert F. Johnson Museum of Art at Cornell University (1973) in Ithaca, New York; and the East Building of the National Gallery of Art (1978) in Washington, D.C. This last's design of two adjoining triangles fitted within the property's trapezoidal lot created a distinctive atrium that catapulted Pei's firm to the forefront of museum design in the United States and beyond. By the time

he received the commission for the Louvre, Pei was an acknowledged master of his profession, having been awarded the Pritzker Architecture Prize in 1983.

Chinese-born Pei graduated from the Massachusetts Institute of Technology in 1940 and earned his Master's in Architecture under Walter Gropius at Harvard Graduate School of Design in 1946. The recipient of several fellowships, he was championed by influential New York developer William Zeckendorf and started his own firm in 1955 with partners Henry N. Cobb (b. 1926) and Eason H. Leonard (1920–2003). Pei remained a partner until retirement in 1990. His firm

was responsible for major buildings throughout the world including the John F. Kennedy Presidential Library (1979) in Boston, the Bank of China Tower (1989) in Hong Kong, and The Gateway twin-tower skyscraper complex (1990) in Singapore. His post-retirement projects include the Miho Museum (1997) in Shigaraki, Japan, and the Museé d'Art Moderne (2006) in Luxembourg.

With his high-profile talent for creating strong geometric forms for beautifully detailed museums, Pei was a natural choice for the Grand Louvre project. This was one of the Grands Projets (Grand Projects) of the 1980s implemented by French President François Mitterrand, influenced by the success of the Centre Georges Pompidou (1971–77; see p. 156) in Paris. These were intended to be major cultural monuments, mostly in Paris, to commemorate the bicentennial of the French Revolution in 1989. They include the Parc de la Villette (1987) by Bernard Tschumi (b. 1944); the Ministry for the Economy and Finance (1988) by Paul Chemetov (b. 1928); the Opéra Bastille (1989) by Carlos Ott (b. 1946); and the National Library of France (1996) by Dominique Perrault (b. 1953). Some were won in competitions, whereas others were commissions. Mitterrand selected Pei in 1984 for the Louvre project.

Pei solved the circulation problems that plagued the museum by connecting its multiple buildings around a central court, the Cour Napoléon. Pei's solution provided rational access for the museum's visitors and an amazing architectural symbol indelibly linked to its brand. The most distinctive feature of this mostly underground series of spaces is the pyramid of stainless steel and glass above the plaza. Visitors descend into this main entry, which acts as a hub to cross-axial underground passages that connect to surrounding museum buildings; it also provides visitor services such as the museum shop and offers glimpses back in time with the foundations from the original medieval castle.

Critics cited the new entry as not appropriate within the surrounding classicist courtyard, its pyramidal shape evoking death and its 666 glass panes associated with Satanic imagery – although the actual count is 675 diamond-shaped and 118 triangular panes.

Despite such objections, the Grand Louvre was a great success for the planned 4 million visitors when opened. The plan was tweaked to accommodate the 7 to 9.3 million visitors the museum sees annually. In 2017 the Grand Louvre was given the Twenty-five Year Award by the American Institute of Architects for rivalling 'the Eiffel Tower as one of France's most recognizable architectural icons'.

ABOVE LEFT Pei's renovated Richelieu Wing features a glazed courtyard, the Cour Marly. Sculptures exhibited here were brought to Paris after the French Revolution of 1789, mostly from King Louis XIV's Château du Marly west of Paris.

ABOVE RIGHT The Louvre dates back to the castle that King Philip II began in 1190 to fortify Paris. With Pei's renovation, the ruins of the castle and its moat were made visible to the public once more.

NATIONAL GALLERY, WASHINGTON, D.C.

Pei's early museum masterpiece was the East Building (left) of the National Gallery of Art in Washington, D.C. He manipulated triangular forms to create an angular atrium. The new wing connects with the classicist main building of 1941 by John Russell Pope (1874–1937) via an underground passage. Pei's wing provides exhibit space for the museum's modern art collection and temporary exhibitions, along with office and research facilities. Visitor service facilities for the museum shop and café are incorporated into the underground passage. The building reopened in 2016 after three years of renovation and the construction of a sculpture garden.

1 COUR CARRÉE

The Cour Carrée is a courtyard built during the sixteenth and seventeenth centuries as the palace expanded from the original castle. It dates to 1546 and the reign of King Francis I. This palace was the design of Pierre Lescot (1515–78). Work continued around the courtyard over the next century and more, essentially being completed by King Louis XIV and the same architects who planned Versailles (1624–1770; see p. 96). Shown just to the right here is the mansard-roofed Pavillon de l'Horloge (Clock Pavilion). Also known as the Pavillon Sully, it is the entry tower to the courtyard and is the work of Jacques Lemercier (c. 1585–1654).

2 UNDERGROUND SHOPPING

As part of Pei's new entry, architectural work included the creation of space under the Louvre's large central Cour du Carrousel in 1993 and later. There were new services for museum visitors and tourists in general, including parking, and a museum shop within a mall of boutiques, shops, and restaurants called the Carrousel du Louvre. Pei credits his associate architect Michel Macary (b. 1936) for substantial input here. The inverted glass pyramid that was Pei's design with engineer Peter Rice is also within, its form intended to add natural illumination to the subterranean level.

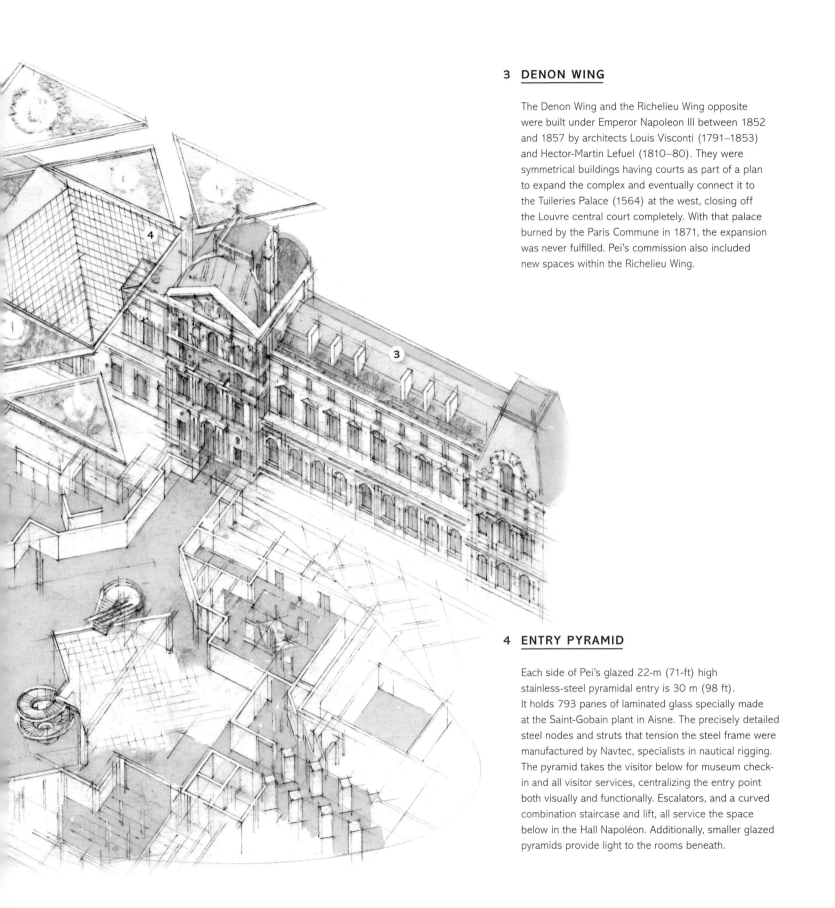

3 DENON WING

The Denon Wing and the Richelieu Wing opposite
were built under Emperor Napoleon III between 1852
and 1857 by architects Louis Visconti (1791–1853)
and Hector-Martin Lefuel (1810–80). They were
symmetrical buildings having courts as part of a plan
to expand the complex and eventually connect it to
the Tuileries Palace (1564) at the west, closing off
the Louvre central court completely. With that palace
burned by the Paris Commune in 1871, the expansion
was never fulfilled. Pei's commission also included
new spaces within the Richelieu Wing.

4 ENTRY PYRAMID

Each side of Pei's glazed 22-m (71-ft) high
stainless-steel pyramidal entry is 30 m (98 ft).
It holds 793 panes of laminated glass specially made
at the Saint-Gobain plant in Aisne. The precisely detailed
steel nodes and struts that tension the steel frame were
manufactured by Navtec, specialists in nautical rigging.
The pyramid takes the visitor below for museum check-
in and all visitor services, centralizing the entry point
both visually and functionally. Escalators, and a curved
combination staircase and lift, all service the space
below in the Hall Napoléon. Additionally, smaller glazed
pyramids provide light to the rooms beneath.

PLAN

This plan is oriented with the east courtyard, or Cour Carrée, on the right and shows the U-shaped complex as it exists today. The construction process unearthed medieval artefacts, original foundations and walls, many of which are exhibited within.

KEY
A   Richelieu Wing
B   Arc du Carrousel
C   Denon Wing
D   Cour Napoleon
E   Cour Carrée

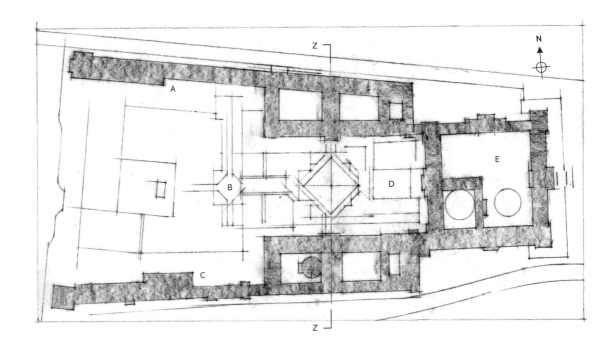

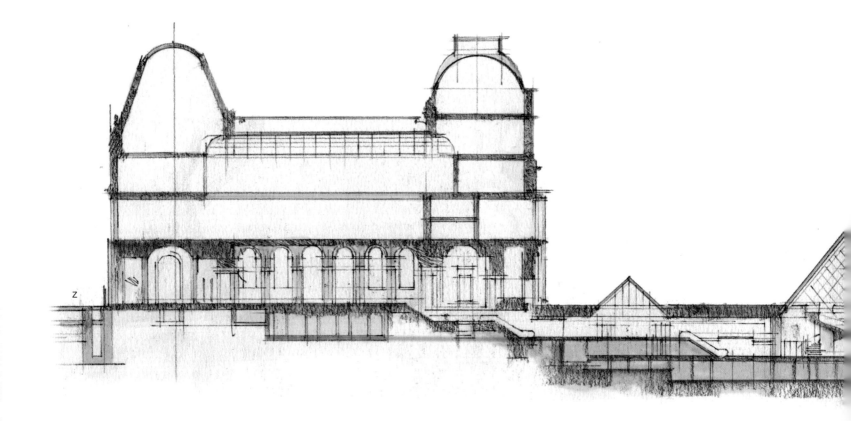

STAIRCASE DETAIL

The spiral staircase to the Hall Napoléon below contains a cylindrical hydraulic lift within its void, whose shaft is sunk well into the ground so that the cab sits on the entry-floor pavement when on the lower level. The staircase is minimally designed, with glazed sides topped by a metal stair rail.

SECTION

This section (marked as z on the plan above left) shows Pei's pyramidal entry and underground spaces looking west, with the Richelieu Wing on the right, and the Denon Wing on the left. Pei's work on the project lasted over fifteen years after he was first hired to be architect for the Grand Louvre renovation in 1984. He was responsible for more than 9 hectares (22 acres) on the site, adding or renovating 62,000 sq m (670,000 sq ft) of space.

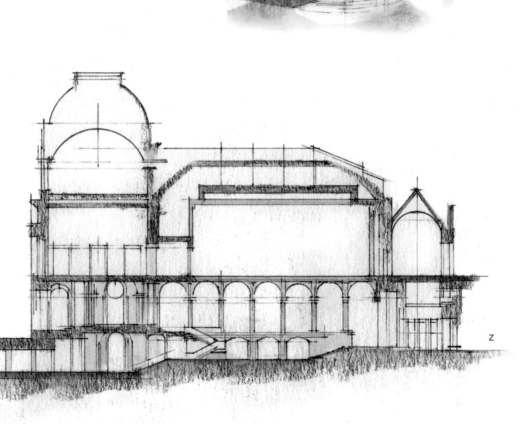

z

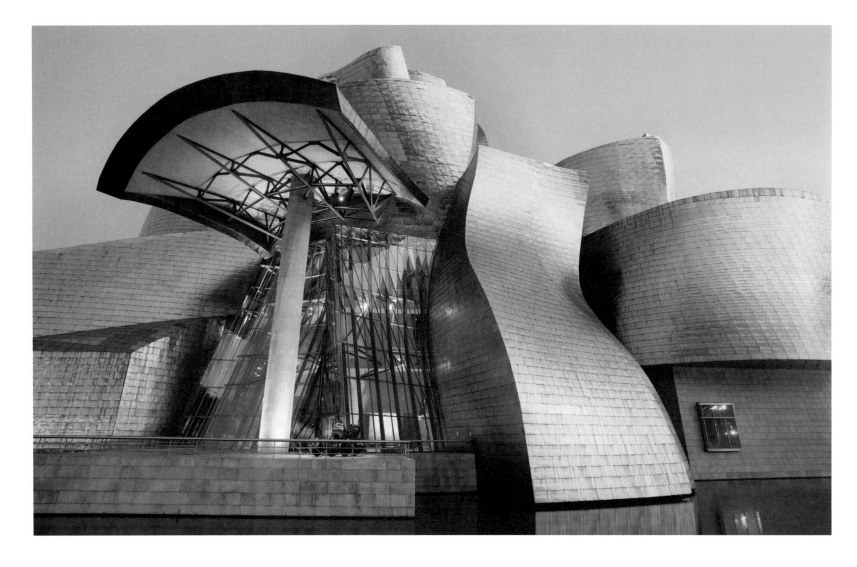

Guggenheim Museum Bilbao

LOCATION	Bilbao, Spain
ARCHITECT	Frank Gehry
STYLE	Deconstructivist
BUILT	1991–97

Knowing that they had commissioned something special, the Guggenheim Foundation had trademarked Guggenheim Museum Bilbao to control commercial use of the building's distinctive image. This does not mean that tourists cannot photograph the building. The owner simply seeks to prevent unauthorized commercial use in creating and selling souvenirs. It was Frank Gehry (b. 1929) who fashioned that distinctive organic shape for them.

Gehry was born in Canada but has lived in California since 1947. He made a splash on the architecture and design scene with cardboard furniture in the late 1960s, as well as his own house in Santa Monica in

1978. The latter utilized common materials such as chain-link fencing and corrugated steel panels to create angular wall planes that heralded this home as an early Deconstructivist project. It eventually led Gehry to larger-scale experiments in angular design such as the California Aerospace Museum (1984) in Los Angeles. His experimentation with computer-aided design programs, particularly his adaptation of Dassault Systèmes' aerospace-engineering software CATIA of 1977, helped launch him on an important career. Using that software as the way to realize his design dreams, he created the Dancing House (1996) in Prague. Its visually distorted towers foreshadowed his later dynamic tower

at 8 Spruce Street (2011) in New York and influenced institutional buildings throughout his career. These range from the Experience Music Project (2000) in Seattle to the Walt Disney Concert Hall (2003) in Los Angeles. The Guggenheim Museum Bilbao is an important part of this institutional sequence as the first major museum building to be designed using this means.

When the project began in 1991, the Basque government supported this partnership with the Guggenheim, providing construction funds of $100 million, as well as operating and art-acquisition funds. The Guggenheim selected Gehry, who provided a dynamically shaped building of titanium, steel, glass and limestone; its plan featured an organic atrium surrounded by nineteen exhibition spaces, ten of which are traditional rectilinear galleries. The total area is 24,000 sq m (260,000 sq ft) and galleries occupy less than half of that space. The remainder includes administration and visitor services such as the restaurant, library and museum shop. On the exterior, materials indicate interior functions: titanium for exhibition spaces and masonry for public services. The titanium acquired from Russia is perhaps the most distinctive exterior feature. It is only .38 mm (.01 in.) thick, and thus easily installed over a waterproof membrane and galvanized steel affixed to the steel structure. It is also less expensive than the originally intended stainless-steel cladding.

The museum opened in 1997 and had a worldwide media impact. It reinforced the Basque government's efforts to support a rebirth of this Spanish industrial city, with additional buildings created between 1995 and 2012 by Santiago Calatrava (b. 1951), Foster and Partners, Arata Isozaki (b. 1931), and Álvaro Siza (b. 1933), among others. The Guggenheim Museum Bilbao was a major spearhead for this effort. It was estimated that it increased Bilbao's economy by $160 million in its first year of operation. With 4 million visitors during the first three years, the taxes collected from that tourism more than paid for the initial construction costs. This so-called Bilbao effect likely led other art museums across the globe to imitate its short-term success by commissioning A-list architects to create exhibition envelopes for their collections in the first decade of the new millennium.

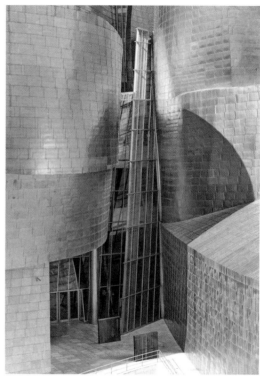

ABOVE LEFT Artist Richard Serra's sculpture *Snake* (1994–97) consists of three enormous ribbons of hot-rolled steel that are permanently installed in the museum's Fish Gallery.

ABOVE RIGHT There is no shortage of compelling curves and adventurous angles throughout the Guggenheim's interior or exterior, the forms themselves becoming works of art.

FRANK GEHRY

Gehry graduated from the architecture school at the University of Southern California in 1954, studying shortly thereafter at the Harvard Graduate School of Design. He first specialized in residential design and furnishings, including an offbeat use of commonplace elements within his home in Santa Monica during the 1970s. Larger commissions came in the 1980s and 1990s, but his adaptation of aerospace-engineering software catapulted him to much more adventurous designs in the late twentieth and early twenty-first centuries.

TITANIUM SKIN

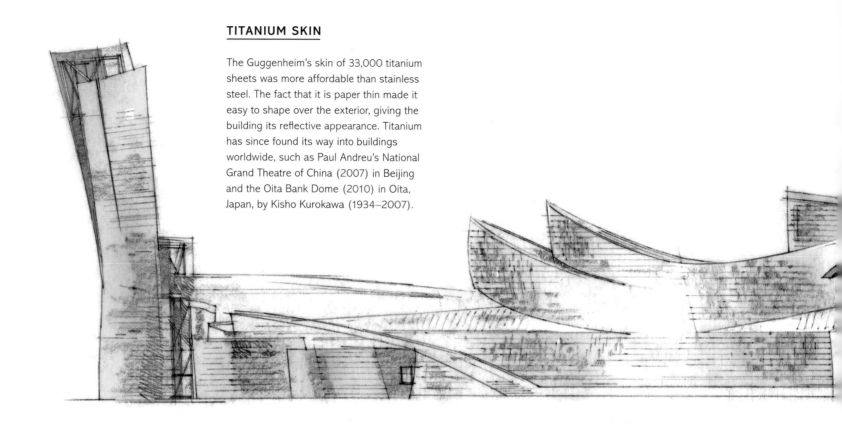

The Guggenheim's skin of 33,000 titanium sheets was more affordable than stainless steel. The fact that it is paper thin made it easy to shape over the exterior, giving the building its reflective appearance. Titanium has since found its way into buildings worldwide, such as Paul Andreu's National Grand Theatre of China (2007) in Beijing and the Oita Bank Dome (2010) in Oita, Japan, by Kisho Kurokawa (1934–2007).

CATIA-GENERATED FORMS

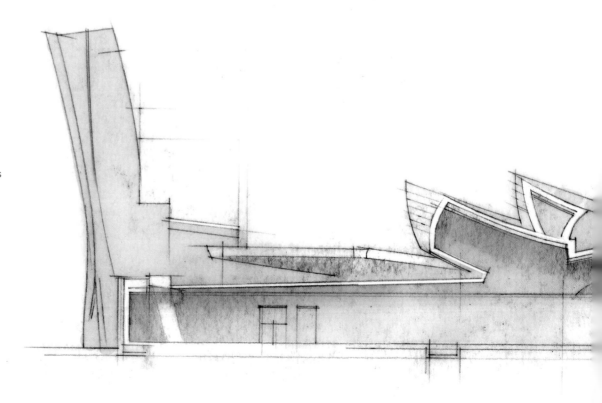

Gehry used an adaption of CATIA aerospace-engineering software to design the extreme intertwining curves and angles of the exterior in relation to similar forms inside. Gehry Technologies was founded in 2002 from his architectural practice. It is based in Los Angeles and has offices around the world. It provides a variety of computer modelling and information services for architects and their clients.

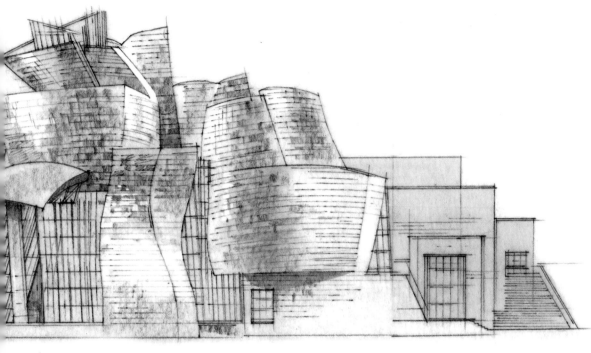

RECTILINEAR SPACES

The wavy exteriors often, though not always, represent curved interiors. Many are used for art installations, including the central organizing atrium. Rectilinear exteriors hold like-shaped interiors. Those are often office and visitor service spaces. These are covered in limestone, not titanium, on the outside. The elevation and section (above and below) show the north, or river, side of the building.

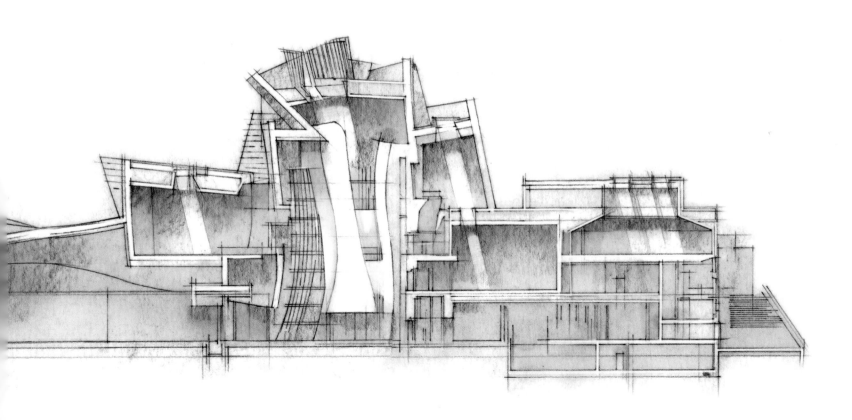

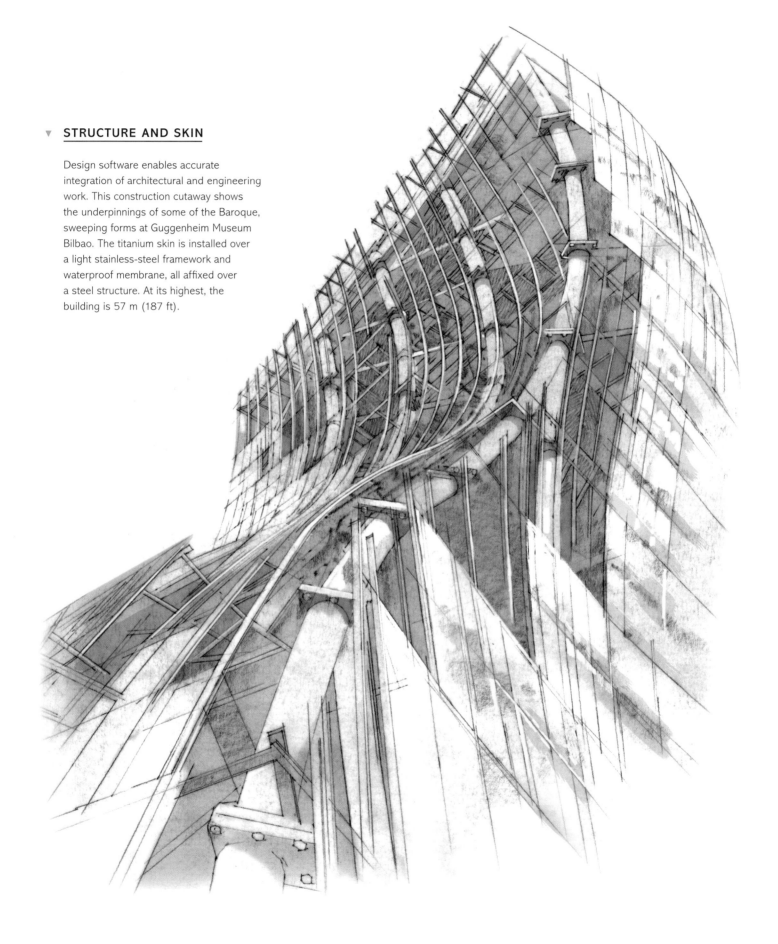

▼ STRUCTURE AND SKIN

Design software enables accurate integration of architectural and engineering work. This construction cutaway shows the underpinnings of some of the Baroque, sweeping forms at Guggenheim Museum Bilbao. The titanium skin is installed over a light stainless-steel framework and waterproof membrane, all affixed over a steel structure. At its highest, the building is 57 m (187 ft).

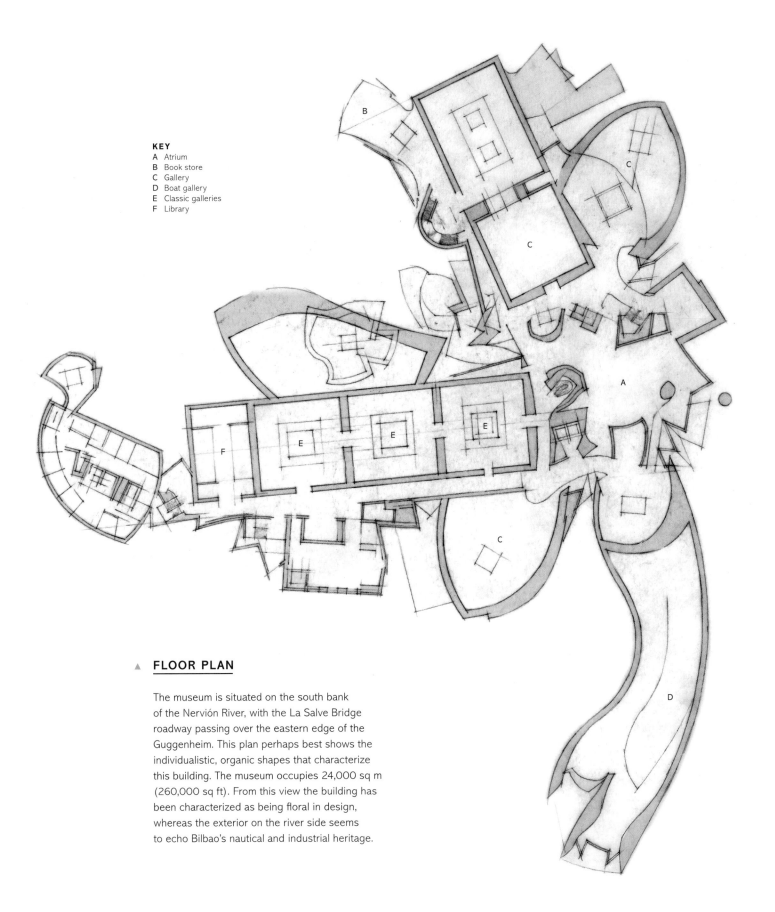

KEY
A Atrium
B Book store
C Gallery
D Boat gallery
E Classic galleries
F Library

▲ **FLOOR PLAN**

The museum is situated on the south bank
of the Nervión River, with the La Salve Bridge
roadway passing over the eastern edge of the
Guggenheim. This plan perhaps best shows the
individualistic, organic shapes that characterize
this building. The museum occupies 24,000 sq m
(260,000 sq ft). From this view the building has
been characterized as being floral in design,
whereas the exterior on the river side seems
to echo Bilbao's nautical and industrial heritage.

National Museum of African American History and Culture

LOCATION   Washington, D.C., United States of America
ARCHITECT David Adjaye
STYLE   Contemporary
BUILT   2009–16

The National Mall in Washington, D.C., is a 1.9-km (1.2-mile) east–west landscaped grass axis between the United States Capitol steps (1792–1891; see p. 34) and the Washington Monument (1885). Its history goes back to a 1.6-km (1-mile) long landscaped 'grand avenue' envisioned as part of a plan by Pierre Charles L'Enfant (1754–1825) for the capital in 1791. It was never really implemented, and subsequent plans led eventually to the McMillan Plan of 1901 to 1902. This created a 91-m (300-ft) wide green vista that connected both of those major monuments, with additional cultural buildings along the axis. That is what is seen today.

The mall on both north and south sides is lined with fourteen major Smithsonian Institution buildings and other national museums. Many of these were designed by major architects. They include the Hirshhorn Gallery and Sculpture Garden (1974) by Gordon Bunshaft (1909–90) of Skidmore, Owings, and Merrill; the East Building of the National Gallery of Art (1978) by I. M. Pei (b. 1917); the United States Holocaust Memorial Museum (1993) by James Ingo Freed (1930–2005) of Pei's office; and the National Museum of the American Indian (2004) by Douglas Cardinal (b. 1934). The National Museum of African American

History and Culture (NMAAHC) was initiated through legislation in 2003 and opened in 2016, to the design of David Adjaye (b. 1966), with the Freelon Group, Davis Brody Bond, and the Smith Group JJR.

Adjaye won the international competition to design the museum in 2009. He was born in Tanzania, the son of a Ghanaian diplomat. Educated in London, he graduated from the Royal College of Art in 1993 with a Master's degree. His London- and New York–based practice has executed designs across the world, from the Idea Store Whitechapel (2005) in London to the Nobel Peace Centre (2005) in Oslo, the Museum of Contemporary Art, Denver (2007), the Moscow School of Management, Skolkovo (2009) and the Aïshti Foundation arts and shopping complex (2015) in Beirut.

The NMAAHC has a striking three-tiered facade inspired by Yoruban caryatids. The tiered Corona consists of 3,600 bronze-toned aluminium panels whose lacy latticework (opposite) is intended to project the image of the ornate ironwork from New Orleans created by enslaved Africans during the nineteenth century. Construction began in 2012. The building is adjacent to the Washington Monument on a 2-hectare (5-acre) site landscaped by Gustafson Guthrie Nichol. The museum contains 37,000 sq m (400,000 sq ft) and cost $540 million for construction, including exhibitions that were designed by Ralph Appelbaum Associates. Major artefacts range from a restored slave cabin of the 1800s to a segregation-era railroad car from the 1920s and Chuck Berry's Cadillac convertible from c. 1973. The five-storey building contains staff offices on the top floor, with galleries and exhibits on the two floors beneath and on the concourse below ground. Theatre and education spaces are on the entry level and floor above, along with visitor services. Energy-saving features include photovoltaic panels to heat water.

At the official opening on 24 September 2016, the NMAAHC welcomed over 30,000 visitors that weekend and more than 1 million visitors within its first five months of operation. Praised in much of the architecture press, the museum fills an important need in the Mall's collection of significant institutions.

ABOVE LEFT The museum's exterior with its distinctive three-tiered inverted pyramid shape was inspired by the Yoruban caryatid, which is a traditional wooden figure that features a crown or corona at its summit.

ABOVE RIGHT A steel staircase connects the main foyer level to the concourse below, where visitors can experience the peaceful space of the Contemplative Court and attend programs at the 350-seat Oprah Winfrey Theater.

NATIONAL MALL, WASHINGTON, D.C.

The National Mall contains the original Romanesque-Revival Smithsonian Institution Building (1855) designed by James Renwick Jr (1818–95). Nicknamed the 'Castle', it was the first of fourteen major museum buildings, the most recent being the National Museum of African American History and Culture. Many are government-funded institutions, with public–private partnership foundations established for additional support. Together, they, and off-site Smithsonian branches, host over 30 million visitors each year.

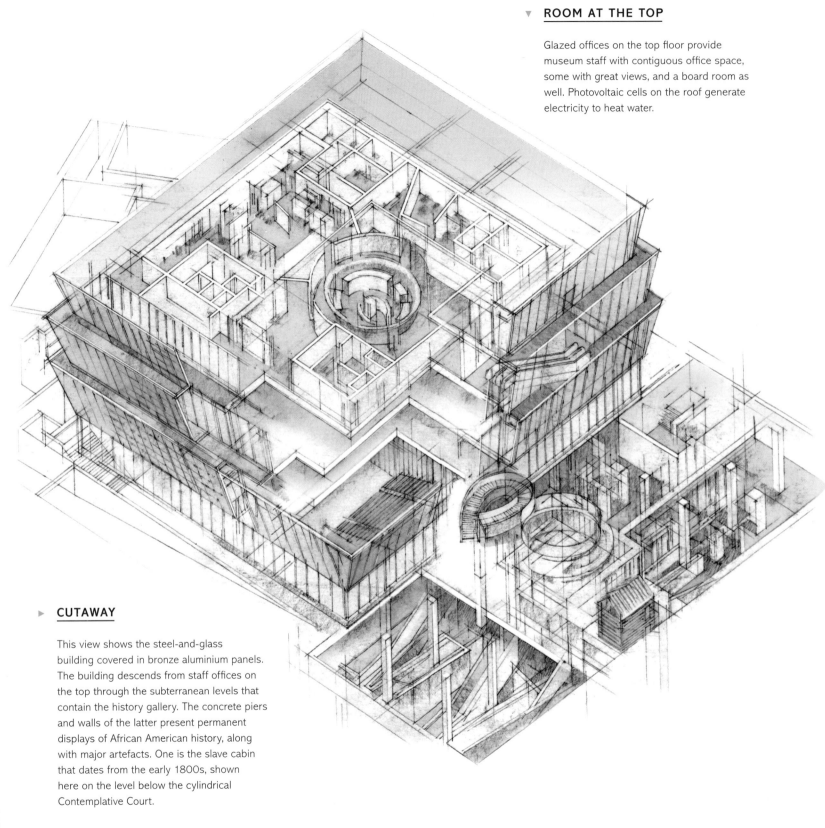

Glazed offices on the top floor provide museum staff with contiguous office space, some with great views, and a board room as well. Photovoltaic cells on the roof generate electricity to heat water.

▶ **CUTAWAY**

This view shows the steel-and-glass building covered in bronze aluminium panels. The building descends from staff offices on the top through the subterranean levels that contain the history gallery. The concrete piers and walls of the latter present permanent displays of African American history, along with major artefacts. One is the slave cabin that dates from the early 1800s, shown here on the level below the cylindrical Contemplative Court.

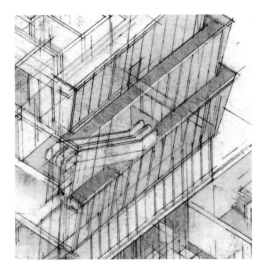

SCREEN FACADE

The lacy, gold-toned screen facade animates the glazed boxlike building behind. Escalators are a circulation feature adjacent, giving users glimpses through the latticework to the outside world. The Corona glows from within at night, serving as a cultural beacon on the mall.

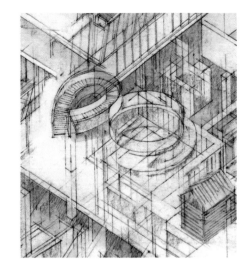

CONCOURSE

The curved stair provides access to the concourse and spaces such as the Oprah Winfrey Theater. Wall panels within the theatre have the same pattern as those on the facade screen. The court has seating arranged around a square fountain with illuminated cascading water. Engraved in the wall opposite is a quote by Martin Luther King Jr: 'We are determined . . . to work and fight until justice runs down like water, and righteousness like a mighty stream.'

▶ FACADE DETAIL

This detail shows a portion of the 3,600 bronze-toned cast aluminium panels that act as a sunscreen and animate the interiors beyond the steel-and-glass curtain wall. The pattern was intended to evoke the appearance of ironwork created by enslaved artisans in the South, particularly New Orleans. The facade material is arranged so that it avoids heat gain yet screens strong warmth generated by the sun.

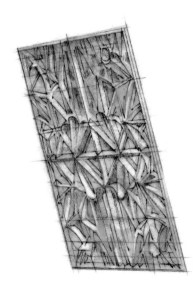

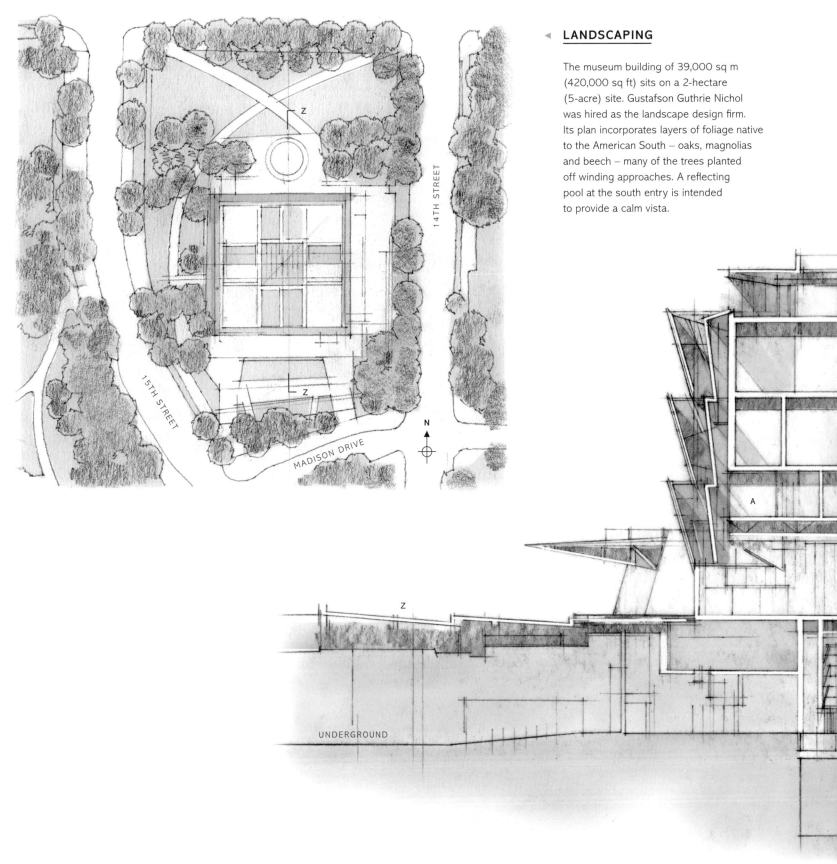

The museum building of 39,000 sq m
(420,000 sq ft) sits on a 2-hectare
(5-acre) site. Gustafson Guthrie Nichol
was hired as the landscape design firm.
Its plan incorporates layers of foliage native
to the American South — oaks, magnolias
and beech — many of the trees planted
off winding approaches. A reflecting
pool at the south entry is intended
to provide a calm vista.

14TH STREET

15TH STREET

MADISON DRIVE

N

Z

A

Z

UNDERGROUND

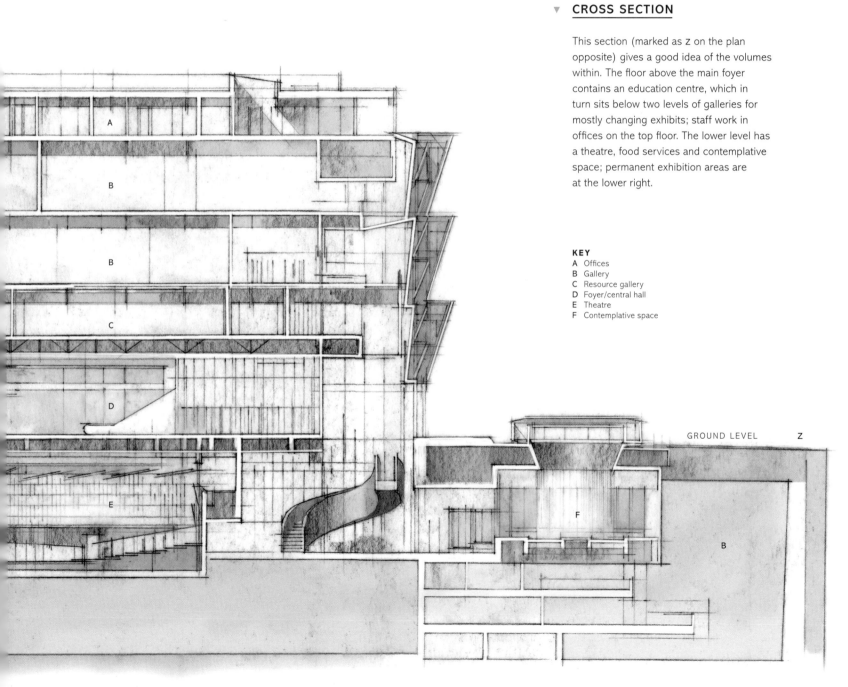

▼ CROSS SECTION

This section (marked as **z** on the plan opposite) gives a good idea of the volumes within. The floor above the main foyer contains an education centre, which in turn sits below two levels of galleries for mostly changing exhibits; staff work in offices on the top floor. The lower level has a theatre, food services and contemplative space; permanent exhibition areas are at the lower right.

KEY
A Offices
B Gallery
C Resource gallery
D Foyer/central hall
E Theatre
F Contemplative space

GROUND LEVEL   Z

Living

'Living it up!' 'Living the high life.' 'Living well is the best revenge.' Maxims such as those connote luxury and extravagance when it comes to lifestyle, including homes and houses. Some of the homes within this chapter validate those phrases, with sites, spaces and vistas that go beyond the mundane implications of the word 'shelter'. But others are on the opposite end of the spectrum, being either the equivalent of a homeless shelter and medical clinic or an efficiently organized and inexpensively constructed small modern home which might well be comparable in cost to today's studio apartment or so-called tiny home.

Of the eleven examples in this chapter, eight are private homes – single-family dwellings. These include the retirement retreat of Villa La Rotonda (1566–1606; see p. 188) in Vicenza, Italy, and a summer or second home such as Villa Mairea (1939; see p. 210) in Noormarkku, Finland. This group represents the creative design forces of the eras in which they were built. They range from Andrea Palladio's fascination with rural Roman prototypes at Villa La Rotonda, the enthusiastic, obsessively intertwined Art Nouveau decorations at the Hôtel Tassel (1893–94; see p. 192) in Brussels, to the open-spaced regional variants of Modernist masterpieces of the 1920s through to the 1940s. These include the Schröder House (1924; see p. 196) in Utrecht, the Netherlands, as well as architects' and designers' own homes, the Casa Luis Barragán (1948; see p. 214) in Mexico City and the Eames House (1949–50; see p. 220) for Charles and Ray Eames in suburban Los Angeles. The Modern movement was a social design movement whose intentions were to reform society by providing supposed universal design solutions, notably in the form of inexpensive materials and construction costs.

Solutions such as these were particularly appropriate in the years after both World Wars (1914–18 and 1939–45), when builders sought to provide housing for returning service personnel. In the 1920s and mid-1940s there were a number of competitions that strove to create the postwar home, with Modernist styles pushing their way into the mix of more traditional residential designs. Examples include the *Chicago Tribune*'s sponsorship of the House Design Competition (1927) and Chicagoland Prize Homes Competition (1945), various European housing exhibitions after the famed *Weissenhofsiedlung* (1927) in Stuttgart, and the Case Study Houses in Los Angeles (1945 and later). Two such innovative yet inexpensive Modernist homes are featured within this chapter, the Schröder and Eames houses. Of all the Modernist single-family homes described here, perhaps the visual correspondence between Villa Mairea by Alvar Aalto (1898–1976) and Frank Lloyd Wright's Fallingwater (1936–39; see p. 206) provides an apt story about Aalto's admiration of Wright's

THE EAMES HOUSE (SEE P. 220)

work and highlights the fascination of both architects to have their buildings respond to the wooded landscape around them.

Those structures are all essentially single-family homes, but three examples within this chapter provide contrasted solutions for multi-occupant spaces in different eras and for different economic levels. The Hôtel-Dieu de Beaune (1443–52; see p. 184) in Beaune, France, was essentially a combination of medical clinic and poor house, its large main hall occupied by beds at the perimeter and long refectory-style tables for communal dining down the centre. The Nakagin Capsule Building (1971–72; see p. 224) in Tokyo, Japan, by Kisho Kurokawa (1934–2007) provided a creatively designed, low-cost solution to prefabricated high-rise dwellings, using the strengths of industry to build self-contained living modules. At the other end of the spectrum, MAD Architects designed individualistic high-end condominiums in Absolute Towers (2007–12; see p. 230) in Mississauga, Toronto, Canada, each with a balcony view – a marketer's dream. Altogether, the chapter features a broad representation of homes and housing, although housing projects could also have been included, such as the renowned horseshoe-shaped Hufeisensiedlung (Horseshoe Estate; 1925–33) in Berlin-Britz by Bruno Taut (1880–1938) and Martin Wagner (1885–1957), or some early communal structures: the Narkomfin Building (1928–30) by Moisei Ginzburg (1892–1946) and the student dormitory at the Communal House of the Textile Institute (1930) by Ivan Nikolaev (1901–79), both in Moscow.

Nevertheless, this chapter gives a picture of what it takes to build and live in these homes. The story does not end here, however, because there are homes and houses throughout some of the other chapters as well. The chapter on Public Life includes the Doge's apartments within his Venetian palace (1340–1614; see p. 28), and the commercial Chrysler Building (1929–30; see p. 38) originally contained an elaborate apartment suite for its owner, Walter P. Chrysler. The chapter on Monuments contains the Palace of Versailles (1624–1770; see p. 96), an example of royal lifestyle and living at its extreme. It also has the famed presidential home Monticello (1796–1809; see p. 102), whose Palladian style bears comparison with Villa La Rotonda here. The chapter on Arts and Education likewise has the individualistically furnished home of John Soane (1792–1824; see p. 116) in London as well as the Modernist Bauhaus (1925–26; see p. 126) in Dessau, Germany, which contained small studio apartments for students. The Louvre (1793, 1984–89; see p. 162) in Paris, also discussed in that chapter, was originally a royal palace and castle before it became an art museum. The final chapter on Worship contains buildings that are each colloquially considered to be a 'House of God'. Beyond that function, they often contained residential quarters for clergy – priests, canons, bishops, monks, mullahs and imams. For instance, the Temple of the Golden Pavilion (after 1397, rebuilt 1955; see p. 256) in Kyoto was planned using residential prototypes, its structure housing a monk's quarters as well as a Buddhist shrine. So the basic human function of shelter or housing can be seen throughout this book as well as across the continents throughout time.

CASA LUIS BARAGÁN (SEE P. 214)

182 LIVING

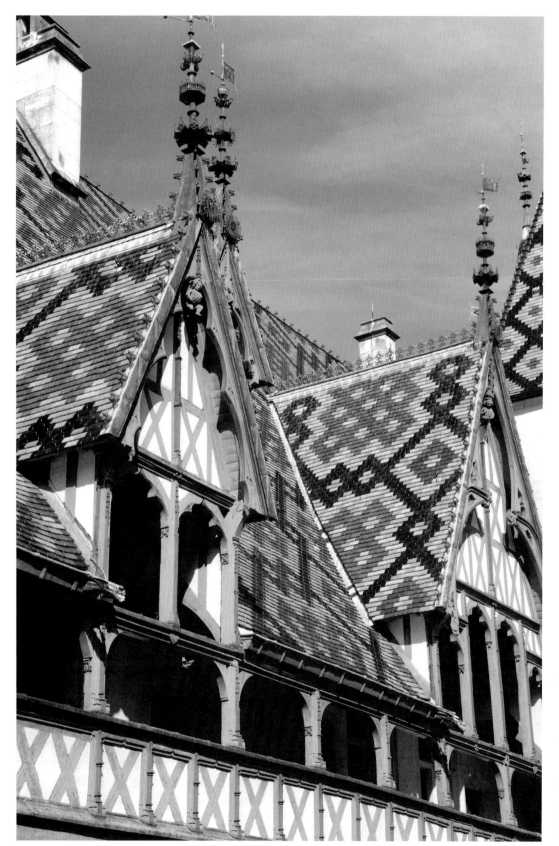

Hôtel-Dieu de Beaune

LOCATION   Beaune, France
ARCHITECT   Jacques Wiscrère
STYLE   Late Gothic
BUILT   1443–52

Medieval 'hotels', hospices or hospitals are comparable to today's private-nonprofit or church-run homeless shelters. They were essentially almshouses for the poor, though also provided medical care and a place for spiritual regeneration. Some were important constructions akin to contemporary buildings such as the Pacific Garden Mission (2007) in Chicago. This large facility was designed by high-profile architect Stanley Tigerman (b. 1930) to include dormitories for more than 900 men and women, a 600-seat dining hall, workshops, an infirmary, a vegetable greenhouse and a chapel. Like other such buildings in medieval Europe, the Hôtel-Dieu de Beaune, or Hospices de Beaune, served similar functions.

The Hôtel-Dieu de Beaune was founded in 1443 by Nicolas Rolin and his third wife, Guigone de Salins, to support, through medical and spiritual care, local people impoverished from the Hundred Years' War (1337–1453) between France and England. Rolin was the chancellor to Philip III, the Duke of Burgundy, whose territories included land in eastern France, Flanders and the Netherlands. Rolin himself was immortalized within a Northern Renaissance painting, the *Madonna of Chancellor Rolin* (*c.* 1435) by Flemish realist master Jan van Eyck, now in the Louvre, Paris, which shows Rolin praying to the Virgin Mary and Christ Child.

The hospice's design and construction are attributed to Jacques Wiscrère. The building was consecrated in 1452 and functioned as an almshouse–hospital until converted into a museum after 1971. The rectilinear two-storey building is arranged around a central courtyard. The small entry portal is on the east side of the building marked by the Gothic finial above. The building contained a kitchen, nuns' quarters, a chapel, a pharmacy and dormitories/wards. The chapel once housed the spectacular *Last Judgment* (c. 1445–50) polyptych, also known as the *Beaune Altarpiece*, by Northern Renaissance painter Rogier van der Weyden, now displayed within its own room in the museum.

Architecturally, however, the most important room is the Grande Salle des Pôvres (Great Hall of the Poor), with its tier-point-arched wood ceiling and polychromed beams, running some 50 m long by 14 m wide and 16 m high (164 × 46 × 52 ft). In this room, beds were arranged at the longitudinal perimeter and the centre contained refectory-like seating for meals.

Reconstructed canopy beds, each likely originally accommodating two occupants, and related furnishings date from the third quarter of the nineteenth century. Floor tiles within are inscribed with the word *seulle*, referring to Rolin's wife as his 'one and only'. In the courtyard the most striking feature is the multicoloured tile roof (opposite) above half-timber galleries. The glazed tiles were repaired and replaced in the early 1900s.

The nonprofit that runs the museum building holds wine auctions every November from its vineyards, its wine reserve being stored in a cellar here. Christie's has managed this exclusive auction since 2005.

BELOW LEFT The Great Hall of the Poor is lined with nineteenth-century reproductions of the canopy beds that accommodated residents, two to a bed, and likely more.

BELOW RIGHT The aerial view from the southeast provides an idea of how spectacular the signature tiled roof was when it was constructed, perhaps even more so than today.

BEAUNE ALTARPIECE

Even more imposing than the roof is the *Beaune Altarpiece*, painted by Northern Renaissance artist Rogier van der Weyden. The painting was originally installed in the chapel on the end of the Great Hall, where those within could easily see it above the altar. Fifteen paintings compose the polyptych that was painted in oil on oak panels, with parts later transferred to canvas. It measures 220 by 546 cm (87 × 215 in.). Considered by many to be the artist's greatest work, the painting was meant to provide both comfort and a warning to patients in the adjacent hall about getting their lives in order before meeting their maker at the Last Judgment, the work's alternative title.

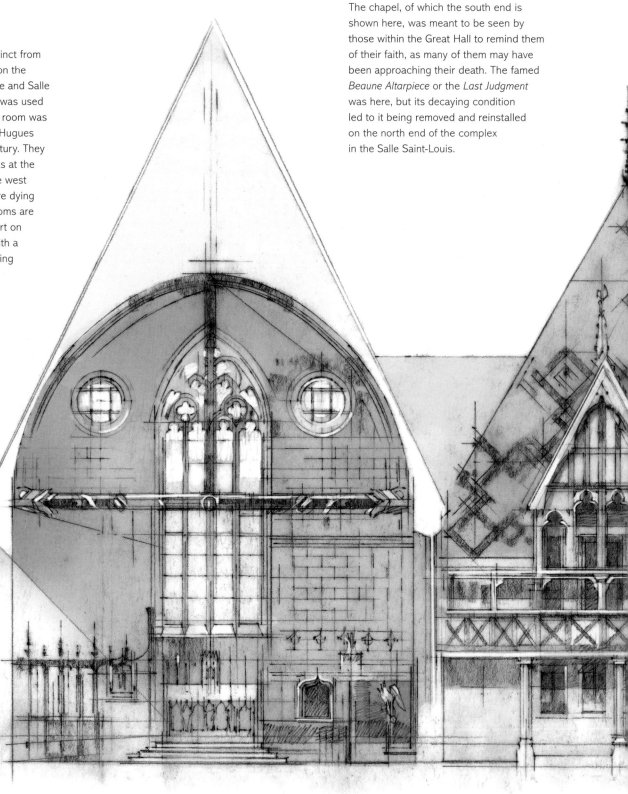

SOUTH WING

This short wing, architecturally distinct from the austere chapel and Great Hall on the east, contains the Salle Sainte-Anne and Salle Saint-Hugues. Sainte-Anne's room was used for affluent patients. Saint-Hugues' room was originally the infirmary, created by Hugues Bétault in the mid-seventeenth century. They connected to the Salle Saint-Nicolas at the southwest corner, technically in the west wing. This was the final place where dying patients were housed. All these rooms are also connected off the internal court on the courtyard and gallery levels, with a corner stair, the gallery also wrapping around the west wing.

▼ CHAPEL

The chapel, of which the south end is shown here, was meant to be seen by those within the Great Hall to remind them of their faith, as many of them may have been approaching their death. The famed *Beaune Altarpiece* or the *Last Judgment* was here, but its decaying condition led to it being removed and reinstalled on the north end of the complex in the Salle Saint-Louis.

▼ TILED ROOF

The roof of the south wing shows the exuberance of the half-timber and coloured tile construction. Tile patterns more typical of central Europe during the late Middle Ages were thought to have inspired these. The central, cobblestone Court of Honour contains an elaborate fountain with Gothic ironwork, and the tiled roofs and half-timber, galleried facade contrast with the sober external appearance of the Great Hall on the left side of the court.

▼ WEST WING

The west wing on the right side of the drawing, the southwest corner of the building shown here in a cutaway, contains the large Salle Saint-Nicolas. This was the last stop before death for many patients. King Louis XIV, in a visit in 1658, was so horrified at the overcrowding of men and women in this space that he provided a gift for another room to be created for women. This space now houses an exhibition on the hospice.

Villa Almerico-Capra – 'Villa La Rotonda'

LOCATION	Vicenza, Italy
ARCHITECT	Andrea Palladio, Vincenzo Scamozzi and others
STYLE	Renaissance–Roman Revival
BUILT	1566–1606

The Villa Almerico-Capra, also known as Villa La Rotonda, was commissioned by papal advisor Canon Paolo Almerico, who wished to retire in his native Vicenza. Almerico hired Andrea Palladio (1508–80) to design what is arguably that architect's most spectacular villa. It was begun in 1566 and completed by Palladio-follower Vincenzo Scamozzi (1548–1616) after Palladio's and Almerico's deaths. Beginning in 1591 Scamozzi and others worked for the next owners, Odorico and Maria Capra, completing the structure in 1606.

The villa was featured in Palladio's treatise *I quattro libri dell'architettura* (*The Four Books of Architecture*, 1570). It was one of a number of farm villas designed and built by Palladio, an aficionado of Roman architecture through his knowledge of *De Architectura* (*On Architecture*, *c*. 30–15 BCE), the writings of Roman architect and civil engineer Vitruvius (*c*. 80–*c*. 15 BCE). In Vicenza, Palladio trained and worked as a stonemason. His buildings included important villas that harked back to simple Roman prototypes. They include Villa Saraceno (1540s) in Agugliaro, Villa Pojana (1549) in Pojana Maggiore, Villa Gazzotti Grimani (1550) in Bertesina and Villa Chiericati (1550–80) in Vancimuglio, all in the Veneto. La Rotonda, built in the words of its owner 'for his pleasure', was constructed on property that was not already functioning agricultural land with related outbuildings. The rustic, arcaded farm buildings on this site were constructed by Scamozzi after the villa changed hands in 1591.

Villa La Rotonda's Greek cross plan features four equal classical facades, each of which has a raised portico of six Ionic columns. Sculptures of classical deities are atop. These facades hark back to those of Roman temples, perhaps in an effort to contrast this simplicity with the more elaborate ecclesiastic architecture in Rome at the time. As with many Palladian villas, this one is built of brick and stucco along with stone. Some of the floors are stucco made with lime and marble fragments, somewhat typical of this region. At the centre is a galleried rotunda with a dome that Palladio intended to be higher, but Scamozzi redesigned to have a lower profile. Staircases in each corner ascend to the third floor and dome at the corners, which was renovated in the eighteenth century. Each floor contains 134 sq m (1,445 sq ft) for a total of some 560 sq m (6,000 sq ft). The main rooms on the piano nobile, or first floor, and the circular space under the dome are covered with frescoes most likely commissioned by the Capra family. Marble mantels and stucco decorations are found throughout. Decorative additions and minor modifications were made between 1725 and 1750. The overall symmetrical plan and appearance are unique among Palladio's constructed villas, though his design for Villa Trissino at Meledo, published in his architectural treatise, bears a direct relationship to his Villa La Rotonda design. The current owners, the Valmarana family, initiated a restoration program in 1976 and operate this world monument as a museum open to the public.

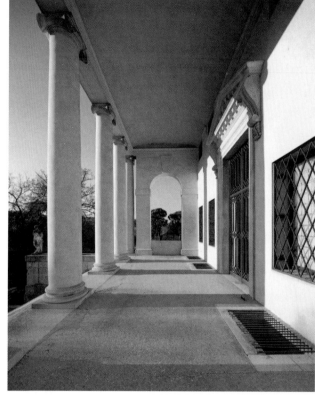

ABOVE LEFT A step inside the central space reminds visitors of the building's nickname, Villa La Rotonda, and gives a glimpse of the spectacular trompe-l'oeil frescoes beyond.

ABOVE RIGHT Like-styled porticoes with Ionic columns project from each side of the cubical central volume, projecting the image of a Roman temple.

PALLADIAN INFLUENCE

Palladio's impact cannot be overestimated, especially in the eighteenth and nineteenth centuries. Anglo-American examples are often the most prominent. Chiswick House (1727; left) in London is arguably among the best known. Built by Richard Boyle, 3rd Earl of Burlington (1694–1753), with the advice of several prominent architects, its central portico, dome and Serlian windows all owe a conscious debt to Palladio.

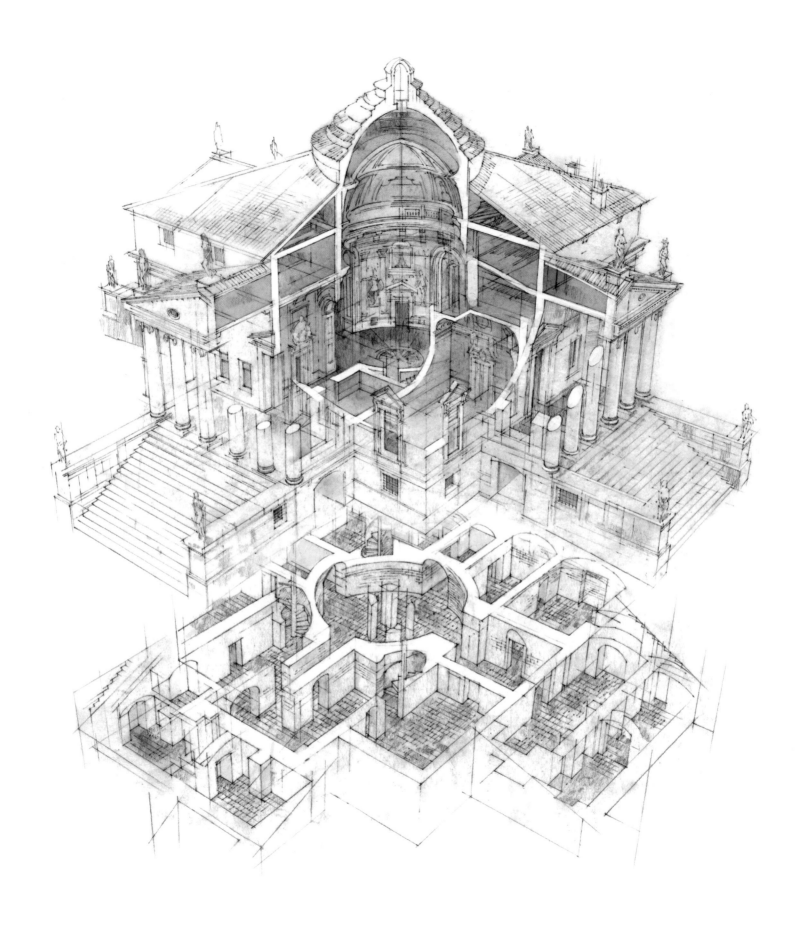

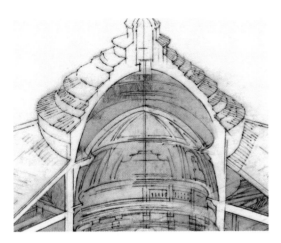

DOME

Palladio designed the dome to be taller, a hemisphere topped with a lantern. But Scamozzi changed the profile to a lower one inspired by the flatter one on the Pantheon in Rome (126 CE). In Villa La Rotonda it is called a *calotte*, a reference to skullcaps. It is a concentrically tiered segmented dome with a tiled roof.

PORTICO

Four symmetrical porticoes, each styled identically with Ionic colonnades, connect to the cubical mass and give the building its simple yet august appearance, much as a public building in ancient Rome would have done. Statues of Roman gods and goddesses at the corners and peak of each pediment reinforce this image.

DRUM

Palladio believed in the visual power of simple geometric forms such as the circle and square. The cylindrical drum at the centre supports the dome and provides a canvas for an explosion of frescoes within both the drum and dome by painter and draughtsman Alessandro Maganza.

▶ **FLOOR PLAN**

The circle and square forms-within-forms are clearly visible in Villa La Rotonda's plan, as is their obsessively quadrilateral arrangement. Ovoid spiral staircases at the corners of the central drum connect the floors. Strong yet simple geometry was a hallmark of Palladio's style; its axial planning is taken to a logical, ordered extreme here.

◀ **LOWER LEVEL**

The ground floor has the same plan as the floor above, with four large rooms connected to small ones, but it has lower ceilings. This was the service and servants' floor, and it includes the kitchen, which has been restored. Direct and indirect sunlight filters down into the spaces. The building sits upon a slight hill so that even the ground floor is raised above the local terrain.

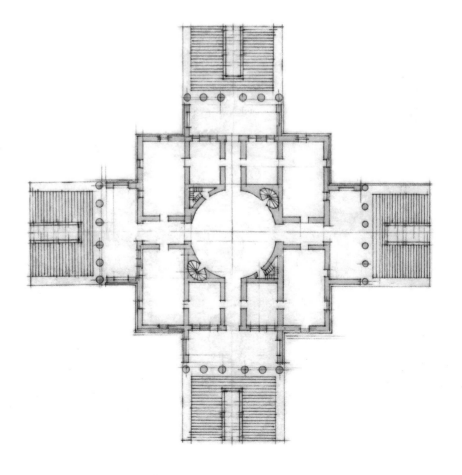

Hôtel Tassel

LOCATION	Brussels, Belgium
ARCHITECT	Victor Horta
STYLE	Art Nouveau
BUILT	1893–94

Each stylistic category in this book might have interpretations and variants, the most frequent related to national and sometimes regional expressions. Such is the case with Art Nouveau of the late nineteenth and early twentieth centuries, which has examples in the UK, Canada and the United States, and that was termed Jugendstil in Germany, Secession in Austria (particularly Vienna) and Liberty Style in Italy. Art Nouveau architects in Europe and North America include Louis Sullivan (1856–1924) in the United States, Hector Guimard (1867–1942) in France, Joseph Maria Olbrich (1867–1908) and Otto Wagner (1841–1918) from Austria, Peter Behrens (1868–1940) in Germany and Giuseppe Sommaruga (1867–1917) in Italy, being just a few. Key Belgian proponents of Art Nouveau include Henry van de Velde (1863–1957) and Victor Horta (1861–1947).

Horta was born in Ghent and had an early fascination with music and architecture. He studied there from 1873 to 1877 as well as in Brussels from 1881 to 1884; in between he had a stint in Paris from 1878 to 1880 working with architect Jules Debuysson. His two years in Paris were likely more impactful than his formal design training; in his own words 'walking the city streets, visiting the monuments and museums threw wide open the windows of my artistic soul'. With his father's death in 1880, Horta went to Brussels to study and work, though in 1889 he visited Paris, where he saw the World's Fair and the newly built Eiffel Tower. In Brussels he taught at the Université Libre de Bruxelles from 1892 to 1911 and designed some of his masterpieces of Art Nouveau, including the Hôtel Tassel. Its importance paved the way for other commissions such as the Hôtel Solvay (1895–1900) and the Volkshuis for the Belgian Workers Party (1899; demolished).

The Hôtel Tassel, designed for Professor Emile Tassel, who taught at the same university as Horta, and Tassel's mother, was the first time Horta incorporated an organically flamboyant iron staircase within a home. It served as a design focal point as well as an example of his own type of 'biomorphic whiplash' – anthropomorphic linear design that characterizes his Art Nouveau work and likely influenced the designs of Guimard and others. Built on a lot 7.8 m wide by 29 m long (25.5 × 95 ft), the townhouse of mostly brick and Euville and Savonnières limestone has steel skylit lightwells within the core for the staircase and winter garden. This spectacular space was opposite the dramatic staircase on the entry floor. Staircase decorations included a statue of Perseus by sculptor Godefroid Devreese and an arabesque mural by painter Henri Baes. As with other architects of the era, Horta's hand was on every curvilinear shape regardless of scale – from door handles to mosaic floor, sculpted capitals, stained-glass windows and exterior ironwork on the bow-front facade.

The home's basement contained utilitarian spaces such as the boiler room, pantry, kitchen, wine cellar and laundry. Three storeys were built above, capped with an attic. The ground floor had the entry, living and dining rooms, as well as a mezzanine with a smoking room within the curved bow-front windows that also served as the equivalent of a home theatre for Tassel's travel slide shows. The next floors above were for bedrooms, study and office. Later the house was used for a variety of purposes, and it was purchased in 1976 by architect Jean Delhaye (1908–93), who had studied with Horta. It underwent a complete restoration from 1982 to 1985 by Delhaye. He was also one of the leading figures to establish a museum within Horta's own home and studio (1898–1901) in Brussels in 1969. Today, Hôtel Tassel is accessible only via private tours.

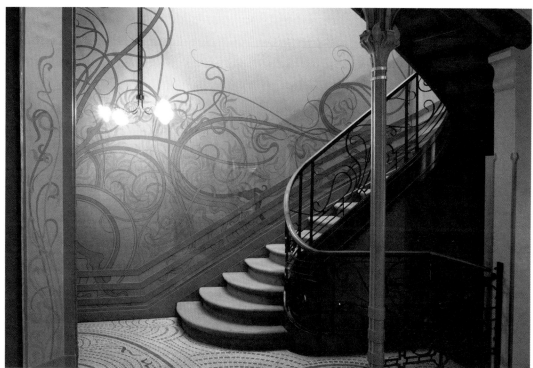

ABOVE LEFT The main entry to the house contains an elaborate mosaic floor, as does the vestibule landing, which leads to similar patterns in the main staircase floor.

ABOVE RIGHT The visual centrepiece of the house, this organically stylized staircase was offset, thus providing increased floor space in rooms above compared with a central stair.

ART NOUVEAU SPLENDOUR

Brussels and Paris are the capitals of European Art Nouveau. The latter has a wealth of highly ornamented structures with slender, stylized natural forms. Simpler yet seductive designs are those by Hector Guimard, such as his entries to the Paris Métro (c. 1905). Later, more elaborate designs include the multistorey domed hall in the Galeries Lafayette (1912, left) department store designed by Georges Chedanne (1861–1940) and Ferdinand Chanut (1872–1961) as a pantheon for shopping.

▼ CROSS SECTION

This section cuts from the street facade on the right to the back of the house on the left. The basement off the street contains the coal cellar, and behind are service spaces such as kitchen and laundry. The main floor street entry above the coal room leads into the porch and vestibule and then up to a landing and the grand staircase. Public rooms tend to be on the main floor to the left of the staircase. Private rooms, mostly bedrooms, are to the left of the staircase above the main floor. The street-side floors above the main floor contain a smoking room-mezzanine above the entry, and a study and office.

◀ EXOTIC ASCENT

The staircase and adjacent winter garden, landing, vestibule and entry form one of the great masterpieces of Art Nouveau. Its stylized organic forms permeate the entire space – floors, walls and decorative ironwork combined – making it a landmark immersive architectural experience with somewhat decadent overtones from the fin de siècle. It is almost like stepping into a French poster from the turn of the nineteenth century.

▲ ART NOUVEAU DETAILS

Miami hotel architect Morris Lapidus (1902–2001) is linked with the phrase 'too much is never enough' when it comes to his flashy designs of the 1950s. But the phrase is equally applicable to the stylized vegetation seen throughout Art Nouveau details. The sketch shown here is of the metalwork from the facade bow-front window.

Schröder House

LOCATION Utrecht, the Netherlands
ARCHITECT Gerrit Rietveld
STYLE Dutch De Stijl Modern
BUILT 1924

Just imagine what the neighbours in the traditional, brick row housing adjacent thought when this structure was being built in 1924. The Schröder House was revolutionary in design and appearance when constructed on a small lot at the end of that row. The radical design was created by architect Gerrit Rietveld (1888–1964). Trained as a carpenter and self-taught in architecture, Rietveld established his furniture and cabinetry business in 1917. His Red–Blue Chair from the same year is arguably the most famous product of this era. His connections to the Dutch modern movement De Stijl (The Style; 1917–31) enabled interaction with other Modernists such as German architect Walter Gropius, famed for designing the Bauhaus (1925–26; see p. 126) in Dessau, Germany. Rietveld's own work beyond the landmark Schröder House shifted away from the primary colours of De Stijl to more monochromatic Modernism in the later 1920s and 1930s, as seen in the multifamily Erasmuslaan (1931–34) in Utrecht and the postwar Van Slobbe House (1961) in Heerlen. He never left his carpentry and furniture roots, however, continuing to design minimal modern pieces such as the Wouter Paap Armchair (1928–30) and the Zig-Zag Chair (1932–34).

Schröder House (1924) is Rietveld's three-dimensional experiment in shifting planes, designed for the recently widowed socialite Truus Schröder. She wanted a home for herself and three children as a place to 'live' and not be 'lived' in, hence the peppy appearance of this small structure. The dynamism of the wall planes and primary colours of the house (left) suggest similar qualities within, where spaces are multifunctional and, at times, separated and even altered by movable walls. Built-in furnishings use that same palette, as do movable furnishings.

The building was constructed mostly of brick and wood, with reinforced concrete used for the foundations and second-floor balcony, and welded steel for the balcony railings. Most of the rooms have rubberized and cork flooring. Rietveld had a particularly low budget for this 110 sq m (1,200 sq ft) home – a mere 9,000 guilders, today worth approximately €65,000 ($73,200). When the building was finished, Rietveld set up a small architectural office on the main floor, where he worked from 1925 to 1933; when his wife died he moved into the home with Truus Schröder and remained there until his death. When Truus died in 1985 she donated the house to a foundation that, with local architect Bertus Mulder (b. 1929), restored it.

Today the Schröder House is operated by the Centraal Museum in Utrecht. In a way, having only one owner has made it an amazing survivor from the 1920s Modern movement and the Dutch variant called De Stijl, which focused on the ideals of geometry in primary colours. It is as much of a unique artwork as any abstract rectilinear painting composition by Rietveld's contemporaries such as Theo van Doesburg and Piet Mondrian.

ABOVE The building projects the image of being a three-dimensional representation of a De Stijl painting, even today being as much a sculpture as it is a house.

LEFT The sliding coloured planes of the interior reflect those on the outside, with built-in storage and flexible, multifunctional rooms

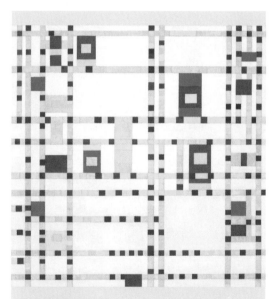

DE STIJL

Artists of the De Stijl movement incorporated abstract, mostly geometric forms and bold primary colours within their works. Mondrian is most associated with those aesthetic principles, particularly after World War I (1914–18). During the 1920s and 1930s he painted a number of gridlike compositions highlighted with colour. Within the first year of World War II (1939–45) he left Europe for New York. *Broadway Boogie Woogie* (1942–43; above) was inspired by the city's architecture, as well as the rhythms of jazz.

▶ TRIUMPH OF RECTILINEARITY

The house is a triumph of rectangles
in structure and wall planes, expressed in
architectural form and colour. This drawing
shows Rietveld's Red–Blue Chairs (1917)
in the corner of the main-floor multifunctional
space as a miniature expression of this
rectilinear victory. The kitchen and dining area
shown below at the corner has built-ins as well.

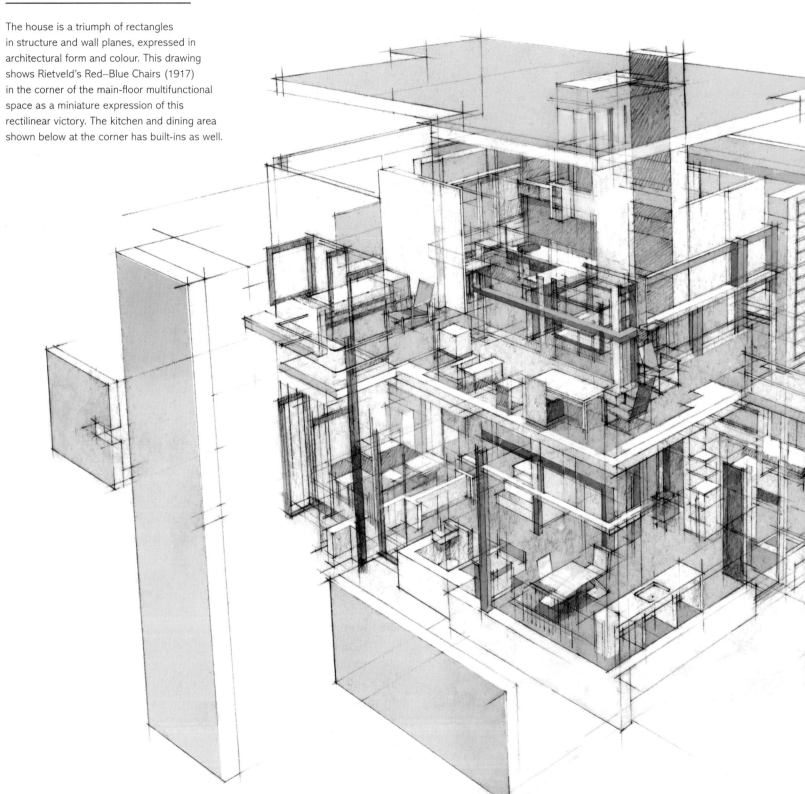

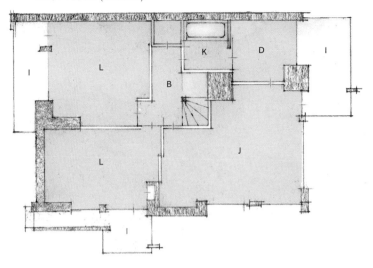

FIRST FLOOR (CLOSED)

▶ FLOOR PLANS

Movable walls and multifunctional or flexible spaces are arranged around a central staircase. The kitchen, dining and living space along with a studio and bedroom are on the ground floor. The next floor contains larger multifunctional spaces that could be subdivided. Even before Rietveld and Schröder officially lived together, he used the ground-floor studio at the rear after the house was built.

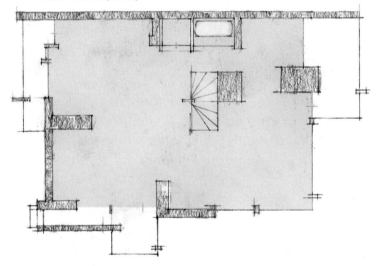

FIRST FLOOR (OPEN)

◀ OPEN SPACE

Like most Modernists, Rietveld found ways to visually bring the outside within. Balconies are an extension of the building's wall planes and windows are designed not only to pivot open but also to occasionally break the corners, suggesting a direct connection to nature, much as Frank Lloyd Wright did at Fallingwater (1936–39; seep. 206) in Pennsylvania. This idea may reflect wider attitudes about open-air tuberculosis treatments during this era and good health in general.

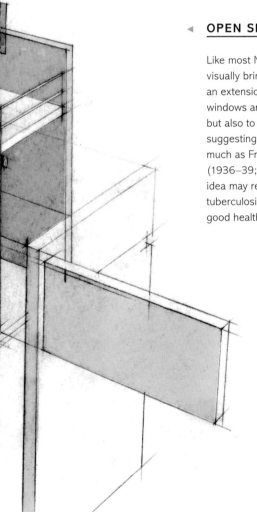

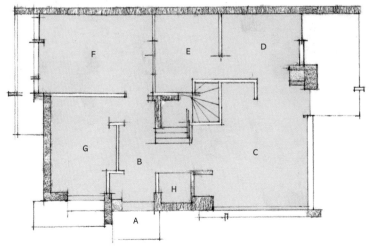

GROUND FLOOR

KEY
A Entrance
B Hall
C Kitchen/dining/living
D Sleeping
E Working
F Studio
G Reading
H Toilet
I Balcony
J Living/dining
K Bath
L Work/sleeping

Maison de Verre

LOCATION   Paris, France
ARCHITECT   Pierre Chareau and Bernard Bijvoet
STYLE   European Modern
BUILT   1928–32

The Maison de Verre (Glass House, 1928–32) in Paris is one of the most interesting and compelling Modernist homes constructed in the years between World Wars I and II. Yet it has often taken a backseat to houses designed by others, such as Le Corbusier (1887–1965), Ludwig Mies van der Rohe (1886–1969), Walter Gropius (1883–1969) and Frank Lloyd Wright (1867–1959). Perhaps this is because its primary designer, Pierre Chareau (1883–1950), is more associated with interior and furniture design than architecture, even though his employee and design associate on this project, Bernard Bijvoet (1889–1979), had a long career designing buildings. Bijvoet was best known at the time for his work with Dutch architect Jan Duiker (1890–1935) on the Grand Hotel Gooiland (1936) in Hilversum, the Netherlands. Another reason might be that Chareau left Paris in 1939 for New York and remained there until his death by suicide.

Chareau studied at the École nationale supérieure des Beaux-Arts from 1900 to 1908, thereafter working for British furniture manufacturer Waring and Gillow in Paris from 1908 to 1913. After military service in World War I (1914–18), he practised in Paris designing interiors and furniture, his designs being known for their use of steel and glass and for sliding panels within spaces. These include the award-winning Office-Library for the French Embassy, shown at the influential Art Deco exhibition of 1925, the Exposition internationale des arts décoratifs et industriels modernes (International Exhibition of Modern Decorative and Industrial Arts). With that favourable level of recognition and previous work for the clients, Dr Jean

Dalsace and his art aficionado wife, Annie, Chareau received the most important commission of his life: the Maison de Verre.

The three-storey house off the Rue Saint-Guillaume includes the doctor's office and patient rooms to the back of the first floor. The structure appears tucked away in this courtyard as a tour de force of steel and glass (opposite). Private quarters are within the two storeys above the public rooms and medical office. The glass block and mechanically pivoting windows energize the steel facade within a modular pattern. The whole house is attached and inserted under the top floor of an existing masonry building, whose occupant could not be evicted. Chareau employed ironworker Louis Dalbert to detail much of the steel work of the building. The interiors feature Chareau's mechanistic touches – sliding-screen walls, folding stairs and a dumb waiter between the kitchen and dining room.

Dr Dalsace was a member of the French Communist Party, and the home's double-storey living-room library with spectacular built-in bookcase served as a meeting place for artists and cultural leaders in Paris during the 1930s, including such prominent figures as painter Max Ernst and actor Louis Jouvet. With the house emptied of its possessions during the German Occupation, the family returned after the liberation of Paris in 1944 and, after repairs and restoration, continued to host political and cultural meetings within.

Since 2006 the Maison de Verre has been owned by a US businessman and collector, Robert Rubin, who has slowly been restoring it and generously opening it to students and scholars. The house is unique among Modernist masterpieces and has influenced a number of other architects, particularly Richard Rogers (b. 1933) and Jean Nouvel (b. 1945), who have each created their own masterpieces in steel and glass.

ABOVE LEFT This space is the double-storey living room with oversized bookcase, the perfect environment for the salons organized by Annie Dalsace.

ABOVE RIGHT The steel-and-glass structure glows from within during the evening and acts as a Modernist beacon in this courtyard off the Rue Saint-Guillaume.

CHAREAU FURNITURE

Chareau trained as a furniture designer and, like the furnishings designed by his Modernist peers, his works are highly valued museum pieces today. Chareau's furniture is characterized by bicoloured parts and planes, at times made up of quirky geometric forms. Often his pieces were fabricated of black-painted steel as well as richly toned or coloured woods. Some are polished wood geometric forms, such as his famous nesting tables. The Maison de Verre still has some Chareau-designed furnishings (left), including rectilinear steel-and-wood built-in cabinetry as well as curved painted-steel side chairs.

GROUND FLOOR

Between the facade ladders at the bottom of the drawing are the main entry and access to public spaces for the doctor's office and waiting room. Patient examination areas wrap around to the rear of the house, the ground floor being essentially for his medical practice. A small black steel staircase leads up to the doctor's private study. The waiting room has pivoting steel-and-glass doors.

KEY
GROUND FLOOR
A Entrance foyer
B Central corridor
C Garden corridor
D Service foyer
E Servants' entrance
F Receptionist
G Waiting room
H Consulting room
I Examination room
J Attendance room
K Auxiliary stair to study
L Stair to kitchen
M Main stair to salon

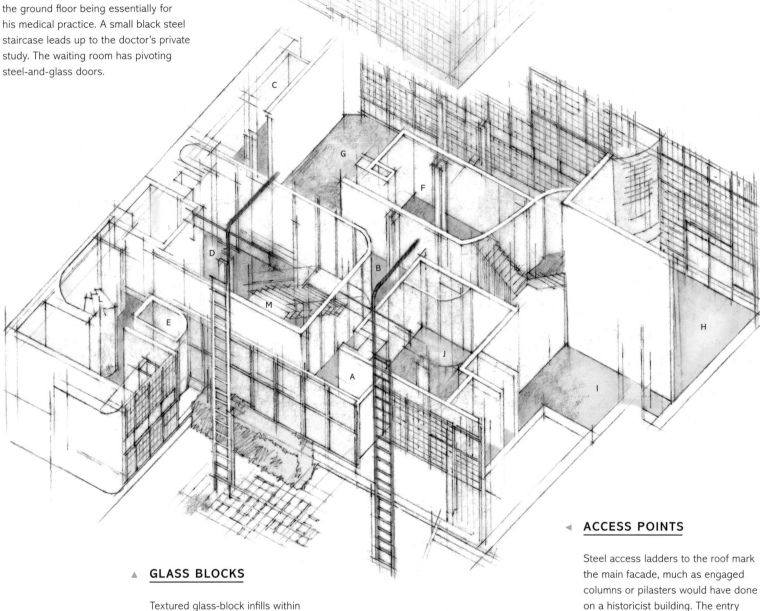

GLASS BLOCKS

Textured glass-block infills within the steel structure as well as backs of operable windows on certain walls characterize this home. They foreshadow the industrial forms within interior spaces.

ACCESS POINTS

Steel access ladders to the roof mark the main facade, much as engaged columns or pilasters would have done on a historicist building. The entry between provides access to the medical office foyer as well as to a main house staircase that connects to space above. The courtyard is accessed by a portal on Rue Saint-Guillaume.

PRIVATE SPACES

The private spaces include the library-living-room salon along with, at the uppermost level, bedrooms and bathrooms. Metal screens and wood panels are used throughout. The bathrooms have built-in shower cubicles, smaller square tiles affixed to the wall planes, glazed cabinets and cylindrical water reservoirs above the fixtures.

KEY
UPPER FLOORS

A Main salon
B Dining area
C Day room
D Study
E Void over foyer
F Void over consulting room
G Kitchen
H Dumbwaiter
I Storage
J Passenger lift

K Auxiliary stair to study
L Stair to kitchen
M Master bedroom
N Bedroom
O Master bathroom
P Shower
Q Toilet
R Guest bathroom
S Workroom
T Maid's bedroom

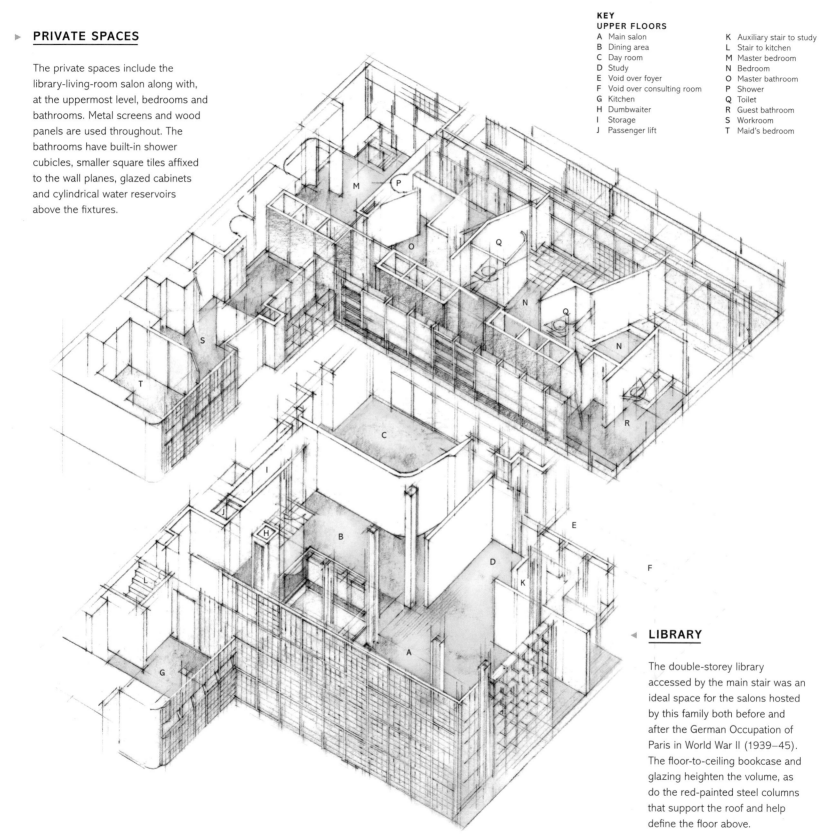

LIBRARY

The double-storey library accessed by the main stair was an ideal space for the salons hosted by this family both before and after the German Occupation of Paris in World War II (1939–45). The floor-to-ceiling bookcase and glazing heighten the volume, as do the red-painted steel columns that support the roof and help define the floor above.

SITE PLAN

The site plan betrays the Maison de Verre's origins with an elongated shape that is typical of eighteenth-century residential buildings in Paris.

GRAVEL PLAY COURT

GRASS AND SHRUBS

GARDEN

KEY

A Tunnel entrance
B Forecourt
C Two-car garage
D Existing eighteenth-century building
E Entrance to the house
F Entrance to the house above
G Service wing
H Garden access

RUE SAINT-GUILLAUME

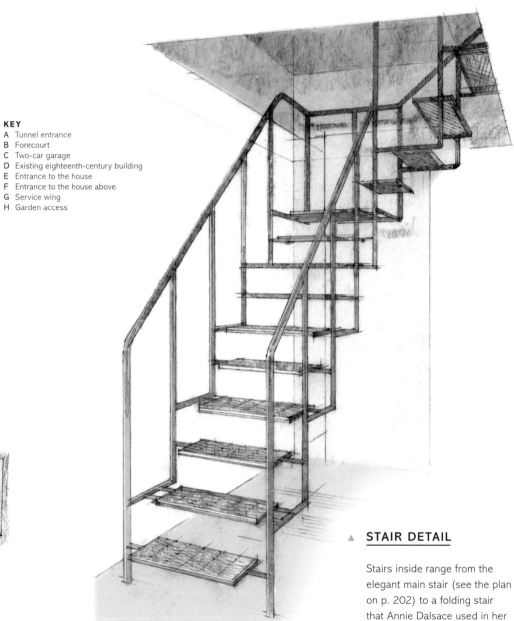

STAIR DETAIL

Stairs inside range from the elegant main stair (see the plan on p. 202) to a folding stair that Annie Dalsace used in her bedroom. The small steel stair sketched here is the one that the doctor used to reach a private study from his office level.

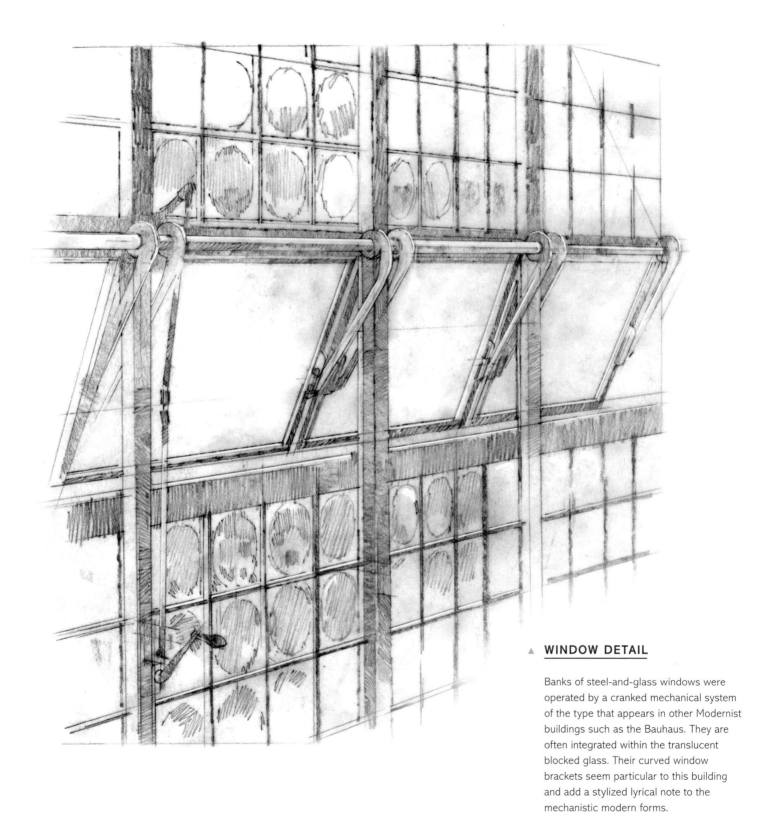

▲ WINDOW DETAIL

Banks of steel-and-glass windows were
operated by a cranked mechanical system
of the type that appears in other Modernist
buildings such as the Bauhaus. They are
often integrated within the translucent
blocked glass. Their curved window
brackets seem particular to this building
and add a stylized lyrical note to the
mechanistic modern forms.

Fallingwater

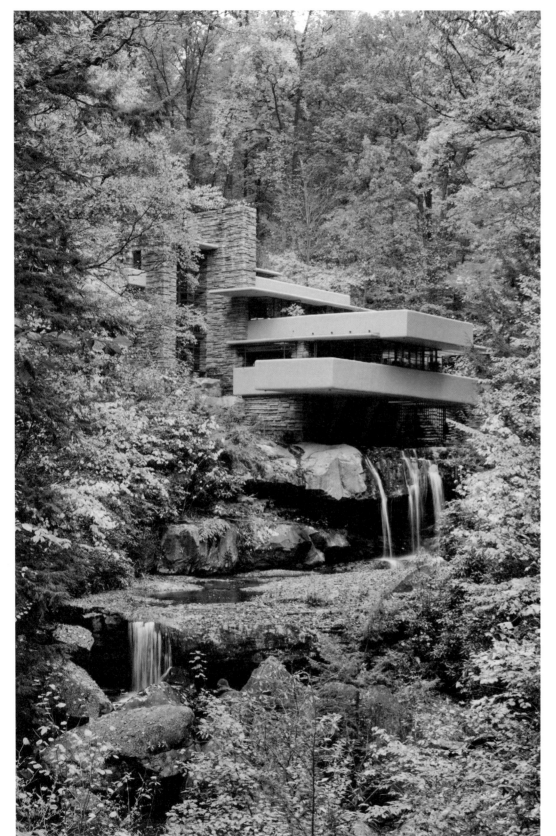

LOCATION	Mill Run, Pennsylvania, United States of America
ARCHITECT	Frank Lloyd Wright
STYLE	Modern
BUILT	1936–39

Frank Lloyd Wright (1867–1959) is arguably the United States' most famous architect, and Fallingwater is his best-known building. He designed it for Edgar and Liliane Kaufmann and their son Edgar Jr, and the house was built between 1936 and 1939. The Kaufmanns lived in Pittsburgh, but this was a holiday home for them in southwest Pennsylvania at a place called Mill Run in the Allegheny Mountains.

The site could not be more dramatic, with a waterfall running under the house. The clients had initially expected the house to be below the falls, so that they would be able to look out on them, but by incorporating the falls below the house, with the building cantilevering out over them, Wright ensured that the occupants would be aware of the water at all times. The idea was to integrate the house in nature, and to this end the house is generously glazed. There is no metal framing between the glazing and the stone walls, with the glass instead running into a recess in the walls.

The concept of the house was also that it should be social, so there is a large living room and several cantilevered balconies. The bedrooms are deliberately small, because Wright's intention was to drive visitors out of them and into the outdoor spaces or the living room. Ceilings are low, in order to direct people's vision outside to their surroundings, and the numerous dark passages are intended to 'compress' visitors' perspective, so that they feel a sense of release when they emerge into the light.

Like most Modernists, Wright continued to find ways to visually communicate with nature. There is a feeling in Fallingwater of a building that is floating in nature, a major achievement in a construction whose main components are stone and concrete. Another of Wright's beliefs was that the hearth should be at the centre of the home, and he designed a large fireplace for the main living room with, in front of it, some large boulders that were originally on the site and never removed. He even designed a special spherical orange kettle to swing over the fire. He also installed a guest house that naturally increases the accommodation and attractively complements the main building.

The actual cost exceeded the initial budget five times over, with the total of $155,000 translating today to about $2.5 million, which may be considered a bargain for a home this size. Almost as soon as it was completed, Fallingwater became internationally famous. It appeared on the cover of *Time* magazine in 1938. It remained in the spotlight, too. In 1991 members of the American Institute of Architects named it 'the best all-time work of American architecture'.

However, the structure has not been without its problems. It is a work of enormous ambition, and ambition is not always successful. Wright fell out with his clients during construction, mainly because they brought in engineers to further reinforce his designs and to make changes to enhance the structural stability. The building leaked from the beginning, and there were problems with the cantilevering balconies. In 1963 the Kaufmanns, tired of the expense and hassle of the upkeep, donated Fallingwater to the Western Pennsylvania Conservancy, which opened it to the public as a museum a year later. There were a series of repairs to the structure, and engineering analyses showed that even with the additional strengthening installed during construction, the reinforcement was still inadequate. A repair solution was carried out in 2002, involving post-tensioning the concrete in a manner that left the inner and outer appearance unchanged. Despite such issues, Fallingwater remains a significant achievement.

LEFT The bold cantilevered levels and deep balconies visually bring the natural environment within the building, almost as if there were no walls beyond those deep recesses.

BELOW Wright designed strip or ribbon window walls to reinforce the horizontality of the design. Some open so that there is no mullion or visible vertical support at the corners, visually dematerializing the structure and letting the outside in.

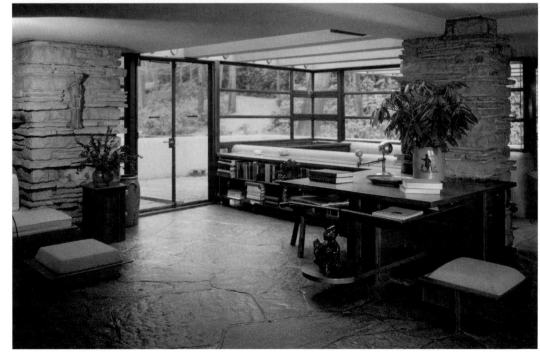

FRANK LLOYD WRIGHT

Wright was mostly self-taught through design apprenticeships in Chicago. His approach to architecture encompassed several creative phases. The early 1900s focused on the Prairie House, whose open spaces were expressions of the rambling, hilly landscape of his native Wisconsin. Wright's first trip to Japan in 1905 greatly influenced his Prairie School designs. The second 1920s phase witnessed concrete zigzag Art Deco–like patterns that related to Native American and Mayan cultures. The third, during the Great Depression of the 1930s and World War II (1939–45), saw the beginnings of more organic forms; the fourth was a further geometric abstraction of that work. Wright's love of nature ran throughout all his buildings.

TOP FLOOR

The top floor of Fallingwater contains a study and a small sleeping area, as well as a generous terrace. Even when at the top of the house, inhabitants were expected to be in touch with the natural environment.

MIDDLE FLOOR

The middle floor of the building has three terraces, with one extending from the master bedroom, one from the guest room and another from the dressing room. In the fourth direction, there is a bridge link by which one can leave the house.

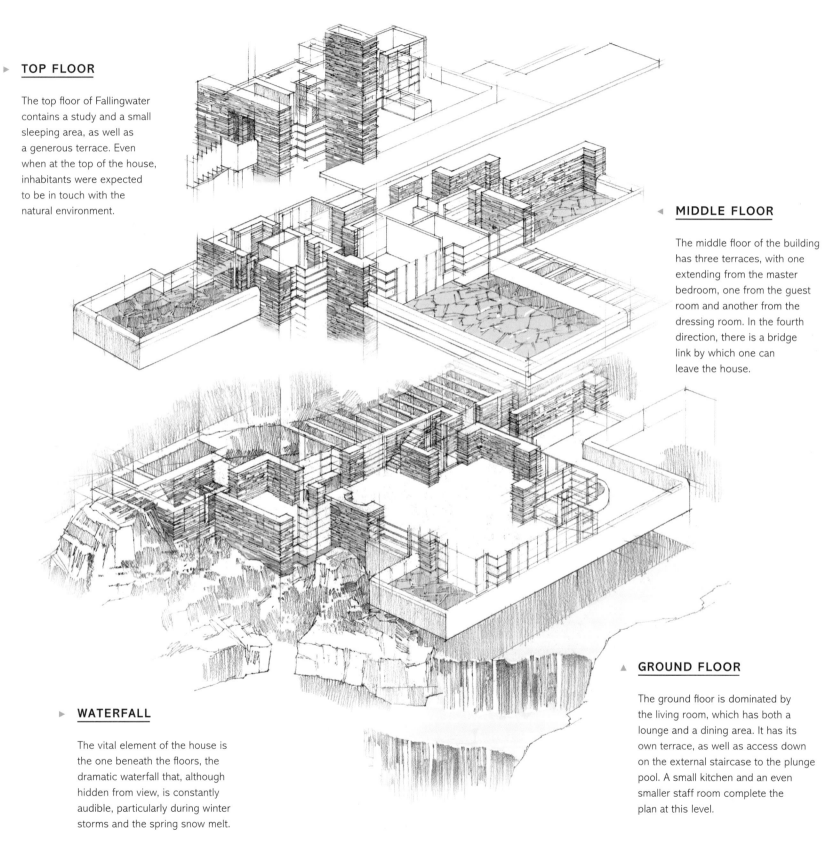

WATERFALL

The vital element of the house is the one beneath the floors, the dramatic waterfall that, although hidden from view, is constantly audible, particularly during winter storms and the spring snow melt.

GROUND FLOOR

The ground floor is dominated by the living room, which has both a lounge and a dining area. It has its own terrace, as well as access down on the external staircase to the plunge pool. A small kitchen and an even smaller staff room complete the plan at this level.

SITE PLAN

This site plan shows the family house at the right (A), and to the left the guest house (B), built a year later, linked by a path that bridges the river. Almost as interesting as the house plans is the topography, showing how the buildings were inserted into the rocky landscape. The house has a total of 495 sq m (5,330 sq ft) of which 268 sq m (2,885 sq ft) is interior space. The guest house is 158 sq m (1,700 sq ft).

PERSPECTIVE CROSS SECTION

This section shows how the land and water fall away beneath the building. The generosity of the outdoor spaces is visible, as is the way in which the house is oriented to make the best of the views to the surrounding landscape. This is a piece of ambitious, single-minded and, at times, foolhardy design – a work of flawed genius in which the defects have been remedied to leave the delight in the way a building can interact with nature so that it is enjoyed and enhanced. Fallingwater has had more than 5 million visitors since 1964, with annual attendance exceeding 167,000.

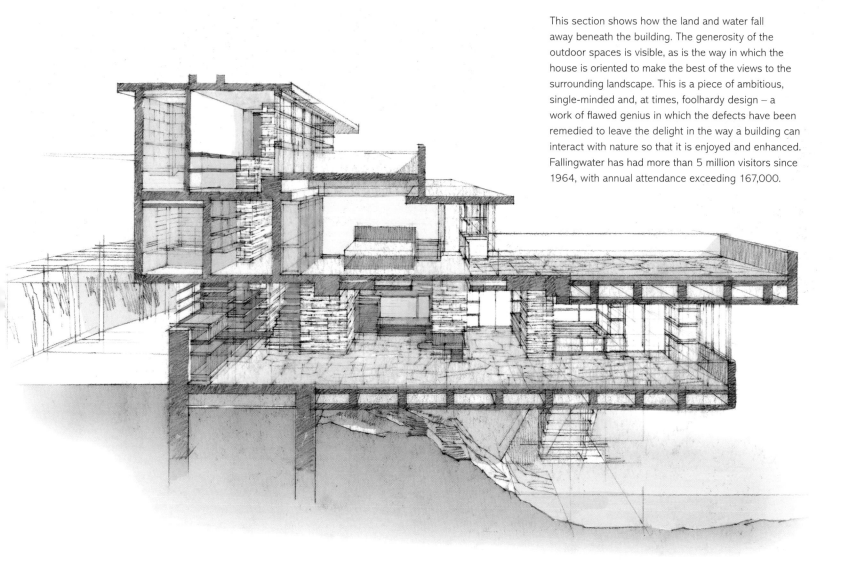

Villa Mairea

LOCATION   Noormarkku, Finland
ARCHITECT   Alvar Aalto
STYLE   Organic Finnish Modern
BUILT   1939

In many ways, Alvar Aalto (1898–1976) is Finland's Frank Lloyd Wright. Both incorporated Japanese elements within their designs; both thought of their designs as an integrated experience, from large scale to small, from buildings to furnishings; both created their designs as an organic response to the natural environment; and both were internationally recognized within their own lifetimes for their distinctive contributions to the field.

Moreover, Aalto's Villa Mairea (1939) and Wright's Fallingwater (1936–39; see p. 206) are comparable in terms of the importance of those buildings within each of their respective careers, as well as their use of natural materials and organic forms that relate to

the landscape. Their impact on their home countries is undisputed in terms of American and Finnish Modernism. Fallingwater was admired by Aalto and in some ways served as a starting point for his Villa Mairea.

Finnish-born Aalto (full name Hugo Alvar Henrik Aalto) is best known for his Finnish Modernist architecture, though his early works tended towards a hybrid of classical and modern forms, as seen in the Jyväskylä Workers' Club (1925). This is perhaps because of his trips to Italy and especially Sweden and the influence of Gunnar Asplund (1885–1940). His designs shifted to a more Modernist expression, though incorporating natural materials in curvilinear forms, in buildings such as the Paimio Sanatorium (1929–33) and the chair of the same name designed with his first wife, Aino (1894–1949), as well as the Viipuri Library (1927–35) in Vyborg, then in Finland but now in Russia. From 1934 to 1935 he built his own home (now part of the Alvar Aalto Museum) in Helsinki, another hybrid Modernist building whose use of stone, wood and brick for a variety of surfaces within and without, and Modernist stucco wall planes, prefigure the more lavish use of these mixed materials at the larger Villa Mairea.

Villa Mairea was the home of industrialist Harry Gullichsen and his wife, Maire. In 1935 Maire co-founded, with the Aaltos, Artek, a home-furnishings company that originally promoted their furniture and glassware designs. Maire was the prime client for the Aaltos on this villa, which bears her name.

It was constructed in wooded Noormarkku in western Finland, the location of the Ahlström company, where Maire's father, Walter Ahlström, was the CEO and board chair, and her husband, Harry, served as a managing director. The Aaltos worked on several projects for that company in Sunila during the late 1930s.

The summer home Villa Mairea was the epitome of Aalto's humanistic or organic Modernism in terms of softening the hard, clean lines of a building through curved forms and extensive use of wood and stone, sometimes with Japanese design precedents. Its plan is centred on an open courtyard or inner garden, which housed an organically shaped pool, almost an enlargement of an Aalto vase. The plan went through a series of several redesigns and spatial compressions, the last of which repositioned some of the rooms and

replaced a separate art gallery with a sauna near the pool. The home and grounds today are managed by the Mairea Foundation and open to the public through guided tours by advance appointment.

With his work for this prominent client, Aalto received important commissions, from the Finnish Pavilion at the New York World's Fair (1939–40) and Baker House at the Massachusetts Institute of Technology (1941–48) in Boston, through postwar jobs that included new buildings at the Helsinki University of Technology (1950 and later), to the Academic Bookstore (1962–69) and Finlandia Hall (1967–71), both in Helsinki.

After the death of Aino, in 1949, Aalto married his second wife, Elissa (1922–94), née Elsa Kaisa Mäkiniemi. Also an architect, she managed a number of Aalto's projects to completion after his death.

ABOVE The living space accommodates all the collective functions of the house as well as the owner's art collections.

ELISSA AALTO

Aalto's second wife was architect Elissa, née Elsa Kaisa Mäkiniemi. They married in 1952 after she graduated from architecture school. Elissa was involved in the office management and the design and restoration of Alvar's buildings. Following Alvar's death in 1976, Elissa oversaw the completion of several of her husband's projects, including the opera house in Essen, Germany, a Danish art museum in Aalborg, a housing estate in Lucerne, Switzerland, and the Riola Church in Grizzana, Italy (1978; above).

WINDOWS

Angular windows for the children's bedrooms also face south above the main entry.

LIBRARY

The irregular trapezoidal plan of this space is at the south wall. It is entered via the larger, more open living room and music room spaces. Harry Gullichsen's library has floor-to-ceiling built-in bookcases and a wood-slat ceiling.

MAIN ENTRY

The understated main entry incorporates typically Aalto-like curves found in many of his designs, from his ubiquitous vases to the pool on this site, as well as in the Finnish Pavilion at New York's 1939 World's Fair. Another feature here is the porch's spindly wood details, comparable to similar Japanese compositions.

JAPANESE INFLUENCE

Slender, irregularly spindly wood verticals define the space around the main staircase of the home, a clear reference to Japanese wood and bamboo structures. The stair thus becomes the tangible focal point of the open plan on the main floor, connecting public space there to private ones above.

FINNISH VERNACULAR

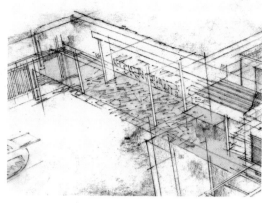

Aalto incorporated numerous elements belonging to traditional Finnish architecture, such as the turfed roof that covers the sauna and attached canopy. The open-plan design is reminiscent of a Finnish *tupa*, the large living room of a farmhouse in which poles were used to mark the boundaries of areas for different activities.

► LAYOUT

This floor plan shows private spaces above the ground floor. It depicts the curved space at the lower right intended to be Maire's studio (A) along with the space below, distinctly separate from Harry's library on the south side of the ground floor. Harry's and Maire's master bedrooms are adjacent (B), being graced with a large terrace. On the short west side of the L-shaped plan are guest rooms (C), with the lower-floor extension indicated for a sauna (D) off the pool. Aalto said: 'An attempt has been made to avoid artificial architectural rhythm in the building.'

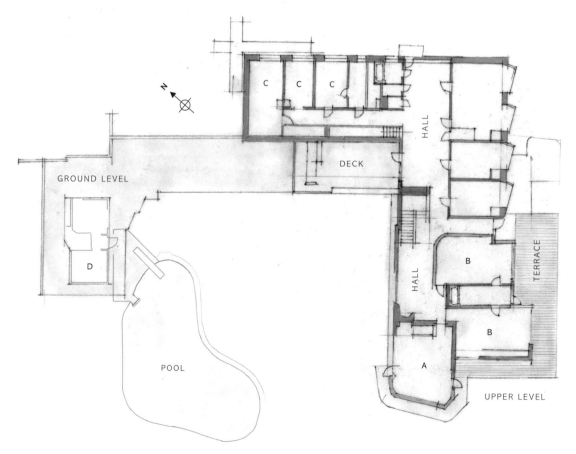

Casa Luis Barragán

LOCATION   Mexico City, Mexico
ARCHITECT   Luis Barragán
STYLE   Mexican Modern
BUILT   1948

Ricardo Legorreta (1931–2011) is often touted as Mexico's great contemporary architect whose highly coloured simple wall planes and geometric forms spanned countries beyond Mexico's borders, from California to South Korea. But he could not have achieved that international status without Luis Barragán (1902–88), whose own strongly geometric and boldly coloured forms made him the pathfinder for Mexican Modernism.

Barragán studied engineering at the Escuela Libre de Ingenieros in Guadalajara, graduating in 1923. In the 1920s and 1930s he travelled to Spain and France, as well as New York. On those travels he met Le Corbusier (1887–1965) and visited gardens designed by writer Ferdinand Bac. He was influenced by the bold colours in Bac's historicist gardens such as Les Colombières (1918–27) in Menton, France, and similar images in his book *Jardins enchantés* (*Enchanted Gardens*, 1925). Barragán worked in architecture in Guadalajara between 1927 and 1936, designing houses there such as Casa Cristo (1929). That home's heavily textured walls, whose forms seem more Arabic than Mediterranean or Mexican, bear bold colour details within the porch as well as interior, similar to Bac's work. In 1936 Barragán moved his practice to Mexico City, adopting a style more influenced by Le Corbusier. Additionally, Barragán's interest in the vernacular combined with his love of simple wall planes and highly coloured forms all combined to shape his architecture of the post–World War II era in Mexico. His home from 1948 in the Tacubaya district of Mexico City was one of the first to combine an interest in Corbusian Modernism with brightly coloured wall planes, all creating an impression that has been compared to architectural compositions in the Surrealist paintings of Giorgio de Chirico. Those paintings project an image of isolation that some feel Barragán experienced while creating his works, since he was trained as an engineer, not an architect.

LEFT The only exterior here with bold colour highlights is the rooftop patio. The space provides opportunity for open-air activity, as does the garden below.

BELOW LEFT The sober street facade is punctuated by a large window, which signals that something different is going on within what might initially appear to be a mundane building.

MEXICAN COLOUR

Mexican design is often thought to be highly colourful as well as decorative. In architecture, brightly coloured wall planes are a hallmark of Barragán, but they achieve a higher level of visibility in the works of Ricardo Legorreta. The latter became Mexico's most prominent architect of the late twentieth century. Examples of his work include the Camino Real Hotel (1968; below) in Mexico City, the IBM Factory (1975) in Guadalajara, Pershing Square (1994) in Los Angeles and the San Antonio Public Library (1995) in Texas.

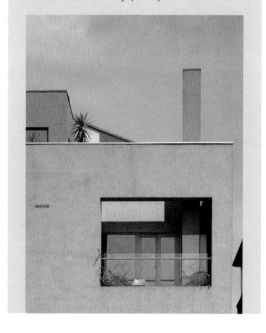

Barragán's home and studio is in Colonia Ampliación Daniel Garza within the Miguel Hidalgo district of Mexico City; its facade is on Calle General Francisco Ramírez 12–14. It is built of plaster over concrete, with a garden space, totalling 1,160 sq m (12,500 sq ft). The north part at number 12 has his studio, and the southern, at 14, his residence. Strong colours illuminated by natural light highlight some of the wall planes from the ground floor up to the rooftop patio. The latter has red and purple walls with reddish-brown tiles for flooring. The concrete street facade's simplicity hides the elegant proportions and dynamically coloured walls within. Interior flooring ranges from

volcanic stone at the entry to hardwood in living spaces (opposite); the living and dining areas and kitchen all access the garden. With his home and studio as a base, Barragán created a number of comparable constructions with simple wall planes that are highly coloured, including Casa Gilardi (1977) in Mexico City.

After Barragán's death, his home and studio were acquired by the state of Jalisco and the Barragán Foundation in 1993, which opened as a museum a year later, complete with the architect's own furnishings, archives and art collection. The complex was restored in 1995 and has become a pilgrimage site for architects and architectural enthusiasts alike.

WALLS

Barragán's solid, simple wall planes often hide the complexity and colour of spaces behind them. The upper-left corner of this drawing indicates the garage on the lower level and guest room atop. Behind those are staircases with access to Barragán's own bedroom, day room and dressing room. The spaces above this on the top floor consist mainly of the roof terrace as well as smaller service and laundry rooms.

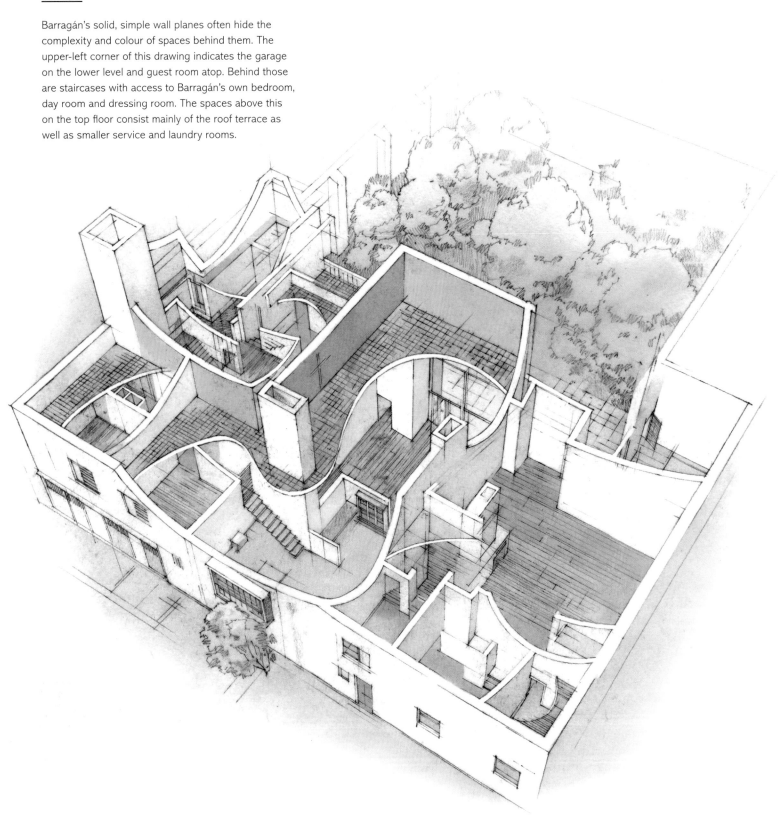

GARAGE

The cream–yellow doors in the street photograph on the previous page
and the doors sketched at the left of the drawing indicate the garage. Bedrooms
are above, and immediately behind is the kitchen, separated by doors and
steps from the garage. Adjacent to the kitchen and connected by a hallway
are the breakfast and dining rooms. The garage has four doors for vehicles.
A single door adjacent is the entry into this private home.

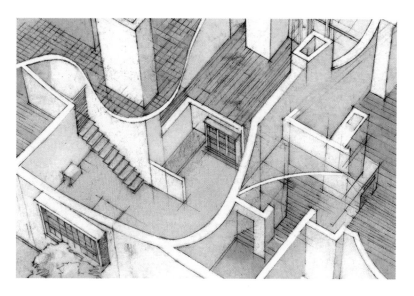

SPACE AND STAIRCASE

The industrial-scaled window on the street facade indicates the library behind. The
staircase on the opposite wall is sculptural, having only risers and treads without
side panels or stair rail. It leads to a small mezzanine room. The wood texture of
the staircase and beamed ceiling contrasts with the yellow floors within. Behind
the library is the living room. The direction of timbers in the beamed ceiling and
wood floors leads visually to the large glazed wall that overlooks the garden.

URBAN GARDEN

The landscaped walled garden occupies a footprint comparable to that of the
home and studio. This is certainly a luxury in any urban environment. Here
a tiled patio across the back of the home leads to a small enclosure with a
fountain called Patio de las Ollas. An *olla* is an unglazed clay pot, and the
area appropriately holds ceramic jugs and amphorae-like vessels under
an overgrown retaining wall.

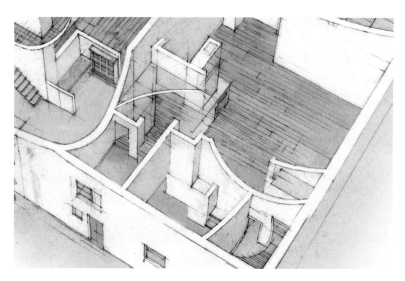

STUDIO

The doorway on the street side with several windows surrounding it is the
entry into Barragán's studio. To the right of the entry vestibule are his secretary's
office and then his own space, with small offices above. Leading on from the
vestibule are small steps that lead to the workroom and then garden beyond.
It is also possible to divert left into the living room–library. On the exterior
this part of the building is the lower one.

KEY
A Breakfast room
B Hall
C Vestibule
D Secretary's office
E Office
F Private office
G Afternoon room
H Dressing room/'Room of the Christ'
I Guest room
J Mezzanine
K Laundry
L Service room

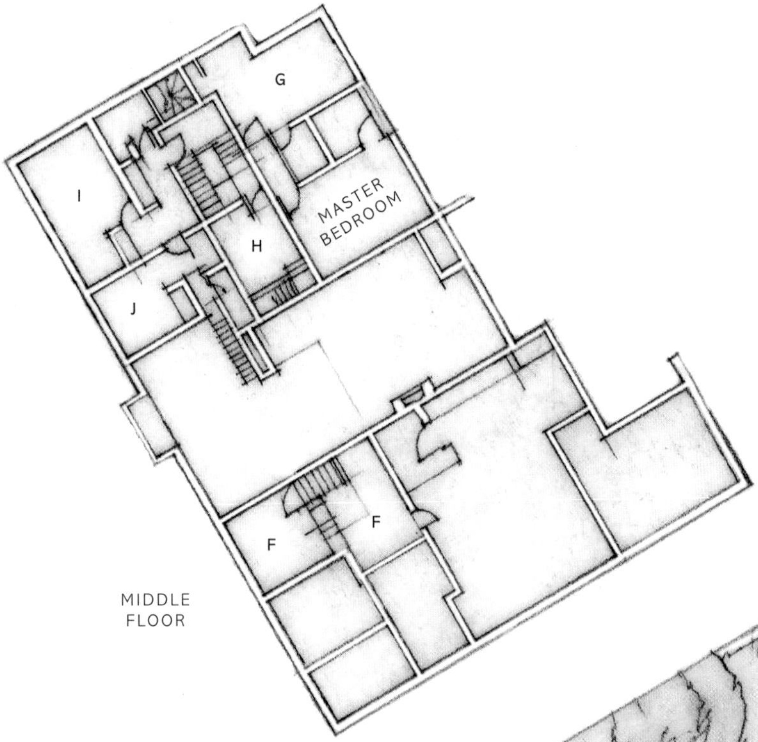

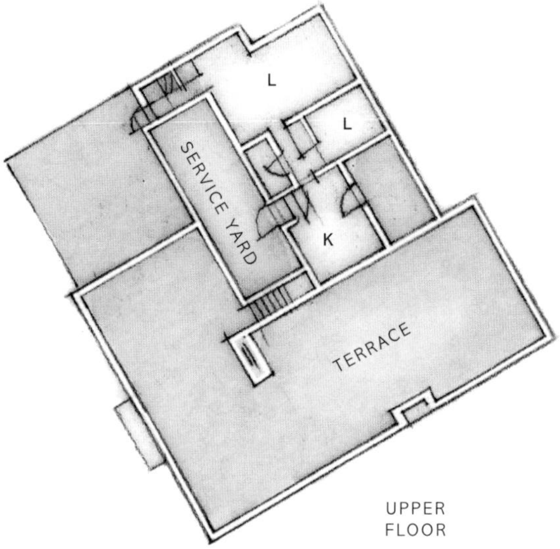

MIDDLE
FLOOR

I

G

H

J

MASTER
BEDROOM

F

F

UPPER
FLOOR

L

SERVICE YARD

L

K

TERRACE

GARAGE

KITCHEN

A

DINING
ROOM

B

C

GARDEN

PATIO

LIVING
ROOM

LIBRARY

C

D

E

STUDY

POTTERY
PATIO

GROUND
FLOOR

Y

Z

Z

Y

▲ **FLOOR PLAN**

This plan clearly shows the substantial
allocation of green space compared with
the footprint of the home and studio.
A large window and door provide actual
and visible access from the living spaces
to the garden. The clever combination
of several properties necessitated
extraordinary thinking in order to
make the manipulation of space work.

These two sections (marked Y and Z on the plan opposite) indicate the floor height and staircase accommodation between the professional and personal divisions of the building. The library acts as both private and work space and is a focal point of the plan, with its location behind its large industrial window.

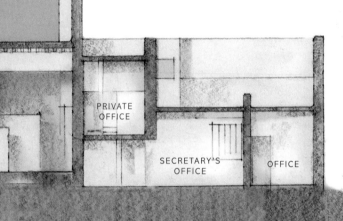

TERRACE   TERRACE

GUEST
ROOM

MEZZANINE

PRIVATE
OFFICE

LIBRARY

GARAGE

SECRETARY'S
OFFICE

OFFICE

Y   Y

TRANSVERSE SECTION (Y)

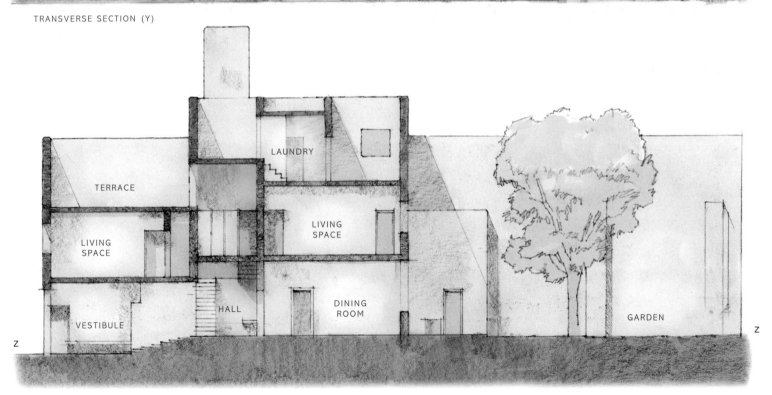

LAUNDRY

TERRACE

LIVING
SPACE

LIVING
SPACE

HALL

VESTIBULE

DINING
ROOM

GARDEN

Z   Z

LONGITUDINAL SECTION (Z)

The Eames House

LOCATION   Pacific Palisades, California, United States of America
ARCHITECT   Charles and Ray Eames
STYLE   International Style, Modern
BUILT   1949–50

The husband and wife team of Charles (1907–78) and Ray (1912–88) Eames made significant contributions to American design in the second half of the twentieth century. After studying briefly at Washington University in St Louis, Charles began practising architecture in 1930. In 1938 he moved to Michigan with his first wife, Catherine, and their daughter so that he could study with Eliel Saarinen (1873–1950) at the Cranbrook Academy of Art. It was there that he met Eliel's son Eero, a future architectural and design collaborator, as well as his second wife, Ray. After divorcing Catherine in 1941, Charles married Ray and

they moved to her native California. Together, they are best known for their furniture and interior design as well as their important contributions to exhibition design, graphic design and instructional films.

Furniture such as their plywood and leather Eames Lounge Chair and Ottoman (1956) for Herman Miller are classics, as are their fibreglass moulded chairs and modular storage units from the early 1950s. Their Tandem Sling Seating airport furniture of 1962, designed at Eero Saarinen's request for Dulles International Airport (1958–62; see p. 44) in Chantilly, Virginia, can still be seen in public spaces around

the world. They created exhibitions that projected US design across the globe, from their multimedia *Glimpses of the USA* (1959) for the American National Exhibition in Moscow to the IBM Pavilion at the New York World's Fair (1964–65) and the travelling exhibit *The World of Franklin and Jefferson* (1975–76), organized in conjunction with the bicentennial of the United States. They also greatly influenced corporate, educational and promotional films with *The Expanding Airport* (1958) made to promote the decentralized design of the new Dulles Airport, *The Information Machine* (1958) created for IBM at the Brussels World's

Fair and their own experimental *The Powers of Ten* (1977). Although their major impact on design is clearly recognized, their architectural work is also significant. Perhaps the most important of these is their own home within the landmark Modernist Case Study Houses.

The Case Study Houses were the brainchild of John Entenza (1905–84), who was the publisher of *Arts & Architecture*. The magazine acquired a 2-hectare (5-acre) site outside Los Angeles to build modern homes as models for the postwar world. The program ran from 1945 to 1966 with designs by noted architects such as Craig Ellwood (1922–92), Richard Neutra (1892–1970), Ralph Rapson (1914–2008), Raphael Soriano (1904–88) and Saarinen. The Eames home was one of the first ten, constructed in 1949 at 203 Chautauqua Boulevard in Pacific Palisades, adjacent to the one that they and Saarinen built for Entenza in 1950, at number 205. The Eames house, or Case Study House Number 8, is best known for being a model of open-plan, black-painted steel and glass shed design that is articulated with coloured plaster inserts and translucent laminates. Their design intent was to make a home for a married couple in the arts and design field, without children living at home. Further, they wished to use minimal materials to create a large volume in two storeys with two buildings for living and working, respectively. Entenza described the house as 'an idea rather than a fixed architectural pattern', likely meaning the use of simple materials to build a dynamic structure within the landscape. Charles and Ray lived there for the remainder of their lives. In 2004 Charles's daughter Lucia established the nonprofit Eames Foundation to manage the house and open it to the public for tours.

ABOVE The double-storey grand space at the home's end is the living room that overlooks the Pacific Coast Highway and the ocean. It has a more intimate seating alcove under the balcony. The upper-floor balcony contains private spaces in bedrooms, bathrooms and a dressing room lined with wardrobe space.

CHARLES AND RAY EAMES

Charles and Ray Eames were truly leaders in US design of the mid-twentieth century. The couple are shown here in their seating alcove off the living room at their home in Pacific Palisades, California, in 1950. Their furniture designs can be seen in museums as well as public spaces and private homes throughout the world. Some of the most famous are a simple moulded and bent birch Plywood Chair (1946); modular steel and plywood ESU Storage Unit bookcase (1949); Moulded Fibreglass Shell Chair (1950); and bent plywood and leather Lounge Chair and Ottoman (1956). Beyond furnishings, their commercial and theoretical films made an international mark in the twentieth century.

STRUCTURE

The simple steel framework was assembled in
less than two days. Eight bays define the home
with porch, and five the workshop–studio. The bay
modules are 6 m high by 6 m wide by 2.3 m deep
(20 × 20 × 7 ft 4 in.). The ceilings within are
5.2 m (17 ft) high. The outside bay of the home
just on the other side of the living room contains
the porch. The seating alcove just beyond the
living room is shown in the drawing, as are
the kitchen and dining rooms beyond. The
steel-and-glass facade has windows that
pivot open on both floors.

▼ UPPER FLOOR

The private spaces above, accessed by the
circular stair, contain two bedrooms, two
bathrooms and a large dressing area with
wardrobe space. Interior finishes throughout
are plywood, and bays throughout the home and
studio have a mixture of infilled spaces, including
plaster, plywood, asbestos, glass and what was
called Pylon, a fibreglass-like material that was
translucent. Bedrooms are closed off from the
living room below with sliding panels.

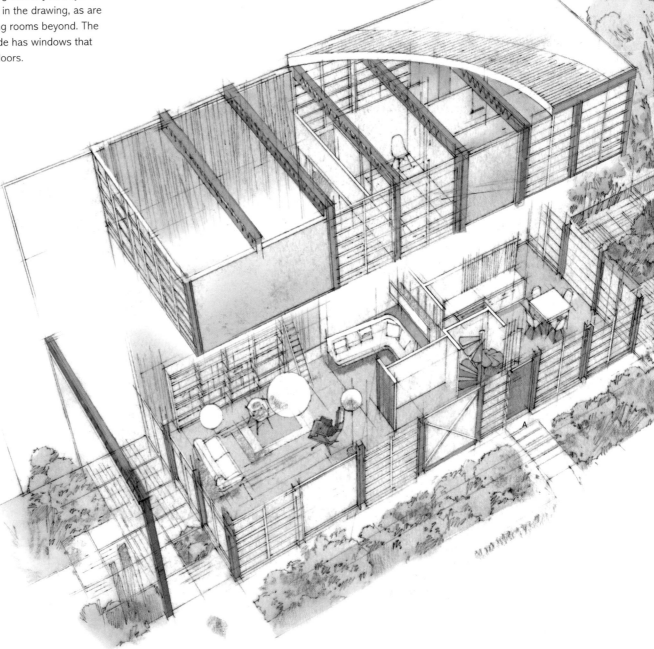

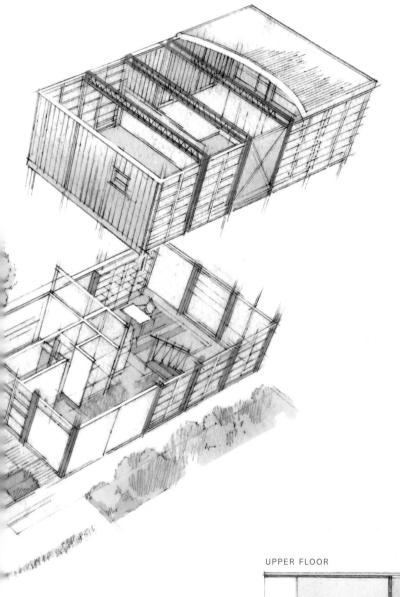

WORKSPACE

The studio workspace building is double-storeyed, entered off a patio, and measures 9.1 by 6 m (30 × 20 ft). The lower level has the studio with a darkroom (B), kitchen and toilet. A ladder connects the double-storey studio space with a storage room atop the kitchen core. The interior features sliding fibreglass shades. There is also a work space outside the studio building.

FLOOR PLAN

This plan shows the simplicity of this home and studio on what is a heavily wooded site of 0.5 hectares (1.4 acres). The house contains 140 sq m (1,500 sq ft). The two levels have a modular arrangement, and the home and studio are clearly separated.

ENTRANCE

The main entry (A) is located between the living and dining areas directly opposite the spiral steel staircase. The staircase is made of an 8.9-cm (3½-in.) vertical steel tube bolted to the concrete slab with a larger diameter flange. Steel brackets fixed with plywood treads cantilever out from the core.

UPPER FLOOR

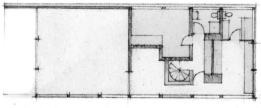

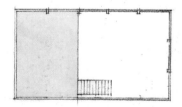

GROUND FLOOR

LIVING ROOM

UTILITY

KITCHEN

DINING ROOM

B

KITCHEN

STUDIO

A

Nakagin Capsule Tower

LOCATION   Tokyo, Japan
ARCHITECT   Kisho Kurokawa
STYLE   Metabolist Modern
BUILT   1971–72

Kisho Kurokawa (1934–2007) was among the most intellectual of Japanese architects during the second half of the twentieth century. He developed his own design philosophies over his career. They include his best known, Symbiosis, which combined aspects from east and west. He published his theories in, among other books, *Architecture of Symbiosis* (1987) and *Intercultural Architecture: The Philosophy of Symbiosis* (1991). Kurokawa was also a crucial figure in founding Metabolism in 1960. This was a Japanese-based movement that promoted prefabrication and mass production to create entire cities that could be replaced or expanded using similar adaptable systems.

Kurokawa was a leader in creating buildings that are tangible expressions of his architectural theories in Asia, the United States and Europe. He was especially prolific in designing museums. Several of the most important are the National Museum of Ethnology (1977) in Osaka; the Saitama Prefectural Museum of Modern Art (1982); the Hiroshima City Museum of Contemporary Art (1988); the Museum of Modern Art in Wakayama (1994); and an addition to the Van Gogh Museum (1998) in Amsterdam. He also created and implemented complicated large-scale projects from skyscrapers and stadiums to airports, such as the Osaka Prefectural Government Offices (1989), Pacific Tower (1992) in La Défense, Paris, Ōita Bank Dome stadium (2001) built for the 2002 World Cup, and Kuala Lumpur International Airport (1998).

Kurokawa's background in architecture helped to lead him down that internationally successful career path. He was the son of a well-respected Japanese architect from the interwar years, Miki Kurokawa. Kisho Kurokawa studied architecture at Kyoto University, graduating in 1957, and then pursued advanced degrees, under the supervision of noted postwar Modernist Kenzō Tange (1913–2005) at the University of Tokyo. He earned his Master's in 1959 and pursued studies towards a doctorate through 1964, being awarded an honorary PhD in 2002 from the Universiti Putra Malaysia. Even while a student he began his own practice in 1962 and was one of the co-founders of Japan's Metabolism movement two years earlier. Kurokawa is especially important here because his Nakagin Capsule Tower (1971–72) in Tokyo is a rare survivor of this movement.

The residential tower was designed from 1969 to 1970 and constructed in about a year, from January 1971 to March 1972. Its two cores are Corten steel and reinforced concrete, using precast concrete for the staircase and lift shaft, the latter also outfitted with the steel framework, all in order to speed construction. Each of the 140 prefabricated, spray-painted steel capsules was manufactured by Daimaru Design and Engineering. Targeted for the single male Japanese office worker, each measures 2.3 by 3.8 by 2.1 m (7 ft 6 in. × 12 ft 6 in. × 6 ft 10 in.) and is fully outfitted in moulded plastic with a kitchen, television, tape deck and tiny bathroom the size of the ones found in sleeping compartments on trains and airplanes. Each capsule was craned to the core and attached with steel brackets and bolts, built from bottom to top in sequence. They are illuminated by porthole windows. Each cost approximately the same as a compact car.

Kurokawa repeated this containerized process in the construction of the ten-storey Sony Tower (1976; demolished 2006) in Osaka, whose limited forty-year lifespan was comparable to that projected by the Metabolists for their constructions. The lifespan of the Nakagin Caspule Tower was only intended to be twenty-five years, and its steel brackets and even the capsules themselves are overdue for replacement. In 2007, 80 per cent of the residents approved demolition while Kurokawa proposed a plan to replace the units and stabilize the structure. Meanwhile, the hot water supply to the building was shut off in 2010 and this international landmark's fate is not yet decided, though occasionally some capsule units are available to rent to architectural adventurers on Airbnb.

METABOLISM AND EXPO 70

Kurokawa secured three pavilions at Expo 70, each of them being expressive of his key role as a proponent of Metabolism. His fair buildings were the modular steel-piped Takara Beautilion of five storeys, designed to be expandable and built within six days; the Capsule House in the Theme Pavilion, a futuristic home suspended from the ceiling; and the two-storey Toshiba IHI Pavilion (above), built of modular expandable steel tetra-frames with a 500-seat domed theatre hung from the steelwork. Unfortunately, they no longer exist within what is now Expo 70 Commemoration Park outside Osaka.

LEFT Every unit has a large operable porthole – an oculus or giant eye that also creates a distinctive pattern on the building's exterior. The prefabricated living pods were created as self-contained units geared to the Japanese 'salaryman', or single male white-collar corporate employee, at that time.

CROSS SECTIONS

These sections indicate how capsules are stacked on the building's core, constructed from bottom to top. Cranes lifted each modular living space into place. The building is 54 m (177 ft) tall, or thirteen floors at the highest, with the other section being slightly lower. The two-storey, tile-clad concrete base contains retail services.

CAPSULES

Each of the 140 capsules has a steel structure and panelled sides, spray-painted as if it were a car. When outfitted with the interior, each weighs four tons. They were trucked to the site and lifted into place by a crane. An oculus within a steel frame illuminates each capsule.

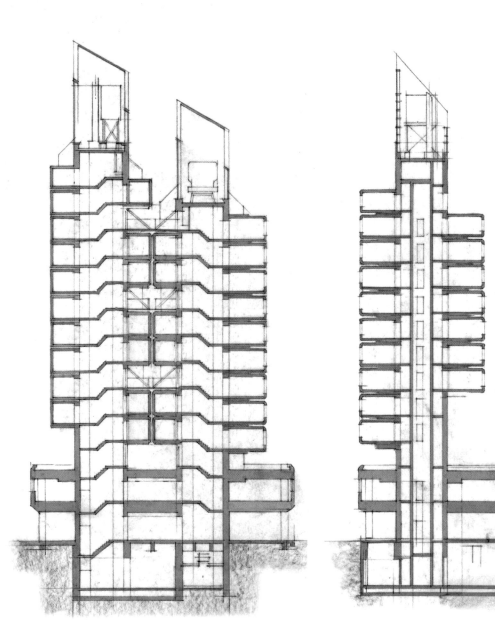

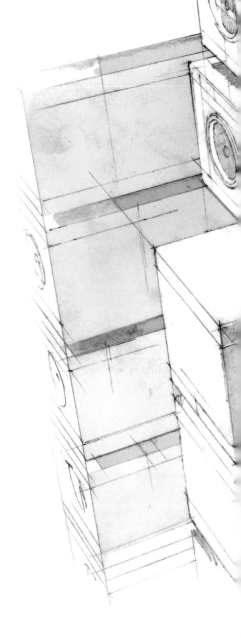

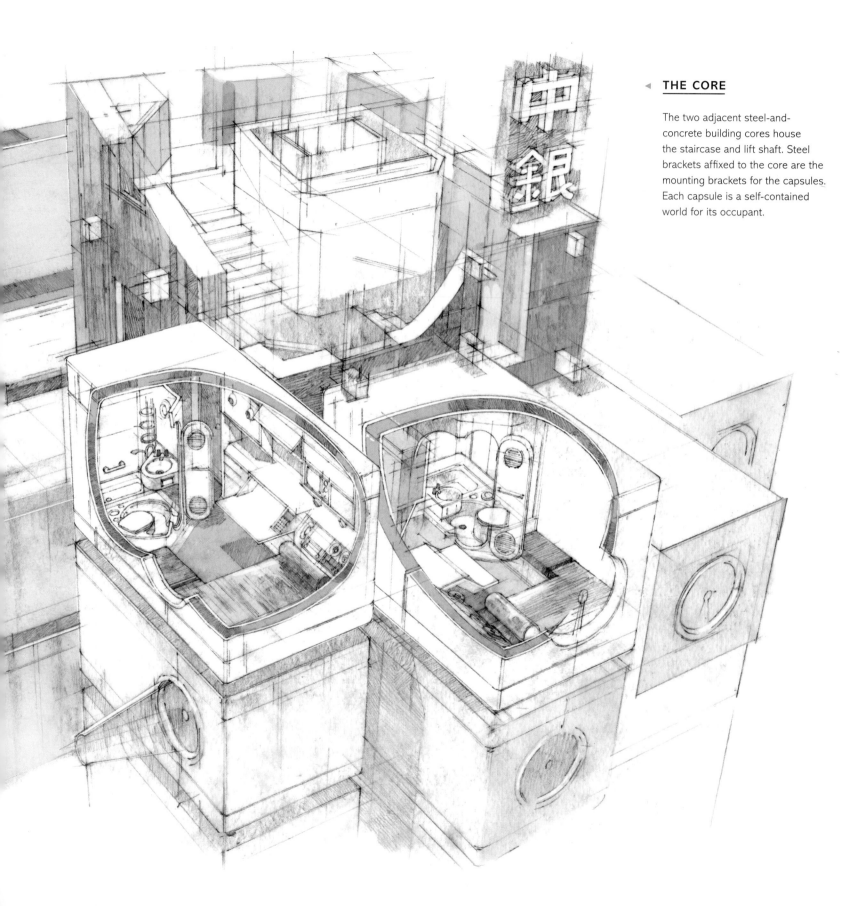

THE CORE

The two adjacent steel-and-concrete building cores house the staircase and lift shaft. Steel brackets affixed to the core are the mounting brackets for the capsules. Each capsule is a self-contained world for its occupant.

CAPSULE AND CORE

Brackets were installed on the concrete core. Capsules were craned up to their location and placed upon two pinned brackets at the bottom, then secured with two others at the top using four high-tension bolts. Even before doing this, prefabricated plumbing racks were installed between the capsule and the core.

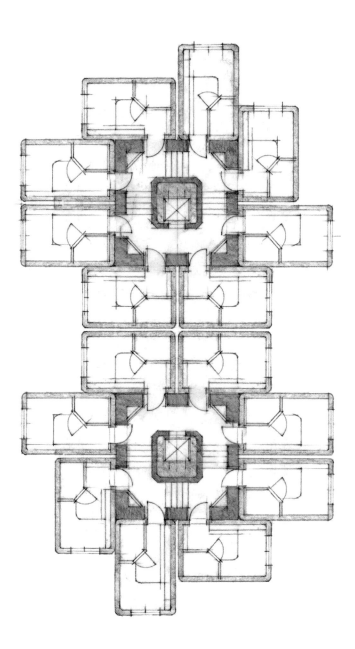

► POD LAYOUT

Capsules included all the modern
amenities – a refrigerator, stove, television
and even a tape deck. Each capsule
contains only approximately 10 sq m
(108 sq ft), with a built-in desk and
efficiently designed bathroom. The latter's
space-saving design is reminiscent of
those in airliners and trains.

The total floor area of the building is 3,091 sq m
(33,271 sq ft). The typical floor plan shows
the various capsules connected to two cores.
Each of the cores contains a lift in the centre
and stairs surrounding it. The stairs and
lifts connect to the building foyer within
a double-storey base.

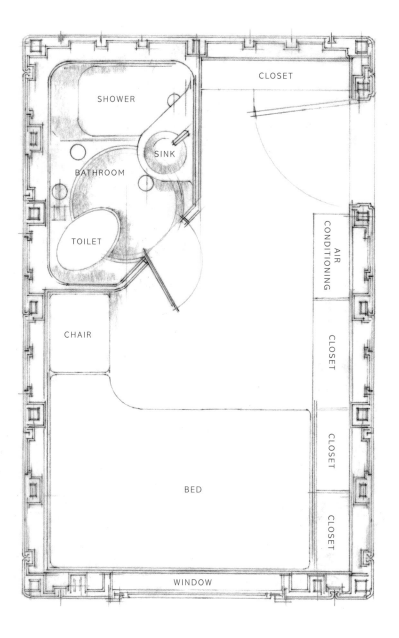

Absolute Towers

LOCATION Toronto, Canada
ARCHITECT MAD Architects
STYLE Contemporary Organic
BUILT 2007–12

When people think of contemporary architecture in China they often instinctively associate it with instant skyscraper cities like Shanghai's Pudong district, which has multiple examples designed by US, Canadian and European architects. But recent years have witnessed the rise of a budding Chinese starchitect whose own designs are being exported to Europe and North America. His name is Ma Yansong (b. 1975).

Yansong was born in Beijing and educated at the Beijing Institute of Civil Engineering and Architecture, also earning a Master's degree in architecture from Yale University. He is the founding partner of MAD Architects, established in 2004 and based in Beijing and Los Angeles. The firm has more than eighty architects managed by Yansong and principal partner Dang Qun. One might think that the name MAD Architects was created as an acronym for Ma and Dang, but Ma Yansong has said, 'I explain it stands for MA Design, but I like MAD (adjective) Architects better. It sounds like a group of architects with an attitude towards design and practice.' Further, he feels that 'architects not only represent social and cultural values, they are ultimately the pioneers of these values.'

MAD Architects, like most designers today, create dynamic architectural forms often realized with the assistance of computer programs, pushing the envelope of what buildings should be. Their most recent major building to receive positive international press coverage is the Harbin Opera House (2015) in China, which the media giant CNN praised as a contemporary equivalent to the landmark Sydney Opera House (1957–73; see p. 150). Their project for the Lucas Museum (2016–17) made press around the world during the search for its home city. The fluidity of both designs as a response to their environment bears comparison with similar projects by Zaha Hadid (see p. 64).

In Absolute Towers, MAD Architects, in association with Burka Architects and structural engineers Sigmund, Soudack and Associates, created high-rise residential units intended as distinctive curvilinear, almost rotating landmarks within a skyline of conventional towers. This was a bold move. Real-estate specialists initially feared that the radical appearance would dissuade condominium buyers in this development of five towers. But others supported the scheme including Hazel McCallion, Mississauga's mayor. Although the distinctive shapes added costs for the developers, Fernbrook Homes and Cityzen Development Group, rising prices for new condominiums helped ensure the sales success of these unique units that vary according to their position in the towers. Sales were not only successful but also quick – both towers were sold out soon after they were announced.

The result of a competition in 2006, for which the public voted on the selected scheme in 2007, the twin towers A, commissioned 2007, and B, commissioned slightly later, contain 45,000 and 40,000 sq m (485,000 and 430,500 sq ft). Tower A is 179.5 m (589 ft) high with fifty-six storeys and 428 units, and tower B is 161.2 m (259 ft) high with fifty storeys and 433 units. Floor plates are mostly the same on each floor but rotated. Steel-and-glass facades have continuous balconies that wrap around their 'sinuous' skins. They have been nicknamed the Marilyn Monroe towers by local residents. In many ways these skyscrapers show how far computer-aided design and engineering integration has progressed from Frank Gehry's Fred and Ginger Dancing House (1996) in Prague and Santiago Calatrava's Turning Torso (2005) in Malmö, Sweden. The seamless fluidity of Absolute Towers led the Council on Tall Buildings and Urban Habitat to vote them the Best Tall Building in the Americas after their completion in 2012.

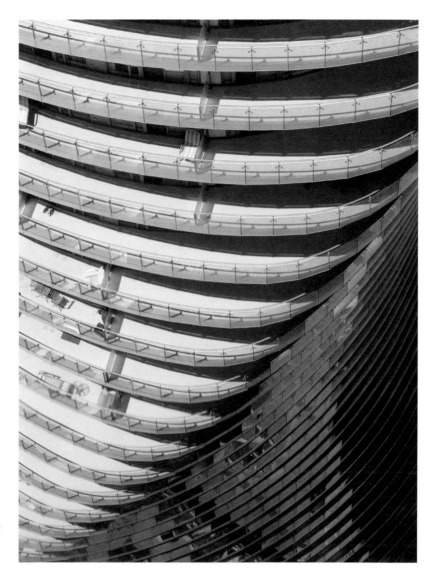

LEFT Real-estate agents know that balcony views are great selling points, and those at Absolute Towers are no exception. They likely helped achieve record-breaking sales only days after the plan was announced.

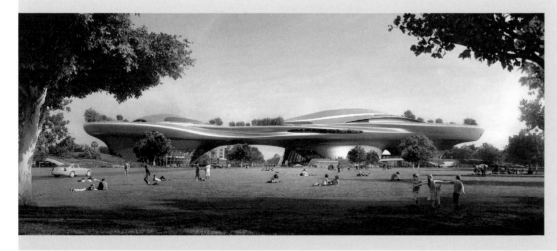

LUCAS MUSEUM

MAD Architects are the designers of the Lucas Museum of Narrative Art in Los Angeles for George Lucas, creator of the popular *Star Wars* franchise. Large, privately funded US museums go back to the robber-baron era of the early twentieth century. Those designed by high-profile architects include the EMP Seattle (2000) by Frank Gehry for Microsoft co-founder Paul Allen, and the Broad (2016) by Diller Scofidio + Renfro for Eli and Edythe Broad. Other locations considered for the Lucas Museum included Chicago and San Francisco, with some sites being opposed by advocacy groups because of the design and scale.

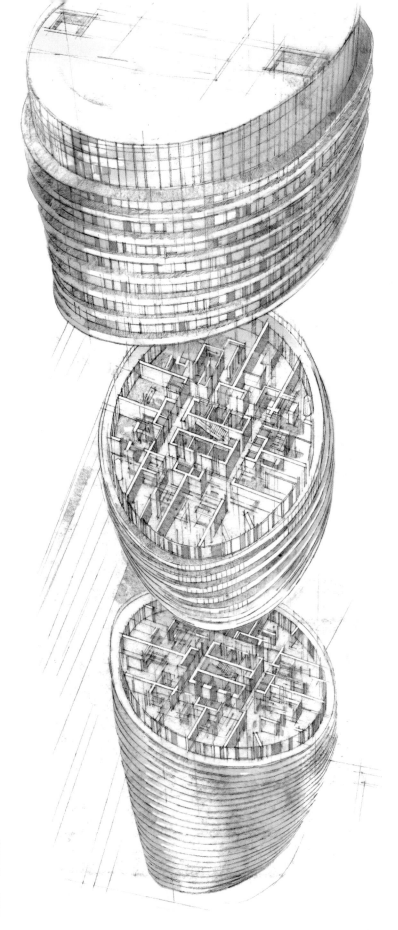

EXTERIOR MEETS INTERIOR

The sinuously curved 'torsional' exterior of the first tower shown here reflects comparable curves on the inside. Residential units also change in size and layout slightly from floor to floor with the varying overall plan form. The building's lift and fire stair core, and surrounding circulation corridor, however, remain rectilinear constants. The latter increases the sense of surprise on entering an apartment's curved space.

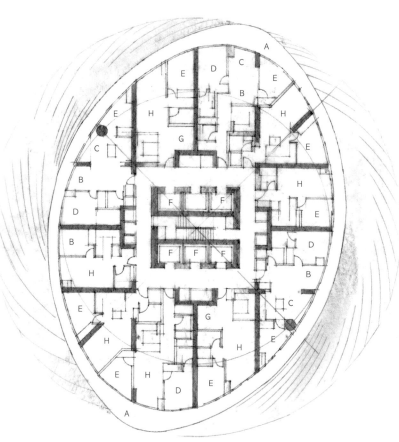

KEY

A   Balcony
B   Living
C   Dining
D   Master bedroom
E   Bedroom
F   Lift
G   Alcove
H   Dining/living

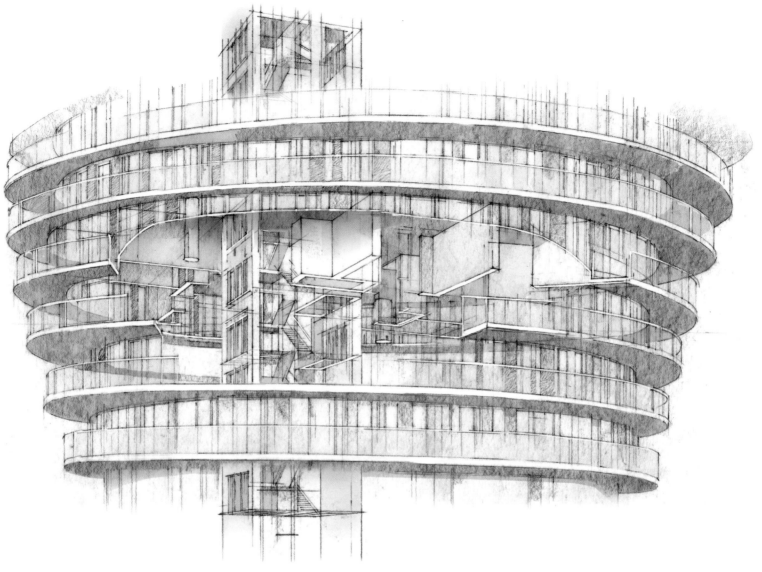

CAD COORDINATION

Computer design software is essential for executing a building such as this. It assists in creating and constructing the overall design, as well as being vital to coordinate architectural, structural and mechanical systems. This is particularly true where vertical pipes and conduits must service floors above and below as unit plans change to accommodate the multidimensional curved design. However, curved rooms and slightly shifting plans sometimes create awkwardly partitioned spaces that might, at times, make furniture placement tricky.

BALCONY VIEWS

The balconies that ring every floor are a real-estate agent's dream in terms of maximum marketability, and they likely helped the tower's sell-out at above-market rates in only a few days. They also provide a brise-soleil for glazed curtain wall spaces behind, thus reducing air-conditioning expenses in the summer. Each oval floor plate is essentially the same but many are rotated to varying degrees, making each unit slightly different. Engineers designed thermal breaks in the floor plates for the main structure and balconies to reduce heat loss in the winter.

Worship

As with the Living chapter, the Worship chapter covers what has been a fact of human life as far back as prehistory. Perhaps the most famous early example of this type of extant structure is Stonehenge (3000–2000 BCE) in Wiltshire, England. Although its function is not particularly tied to any known deity, its use is thought by some to have related to the solstice and the natural progression of life on earth, linking it to spiritual more than practical concerns.

Other outdoor Neolithic temples have been found in the Orkney Islands, Scotland, such as the Ness of Brodgar (c. 3500 BCE), and recently excavated at Göbekli Tepe (c. 10,000 BCE) in Turkey. Egyptian temples dedicated to specific gods, particularly the chief deity Amun, seem to be the first of this type, with examples built by pharaohs Thutmose III at Amada (15th century BCE) and Seti I at Abydos (after 1279 BCE), as well as the much-visited Luxor Temple (1400 BCE) in Thebes. The earliest religious structure in this survey is within the chapter on Monuments, the Parthenon (c. 447–432 BCE; see p. 80) on the Acropolis in Greece, which served as a temple dedicated to Athena and, in subsequent centuries, as a church and then a mosque. This multifaceted, sequential use also applies to two early buildings within this chapter. The first is the massively domed Hagia Sophia (see p. 238) in Istanbul, built as a church between 532 and 562, and then converted into a mosque in 1453. By comparison the strikingly arcaded Mosque Cathedral of Córdoba (see p. 244) was begun as a mosque in 785 and converted

and renovated into a cathedral in 1523. In cases such as those there is no reason to wastefully demolish a spectacular building simply because different cultures practice different religions.

When thinking of Western religious structures, cathedrals often come first to mind. This chapter includes several. They range from a Gothic classic, Chartres Cathedral (1194–1260; see p. 250) in France, and the mostly Early Renaissance Florence Cathedral (1296–1461; see p. 260), to the massive High Renaissance and Baroque St Peter's Basilica (1506–1626; see p. 270) in Rome – though technically not a cathedral – and the Baroque and Neoclassical St Paul's Cathedral (1675–1720; see p. 276) in London. There is also the wildly expressionist Sagrada Familia (begun 1883; see p. 288) in Barcelona, and the compellingly Late Gothic monastery at Batalha (1386–1533; see p. 266) in Portugal. Many of these buildings, particularly St Peter's and St Paul's, have been long-term record-holders for the height of their massive domes. Their silhouettes were often included in later nineteenth-century comparative drawings of the world's biggest buildings.

In everything cited thus far, including those eight buildings described in this chapter, there are certain types of structure that are mostly predictable in terms of style and form. After all, religious architecture is often culturally and liturgically based, so there are usually no surprises. It is generally a conservative building type in terms of design. This is also the case for the pagoda-like forms of the tiny wooden Golden Pavilion (after 1397; rebuilt 1955) in Kyoto (see p. 256). This Buddhist shrine had to be rebuilt after being destroyed by fire. Two interesting aspects of this building are: it was designed when Florence Cathedral was being built; and in being rebuilt, it reminds us that even cathedrals and mosques have been under constant repair, restoration and renovation over their lifetimes. Chartres, for instance, has long lost its original medieval timber-framed roof, the current one being a copper-clad iron structure dating from the Industrial Revolution. Earthquakes in Istanbul created work for both early Christian and Islamic architects to reinforce Hagia Sophia's various domes soon after it was built and through much of its life as a religious structure. This should not be a surprise to anyone who has owned an older home. Historic buildings are in need of constant maintenance and repair, and religious structures often are held to a higher standard for repairs and restorations.

With this generally conservative design background in mind, there have been instances when religious architecture has moved ahead in terms of design. The growth of the new Gothic style in the twelfth and thirteenth centuries, with its light-filled spaces defined by slender structural members, seemed a quantum leap from the heavily walled Romanesque architecture of a century before. Likewise, Modernist and contemporary-styled religious buildings, as opposed to their historicist predecessors, were likely first seen in the years between World War I (1914–18) and World War II (1939–45). This is so for the new Weimar Republic (1919–33), which attempted to leave the trappings of imperial Germany behind as it entered a new democratic era after World War I. Several architects specialized in such Modern churches. Dominikus Böhm (1880–1955) in the Immakulata-Kapelle (1928; demolished) in Cologne and St Engelbert (1930) in Cologne-Riehl, Martin Weber (1890–1941) with St Boniface Frankfurt (1926–32), and Otto Bartning (1883–1959) with Cologne's Stahlkirche (1928; demolished) and Berlin's Gustav-Adolf-Kirche (1934; rebuilt 1951) are just a few. Likewise, postwar Germany also left the Third Reich behind with very modern churches such as Berlin's Kaiser Wilhelm Memorial Church (1963) by Egon Eiermann (1904–70). France experienced something similar, with the Perret brothers, Auguste (1874–1954) and Gustave (1876–1952), and their Notre-Dame du Raincy Church (1923) and Auguste's St Joseph's Church in Le Havre (1951–57). This context supplies the foundation for one of the truly revolutionary church designs: Le Corbusier's Notre-Dame-du-Haut Chapel (1950–54; see p. 282) at Ronchamp. Many other ecclesiastic designers often created simplified wall planes that are Modernist in appearance, yet the building's massing duplicates the basilica and tower forms of traditional churches. The Modernist pioneers in France and Germany during the 1920s and early 1930s created the environment for this style to flower after the war. Albeit less daring, they paved the way for this masterpiece of Modernism, distinct even within Le Corbusier's oeuvre. Contemporary design in churches, synagogues, mosques and even Buddhist and Baháʼí temples today owes a debt of gratitude to Le Corbusier's bold statement at Ronchamp more than six decades ago.

MOSQUE CATHEDRAL OF CÓRDOBA (SEE P. 244)

Hagia Sophia

LOCATION Istanbul, Turkey
ARCHITECT Anthemius of Tralles, Isidore of Miletus and others
STYLE Byzantine and Islamic
BUILT 532–62, altered as mosque, begun 1453

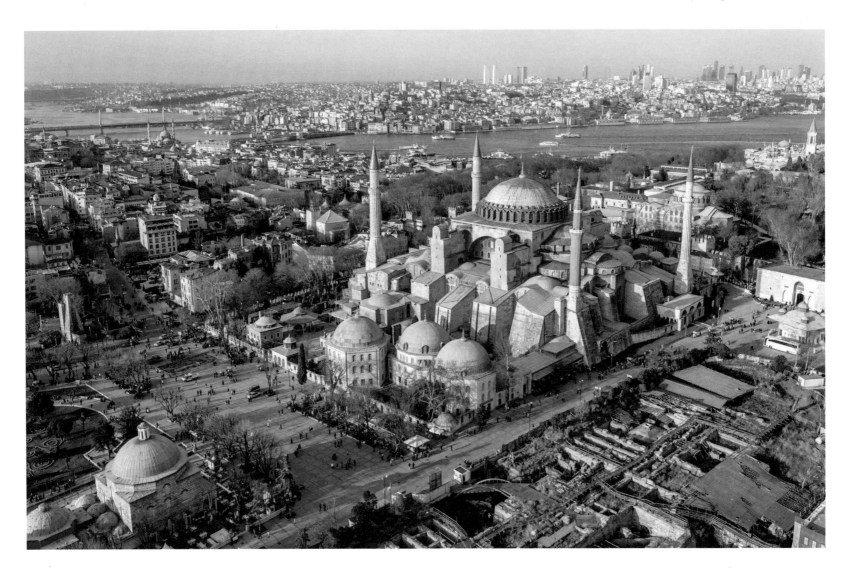

A key turning point in the history of what was the Roman and then Byzantine Empire occured on 29 May 1453. That day, the Ottoman army of Sultan Mehmed the Conqueror (Mehmed II) entered Constantinople as victors after a more than seven-week-long siege. What was a city named after its Emperor Constantine the Great became afterwards Islambol, meaning 'where Islam abounds'. The city officially received its current name, Istanbul, in 1930.

After his armies sacked the city for three days, the sultan declared that they halt their looting and that citizens should return to their homes. They were permitted to practise their Christian Orthodox religion under his rule, but some prime religious properties were soon recycled into mosques. Hagia Sophia, or Church of the Holy Wisdom, was one of them. During the period 1453 to 1931 minarets were added, the eastern apse was converted into a mihrab, Christian murals were covered and various sultans were buried nearby. Ironically, the massive church was later used as the base plan for several large mosques.

As to its original construction, the gigantic masonry domed building replaced two earlier churches. Nothing remains of these except archaeological remnants from the second church of 415. The third Hagia Sophia, or current building, measures approximately 82 m long by 73 m wide (269 × 240 ft). Its dome is 33 m (108 ft) in diameter and approximately 55 m (180 ft) high. The structure is built of stones from all over the empire, including Egypt, Syria, the Bosphorus and Thessaly. The massive interior space could hold some 10,000 worshippers. Emperor Justinian I commissioned the church in 532, with geometrician Anthemius of Tralles and physicist Isidore of Miletus serving as architects. Justinian I and Patriarch Menas of Constantinople performed the dedication on it on 27 December 537.

The structure was finished later in the reign of Justinian II, including the spectacular mosaics. Earthquakes in 557 and 558 collapsed the main dome and caused structural damage to others. Isidorus the Younger, nephew of Isidore of Miletus, rebuilt the dome and strengthened the supporting walls in *c.* 560, installing gigantic granite columns recycled from the Roman Temple of Jupiter in Baalbek, Lebanon. A subsequent earthquake damaged the western dome in 989, and Emperor Basil II commissioned architect Trdat (*c.* 950–1020) to rebuild it in 994. At this time, the mosaic decorations were all refreshed and repaired.

In 1204 the building suffered additional damage during the Fourth Crusade (1202–04) and underwent several major repairs in the fourteenth century.

With the Ottoman sack of Constantinople, the church was looted and then officially converted into Hagia Sophia mosque on 1 June 1453. Minarets were constructed after 1481 but mostly in the sixteenth century, and additional repairs were made to the building by architect Mimar Sinan (*c.* 1489–1588). Around this time buildings surrounding the mosque were demolished to provide space for a variety of tombs for sultans and Ottoman princes. Rulers in the

seventeenth and eighteenth centuries renewed the plaster that preserved many of the early Christian mosaic murals. Sultan Abdülmecid I commissioned architect brothers Gaspare (1809–83) and Giuseppe (1822–91) Fossati to implement a full restoration from 1847 to 1849, which also equalized the minaret heights. Turkish president and founder of the republic Mustafa Kemal Atatürk spearheaded the conversion of the mosque into a museum, a tribute to its Byzantine and Ottoman Islamic heritage. Restorations and repairs were undertaken in 2006, and more than 3 million people visit annually.

RIGHT Named after Emperor John II Comnenus, who is depicted on the left, this mosaic dates from 1122. The Virgin Mary holds the Christ Child, and John's wife, Empress Irene of Hungary, is to the right.

BELOW The interior is dominated by the mostly Byzantine mosaics and decorations, as well as some Islamic additions, including eight calligraphic roundels from the mid-1800s, each approximately 7.5 m (24 ft 6 in.) in diameter.

OTTOMAN EMPIRE

The Ottoman Empire lasted from the late thirteenth century until after World War I (1914–18), ending with Turkish independence in 1922. It covered North Africa and the Middle East through Turkey and the Balkans, and was administered from Istanbul after 1453. This illustration by nineteenth-century Greek painter Panagiotis Zografo depicts the Fall of Constantinople in 1453, showing Sultan Mehmed II. The empire reached its peak, especially in terms of the arts, under Suleiman I, known as 'The Magnificent'. He ruled from 1520 until his death in 1566. The Byzantine architecture of the Hagia Sophia served as inspiration for many Ottoman mosques.

BYZANTINE ARCHITECTURE

Byzantine religious architecture is often characterized by multiple-domed spaces that are highly decorated with mosaics. Domes are typically arranged in a centrally planned, equilateral Greek cross. In addition to the extensive use of mosaics, structural elements were often highly decorative, featuring grained marbles and extensive inlays. Altogether, the lavish materials and enormous scale of Hagia Sophia must have projected the image of an otherworldly experience, as befitting an imperial church.

MINARETS

Minarets are towers at mosques from which the call to prayers is made. Those of Hagia Sophia were added after the sack of Constantinople in 1453, when the church was converted into a mosque. The Christian mosaics were plastered over during Sultan Mehmed II's reign, but the plaster preserved them and they were uncovered and restored when the building was made into a museum in 1935.

FLOOR PLAN

The dark-coloured elements of the plan show the entry at the bottom, with the semicircular apse, later the mihrab, at the top. Minarets (A) are at the corners, as are: the former baptistery (B), which later held the tombs of sultans Mustafa and Ibrahim; the *metatorium* (C), or space designated for the emperors; and the *skeuophylakion*, or treasury (D). Buildings surrounding the baptistery, which are now tombs, also include mausolea for sultans Selim II, Mehmed III and Murad III.

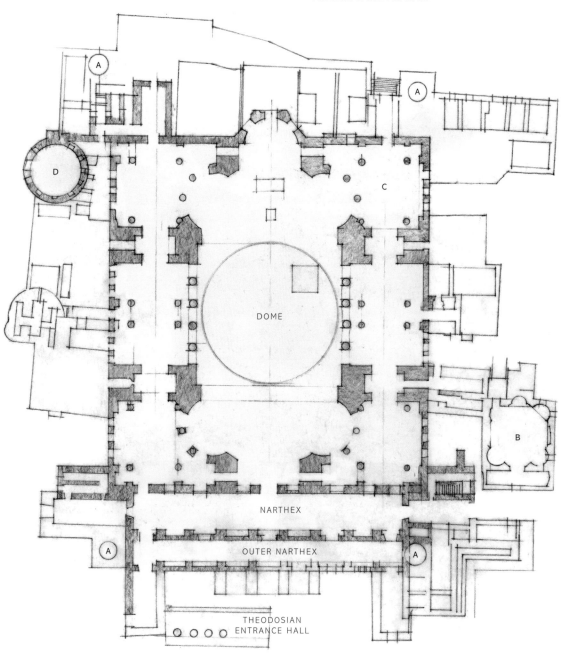

DOME

NARTHEX

OUTER NARTHEX

THEODOSIAN
ENTRANCE HALL

DOMICAL SPACE

Typical of much Byzantine architecture, the central dome rests on pendentives, triangular segments of a sphere. These give the dome a higher profile and likely act in channelling forces better than a typical drum. The dome is 33 m (108 ft) in diameter and approximately 55 m (180 ft) high. The nave column capitals are carved of marble from Marmara island almost 160 km (100 miles) southwest of Istanbul. The monumental nave columns, some with inscriptions indicating that they were recycled from Roman monuments, are 17 m (56 ft) high and were shaped of richly grained marble from quarries near Thessaly, Greece.

CROSS SECTION

This section looking towards the apse or mihrab shows on the left the treasury, with an underground vault, and on the right the massive masonry buttresses throughout that help support the building within what is an earthquake zone. The drawing clearly shows the double-height vaulted galleries on either side of the nave, as well as some of the forty ribs used within the brick dome.

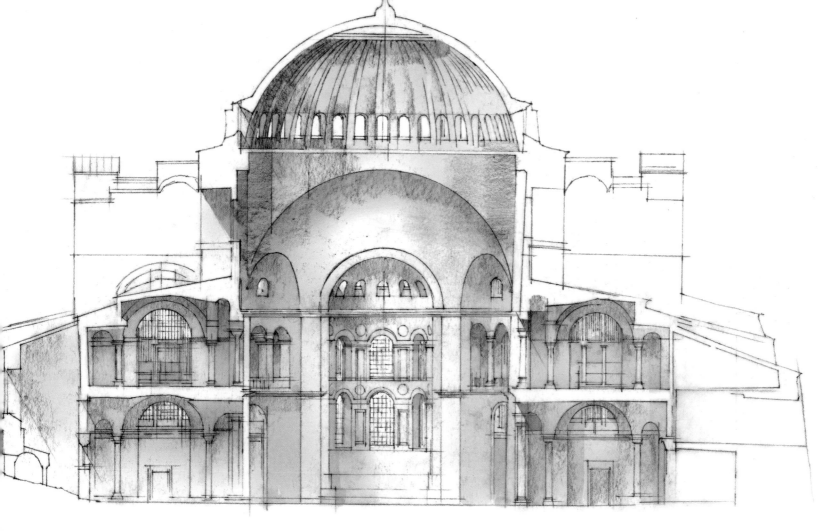

Mosque Cathedral of Córdoba

LOCATION   Córdoba, Spain

ARCHITECT   Unknown (mosque); Hernán Ruiz II (cathedral additions)

STYLE   Mozarabic with Renaissance alterations

BUILT   785 (hypostyle hall of mosque begun); 1523 (cathedral begun)

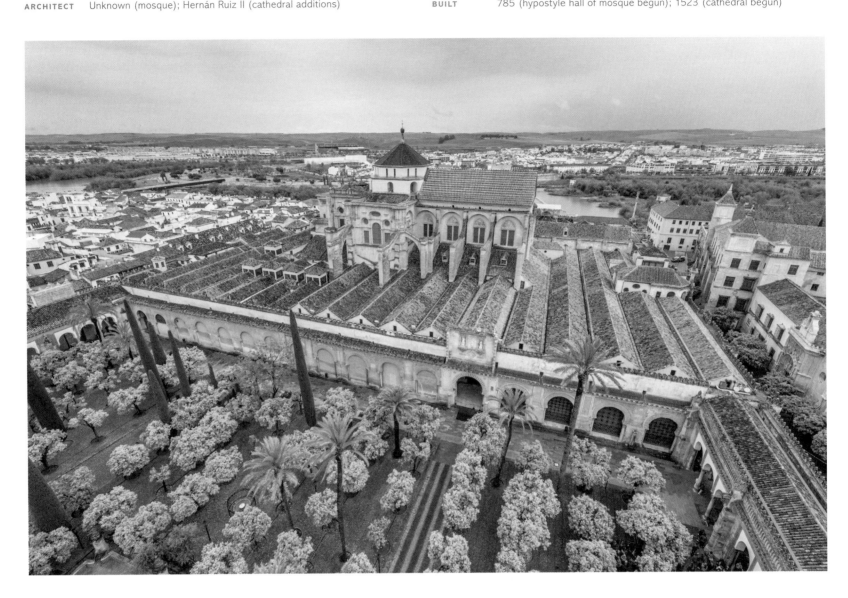

Sanctioned by Umayyad Caliph Al-Walid I headquartered in Damascus, and led by Tariq ibn-Ziyad, the Moors' invasion of Spain from North Africa began in 711 with the capture of Gibraltar, whose name derives from the Arabic *Jabal Ṭāriq* (Mt Tariq). Tariq won the subsequent Battle of Guadalete (*c.* 711), which led to the rout of Visigothic forces in Spain and the capture of Córdoba and other Spanish cities. Córdoba was established as the capital of Al-Walid's province of

Spain, known as Al-Andalus, and in 756 it became an independent emirate under Abd Al-Rahman I. His grandson Abd Al-Rahman III established the Caliphate of Córdoba in 929. Both men, especially the younger, helped make the city an arts, cultural and intellectual centre of Muslim Spain, which extended from the Mediterranean Sea to cities such as Salamanca, Segovia, Guadalajara, Zaragoza and Tarragona in the north.

Córdoba was said to have more than 3,000 mosques but the centrepiece was, and still is, the Great Mosque, now a cathedral. After the conquest of Córdoba in 711, a Visigothic church on the site was shared by Christians and Muslims for worship. It was purchased by Abd Al-Rahman I and demolished to begin the Great Mosque in 784, with construction continued under his successors through warrior regent Muhammad ibn Abu Amir Al-Mansur. The Great Mosque consists of five interconnected prayer halls with spectacular polychromed masonry arcades, built as the site expanded under various rulers, as well as a courtyard and minaret tower, erected under Abd Al-Rahman III and later subsumed within a Renaissance tower. The first prayer hall of Abd Al-Rahman I consists of eleven corridors or naves running northwest to southeast, with 110 columns and capitals made from granite, jasper and marble reused from Roman and Visigothic ruins. The horsehoe arches within are Visigothic-style, with unique doubled arches being used to support higher ceilings. By the time of Al-Mansur the building had tripled in size with the addition of further prayer halls, which brought the total number of columns to 856, and the dynamically vaulted treasury and mihrab had been added to the southeast side of the complex.

The power of the caliphate waned after Al-Mansur and eventually a series of battles of the so-called Reconquista, from the mid-eighth through to the fifteenth centuries, culminated in the Treaty of Granada in 1491, after which the Moors surrendered that city, leaving Spain altogether. As part of those campaigns, Córdoba was reconquered in 1236 by King Ferdinand III of Castile and the mosque was converted into a church. Various kings made subsequent alterations, the most visually prominent being the insertion of a Renaissance cathedral within the centre of the prayer halls and bell tower that encased the remains of the minaret. Architect Hernán Ruiz II (c. 1514–69) built the cathedral in 1547 and remodelled the tower. Renovation work continued on the tower in the seventeenth century, with Juan Sequero de Matilla creating the

clock portion and Gaspar de la Peña repairing it again, and incorporating the bell chamber, in 1664. The sculpture of St Rafael at the top was the work of Bernabé Gómez del Río and Pedro de la Paz.

When Holy Roman Emperor Charles V visited the new cathedral he said, 'They have taken something unique in all the world and destroyed it to build something you can find in any city'. Indeed, even today the architecture of the mosque is what makes this a distinct landmark, compared with that of the cathedral. Controversies continue about whether Muslim services should be permitted within, but one thing is certain. The 1.5 million annual visitors acknowledge the importance of both Muslim and Christian cultures in shaping Spain and this distinct house of worship.

ABOVE LEFT The rotated geometry of the ribs within this and the flanking domed spaces next to the prayer niche, along with the elaborate abstract decorations, is typical of Islamic architecture of the Umayyad Caliphate, especially within mihrabs.

ABOVE RIGHT The rows of horseshoe-shaped arches characterize the architecture of Córdoba's mosque from the early Middle Ages and are typical of Visigothic architecture in southern France and Spain from the fifth and sixth centuries.

ISLAMIC SPAIN

In William Shakespeare's *Othello* (1603), the title character is a North African commander in the Venetian army. Arabic forms and customs were common in much of Spain over some 800 years after the Arab Moorish invasion in 711. Under the Moors, Córdoba was far ahead of its European counterparts, having paved streets, night illumination and more than 900 baths. Oranges were one of the provisions they introduced in Spain. The Patio de los Naranjos (left), or orange tree courtyard, is thought to correspond approximately to the area of the old mosque.

1 CATHEDRAL CUTAWAY

Architects Hernán Ruiz the Elder (d.1547)
and his son, Hernán Ruiz the Younger,
built the cathedral in 1523 right in the
centre of the former mosque. It has Gothic
and Renaissance details with a classical
dome. The altar, by Álonso Matias,
dates from the seventeenth century and
eighteenth-century pulpits were created
by sculptor Miguel Verdiguier.

2 TOWER IN THE GARDEN

The Patio de los Naranjos (orange tree courtyard)
on the northwest side of the complex, with fountains,
is a traditional space for ablutions before worshippers
entered the mosque for prayers. The 93-m (305-ft)
high Torre del Alminar minaret, from the mid-fifteenth
century and later, encases remnants of the original
minaret. This was begun during the reign of Abd
Al-Rahman III in the first half of the tenth century, as
was the arcaded courtyard. Both were finished by his
successor Hisham Al-Reda. The courtyard had palm
trees in the thirteenth century and orange trees in
the fifteenth, with cypress trees added later.

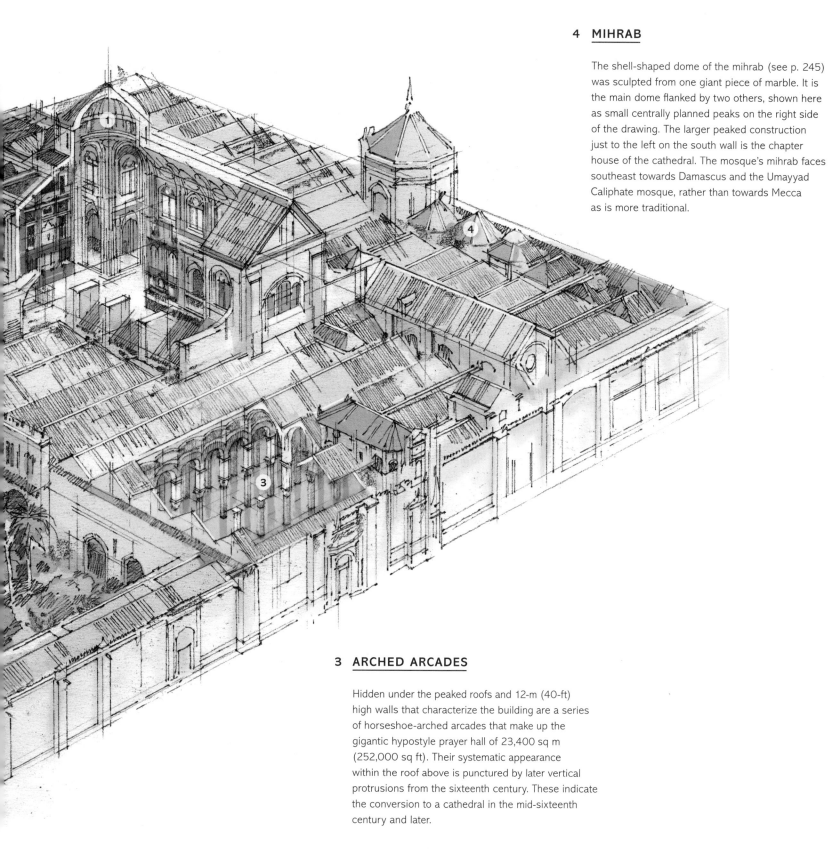

4 MIHRAB

The shell-shaped dome of the mihrab (see p. 245) was sculpted from one giant piece of marble. It is the main dome flanked by two others, shown here as small centrally planned peaks on the right side of the drawing. The larger peaked construction just to the left on the south wall is the chapter house of the cathedral. The mosque's mihrab faces southeast towards Damascus and the Umayyad Caliphate mosque, rather than towards Mecca as is more traditional.

3 ARCHED ARCADES

Hidden under the peaked roofs and 12-m (40-ft) high walls that characterize the building are a series of horseshoe-arched arcades that make up the gigantic hypostyle prayer hall of 23,400 sq m (252,000 sq ft). Their systematic appearance within the roof above is punctured by later vertical protrusions from the sixteenth century. These indicate the conversion to a cathedral in the mid-sixteenth century and later.

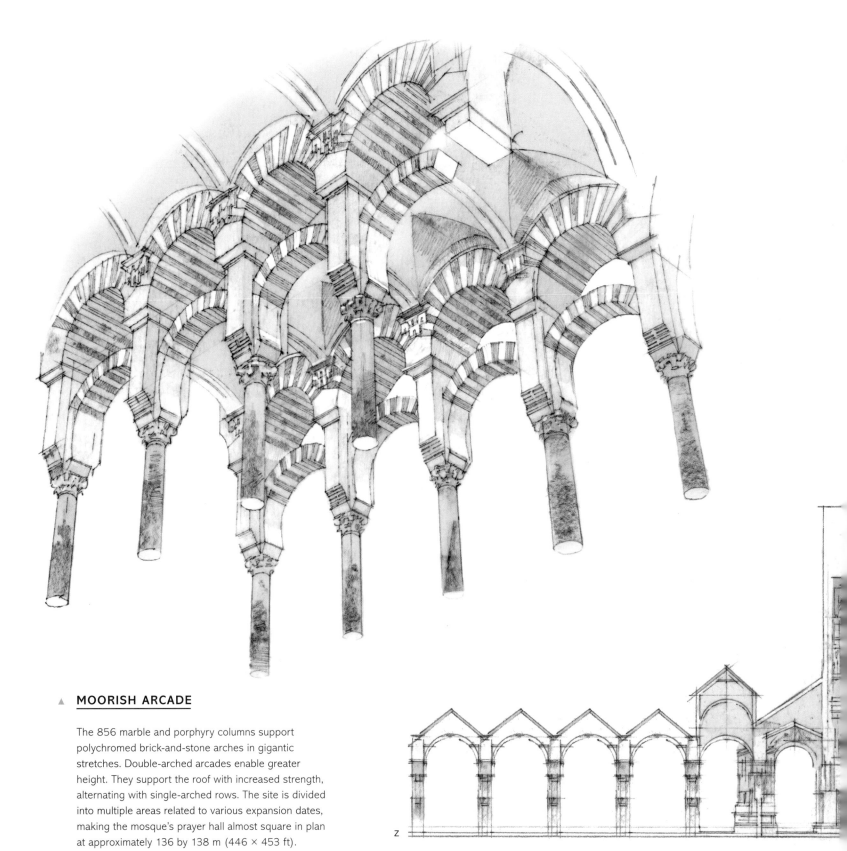

MOORISH ARCADE

The 856 marble and porphyry columns support polychromed brick-and-stone arches in gigantic stretches. Double-arched arcades enable greater height. They support the roof with increased strength, alternating with single-arched rows. The site is divided into multiple areas related to various expansion dates, making the mosque's prayer hall almost square in plan at approximately 136 by 138 m (446 × 453 ft).

Z

► FLOOR PLAN

This labelled plan gives an idea of spaces within the building, both Christian and Muslim. Various chapels pepper the inside spaces beyond the cathedral insertion, as the building's religious use changed. Today it remains a great monument to Spain's history and both faiths.

KEY
A Patio de los Naranjos
B Cathedral
C Chapter House
D Mihrab
E Mosque arcades

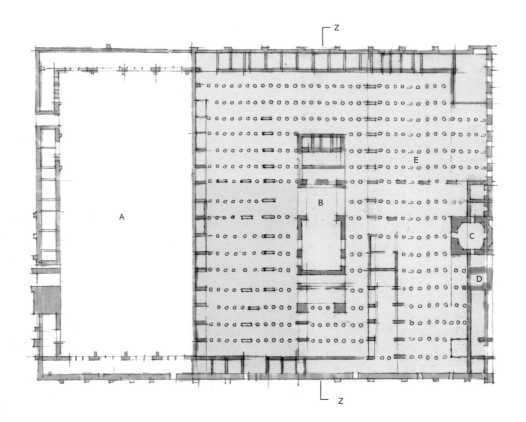

▼ CATHEDRAL SECTION

This drawing shows the longitudinal section of the cathedral looking north (marked as z on the plan above). The bird's-eye view cutaway (see p. 247) gives an idea of the insertion of this structure within the lower-scaled mosque. The detailing also suggests how the building moves from a simpler late Gothic nave arcade to more elaborate Renaissance and Baroque forms towards the crossing dome.

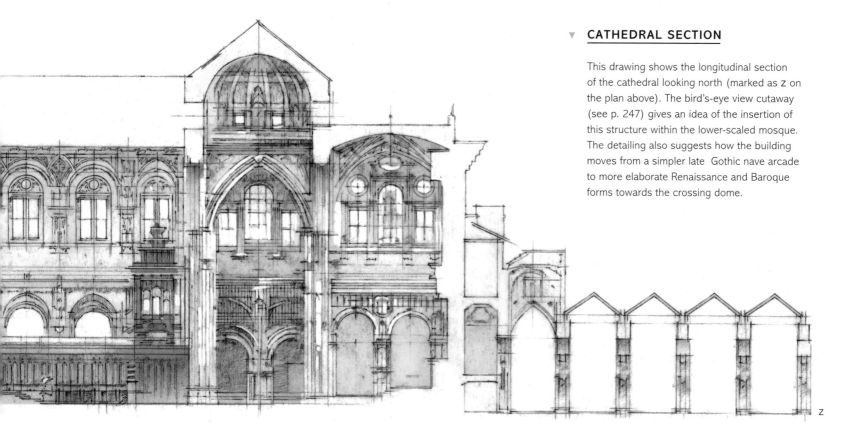

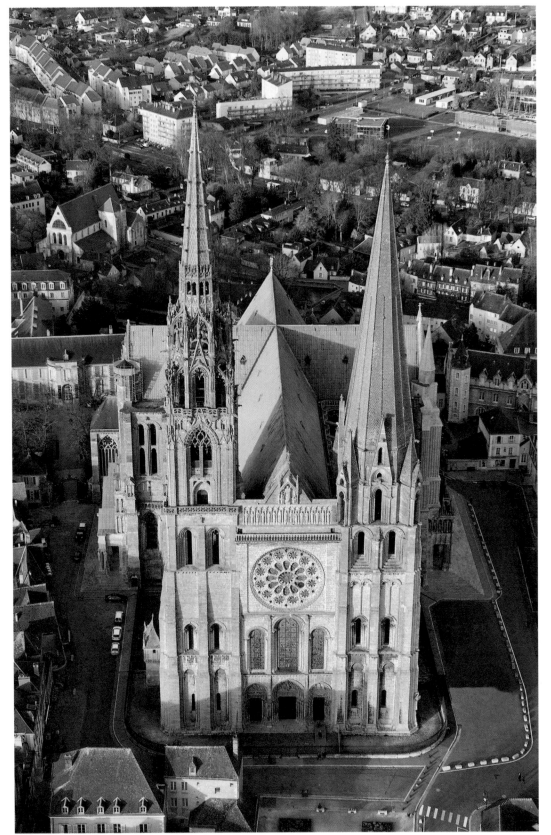

Chartres Cathedral

LOCATION	Chartres, France
ARCHITECT	Unknown
STYLE	Gothic
BUILT	1194–1260

It was a case of 'you can't fire me because I quit', when French architect Jean Mignot admonished clerical clients at Milan Cathedral in 1401 with the statement '*Ars sine scientia nihil est*' or 'Art without science is nothing'. He was their third cathedral builder who walked off the job, the others being German master masons Heinrich Parler (*c*. 1310–*c*. 1370) and Ulrich von Ensingen (*c*. 1350–1419). Mignot's statement criticized the appearance and structural stability of a building that did not follow rational rules of how cathedrals were designed and built. This *scientia* – the geometric proportioning of buildings and structural members such as flying buttresses –made tall cathedrals stand up. It is why the wedding-cake Milan cathedral looks so different from other Gothic cathedrals of the era in continental Europe, particularly those in France, where this design movement started two centuries before.

The earliest example of Gothic architecture can be found in the Abbey of St Denis (*c*. 1135–44) outside Paris. St Denis has arches that hesitatingly morph from round to pointed. Their rib-vaulted bays spring from columns rather than thick walls, allowing large stained-glass windows to illuminate the space. St Denis's Abbot Suger (1081–1151) worked with his now unknown master mason to build the west facade and, more importantly, enlarge the choir. This created open, well-lit spaces that could, in his words, 'shine with the wonderful and uninterrupted light of most luminous windows. . . '. Gothic's increasingly pointed arches were likely adapted from earlier forms in Islamic architecture. Skeletal members such as rib vaults supported by flying buttresses found expression in what many feel is the epitome of French High Gothic in Amiens Cathedral (*c.* 1220–70). Chartres is a bridge between Suger's St Denis and Amiens, as well as many French cathedrals that followed in the 1200s. They tended to be light and open, created with elements that were increasingly slender, visually complex and diagonal, whereas earlier Romanesque buildings had thicker walls, smaller windows and planar, often rectilinear forms.

Notre-Dame de Chartres, dedicated to the Virgin Mary and an important pilgrimage shrine that holds a relic of her cloak, is approximately 80 km (50 miles) southwest of Paris. It is 131 m (430 ft) long and has a nave height of 37 m (121 ft). It replaced an earlier cathedral that dated mostly from the eleventh century whose choir and nave were greatly damaged by fire on 10 June 1194; its west facade and royal portal (1136–41), as well as crypt from the previous century, were spared. Although the masons have not been identified, studies indicate that some 300 worked in various teams on the limestone building over more than six decades, from 1194 to its consecration on 24 October 1260, though the choir was completed by 1221. The nave, like those in cathedrals at Amiens and Reims, has a labyrinth that was symbolically used to represent a pilgrim's life journey past temptations and diversions in search of God.

Because Chartres has had few additions, its interior is what visitors likely saw in the later thirteenth century – a tripartite nave and choir elevation where each bay has a single high arch, a middle-level blind arcade triforium and a spacious windowed clerestory of richly coloured glass. The clerestory and various rose windows number 176, the majority fabricated between 1205 and 1240. They were removed at the start of World War II (1939–45) and replaced after. They make Chartres an exceptional experience akin to what Suger intended at St Denis – a spatial and sensory representation of the New Jerusalem.

VILLARD DE HONNECOURT

Medieval architects would create architectural drawings on parchment as well as plaster floors or walls that, once filled, could easily be replastered to create a new drawing surface. But one mid-thirteenth-century Frenchman, likely a craftsman if not an architect–mason, named Villard de Honnecourt kept a sketchbook of some 250 drawings, which is now in the Bibliothèque nationale de France. Architectural subjects within record his travels to Laon, Lausanne, Meaux, Reims and of course Chartres. At Chartres he sketched the rose window of the west facade (above).

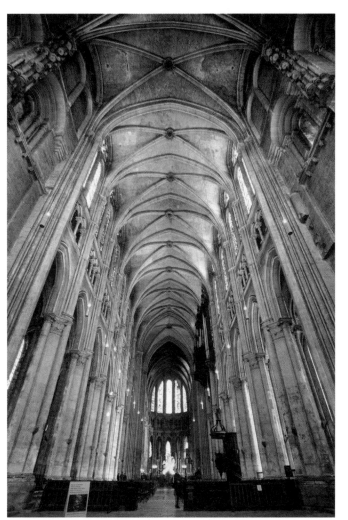

LEFT In the nave, slender ribbed vaults atop visually uninterrupted piers transfer gravitational forces below, as well as to the perimeter through flying buttresses.

BELOW The rose window of the south transept from *c.* 1225 measures almost 10.8 m (35 ft 6 in.) in diameter.

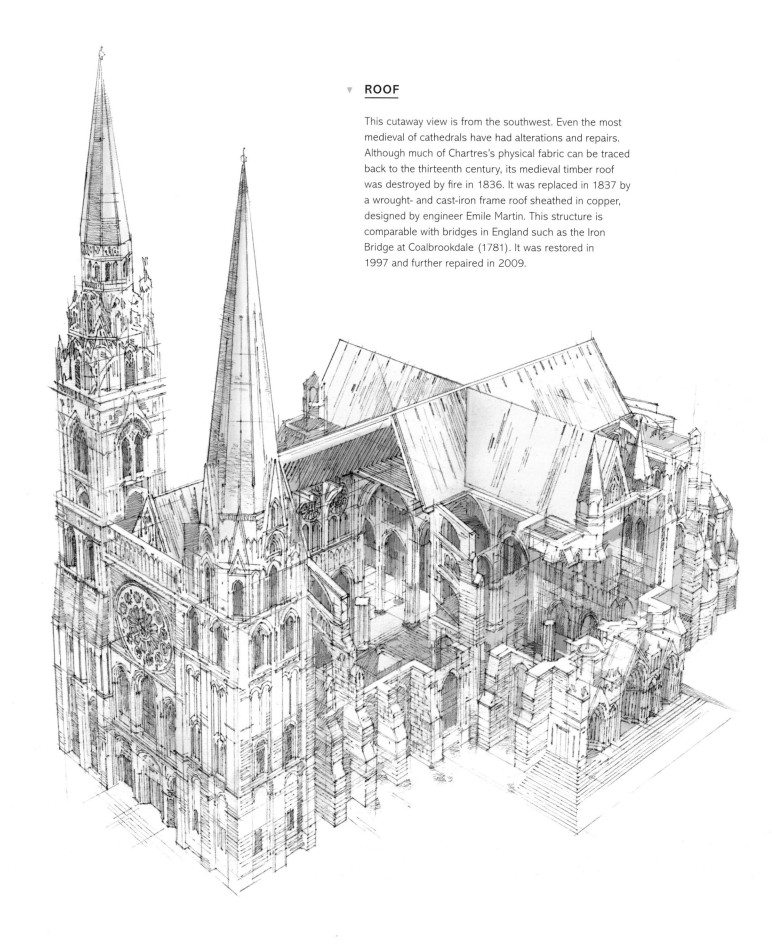

▼ ROOF

This cutaway view is from the southwest. Even the most medieval of cathedrals have had alterations and repairs. Although much of Chartres's physical fabric can be traced back to the thirteenth century, its medieval timber roof was destroyed by fire in 1836. It was replaced in 1837 by a wrought- and cast-iron frame roof sheathed in copper, designed by engineer Emile Martin. This structure is comparable with bridges in England such as the Iron Bridge at Coalbrookdale (1781). It was restored in 1997 and further repaired in 2009.

▼ FLYING BUTTRESSES

This cross section shows the nave and vault
structure as well as the nineteenth-century
roof. Two levels of flying buttresses arch
from the walls on both sides of the nave,
directing the gravitational forces into large
setback piers on the outside walls of the
aisles. This system enabled Gothic architects
to empirically create even taller, more skeletal
structures until the collapse of the choir at
Beauvais Cathedral in 1284 caused architects
to make them somewhat thicker.

NAVE ELEVATION

This elevation shows the use of what became a fairly standard tripartite formula for cathedral design. A Gothic arcade with bundled columns and elaborate capitals has vertical piers springing above, becoming ribs of the vault bays. Cross ribs highlight and support the groin vaults. The shorter middle level of the unilluminated triforium arcade sits underneath the large clerestory level. There, arcuated and rose windows of leaded stained glass, much of it original, bathe the interiors with otherworldly light, as does similar fenestration in the aisle below.

LABYRINTH AND FLOOR PLAN

The plan shown here became more or less formulaic, at least for French cathedrals. Aside from the rectilinear St Piat Chapel (1323), which was added off the choir, the apse and various chapels on the east end of the semicircular choir are the religious culmination of any cathedral. Basilical in plan, with a large central nave and flanking side aisles, Chartres, like many other cathedrals, has transepts that cross the nave and choir. These are often where there is a larger crossing groined vault with sometimes a large tower atop. The original labyrinth (c. 1205) in the nave towards the west end of the cathedral represents a pilgrim's arduous journey to God through life's diversions. Labyrinths can be found in other cathedrals such as Amiens and Reims, as well as in Villard de Honnecourt's sketchbook.

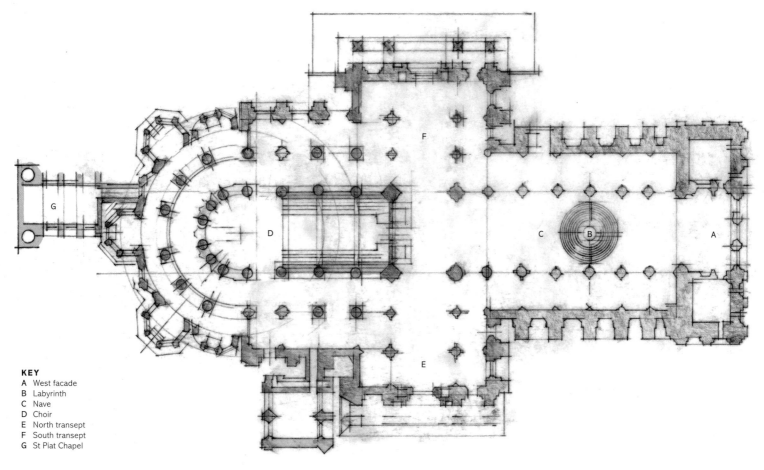

KEY
A West facade
B Labyrinth
C Nave
D Choir
E North transept
F South transept
G St Piat Chapel

Temple of the Golden Pavilion

LOCATION   Kyoto, Japan
ARCHITECT   Unknown
STYLE   Zen Buddhist
BUILT   After 1397; rebuilt 1955

For over a year, through the second half of 1944 until Japan's surrender in August 1945, Japanese cities were the targets of some 145,000 tonnes (160,000 tons) of bombs, with well over 300,000 casualties. These statistics are separate from the nuclear bombing of Hiroshima and Nagasaki that caused the destruction of both cities and a total of some 200,000 deaths. Kyoto was on the nuclear target list but somehow was removed. Many think that US Secretary of War Henry L. Stimson interceded with President Harry S. Truman to spare the ancient Japanese capital from atomic holocaust because of its non-military function and its host of historic structures and shrines. Indeed, today Kyoto is the renowned tourism destination for those wishing to glimpse ancient Japan's built environment, more so than many other Japanese cities. The city has seventeen sites dating from the tenth to the nineteenth centuries included on UNESCO's World Heritage List. One is the Rokuon-ji (Deer Garden Temple), also called Kinkaku-ji (Temple of the Golden Pavilion), the subject of countless tourist images and souvenirs, from refrigerator magnets to an N-scale hobby kit.

The Golden Pavilion dates from after 1397, when this site was acquired by Shogun Ashikaga Yoshimitsu, who constructed a large villa complex along with Buddhist shrines, one of which is the pavilion. The mostly cypress pavilion is situated on a pond within a large garden of the Muromachi period (1338–1573). The second and especially third floors of its three-storey, 12.5-m (41-ft) high frame have been linked to Zen Buddhist shrines and Chinese pagodas. The first stage features elements of earlier medieval Japanese residential architecture, suggesting to some that the pavilion may have been a remodelling. The gilt wooden construction projects a distinctive appearance and water reflection within its natural setting. A small dock was supposedly used for fishing. The pavilion's overall appearance served as a prototype for the tiny Ginkaku-ji (Silver Pavilion Temple; 1490), also in Kyoto.

The Golden Pavilion survived the Onin War (1467–77), which destroyed many of the buildings nearby. It was also spared from war damage in the 1940s through the removal of Kyoto from the atomic bombing target list. But on 2 July 1950, it was destroyed in a fire set by a disturbed novice monk, Hayashi Yoken. He then attempted suicide, but survived and was prosecuted, serving a prison sentence. The Golden Pavilion was rebuilt in 1955 based, in part, on vintage photographs as well as survey drawings made during a restoration conducted in 1906. Its essentially crisp appearance today is surprising but presents a reminder of what it may well have looked like in late medieval Japan.

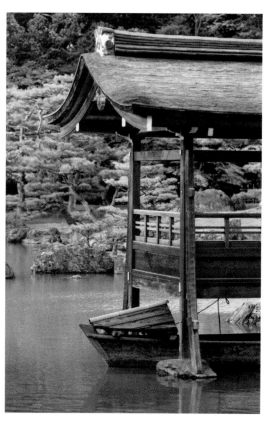

WAR MEMORIAL

Unveiled in 1955, Ryozen Kannon in Kyoto is a memorial to the Japanese casualties from World War II (1939–45). Choun Yamazaki and Hirosuke Ishikawa created this 24-m (80-ft) high concrete Buddha. A memorial hall holds Japan's Tomb of the Unknown Soldier and memorial tablets that commemorate the 2 million Japanese who died during the war. In addition, there is a memorial to the 48,000 foreign soldiers who died in the Pacific theatre.

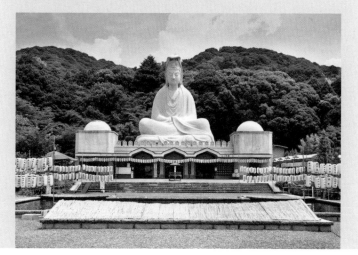

ABOVE LEFT The phoenix is a symbol of rebirth. It is appropriate here since the original building was destroyed in a 1950 fire, but was rebuilt in 1955.

ABOVE RIGHT The small covered pier on the west side of the pavilion's ground floor is said to have been a fishing porch. Today it provides convenient waterside access for a tiny dinghy.

TOP FLOOR

The gilt curved pavilion roofs have been associated with Chinese pagoda architecture and Zen Buddhist temples, particularly when the uppermost level was occupied. This ensemble may have been a Zen priest's quarters. The floor of the room is lower than that of the surrounding veranda, suggesting a structural support role for the surrounding lower roofline.

MIDDLE FLOOR

The L-shaped structure allows also for a large porch facing south, as on the floor below. The little structure here functioned as a religious space, with an altar inside that probably housed a statue of Buddha. The room had decorative paintings of clouds and birds, but these are not shown in the reconstruction.

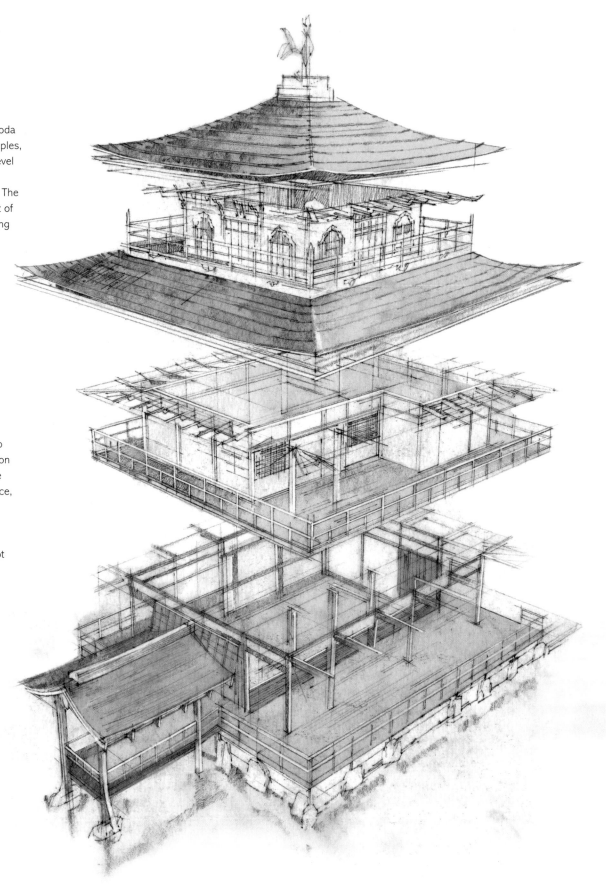

◄ GROUND FLOOR

The view from the southwest shows
the small fishing porch. This main floor is
unfinished cypress, contrasted with the gilt
structure above. It has a generous porch
on the south side. The veranda floor that
surrounds the offset main-floor structure
is lower than that of the interior space.
Creating south-facing porches on Japanese
homes dates to the Heian era (794–1185).

▲ ROOFTOP HOME

The pagoda-like roof has a double-storey space
within, generously lit and ventilated with large
windows. The roof is shingled and has an intricate
structure underneath. The elaborate details on this
level contrast with the greater simplicity of levels
below. Drawings of the details of this level were
included within early surveys such as *Japanese
Architecture: A Short History* (1941) by the
pioneering Japanologist A. L. Sadler.

Florence Cathedral

LOCATION Florence, Italy
ARCHITECT Arnolfo di Cambio (nave), Giotto di Bondone (bell tower), Francesco Talenti (apse), Filippo Brunelleschi (dome)
STYLE Gothic and Early Renaissance
BUILT 1296–1461

It seems that Italy never quite understood the concept of Gothic architecture. Examples were either over-the-top wedding cakes such as Milan Cathedral (1386 and after) or hybrid attempts to combine the structural members of Gothic with the masonry reassurance of Romanesque, all with surface decorations akin to Byzantine architecture.

This emphasis on wall surface over wall penetration may have something to do with the heat of the Tuscan summers, as opposed to the dark coldness of northern European winters. Whatever the reason, it is what one sees in the nave of the cathedral designed by Arnolfo di Cambio (*c.* 1240–*c.* 1310) and its bell tower by Giotto di Bondone (*c.* 1270–1337) in early Renaissance Florence.

Arnolfo was a sculptor and architect who apprenticed with sculptor Nicola Pisano in Pisa. Arnolfo's best-known work with Pisano is the pulpit (1265–68) for Siena Cathedral (1348). Arnolfo's sculptural style has been characterized as classical, blocky and planar with Roman overtones, which certainly comes across in the nave of the Cathedral of Santa Maria del Fiore in Florence, the Duomo di Firenze. The cathedral replaced an earlier one dedicated to St Reparata, with most of its construction occurring in the eighth and ninth centuries, with eleventh-century additions. Although the detached octagonal baptistery from 1128 was spared demolition, this smaller, older cathedral needed to be replaced. It was almost 58.5 m (192 ft) long whereas the length of the new cathedral is almost 153 m (502 ft).

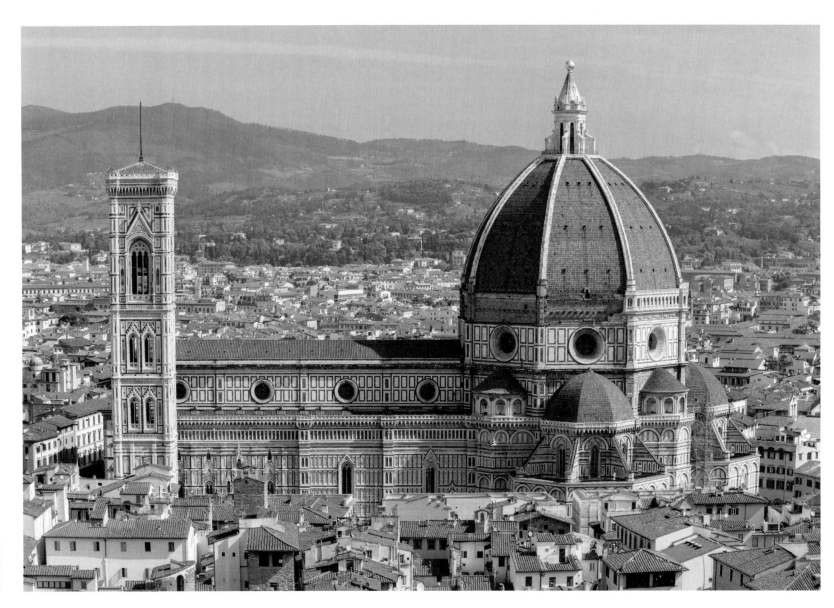

The current basilica's cornerstone was laid on 9 September 1296. As expected, the nave favours more wall than glass, and building materials are polychromatic stone. Upon Arnolfo's death, the famed painter Giotto continued work on the cathedral after a three-decade stoppage. Giotto's most famous contribution is the bell tower that he designed in 1334, being mostly completed after his own death by sculptor and architect Andrea Pisano (*c.* 1295–*c.* 1348). It stands 84.7 m (278 ft) high and is decorated throughout with sculpted rectilinear panels, the higher levels being finished by architect and sculptor Francesco Talenti (*c.* 1300–69). It was Talenti who enlarged Arnolfo's plan of the cathedral to the east. Other architects such as Giovanni di Lapo Ghini (d.1371) joined in, with the nave completed in 1380 and the cathedral mostly finished in 1418, except for its dome.

To many, the dome designed by Filippo Brunelleschi (1377–1446) and constructed between 1420 and 1436 is what really makes this building. It was the largest in Europe when built, measuring 44 m (144 ft) across and, with its lantern atop, 114 m (374 ft) high. Its height still did not surpass cathedral spires in Salisbury, England, at 123 m (404 ft) from 1330, and Strasbourg, France, at 142 m (466 ft) from 1439.

Brunelleschi created buildings that referenced Roman classicism, such as the arcaded Hospital of the Innocents (1419–45) in Florence. His design for the Florence Cathedral dome won a competition in 1418, supposedly with a large brick model, though there had been plans for a dome since 1357, with the current dome's span and height predetermined in 1367. His proposal's genius lies in its octagonal shape, with an interior supported itself through the curvature of the eight shells. Two spherical vaults were placed one atop the other and connected by bricks, with stones used at the bottoms and lighter bricks above. The bricks were interlocked in a parquet pattern to provide strength. Multiple chain and stone rings mortared around the perimeter reinforced the dome. Brunelleschi intended the exterior exedra, designed in 1439, to buttress the base of the dome. The completed dome's height made it a target to beat for the papacy and Michelangelo (1475–1564) when he designed St Peter's Basilica (1506–1626) in Rome (see p. 270).

ABOVE The interior of the dome has a fresco, *The Last Judgment* (1568–79), painted by Giorgio Vasari and Federico Zuccari, which covers 3,600 sq m (38,750 sq ft).

THE GATES OF PARADISE

The octagonal baptistery of St John lies just west of the cathedral. It is best known for its bronze doors, especially the *Gates of Paradise* (1425–52) series by Lorenzo Ghiberti, who won the commission in a competition in 1401 over the entry by Brunelleschi. Earlier, while serving as cathedral architect, Giotto recommended Andrea Pisano to design the first of the baptistery's bronze doors from 1330 to 1336. These sets of bronze reliefs by Pisano and Ghiberti are among the great masterpieces of Renaissance sculpture.

1 NAVE

Arnolfo di Cambio designed the cathedral's nave, begun in 1296, but it was essentially built by his three successor architects: Giotto, Pisano and Talenti. This cutaway view adjacent to the campanile indicates substantial yet simple wall planes illuminated by oculi, rather than large stained-glass clerestory windows as in French cathedrals of the same era. The four nave bays were built west to east between 1366 and 1380. The crypt of the former cathedral of St Reparata, along with Brunelleschi's tomb, lies under the first two bays on the west. It was excavated in 1973.

2 APSIDAL CHAPELS

Three polygonal apses, each containing five chapels, flank the dome. They were constructed from c. 1380 to 1418. They were pushed eastwards by at least one bay and more from Arnolfo's original design when Talenti became the cathedral architect. The domical apses and adjacent domed exedra help support the drum and, in turn, the dome.

3 CAMPANILE

Giotto designed the cathedral's campanile, or bell tower (1334), which was completed after his death; the very top was by Talenti. Giotto's original drawing housed in the cathedral museum shows it as having a more pointed Gothic spire, but Talenti finished it with a more rectilinear, panelled design. The tall, multistorey spaces at various stair landings have groin-vaulted ceilings.

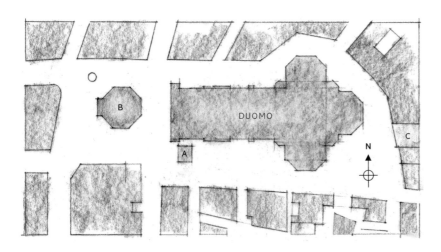

SITE PLAN

This plan of the cathedral plaza gives an idea of the building's east–west orientation in its urban environment relative to other structures of the complex, such as the campanile (A) and baptistery (B). Treasures from the cathedral are within the church itself but are also on exhibit and as in storage in the recently renovated Opera Duomo Museum (C) east of the cathedral. The 6,770 sq m (72,870 sq ft) museum was renovated in 2015 by firms Natalini Architetti and Guicciardini and Magni.

BAPTISTERY

The baptistery of St John just west of the cathedral's entry facade dates from 1128. It is an octagon built of Carrara and green marble, with a pyramidal roof. Inside the roof is a spectacular dome mosaic from the thirteenth century.

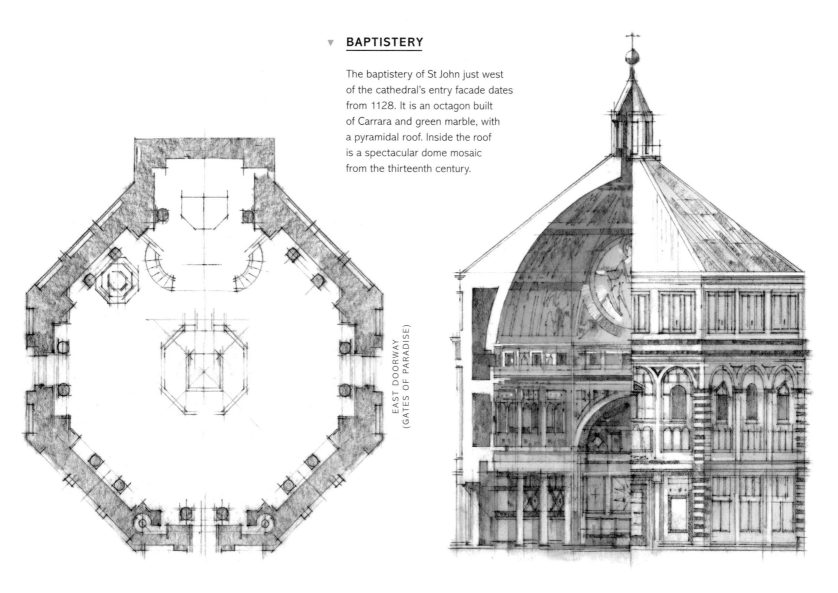

EAST DOORWAY
(GATES OF PARADISE)

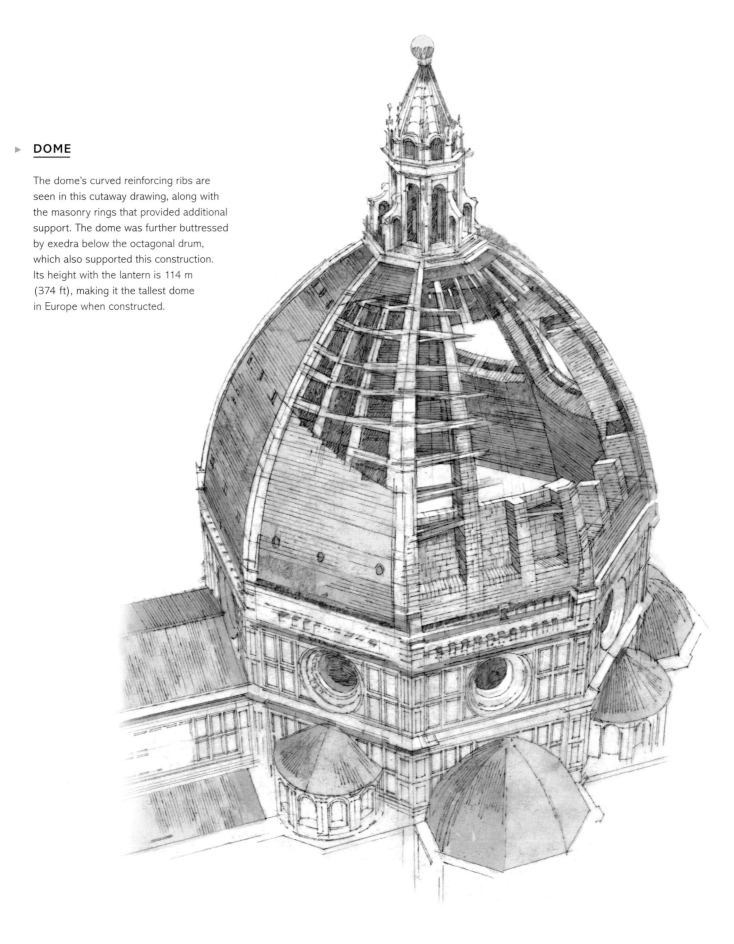

▶ DOME

The dome's curved reinforcing ribs are seen in this cutaway drawing, along with the masonry rings that provided additional support. The dome was further buttressed by exedra below the octagonal drum, which also supported this construction. Its height with the lantern is 114 m (374 ft), making it the tallest dome in Europe when constructed.

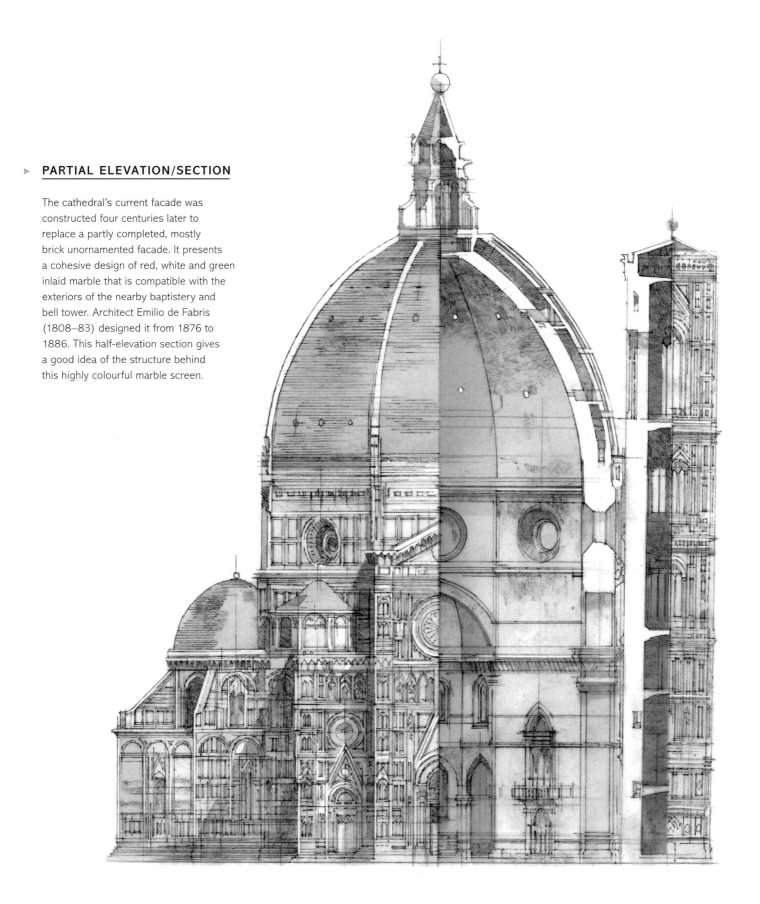

► PARTIAL ELEVATION/SECTION

The cathedral's current facade was
constructed four centuries later to
replace a partly completed, mostly
brick unornamented facade. It presents
a cohesive design of red, white and green
inlaid marble that is compatible with the
exteriors of the nearby baptistery and
bell tower. Architect Emilio de Fabris
(1808–83) designed it from 1876 to
1886. This half-elevation section gives
a good idea of the structure behind
this highly colourful marble screen.

Batalha Monastery

LOCATION   Batalha, Portugal
ARCHITECT   Afonso Domingues and others
STYLE   Late Gothic
BUILT   1386–1533

Batalha's Monastery was built to commemorate the Battle of Aljubarrota, fought between Portugal and Castile on 14 August 1385. King John I of Portugal's army, with English support through his wife, Philippa of Lancaster, successfully battled the army of King John I of Castile, which was reinforced by a host of troops from Italy and France. The battle, in some ways part of the ongoing Hundred Years' War (1337–1453) between England and France, demonstrated the success of English defensive tactics and archery against French cavalry despite the smaller force of the defenders, the Portuguese being outnumbered by five men to one. The battle ensured Portugal's independence from Spain. In thanks for this victory, the Portuguese king founded the town of Batalha, meaning 'battle', and the Monastery of St Mary of the Victory of Batalha in 1386, some 18 km (11 miles) north of the battleground.

Afonso Domingues (d.1402) planned the monastery and worked on it from 1388 until his death. His planning and design details were influenced by English style and precedents, especially the rectilinear screen facade and centrally planned chapter house off the cloister. Architect David Huguet (1416–38) succeeded him until his own death. He is credited with the nave vaults at more than 32.3 m (106 ft) high, the plan of the unfinished eastern chapels, or *Capelas Imperfeitas*, parts of the cloister including the dome of the chapter house, and the founder's chapel. This last

is a spectacularly vaulted gem from 1426 that includes the ornate tombs of King John and Queen Philippa. The tombs of various princes and their spouses are in the ambulatory at the perimeter.

Works continued under other architects. A second cloister farther from the monastery was added by Fernão d'Évora between 1448 and 1477. Mateus Fernandes the Elder (d.1515) designed the elaborate portal to the unfinished chapels from *c.* 1503 to 1509, with João de Castilho (1470–1552) continuing work on that, and Miguel de Arruda (d.1563) creating their balcony after 1533. However, they were the last. The church remains unfinished because Portuguese rulers such as King Manuel I and King John III diverted

funds to other sites including the Jerónimos Monastery (1495–1601) at Belém outside Lisbon (now part of the National Maritime and Archaeology Museums). The ornate Late Gothic style of that building has often been called Manueline, after King Manuel, and comparable details from the sixteenth century can also be seen in Batalha. Some speculate that exuberant, even outlandish detailing in sixteenth-century Gothic, from King's College Chapel (1515) in Cambridge, England, through the Frauenkirche (1515–20) chapel vaults in Ingolstadt, Germany, heralded the end of the Gothic era as many nations shifted their tastes to simpler Italian Renaissance architecture or their own regional variants of that style.

The monastery at Batalha was damaged in 1810 during the Napoleonic Wars (1803–15) and then abandoned after 1834 with the country's dissolution of the monasteries. King Ferdinand II, upset at the decaying monument, pressured the government to commit to its restoration, which it did in 1840. Work continued through the nineteenth century, with a focus on the monastery and cloisters from the fifteenth and sixteenth centuries and removal or demolition of a number of adjacent structures that had changed the context of this major monument, a museum since 1980. The former chapter house today contains Portugal's Tomb of the Unknown Soldier, whose remains were brought from Flanders and Portuguese Africa in 1921.

ABOVE LEFT The Royal Cloister, part of the original plan by Afonso Domingues, includes this vaulted gemlike fountain room at the northwest corner.

ABOVE RIGHT The second architect, Huguet, raised the vaults of the narrow nave and choir between 1402 and 1438 to its current height of more than 32.3 m (106 ft).

BATTLE OF ALJUBARROTA

The Battle of Aljubarrota between Portuguese and Spanish armies and their allies has been memorialized in manuscript illuminations. The battle is legendary because it secured Portugal's independence from Spain. It also was one of several battles in which English tactics and archers defeated a superior force. In some ways, it prefigured the English victory over France at the Battle of Agincourt in 1415.

CAPELAS IMPERFEITAS

Beyond the fourteenth-century church's apse stand
the *Capelas Imperfeitas* (Unfinished Chapels), likely
begun in 1434 or after by Huguet and continued by
Fernandes in the early sixteenth century. They were
intended by King Edward to be his funerary pantheon
equal to that of the founder's chapel. These incomplete
chapels are the most memorable of the constructions
because they appear to be an oversized planned
ruin, yet they were never completed, though later
kings continued the work. Reconstructions show the
proposed cappings of the chapels with slender towers.

1 CLOISTERS

There were three cloisters at the monastery.
The first, on the right, is the Royal Cloister adjacent
to the church designed by Domingues and completed
by others, including Fernandes and Diogo Boitac, who
executed the tracery within the arcades. This cloister
also has the monastery's chapter house off the eastern
wing, shown in this cutaway. The centrally planned
chapter house, likely finished by Martim Vasques
(1235–1335), was influenced by English precedents.
The cloister shown to the left, or north, of the Royal
Cloister is the double-storey Cloister of King Afonso V,
designed by Fernão d'Évora between 1448 and 1477.
The third cloister, adjoining this one to the east, was
destroyed in 1810 by French troops.

2 NAVE

The nave has been compared to fourteenth-century designs at York Minster (1230–1472) in England. The monastery's squared-off west facade, octagonal east end chapels and centrally planned chapter house and founder's chapel have English rather than French associations. Historians have likened the founder's chapel to the chapter house of Old St Paul's (1332) in London by William Ramsey (d.1349). The plan for the Unfinished Chapels may relate to the octagon at Ely Cathedral (after 1322) by Alan of Walsingham (d. c. 1364) and master carpenter William Hurley.

3 FOUNDER'S CHAPEL

The chapel, reminiscent of polygonal English chapter houses, is the pantheon of Portuguese royalty. It was an addition by King John I, and the creation of David Huguet, between 1433 and 1434. The plan morphs from a square into an octagon with a ribbed vault that encompasses the space for the tombs of the king and his wife. There are tombs within and adjacent to the entry for their children. Additional architectural tombs were created for the founder's heirs in the early twentieth century.

St Peter's Basilica

LOCATION Vatican, Rome, Italy
ARCHITECT Michelangelo and others
STYLE High Renaissance and Baroque
BUILT 1506–1626

Viewers are often amazed at the scale of the complex of St Peter's Basilica, especially during papal appearances. The square can hold some 250,000 visitors, giving credence to statements that it is one of the world's largest religious sites. A review of the architects who created this remarkable construction might lead some to say that it was designed by committee, but a committee of the 'A-list' architects and artists of the Italian Renaissance.

The elaborate Renaissance and Baroque construction of today was built on the site of the smaller Early Christian style Old St Peter's Basilica (326–333 CE), constructed by the Emperor Constantine at the site of the tomb of St Peter after his martyrdom under Emperor Nero in 64 CE. The new building replacing it was begun in 1506 and completed in 1626. St Peter's tomb as well as papal tombs and shrines are on a grotto level between the archaeological remains of the Constantinian church and the current Renaissance–Baroque one. Depictions of St Peter's Basilica in the nineteenth century show it as one of the largest buildings in the world, its dome reaching a height of 136.6 m (448 ft). The massive, mostly marble construction below occupies a footprint some 220.5 m (730 ft) long and 152.4 m (500 ft) wide. Services inside are sometimes attended by tens of thousands of people. The scale and elaborate classical imagery throughout was a tangible expression of the Counter-Reformation

(1545–1648), which attempted to reassert papal authority and the importance of Catholic theology. The movement acted as a direct response to the expansion of Protestantism, which culminated in the Thirty Years' War (1618–48).

The new basilica was initially planned for expansion in the fifteenth century by Leon Battista Alberti (1404–72) and Bernardo Rossellino (1409–64) for Pope Nicholas V. Little was accomplished until Pope Julius II decreed the demolition of the old church in 1505 and staged a competition that was won by Donato Bramante (1444–1514). He created a Greek cross plan for the new church with a dome similar to that of the Roman Pantheon (18–128 CE). After Julius's death in 1513 others were hired, including painter Raphael (1483–1520), who changed the plan to a Latin cross variant. With the Sack of Rome in 1527, political problems, and structural problems with earlier foundation work, Pope Paul III appointed Michelangelo (1475–1564) in 1547. Michelangelo solved the existing structural problems, returned the church plan back to a Greek cross variant of Bramante's plan, redesigned the dome to rival that of Florence Cathedral (1296–1461; see p. 260) and continued construction. Much of what is seen today is his design. With the death of Michelangelo, Giacomo della Porta (c. 1533–1602) and Domenico Fontana (1543–1607) completed the dome in 1590. Later additions made the complex what it is today. They include the nave extension and atrium facade (1608–12) by Baroque architect Carlo Maderno (1556–1629), as well as the baldachin under the dome (1623–33) and St Peter's Square (1655–67), both by Baroque master Gian Lorenzo Bernini (1598–1680).

St Peter's has had a version of an architectural committee to care for its physical fabric since 1523, though the focus was not exclusively on architectural repairs until the early twentieth century. Pope John Paul II created a successor committee in 1988 to care for, repair and maintain the building as well as regulate the behaviour of church employees, visitors and pilgrims. Later work included a $5 million restoration and cleaning of the facade in 1999.

LEFT The dome decorations are not frescoes but mosaics. Most were designed by Giuseppe Cesari and executed by various mosaic artists.

BELOW The elaborate bronze baldachin executed between 1624 and 1633 by Bernini is approximately 29.3 m (96 ft) high and weighs some 45,500 kg (100,000 pounds).

MICHELANGELO

Michelangelo, or Michelangelo di Lodovico Buonarroti Simoni, is arguably the greatest among great Italian artists, his rival being Leonardo da Vinci. Apprenticed with artists, the Florentine-raised Michelangelo created some of the most lauded sculptures of the Italian Renaissance such as the *Pietà* (1498–99) and *David* (1501–04). His painted masterpiece is the ceiling of the Vatican's Sistine Chapel (1508–12), which includes 300 monumental figures and covers more than 460 sq m (5,000 sq ft). Architecturally, he also created the funerary chapel for the Medicis within Florence's San Lorenzo (1521–24 and later).

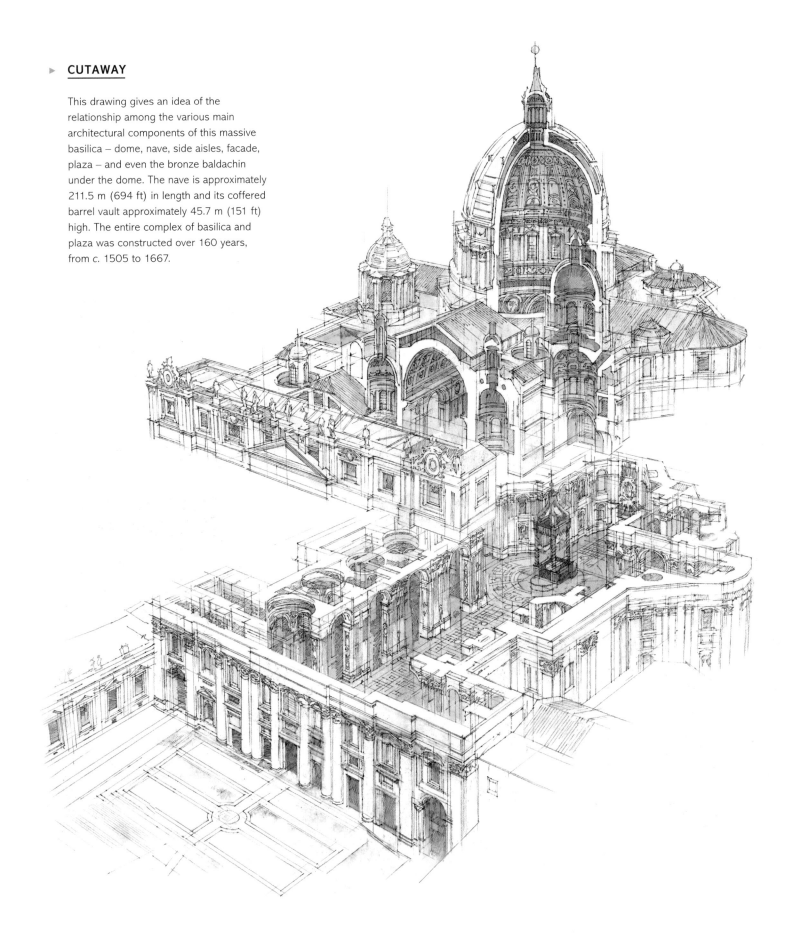

► **CUTAWAY**

This drawing gives an idea of the
relationship among the various main
architectural components of this massive
basilica – dome, nave, side aisles, facade,
plaza – and even the bronze baldachin
under the dome. The nave is approximately
211.5 m (694 ft) in length and its coffered
barrel vault approximately 45.7 m (151 ft)
high. The entire complex of basilica and
plaza was constructed over 160 years,
from *c.* 1505 to 1667.

DOME

The dome was intended to rival that at Florence Cathedral (see p. 260). Michelangelo designed it in 1547 and it was finished in 1590 by della Porta and Fontana. It rises to a total height of 136.6 m (448 ft) from the floor of the basilica to the cross atop its lantern; it is the tallest dome in the world. Like Florence's great dome, this one is constructed with a brick double shell and a sixteen-rib stone structure.

BALDACHIN

The gilt-bronze baldachin designed by Bernini was based on the ciborium, a small, shrinelike cover for the host used in the Eucharist. It was also inspired by the canopy carried over the pope. The twisting columns harken back to those at the biblical Temple in Jerusalem. The structure includes gold-leaf bee symbols, the emblem of Pope Urban VIII.

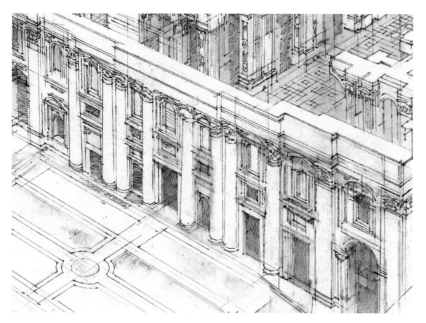

FACADE

Maderno designed the facade between 1608 and 1615. More than 700 workers constructed it of travertine, its dimensions being 114.6 m wide by 45.4 m high (376 × 149 ft high). Immediately behind the facade is a barrel-vaulted narthex. It acts as a vestibule for the basilica.

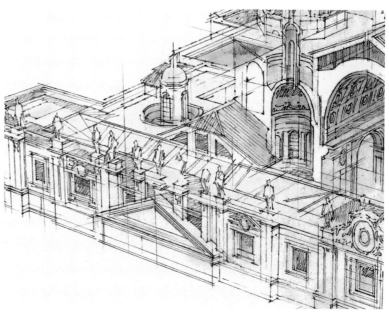

SCULPTURES

There are a vast number of decorations and sculptures at St Peter's. Even above the entry Maderno placed a series of thirteen works depicting Christ, St John the Baptist and eleven apostles. St Peter's statue is near the main entry below. The pedimental inscription honours Pope Paul V.

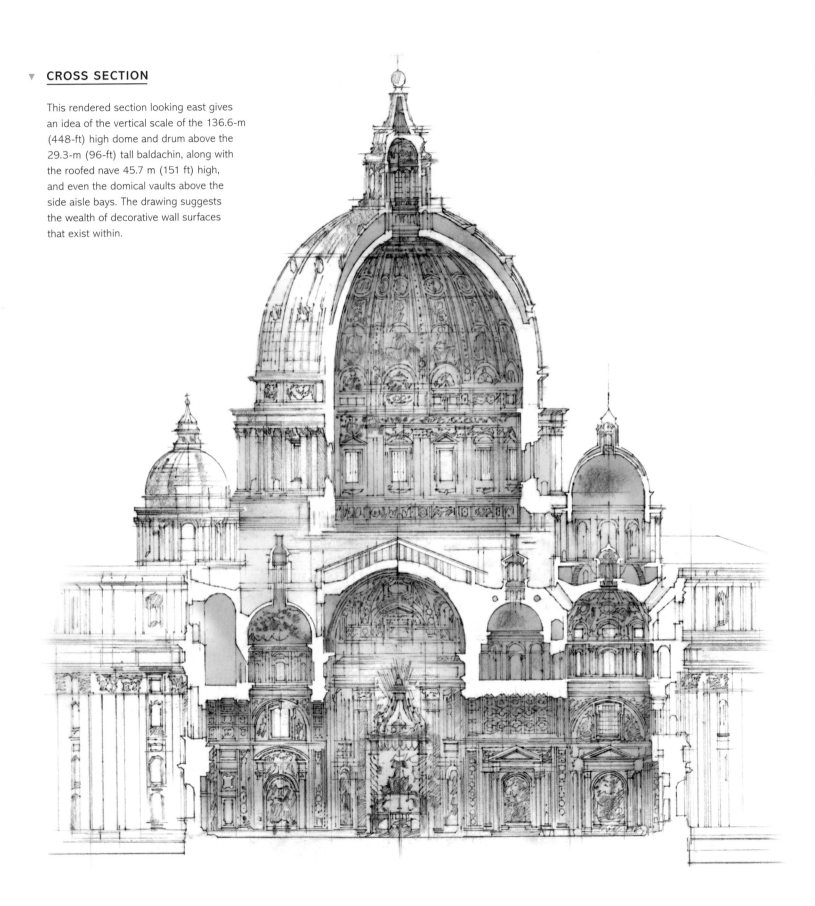

CROSS SECTION

This rendered section looking east gives an idea of the vertical scale of the 136.6-m (448-ft) high dome and drum above the 29.3-m (96-ft) tall baldachin, along with the roofed nave 45.7 m (151 ft) high, and even the domical vaults above the side aisle bays. The drawing suggests the wealth of decorative wall surfaces that exist within.

LONGITUDINAL SECTION AND FLOOR PLAN

This drawing illustrates the relationship between St Peter's and the massive square at the entry to the basilica. The latter measures 339.8 m long by 239.8 m wide (1,115 × 787 ft). Bernini designed it from 1656 to 1667. Its curved shape has been likened to the welcoming arms of the Catholic Church. The site includes the reuse of an Egyptian obelisk that was said to have been connected with St Peter's crucifixion. The obelisk is one of several that were transferred to Rome as trophies. It is almost 25.5 m (84 ft) high and weighs 326 tonnes (359 tons). It took more than a year to bring it to this site.

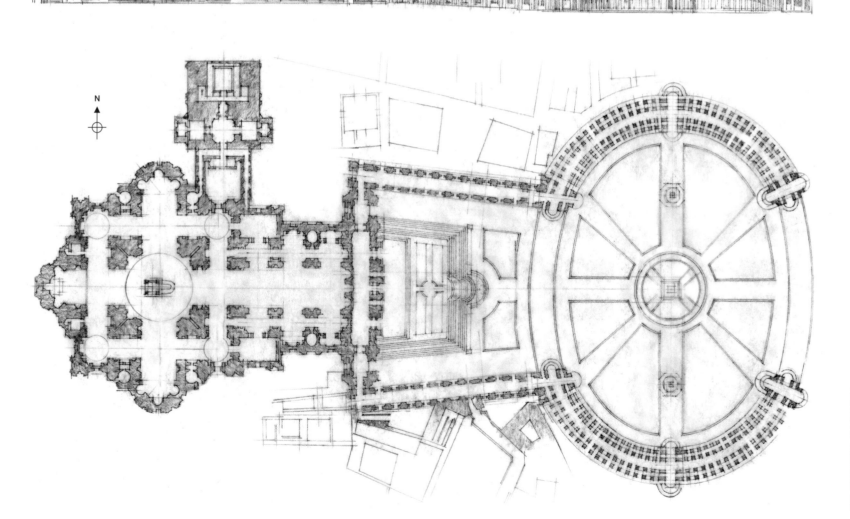

N

St Paul's Cathedral

St Paul's Cathedral sits in the heart of the City of London, the main business and banking district. Its prominence is considered so vital that the planning system protects views to the cathedral when any new development is proposed. Built in its present form between 1675 and 1711, it was commissioned after its predecessor was destroyed in the Great Fire of London in 1666. Its architect, Christopher Wren (1632–1723), who had been appointed to work on the previous church before the fire, set out to design a new cathedral. He also designed a large number of city churches, such as St Mary Aldermary (1679–82) and St Stephen Walbrook (1672–79), and created much of the character of that part of London. St Paul's was unique among British cathedrals at the time for having been designed by a single architect and completed in his lifetime.

LOCATION London, United Kingdom
ARCHITECT Christopher Wren
STYLE English Baroque
BUILT 1675–1720

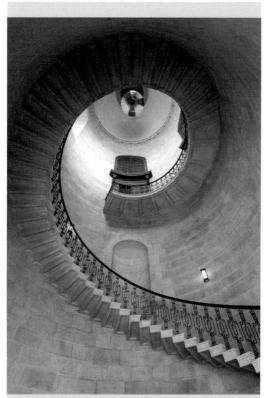

Wren's first design was in the form of a Greek cross, with four equal arms, but this plan was rejected by the ecclesiastical authorities. A second design, substantially as built today, was then accepted. This design, in the form of a cross with a dome at the centre, above where the two arms meet, was the first of its kind in England, and there are still no comparable buildings anywhere in the country. Wren had been inspired by the architecture of Andrea Palladio, but married it with some of the traditions of English church building.

The cathedral was erected in stages, with walls of Portland stone; the design of the dome was the last to be settled, although it was intended to be the crowning achievement. Wren faced two problems in his design, one aesthetic and the other technical. He wanted the dome to tower over London, but this tall dome, while impressive from the outside, would be too steep from the inside. The answer was to create a double dome, with a profile on the inside different from that on the outside. Instead, this became the world's first triple dome, with a hidden brick interior dome supporting both the external timber dome and the stone lantern.

In this way, Wren was able to reduce the weight of the dome, which was essential, because the foundations of the previous building on the same site were beginning to subside.

Other important features of the cathedral include the majestic portico on the west front, with its twin towers, and the richly decorated interior decorated with sculpture, elaborate metalwork and mosaics. Both Horatio Nelson and Arthur Wellesley, 1st Duke of Wellington, are buried there, and there are numerous memorials, including one deciated to Wren, whose epitaph reads: *Si monumentum requiris, circumspice* ('If you seek his monument, look around').

St Paul's Cathedral has continued to play a significant role in the life of the nation. It became a symbol of hope in World War II (1939–45), surviving (rather fortuitously) the destruction that occurred around it during the Blitz, the sustained program of bombing carried out by the German Luftwaffe (air force). Although it is one of the least English of buildings in terms of design, St Paul's has found a place at the heart of the British establishment.

GEOMETRIC STAIRCASE

The Geometric Staircase in the southwest tower, also known as the Dean's Stair, is one of the longest examples of a staircase type that fascinated Renaissance architects. Built in 1705, it links the cathedral floor to the triforium. It has no central support and appears to cantilever out from the supporting wall (these are often described as cantilever stairs), although most of the load bearing is done by the weight of one stair atop the one below. There are two flights, the upper of which consists of eighty-eight steps with no intermediate landing.

▼ ISOMETRIC CUTAWAY

St Paul's Cathedral is built on London clay, not the best foundation for a heavy structure. Its crypt – the largest in Europe – was designed to house the massive columns that support the more slender columns above, helping to spread the load. Eight piers support the dome (two on each side), whereas most domes have only four supports. This was an attempt to spread the load widely. The low-pitched roofs are designed to be hidden by the parapets when the building is viewed from ground level.

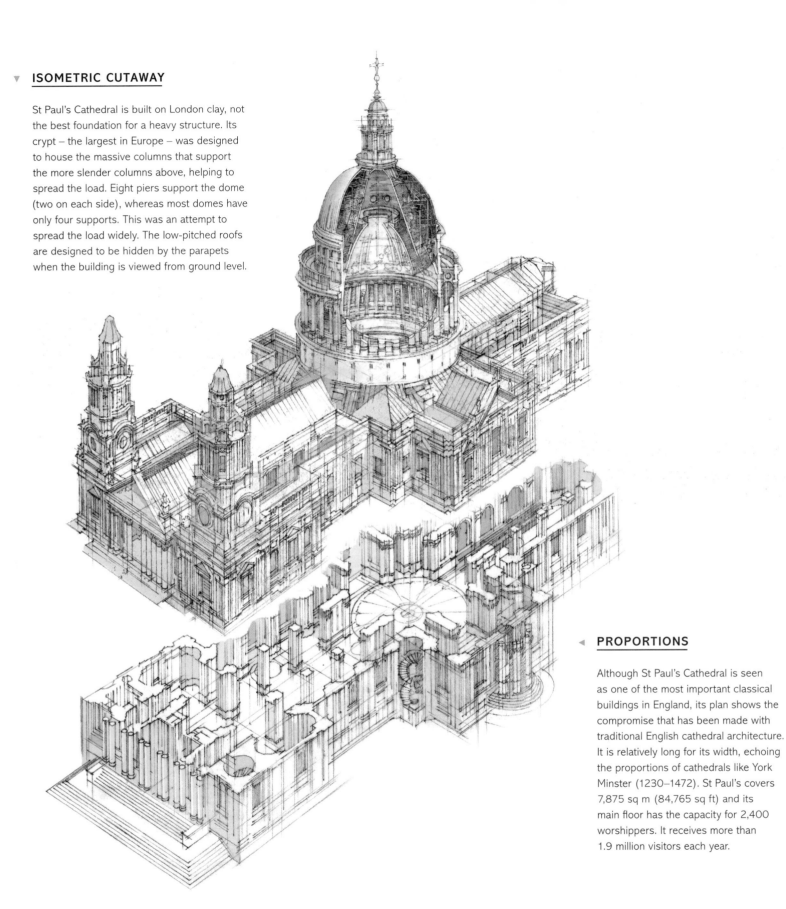

◄ PROPORTIONS

Although St Paul's Cathedral is seen as one of the most important classical buildings in England, its plan shows the compromise that has been made with traditional English cathedral architecture. It is relatively long for its width, echoing the proportions of cathedrals like York Minster (1230–1472). St Paul's covers 7,875 sq m (84,765 sq ft) and its main floor has the capacity for 2,400 worshippers. It receives more than 1.9 million visitors each year.

▶ CROSS SECTION

This section shows the triple form of the dome, an innovation that allowed Wren to reduce weight while still providing very different profiles inside and out. There is a gallery at the top of the inner dome, although it is no longer accessible to the public. Artist James Thornhill decorated the inside of the dome, painting it with false coffering, which gives a very impressive trompe-l'oeil impression of depth. The triple dome enabled Wren to capture the building height record for London at 111.3 m (365 ft) until 1963, when the Millbank Tower, 118 m (387 ft) high, designed by Ronald Ward and Partners, was constructed.

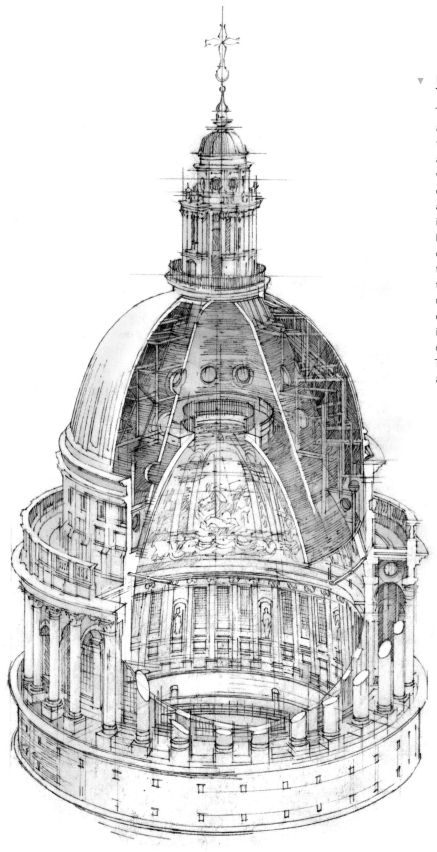

DOME CUTAWAY

The dome of St Paul's rises to 111.3 m (365 ft) at the upper tip of the cross on its summit. In order to save weight, there is a thin, inner dome of brick and an outer dome of timber covered in lead. But Wren was determined to have a stone lantern on top of the dome, and a timber structure would not have been able to support it. So he built the conical masonry inner dome, directly supporting the lantern and hidden from the view of everyone except people climbing the stairs, who pass between this dome and the outer dome. In order to resist the 'hoop stresses' that would try to push this conical dome outwards under the load that it supported, Wren embedded chains within bands of stone, the largest of which is known as the Great Chain, which is near the base of the dome. The rest of the cone is built of brick. There is an oculus at the top of the inner dome, which allows light into the space below.

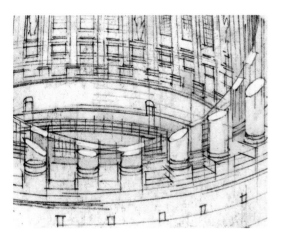

WHISPERING GALLERY

Visitors climbing the dome of St Paul's first reach the Whispering Gallery, an internal space at the base of the inner dome, after ascending 259 steps. It acquired its name because of an acoustic quirk; if a person says something quietly on one side of the gallery, it can be heard on the other side.

STONE GALLERY

The Stone Gallery is the first of two external galleries, sitting at the base of the external dome. It is reached by 378 steps and is at a height of 53.4 m (173 ft) above ground level. As well as the views it offers over London, it is a good vantage point from which to admire the outer dome close up.

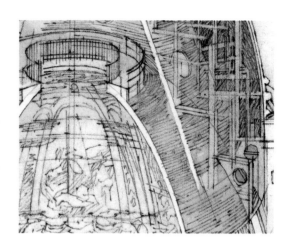

INNER BRICK DOME

The inner dome is roughly hemispherical and just 46 cm (18 in.) thick – the length of two standard bricks. Special bricks were made, whose length was equivalent to the thickness of the dome, to help hold the structure together. Wren did not approve of the decoration to the interior of the dome.

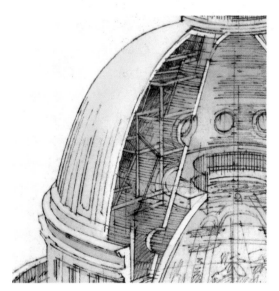

TIMBER OUTER DOME

Wren reworked the magnificent outer dome of St Paul's in order to get it exactly as he wished it to be. He built several detailed scale models and worked closely with mathematician Robert Hooke on various mechanical theories that could not be entirely proved, but which were tested on a trial-and-error basis. The result was a dome with a difference and a prominent landmark.

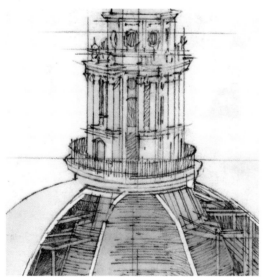

GOLDEN GALLERY

The Golden Gallery is the highest point that visitors can reach today at 528 steps or almost 85.4 m (280 ft) above the floor. It is a small external viewing platform at the top of the outer dome and offers a magnificent vista over London. The stairs to reach it pass through the space between the outer and central domes. Just before going out onto the gallery, visitors can look through an oculus down to the floor of the cathedral.

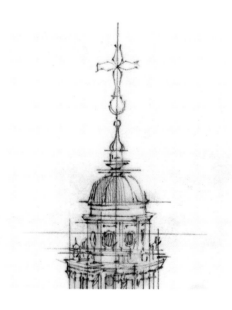

THE BALL AND LANTERN

The original ball and cross were erected by Andrew Niblett, Citizen and Armourer of London, in 1708. They were replaced in 1821 by a new ball and cross designed by the Surveyor to the Fabric, C. R. Cockerell, and executed by R. and E. Kepp. When Wren designed the lantern, he had no plans to glaze it; the glass was added sometime later, after it was found that water was dripping into the building.

Notre-Dame-du-Haut Chapel

LOCATION Ronchamp, France
ARCHITECT Le Corbusier
STYLE Organic Modern
BUILT 1950–54

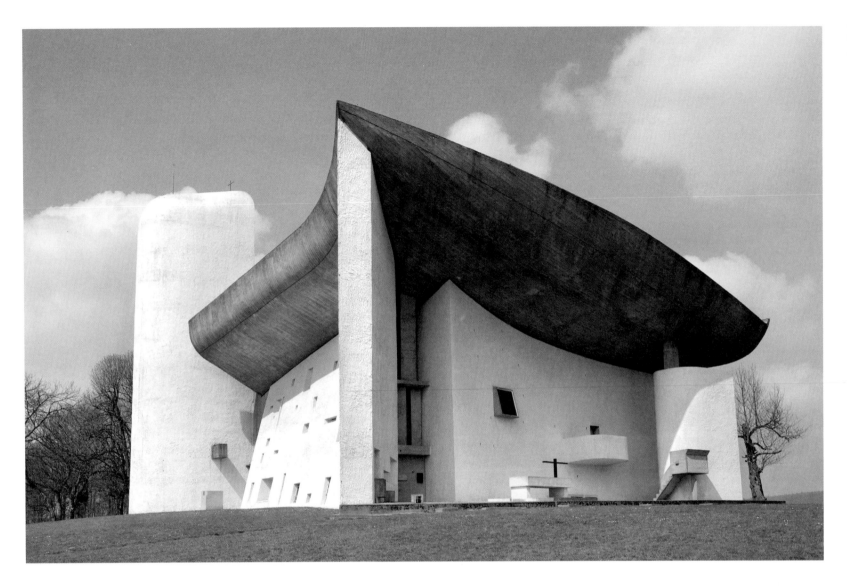

The summer of 1944 marked the invasions of France on 6 June with Operation Overlord, known as D-Day, in Normandy, and Operation Dragoon near Marseille on 15 August. Over the next few months Allied armies pushed the German Wehrmacht (army) to Germany's borders, but not without considerable casualties and effort. In Ronchamp, the Germans occupied the earlier Neo-Gothic pilgrimage chapel in September 1944. In the subsequent drive to liberate Champagney east of Ronchamp, the 1st Free French Division, supported by Algerian and colonial French troops, pushed the

Germans eastwards from October to November 1944. The church at Ronchamp remained, in effect, a ruin by the end of this operation.

The immediate postwar period saw the removal of church officials in the region who collaborated with the pro-German Vichy government. Plans were made to provide Ronchamp with a new chapel, an initial proposal in 1949 being a traditionally styled one by architect Jean-Charles Moreux (1889–1956). At the same time this was being discussed, Le Corbusier (1887–1965) promoted modern designs for

war-ruined French churches such as that for Saint-Dié Cathedral (1948) in Lorraine to reflect a new, postwar France. This was comparable, in intent, to what Basil Spence (1907–76) did for Coventry Cathedral (1962) in postwar Britain and Egon Eiermann (1904–70) did for West Germany with the Kaiser Wilhelm Memorial Church (1970) in Berlin. As part of a reform movement within the regional church, Dominican priest Father Marie-Alain Couturier, an accomplished artist in modern stained glass, was instrumental in supporting the commission for Le Corbusier's new pilgrimage church at Ronchamp, as well as helping to secure the commission for that architect's Sainte-Marie de La Tourette (1960).

Le Corbusier was inspired for his overall design of 1950, and particularly the distinctive roof, by a crab shell found on a Long Island, New York, beach in 1946 that he had saved on his drafting table. He intended the curved roof and wall forms as a response to the wooded, natural landscape. The walls themselves contain rubble of the ruined church faced with whitewashed gunite over concrete. Punctuated with a variety of rectilinear windows in illuminated stained glass, these thick, tapering walls give the impression of an otherworldly spiritual experience with shafts of light, much as stained glass did within early Gothic cathedrals. A thin clerestory band of light makes the large curved roof appear to float, even though it is supported on concrete columns embedded within the walls. The shape of roof suggests an enormous thickness of some 2.1 m (7 ft) but the concrete shell is hollow, supported by concrete ribs with the entire roof clad in aluminium. Le Corbusier also created an exterior altar space on the east side of the chapel to face an open clearing for pilgrimage services. The northeast open area has a monument dedicated to those who died in 1944 for the liberation of Ronchamp. Here the chapel exterior has a niche for a historic statue of the Virgin Mary salvaged from the original church.

In all, Le Corbusier's individualistic expression at Ronchamp contrasts with the more modular and mechanized approach to some of his designs in concrete. In religious as well as individual architectural pilgrimages, the church witnesses more than 80,000 visitors annually.

In 2014 vandals smashed one of the windows in the church. Although condemned by architects and historians around the world, this act brought to light the landmark's state of preservation and paucity of funds allocated for it, when compared with the much larger monies of over €10 million ($10.8 million) spent in building the nearby convent, visitor centre and hostel in 2011, all designed by Renzo Piano.

ABOVE LEFT Recessed windows, seemingly placed in a haphazard way, provide dramatic bands of light within the organically shaped space.

ABOVE RIGHT Le Corbusier often created painted or enamelled portals within his projects as if they were oversized paintings hung on a concrete wall. This photo shows the main, or south entry, door that pivots on a central shaft.

LE CORBUSIER

Le Corbusier was born Charles-Édouard Jeanneret in La Chaux-de-Fonds, Switzerland. Although not formally trained, he was arguably the most influential architect of the twentieth century. His earliest houses before World War I (1914–18) were blocky, simple, yet historicist. His Parisian move and postwar period there led him to an appreciation of Cubist art as well allowing him to develop his own theories on modern architecture and urbanism. His architectural writings such as *Vers une architecture* (*Towards an Architecture*, 1923) and buildings of the 1920s such as the Villa Savoye (1928–31) in Poissy, on the outskirts of Paris, espoused a cool, purist Modernism that he replaced after World War II (1939–45) with a more organic approach to design.

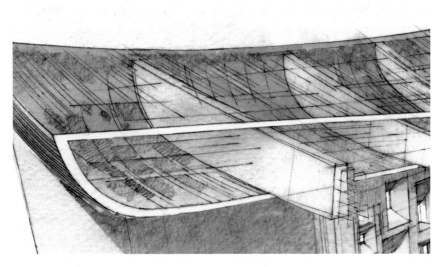

CURVED ROOF

The roof, with its dramatically sweeping curve, projects the image of a massive concrete wave some 2.1 m (7 ft) thick that seems to mystically float above the building because of a thin clerestory band. Yet in reality it is not one solid casting but rather a concrete shell with curved internal ribs, the outside being clad in aluminium. Rainwater drains from the roof through two pipes at the west end of the church. Observers often liken the roof to a nun's habit, but Le Corbusier stated that he was inspired by a crab shell found on a Long Island, New York, beach in 1946.

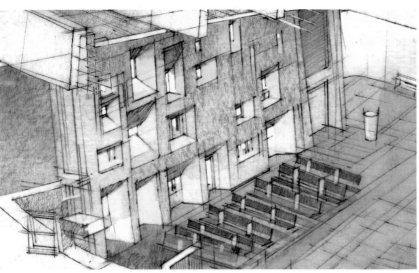

WINDOWS

The south wall, also of hollow construction, is covered in gunite, as is most of the building. It varies in thickness from 1.2 to 3.6 m (4 to 12 ft). The twenty-seven rectilinear windows that puncture the structure offer a random pattern of illumination within the space. The windows are generally clear, although some have coloured highlights. The church seating angles within the organic volume as well. The concrete paved floor slopes down to the altar, following the terrain of the site. Multiple curves within the church space create a three-dimensional organic design experience, and the curved walls are self-buttressed.

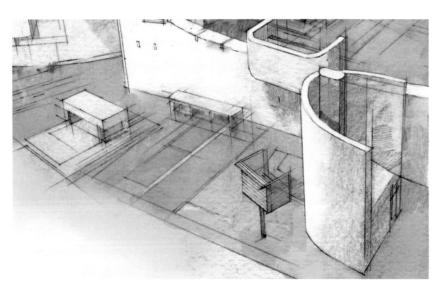

EXTERIOR ALTAR AND PULPIT

The church's main altar is inside at the east end. But there is also an exterior altar as well as a pulpit for outdoor services for larger crowds of pilgrims. Le Corbusier also accommodated, in a niche near the east entry of the outdoor worship space, a polychromed wood statue of the Virgin Mary that was salvaged from the ruined church. The outdoor worship platform also faces towards an open green, with the pyramid of peace designed by Le Corbusier as a memorial to those who died here in the liberation of Ronchamp in October 1944.

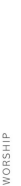

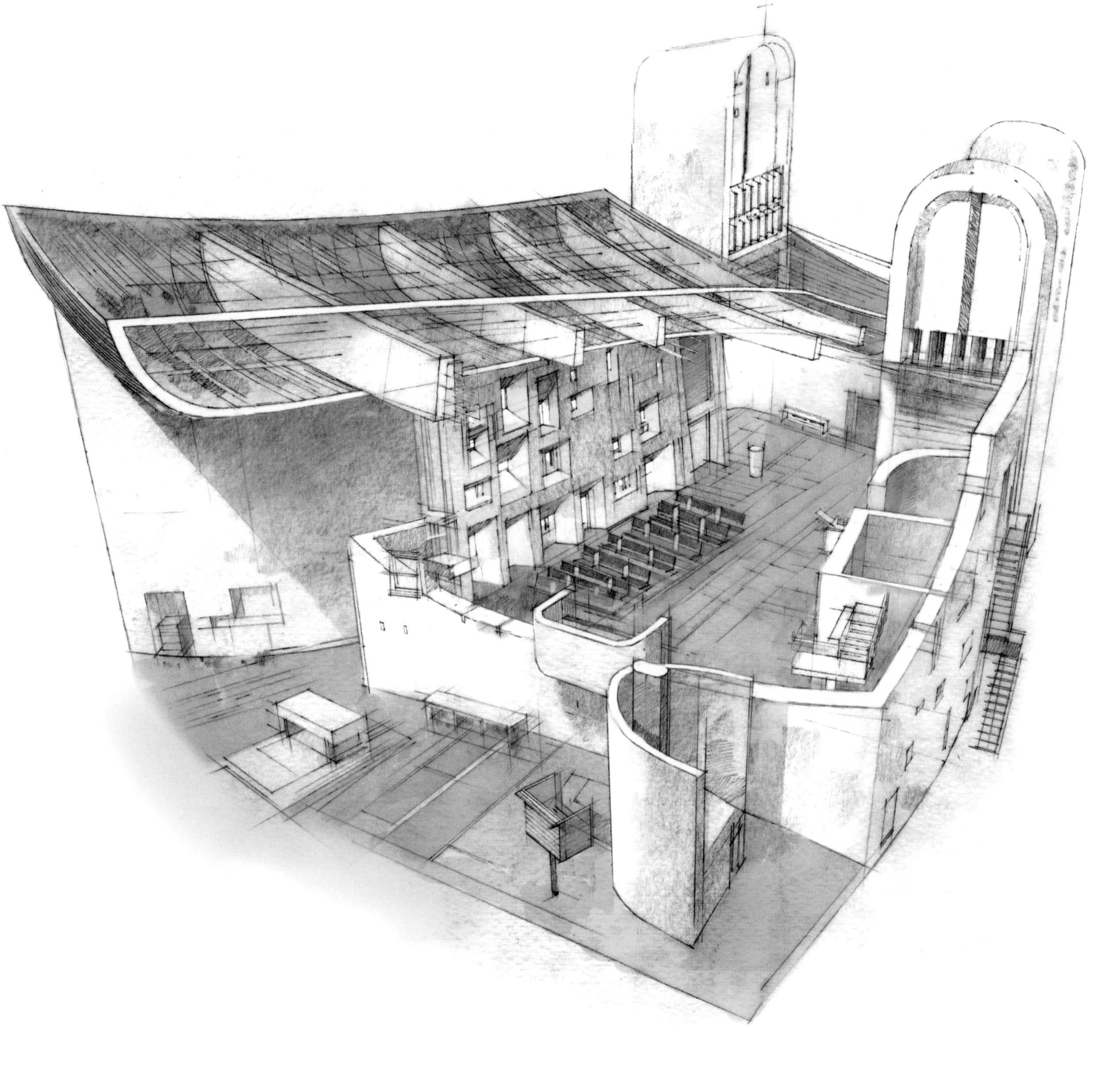

CROSS SECTION

The towers at Ronchamp are up to 26.8 m (88 ft) high or more. This cutaway view shows the hollow roof as well as the south wall; the remaining church walls used rubble from the previous church left in ruins by wartime fighting in 1944. Opposite the seating area to the north of it is the open choir space. The rubble-wall multistorey spaces to the right include a chapel and sacristy. The doors at the end are confessional booths.

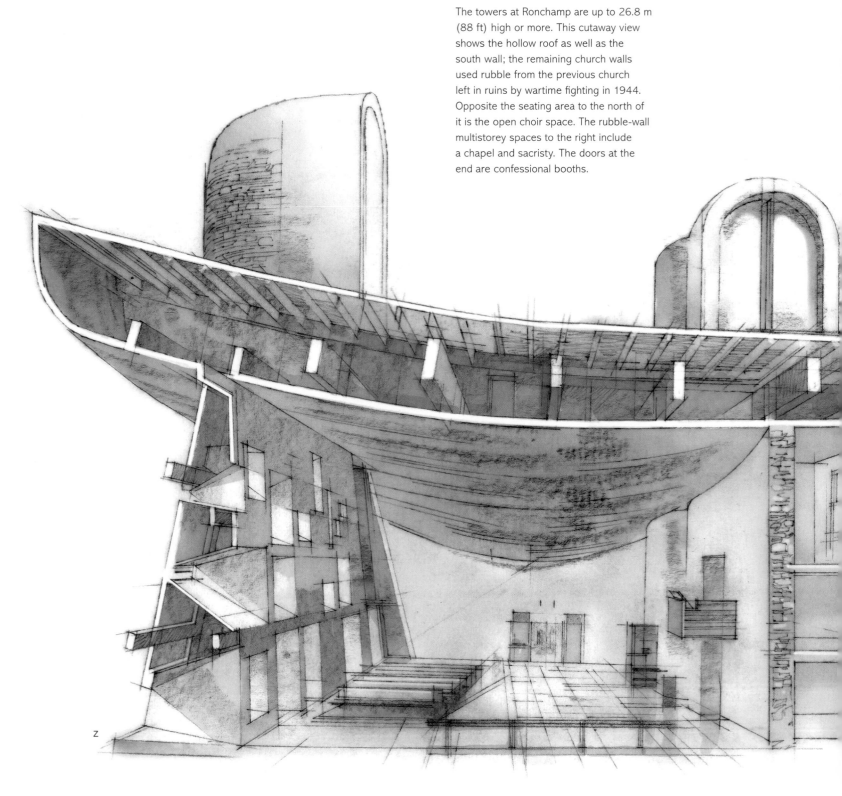

▼ FLOOR PLAN

The church is on a site that measures about 30 by 40 m (98 × 131 ft). It can accommodate 200 worshippers within. Outside on the east end, shown on the left of the plan, is an open space for more than 1,000 worshippers with an exterior altar. The curved tower spaces at the west end have chapels with confessionals niched within the wall. The plan also shows the main entry pivoting door on the southwest, as well as a smaller secondary door diagonally opposite on the north wall.

KEY
A Altar
B Choir
C Sacristy
D Main entrance
E South side chapel
F Confessionals
G West side chapel
H North entrance
I East side chapel
J East entrance
K Exterior altar and pulpit

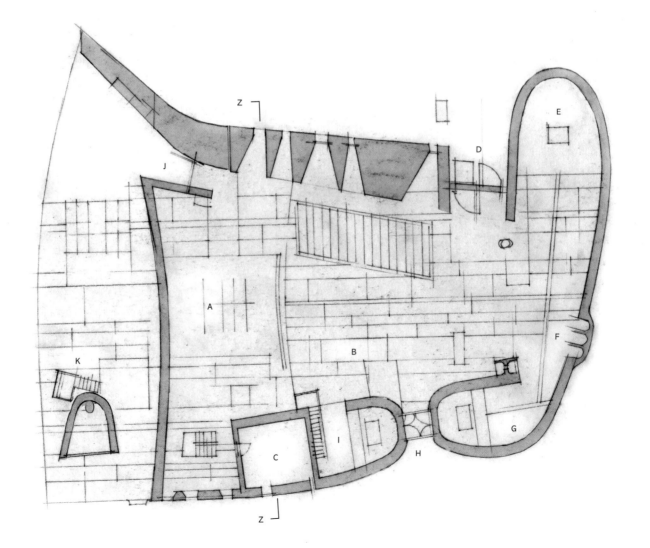

Sagrada Familia

LOCATION   Barcelona, Spain
ARCHITECT   Antoni Gaudí

STYLE   Individual
BUILT   Begun 1883

It may seem strange that the Sagrada Familia ends this chapter when it was begun in 1883. However, the completion is expected in 2026. This fourteen-decade-plus construction time is one of the sources of controversy that surrounds this structure. But when it comes to building timelines, it is worth remembering that some medieval cathedrals were also created over many decades. Construction of Cologne Cathedral, for example, began in 1248 and stopped over two centuries later in 1473, then resumed in the nineteenth century. The facade towers were completed to the

original design in 1880. Modern cathedrals are not exempt from such time frames. Washington National Cathedral, begun in 1907, was completed only in 1990. Others remain incomplete, such as St John the Divine in New York, begun in 1892 but whose design changed in 1909, earning it the nickname 'St John the Unfinished'. The Sagrada Familia is comparable to the latter because the design changed, though in this case from a predictably rational Gothic style to the personal, expressionist masterpiece seen today, still under construction.

Sagrada Familia, meaning 'Holy Family' (officially Basílica i Temple Expiatori de la Sagrada Família), was the life's passion and masterpiece of Antoni Gaudí (1852–1926). He graduated in 1878 from the Barcelona Higher School of Architecture, augmenting those studies while serving as a draughtsman. Although a mediocre student, Gaudí excelled in his own practice, which incorporated craft detailing and a love of natural forms; he created geometric abstractions of the latter in multicoloured ceramics that display Gothic, Asian and Islamic overtones. Some of his most famous early creations include the Güell Pavilions (1887) and Casa Vicens (1888), both in Barcelona. His own version of expressionistic naturalism can best be seen in Barcelona's Casa Batlló (1906), Casa Milà (1912) and Park Güell (1914).

Gaudí drew some of his buildings, but his passion for three-dimensionality made him prefer models and plaster casts, some of which still survive for Sagrada Familia. Although Gaudí began his own work on the church in 1883, he devoted much of his time from 1915 to 1926 to that project, becoming an increasingly devout Catholic. He reshaped the building from the preexisting traditional Gothic crypt of 1882 designed by Francisco de Paula del Villar y Lozano (1828–1901) to his more individual scheme, with his five-aisled nave envisioned as a forest of trees under a canopy of hyperboloid, or elliptical, vaults. The organic entry facades, particularly the Nativity facade of his own design, have expressionist sculptures related to his personal vision of what Gothic cathedrals should include. Gaudí's church plan incorporated a total of eighteen towers. His changing design for Sagrada Familia was informed by his own stylistic shift to a more organic architecture at the turn of the century, particularly in his unexecuted design for the Church of the Colònia Güell (1890–1918) near Barcelona and his proposed Hotel Attraction (1908) skyscraper in New York, whose multiple towers would have been 360 m (1,180 ft) high.

Gaudí was hit by a tram on 7 June 1926, and died several days later. This led to a continuation of work on Sagrada Familia under Gaudí's assistant, Domènec Sugrañes (1878–1938). Although Gaudí's workshop with models and drawings was ransacked during the Spanish Civil War (1936–39), work continued under a variety of architects including Lluís Bonet i Gari (1893–1993) and, more recently, his son Jordi Bonet i Armengol (b. 1925). The nave was completed in 2000, and 2006 saw the tower and crossing supports constructed, with one of the domed sacristies finished in 2016. The current chief architect, Jordi Faulí i Oller (b. 1959), estimates that the structure will be finished in 2026 with visitor-entry fees supporting the €25 million ($28 million) final cost.

ABOVE LEFT This is a detail of the Nativity Portal. Its sculptures were completed in 1905 under the direct supervision of Gaudí. This facade and the original crypt have been designated UNESCO World Heritage Sites.

ABOVE RIGHT Tree branch columns define the nave and expressionist vaults. The capitals are stylized equivalents of the knots and bark of *Platanus hispanica*, the London plane tree.

MEJORADA DEL CAMPO CATHEDRAL

Gaudí's lifelong work at Sagrada Familia likely inspired the 50 by 25-m (164 × 82-ft) cathedral of Mejorada del Campo. Justo Gallego Martínez (b. 1925) built it of scrap construction materials over fifty years. He is a former farmer, bullfighter, Trappist monk and self-taught architect–builder who has dedicated his life to building this church around 20 km (12 miles) from Madrid. He named it Nuestra Señora del Pilar, or Our Lady of the Pillar, relating to the Virgin's and Christ's appearance to the apostle St James the Greater as he was preaching in the Roman province of Hispania.

◄ HEIGHT

Multiple planned and partially executed towers define the church's profile. Of the eighteen planned, eight are complete. The highest one so far is a facade tower 106.9 m (351 ft) high, but the main Jesus Tower is planned to be some 170.6 m (560 ft) high. The other spires here are dedicated to the Virgin Mary as well as apostles. This drawing shows the complexity of the planned structures, with sepia-toned elements indicating the parts that are complete. This includes the original Nativity facade of 1905 designed by Gaudí, as well as one of the sacristies finished in 2016.

JESUS TOWER

The main tower dedicated to Jesus and buttressed, in a way, by the smaller surrounding towers bears a relationship to Gaudí's own design in 1908 for the parabolic towers of a skyscraper hotel in Lower Manhattan, to be built on the site of the later World Trade Center (1973; destroyed 2001). The Jesus Tower has progressed only to its base, which is essentially the crossing vault. In 2006 the crossing-vault concrete was ready to be poured within the formwork and reinforcing rods in place.

FLYING BUTTRESSES

Like many Gothic cathedrals, the church contains flying buttresses, though here they are more for aesthetic effect than structural necessity. The stacked gables of the nave clerestory walls are already constructed without the intended buttresses. The design of the latter features intersecting paraboloids for support.

SACRISTY

The sacristy was finished in 2016. This small multistorey tempietto is approximately 46 m (150 ft) high. It is used for an exhibition space displaying the building's history and relevant artefacts. A vintage maquette for the sacristy was published in 1951.

▶ FLOOR PLAN

What may seem like an irrational placement of architectural members on a rectilinear block shows a traditional, almost French cathedral plan within. A nave flanked by two aisles on each side is within a Latin cross plan, along with what would be traditional transepts, crossing, and choir or chevet with apsidal chapels beyond. The plan's orientation is akin to that of the perspective cutaway on the page opposite.

KEY
A Doorway of the Passion
B Doorway of the Nativity
C Doorway of Majesty
D Entrance
E Altar (Crypt below)
F Chapel of Resurrection
G Baptistery
H Chapel of the Sacrament

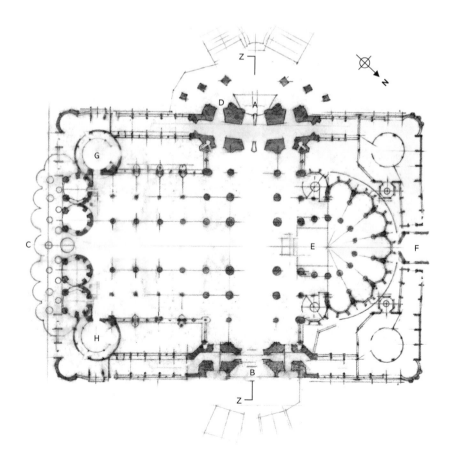

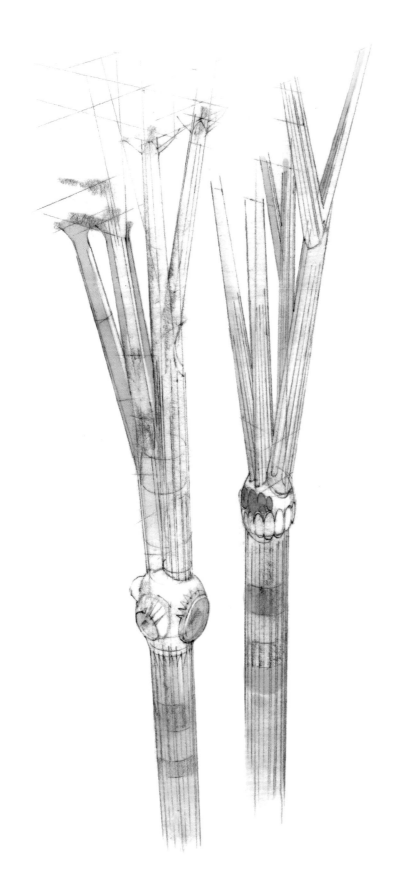

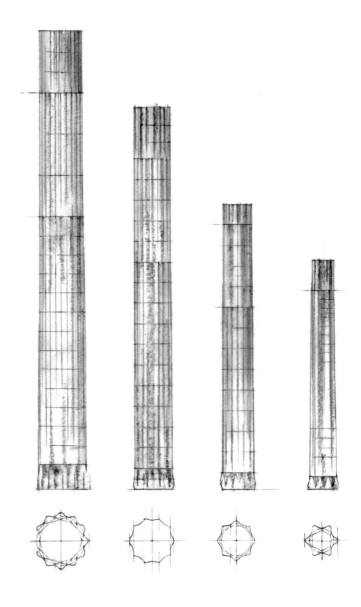

NAVE COLUMNS

Gaudí went through three design phases in his maquettes before finalizing the design of the columns with their distinctive nodelike capitals and expressive skeletal ribs. They were abstracted versions of natural sources, in this case the texture of *Platanus hispanica*, or the London plane tree. Tropical natural forms are found throughout the complex, from the rootlike columns and sculptures of the Passion facade (planned 1917; executed 1986 and later), which are based on kapok trees, and the scalloped turret tops that were inspired by aloe plants. Although Gaudí's maquettes are recorded in photographs and designs of these columns exist, CAD versions have been made to facilitate their construction as well as analyze the structural forces within.

Gaudí's drawings are somewhat impressionistic in execution, not overly sketchy (though some do exist), but rather expressive of detail and design. The drawn section here (marked as z on the plan on p. 291) captures some of that spirit. The spiky tower tops are indicated. The facade towers that have been built on the east and west sides have reflective minerals encrusted within their surfaces, such as pyrite, galena and fluorite, an extension of Gaudí's fascination with natural materials and forms as the basis of his architecture. An extensive full crypt is below the building's footprint.

Selected Sources

Nowadays, much of what anyone needs to learn about architecture can be found online, although traditional publications still offer invaluable information when it comes to in-depth study. As regards websites, rather than list URLs that can change over time, we encourage keyword searches related to subjects covered within this book. Of websites currently available, those on Robbie Polley, various contemporary architects whose work is published here, and organizations such as UNESCO's World Heritage Centre are invaluable, as are entries in Wikipedia and Encyclopedia Britannica. Many of the buildings that are museums, cultural organizations and historic landmarks also have their own websites. For any additional information, we have listed selected publications that are arranged according to this volume's sequence of sites. Comprehensive surveys of architecture are too numerous to list. They range from the venerable *A History of Architecture on the Comparative Method* by Sir Banister Fletcher (1896; numerous editions through 1996) to *Architecture: The Whole Story* (2014), edited by Denna Jones. These books and other relevant titles were located during the course of this research within the Ryerson and Burnham Libraries of The Art Institute of Chicago.

PUBLIC LIFE

Colosseum
Keith Hopkins and Mary Beard. *The Colosseum*. Cambridge, Massachusetts, 2005.

Palace of Diocletian
Iain Gordon Brown. *Monumental Reputation. Robert Adam & the Emperor's Palace*. Edinburgh, 1992.
Marco Navarra, ed. Robert Adam. *Ruins of the Palace of the Emperor Diocletian*, 1764. Cannitello, Italy, 2001.

Doge's Palace
Giandomenico Romanelli, ed. *Palazzo Ducale Storia e Restauri*. Verona, 2004.
Wolfgang Wolters. *The Doge's Palace in Venice*. Berlin, 2010.

Capitol Building
William C. Allen. *The Dome of the United States Capitol: An Architectural History*. Washington, D.C., 1992.
Henry Hope Reed. *The United States Capitol, Its Architecture and Decoration*. New York, 2005.

Chrysler Building
Donald L. Miller. *Supreme City*. New York, 2014.
David Stravitz. *The Chrysler Building: Creating a New York Icon*. New York, 2002.

Dulles International Airport
Jayne Merkel. *Eero Saarinen*. London, 2005.
John Zukowsky, ed. *Building for Air Travel*. Munich, 1996.

Palace of Assembly
H. Allen Brooks, ed. *The Le Corbusier Archive*, vols. XXII–XXV. New York, 1983.

Jaspreet Takhar, ed. *Celebrating Chandigarh. 50 Years of the Idea*. Chandigarh-Ahmedabad, 1999.

National Assembly Building of Bangladesh
Kazi Khaleed Ashraf and Saif Ul Haque, *Sherebanlanagar: Louis Kahn and the Making of a Capital Complex*. Dhaka, 2002.
Grischa Rüshchendorf. *Louis Kahn House of the Nation*. San Francisco, 2014.

Reichstag
Michael S. Cullen. *The Reichstag: German Parliament between Monarchy and Feudalism*. Berlin, 1999.
David Jenkins, ed. *Rebuilding the Reichstag*. London, 2000.

London Aquatics Centre
Yoshio Futagawa. *Zaha Hadid*. Tokyo, 2014.

World Trade Center Transit Hub
Joann Gonchar. 'Talk of the Town', *Architectural Record* (April 2016), 50–53.
Alexander Tzonis. *Santiago Calatrava. The Complete Works*. New York, 2011.

MONUMENTS

Parthenon
Jenifer Neils, ed. *The Parthenon: From Antiquity to the Present*. Cambridge, England, 2005.

Angkor Wat
Eleanor Mannikka. *Angkor Wat. Time, Space and Kingship*. Honolulu, 1996.
K.M. Srivastava. *Angkor Wat and Cultural Ties with India*. New Delhi, 1987.

Taj Mahal
Ebba Koch. *The Complete Taj Mahal*. London, 2006.

Palace of Versailles
Jean and Louis Faton. *La Galerie des Glaces. Histoire & Restauration*. Dijon, 2007.
James Arnot and John Wilson. *The Petit Trianon Versailles*. New York, 1929.

Monticello
Beth L. Cheuk. *Thomas Jefferson's Monticello*. Chapel Hill, North Carolina, 2002.
Susan R. Stein. *The Worlds of Thomas Jefferson at Monticello*. New York, 1993.

Einstein Tower
Norbert Huse, ed. *Mendelsohn, der Einsteinturm: die Geschichte einer Instandsetzung*. Stuttgart, 2000.

ARTS AND EDUCATION

Sir John Soane's Museum
Helene Mary Furján. *Glorious Visions: John Soane's Spectacular Theater*. New York, 2011.
Susan Palmer. *The Soanes at Home. Domestic Life at Lincoln's Inn Fields*. London, 1997.

Glasgow School of Art
William Buchanan, ed. *Mackintosh's Masterwork. The Glasgow School of Art*. Glasgow, 1989.

Bauhaus
C. Irrgang. *The Bauhaus Building in Dessau*. Leipzig, 2014.
Monika Margraf, ed. *Archäologie der Moderne : Sanierung Bauhaus Dessau*. Berlin, 2006.

Barcelona Pavilion
Franz Schulze. *Mies van der Rohe: A Critical Biography.* Chicago, 1985, rev. 2012.

Solomon R. Guggenheim Museum
Alan Hess. *Frank Lloyd Wright. Mid-Century Modern.* New York, 2007.

Berliner Philharmonie
Peter Blundell Jones. *Hans Scharoun.* London, 1995.
Wilfrid Wang and Daniel E. Sylvester, eds. *Hans Scharoun Philharmonie.* Berlin, 2013.

Kimbell Art Museum
Patricia Cummings Loud. *The Art Museums of Louis I. Kahn.* Durham, North Carolina, 1989.

Sydney Opera House
P. Murray. *The Saga of Sydney Opera House.* New York, 2004.

Centre Georges Pompidou
Kester Rattenbury and Samantha Hardingham. *Richard Rogers. The Pompidou Centre.* New York, 2012.

Grand Louvre
Philip Jodidio and Janet Adams Strong. *I.M. Pei Complete Works.* New York, 2008.
I.M. Pei and E.J. Biasini. *Les Grands Desseins du Louvre.* Paris, 1989.

Guggenheim Museum Bilbao
Coosje van Bruggen. *Frank O. Gehry, Guggenheim Museum Bilbao.* New York, 1998.

National Museum of African American History and Culture
Mabel Wilson. *Begin with the Past: Building of the National Museum of African American History and Culture.* Washington, D.C., 2016.
Okwui Enwezor and Zoë Ryan, in consultation with Peter Allison, eds. *David Adjaye: Form, Heft, Material.* Chicago, 2015.

LIVING

Hôtel-Dieu de Beaune
Nicole Veronee-Verhaegen. *L'Hôtel-Dieu de Beaune.* Brussels, 1973.

Villa Almerico-Capra – 'Villa La Rotonda'
Gian Antonio Golin. *La Rotonda: Andrea Palladio.* Venice, 2013.

Renato Cevese, Paola Marini, Maria Vittoria Pellizzari. *Andrea Palladio la Rotonda.* Milan, 1990.

Hôtel Tassel
François Loyer and Jean Delhaye. *Victor Horta: Hotel Tassel, 1893–1895.* Brussels, 1986.

Schröder House
Bertus Mulder. *Rietveld Schröder House.* New York, 1999.

Maison de Verre
Yukio Futagawa, ed. *Pierre Chareau Maison de Verre.* Tokyo, 1988.

Fallingwater
Lynda Waggoner, ed. *Fallingwater.* New York, 2011.

Villa Mairea
Göran Schildt. *The Architectural Drawings of Alvar Aalto 1917–1939, vol. 10.* New York, 1994.

Casa Luis Barragán
Luis Barragán. *Luis Barragan: His House.* Mexico City, 2011.

The Eames House
Elizabeth A.T. Smith. *Blueprints for Modern Living: History and Legacy of the Case Study Houses.* Los Angeles, 1989.
James Steele. *Eames House: Charles and Ray Eames.* London, 1994.

Nakagin Capsule Tower
Peter Cachola Schmal, Ingeborg Flagge, Jochen Visscher, eds. *Kisho Kurokawa: Metabolism and Symbiosis.* Berlin, 2005.

Absolute Towers
Ma Yansong. *MAD Works MAD Architects.* London, 2016.

WORSHIP

Hagia Sophia
Heinz Kähler and Cyril Mango. *Hagia Sophia.* New York, 1967.
Roland Mainstone. *Hagia Sophia.* London, 1988.

Mosque Cathedral of Córdoba
Antonio Fernández-Puertas. *Mezquita de Córdoba: su estudio arqueológico en el siglo XX.* Granada, 2009.
Gabriel Ruiz Cabrero. *Dibujos de la Catedral de Córdoba: Visiones de la Mezquita.* Cordoba and Madrid, 2009.

Chartres Cathedral
Philip Ball. *Universe of Stone: A Biography of Chartres Cathredral.* New York, 2008.
Brigitte Kurmann-Schwarz and Peter Kurmann. *Chartres: la cathédrale.* Saint-Léger-Vauban, 2001.

Temple of the Golden Pavilion
Jiro Murata. 'The Golden Pavilion', *Japan Architect* (March 1963), 90–97.

Florence Cathedral
Eugenio Battisti. *Brunelleschi: The Complete Work.* London, 1981.
Francesca Corsi Massi. *Il ballatoio interno della Cattedrale di Firenze.* Pisa, 2005.
Marvin Trachtenberg. *Giotto's Tower.* New York, 1971.

Batalha Monastery
Vergilio Correia. *Batalha. Estudo Historico-Artistico-Arqueologico do Mosteiro da Batalha.* Porto, 1929.
Ralf Gottschlich. *Das Kloster Santa Maria da Vitoría in Batalha und seine Stellung in der Iberischen Sakralarchitektur des Spätmittelalters.* Hildesheim, 2012.

St Peter's Basilica
Barbara Baldrati. *La Cupola di San Pietro. Il Metodo Costruttivo e il Cantiere.* Rome, 2014.
Paul Letarouilly. *The Vatican and Saint Peter's Basilica of Rome.* New York, 2010, orig. Paris, 1882.

St Paul's Cathedral
Derek Keene, Arthur Burns, Andrew Saint, eds. *St Paul's: The Cathedral Church of London, 604–2004.* New Haven, 2004.
Ann Saunders. *St Paul's Cathedral: 1400 Years at the Heart of London.* London, 2012.

Notre-Dame-du-Haut Chapel
Le Corbusier. *Ronchamp, Maisons Jaoul, and Other Buildings and Projects 1951–52.* New York and Paris, 1983.
Danièle Pauly. *Le Corbusier: La Chapelle de Ronchamp.* Paris and Boston, 1997.

Sagrada Familia
I. Puig Boada. *El Templo de la Sagrada Familia.* Barcelona, 1952.
Jordi Cussó i Anglès. *Disfrutar de la Naturaleza con Gaudí y la Sagrada Familia.* Lleida, 2010.
Nicolas Randall. *Sagrada Família: Gaudi's Opus Magnum.* Madrid, 2012.

Glossary

arch
A curved, open construction, whose lateral thrust on its two sides is contained by abutments. Open arches such as bridges require inward thrust to keep the ends from spreading, with anchorage provided by either natural (riverbanks, canyons) or artificial (buttresses) sources. Used in Western and Islamic architecture, types common to both include the pointed arch. Those more specific to Islamic architecture include the horseshoe and poly-lobed arches, while those particular to the West include the lancet, trefoil and Tudor.

baldachin
An interior canopy placed over a secular throne or religious altar. It can be suspended, free standing or projected from a wall.

Beaux-Arts
An eclectic style of the late nineteenth and early twentieth centuries that borrowed and adapted the monumentality and rich decorative detail of French architecture from the sixteenth to the nineteenth centuries.

brise soleil
A permanent sun-break feature used to shade windows (often vertical or horizontal fins, but also including open-patterned masonry blocks), particularly in hot climates. It was popularized by Le Corbusier, but has roots in vernacular Islamic architecture.

buttress
A masonry or brickwork mass that supports a wall. Buttress types include 'clasping', which creates a flush embrace to a building angle, and 'flying', which is an arch or half-arch brace that repels the building's outward thrust. More basic buttresses include timber planks wedged at 45-degree angles against walls.

cella
The inner area of an ancient Greek or Roman temple, which housed the image of the deity. Also known as the naos.

chhatri
A dome-shaped pavilion on the roof of a building. It is commonly associated with Indian architecture, particularly the Rajput architecture of Rajasthan.

ciborium
An interior canopy over a Christian altar that is supported on columns. It is similar to the baldachin.

clerestory
A windowed area in the upper part of a church nave, above the aisle roofs. Its unimpeded location enables light to infiltrate the interior. The term is also used to describe similar arrangements that are found in secular buildings and domestic architecture.

exedra
An outdoor bench in a semicircular or rectangular recess. It can also refer to the apse of a church or to a niche therein.

formwork
Also known as 'shuttering', formwork is a temporary or permanent mould that holds and shapes poured concrete until it cures to create precast concrete. The formwork's texture, particularly timber, will imprint on the concrete. Intentional textures and raised-profile finishes are created with bespoke formliners placed inside the mould.

gambrel
A roof with two sides, each of which has two slopes. On both sides a shallower slope sits above a steeper one.

gunite
A mixture of cement, sand and water that is sprayed through a pressure hose, producing a dense, hard layer of concrete.

High-Tech
A style of architecture inspired by the materials and techniques associated with engineering and other technologies. The term was adopted from the interior design book *High Tech: The Industrial Style and Source Book for the Home* (1978) by Joan Kron and Suzanne Slesin, and replaced the 'Industrial Style' label that was used to describe such architecure in the 1970s.

International Style
An architectural style that emphasized form over social context, as first defined by Henry Russell Hitchcock and Philip Johnson in 1932. Lasting from approximately 1925 to 1965, the style emerged from the European Modernist movement and the Bauhaus. Focus then shifted to the United States, from where the style was exported globally. Influential typologies include the corporate skyscraper.

mansard roof
A double slope roof where the lower slope on each of its four sides is taller and more acutely angled than the smaller four-sided upper slope, whose lower pitch can conceal it from casual observation. The design is characteristic of the French Renaissance and was a common feature of nineteenth-century Second Empire architecture in France.

metopes
A square space between the triglyphs of a Doric frieze, often decorated with carved work.

naos
See *cella*.

narthex
A general term for the antechurch (porch) at the entrance of a medieval Christian church. Two types of narthex are found in Byzantine churches: the esonarthex, which precedes the nave and aisles, and the exonarthex, which precedes the facade. For both types, the division is made clear by columns, rails or a wall between the zones.

oculus (plural oculi)
A circular opening located at the apex of a dome.

opisthodomos
The room positioned at the rear of an ancient Greek temple, farthest from the main entrance.

piano nobile
The main floor of a grand house, containing public reception rooms. Generally it is located on a raised ground floor and has higher ceilings than the storeys above.

pilotis
Pillars, columns or stilts that support the raised floor of a building, leaving open circulation beneath. Popularized by Le Corbusier, their origins lie in vernacular architecture. Variations include Brazilian architect Oscar Niemeyer's V-shaped and W-shaped pilotis.

pishtaq
A prominent projecting gateway or portal of a mosque, often an arched doorway set within a flat rectangular 'frame'. It served to emphasize a building's presence.

pronaos
An anteroom at the front of an ancient Greek temple, forming a portico immediately in front of the cella.

quadriga
A two-wheeled chariot drawn by four horses abreast.

reinforced concrete
A type of concrete in which metal bars or wire are embedded to increase its tensile strength.

Serlian window
A three-part window consisting of a central window with an arched head flanked on either side by a usually narrower window with a square head. It is named after Sebastiano Serlio, who described the design in *L'architettura* (1537). It is also known as a Palladian window, as similar openings were common in the work of Andrea Palladio.

tempietto
A small, temple-like building, often circular.

trabeated system
A basic construction method also known as the post-and-lintel system, where two upright posts support a bridging horizontal lintel across their top surfaces.

triforium
An arcade above the arches of the nave of a church, forming an upper storey to the aisle between the nave and the clerestory.

tympanum
The semi-circular or triangular area above a doorway, bounded by a lintel and arch. It is often decorated with relief sculpture.

Greek Architectural Orders

The columns in ancient Greek buildings fall into three distinct architectural orders: Doric, Ionic and Corinthian.

Doric

The Doric order was established by the first quarter of the sixth century BCE and was characterized by a fluted column that rested directly on the floor of the temple without a base, topped by a plain, unadorned capital.

Ionic

The Ionic order originated in Ionia (today part of Turkey) during the mid-sixth century BCE, and featured a slimmer profile with a greater number of flutes on the pillar. The bottom of the column rested on a moulded base, while the capital at the top was decorated with volutes (scroll-like ornaments).

Corinthian

The Corinthian order developed in the fifth century BCE and went on to become the favoured style of the Romans. It was distinguished by its elaborate capital, which was carved with two staggered rows of stylized acanthus leaves and four scrolls.

Index

Picture Credits

Illustrations by Robbie Polley. Photographs supplied by the following sources:

(Key: top = **t**; bottom = **b**; left = **l**; right = **r**; centre = **c**; top left = **tl**; top right = **tr**; centre left = **cl**; centre right = **cr**; bottom left = **bl**; bottom right = **br**)

2 Architectural Images/Alamy Stock Photo **12** Fotofeeling/Getty Images **15** James Ewing/OTTO Archive **16** Denis Polyakov/Alamy Stock Photo **17t** phxart.org/Wikimedia Commons **17bl** Evan Reinheimer/Getty Images **17br** J. Pie/Alamy Stock Photo **22** Mrak.hr/Shutterstock **23tl** DEA Picture Library/Getty Images **23bl** Tuomas Lehtinen/Alamy Stock Photo **23r** Peter Noyce ITA/Alamy Stock Photo **28** @Didier Marti/Getty Images **29tl** Roland Liptak/Alamy Stock Photo **29tr** dominic dibbs/Alamy Stock Photo **29b** Photo by H.N. Tiemann/The New York Historical Society/Getty Images **34** © Corbis/VCG/Getty Images **35tl** Thornton, William, Architect. [U.S. Capitol, Washington, D.C. East elevation, low dome]. Washington D.C, None. [Between 1793 and 1800] Photograph. Retrieved from the Library of Congress, https://www.loc.gov/item/92519533/ **35bl** Irene Abdou/Alamy Stock Photo **35r** Photo by Library of Congress/Corbis/VCG via Getty Images **38** Cameron Davidson/Getty Images **39l** Elizabeth Wake/Alamy Stock Photo **39c** Nathan Benn/Corbis via Getty Images **39r** Iconic New York/Alamy Stock Photo **44** Connie Zhou/OTTO Archive **45tl** Balthazar Korab/OTTO Archive **45tr** Granger Historical Picture Archive/Alamy Stock Photo **45b** Connie Zhou/OTTO Archive **48** James Ewing/OTTO Archive **49t** (c) Stephane Couturier/Artedia/VIEW **49b** ITAR-TASS Photo Agency/Alamy Stock Photo **54** David Greedy/Lonely Planet Images/Getty Images **55t** VIEW Pictures Ltd/Alamy Stock Photo **55bl** Phillip Harrington/Alamy Stock Photo **55br** Majority World/UIG via Getty Images **58** (c) Werner Huthmacher/Artur/VIEW **59tl** VIEW Pictures Ltd/Alamy Stock Photo **59tr** dpa picture alliance/Alamy Stock Photo **59b** akg-images/Alamy Stock Photo **64** Hufton+Crow/Corbis Documentary/Getty Images **65tl** Hufton+Crow/Corbis Documentary/Getty Images **65tr** View Pictures/REX/Shutterstock **65b** Loop Images Ltd/Alamy Stock Photo **70** James Ewing/OTTO Archive **71tl** Peter Aaron/OTTO Archive **71tr** Leonardo Mascaro/Alamy Stock Photo **71b** Kim Karpeles/Alamy Stock Photo **76** Pakawat Thongcharoen/Moment/Getty Images **79** charistoone-travel/Alamy Stock Photo **80** Ren Mattes/hemis.fr/Getty Images **81t** Nick Dale/Design Pics/Getty Images **81bl** akg-images/Peter Connolly **81br** Brian Jannsen/Alamy Stock Photo **86** Boy_Anupong/Moment/Getty Images **87t** imageBROKER/Alamy Stock Photo **87bl** Robert Holmes/Alamy Stock Photo **87br** VW Pics/Universal Images Group/Getty Images **92** Wildviews/Charles Tomalin/Alamy Stock Photo **93tl** Diana Mayfield/Lonely Planet Images/Getty Images **93tr** david pearson/Alamy Stock Photo **93b** khairel anuar che ani/Moment/Getty Images **96** Guillaume Baptiste/AFP/Getty Images **97tl** Hemis/Alamy Stock Photo **97tr** Loop Images/Tiara Anggamulia/Passage/Getty Images **97b** Kalpana Kartik/Alamy Stock Photo **102** Albert Knapp/Alamy Stock Photo **103tl** Buddy Mays/Alamy Stock Photo **103tr** Evan Sklar/Alamy Stock Photo **103b** Philip Scalia/Alamy Stock Photo **108** akg-images/Bildarchiv Monheim/Opitz **109t** Photo Scala, Florence/bpk, Bildagentur fuer Kunst, Kultur und Geschichte, Berlin **109c** ullstein bild/ullstein bild via Getty Images **109b** Photo Scala, Florence/bpk, Bildagentur fuer Kunst, Kultur und Geschichte, Berlin **112** Brad Feinknopf/OTTO Archive **114** Jannis Werner/Alamy Stock Photo **116** Mark Lucas/Alamy Stock Photo **117t** Arcaid Images/Alamy Stock Photo **117bl** Mieneke Andeweg-van Rijn/Alamy Stock Photo **117br** Archimage/Alamy Stock Photo **122** John Peter Photography/Alamy Stock Photo **123tl** Leemage/Universal Images Group/Getty Images **123tr** VIEW Pictures Ltd/Alamy Stock Photo **123b** John Peter Photography/Alamy Stock Photo **126** ullstein bild/Getty Images **127tl** Ton Kinsbergen/Arcaid Images **127tr** Jannis Werner/Alamy Stock Photo **127b** LianeM/Alamy Stock Photo **130** imageBROKER/Alamy Stock Photo **131t** Campillo Rafael/Alamy Stock Photo **131c** imageBROKER/Alamy Stock Photo **131b** Arthur Siegel/The LIFE Images Collection/Getty Images **134** imageBROKER/Alamy Stock Photo **135tl** Art Kowalsky/Alamy Stock Photo **135tr** Peter Aaron/OTTO Archive **135b** Historic American Buildings Survey, Creator, Frank Lloyd Wright, and V C Morris. V.C. Morris Store, 140 Maiden Lane, San Francisco, San Francisco County, CA. California San Francisco San Francisco County, 1933. Documentation Compiled After. Photograph. Retrieved from the Library of Congress, https://www.loc.gov/item/ca1392/ **140tl** View Pictures/Universal Images Group/Getty Images **140bl** akg-images/euroluftbild.de/bsf swissphoto **141** Iain Masterton/Alamy Stock Photo **146** Ian G Dagnall/Alamy Stock Photo **147t** Richard Barnes/OTTO Archive **147b** Randy Duchaine/Alamy Stock Photo **150** Michael Dunning/Photographer's Choice/Getty Images **151tl** Ivo Antonie de Rooij/Shutterstock **151tr** Blaine Harrington III/Alamy Stock Photo **151b** French+Tye/Bournemouth News/REX/Shutterstock **156** Connie Zhou/OTTO Archive **157tl** Atlantide Phototravel/Corbis Documentary/Getty Images **157tr** Hemis/Alamy Stock Photo **157** Photononstop/Alamy Stock Photo **162** Sebastien GABORIT/Moment/Getty Images **163tl** Richard I'Anson/Lonely Planet Images/Getty Images **163tr** Hemis/Alamy Stock Photo **163b** nobleIMAGES/Alamy Stock Photo **168** Kevin Schafer/Corbis Documentary/Getty Images **169tl** View Pictures/Universal Images Group/Getty Images **169tr** Senior Airman Christophe/age fotostock/Superstock **169b** Art Streiber/OTTO Archive **174** REUTERS/Alamy Stock Photo **175tl** Brad Feinknopf/OTTO Archive **175tr** Brad Feinknopf/OTTO Archive **175b** Buyenlarge/Archive Photos/Getty Images **181** Danica Kus/OTTO Archive **182** Peter Aaron/OTTO Archive **184** JAUBERT French Collection/Alamy Stock Photo **185tl** Pol M.R. Maeyaert/Bildarchiv-Monheim/Arcaid Images **185tr** Hemis/Alamy Stock Photo **185b** Wikimedia Commons **188** David Madison/Photographer's Choice/Getty Images **189tl** Bildarchiv Monheim GmbH/Alamy Stock Photo **189tr** Fabio Zoratti/Getty Images **189b** Pat Tuson/Alamy Stock Photo **192** Karl Stas/Wikimedia Commons, CC-BY-SA-3.0 **193tl** © Our Place The World Heritage Collection **193tr** © Our Place The World Heritage Collection **193b** Charles LUPICA/Alamy Stock Photo **196** Arcaid Images/Alamy Stock Photo **197tr** Anton Havelaar/Shutterstock **197cl** Digital image, The Museum of Modern Art, New York/Scala, Florence **197b** Image & copyright: Centraal Museum Utrecht/Kim Zwarts 2005 **200** © Rene Burri/Magnum Photos **201tl** © Rene Burri/Magnum Photos **201tr** Arcaid Images/Alamy Stock Photo **201b** Digital image, The Museum of Modern Art, New York/Scala, Florence **206** Connie Zhou/OTTO Archive **207tl** Wim Wiskerke/Alamy Stock Photo **207bl** HABS PA,26-OHPY.V,1--93 (CT), Library of Congress Prints and Photographs Division Washington, D.C. 20540 USA http://hdl.loc.gov/loc.pnp/pp.print **207r** Alfred Eisenstaedt/The LIFE Picture Collection/Getty Images **210** Lehtikuva Oy/REX/Shutterstock **211l** Lehtikuva Oy/REX/Shutterstock **211r** Arcaid Images/Alamy Stock Photo **214** Peter Aaron/OTTO Archive **215tl** Peter Aaron/OTTO Archive **215cl** Peter Aaron/OTTO Archive **215br** Arcaid Images/Alamy Stock Photo **220** Walter Bibikow/Photolibrary/Getty Images **221t** EWA Stock/Superstock **221b** Peter Stackpole/The LIFE Picture Collection/Getty Images **224** Arcaid Images/Alamy Stock Photo **225l** urbzoo/Wikimedia Commons, CC-BY-2.0 **225r** Paul Almasy/Corbis Historical/Getty Images **230** VIEW Pictures Ltd/Alamy Stock Photo **231t** VIEW Pictures Ltd/Alamy Stock Photo **231b** Lucas Museum of Narrative Art/ZUMA Wire/REX/Shutterstock **234** Thoom/Shutterstock **237** Pascal Saez/VWPics/Alamy Stock Photo **238** Ali Kabas/Corbis Documentary/Getty Images **239tl** Ayhan Altun/Alamy Stock Photo **239bl** Siegfried Layda/The Image Bank/Getty Images **239r** Science History Images/Alamy Stock Photo **244** Benny Marty/Alamy Stock Photo **245tl** Gonzalo Azumendi/Photolibrary/Getty Images **245tr** John Turp/Moment/Getty Images **245b** Perry van Munster/Alamy Stock Photo **250** Arnaud Chicurel/hemis.fr/Getty Images **251tr** Photo (C) BnF, Dist. RMN-Grand Palais/image BnF **251bl** Martin Siepmann/imageBROKER/REX/Shutterstock **251br** funkyfood London - Paul Williams/Alamy Stock Photo **256** Joshua Davenport/Alamy Stock Photo **257tl** Mariusz Prusaczyk/Alamy Stock Photo **257tr** Alex Timaios Japan Photography/Alamy Stock Photo **257b** David Clapp/Photolibrary/Getty Images **260** Panther Media GmbH/Alamy Stock Photo **261l** Cristina Stoian/Alamy Stock Photo **261r** Gunter Kirsch/Alamy Stock Photo **266** © Aiisha/Dreamstime **267tl** Florian Kopp/imageBROKER/REX/Shutterstock **267tr** GM Photo Images/Alamy Stock Photo **267b** British Library/Robana/REX/Shutterstock **270** Eric Vandeville/Gamma-Rapho/Getty Images **271tl** Mark Williamson/Stockbyte/Getty Images **271bl** imageBROKER/Alamy Stock Photo **271r** De Agostini Picture Library/Getty Images **276** Peter Macdiarmid/Getty Images News/Getty Images **277l** Ludovic Maisant/hemis.fr/Getty Images **277r** VIEW Pictures Ltd/Alamy Stock Photo **282** Oleg Mitiukhin/Alamy Stock Photo **283tl** Annet van der Voort/Bildarchiv-Monheim/Arcaid Images **283tr** Bildarchiv Monheim GmbH/Alamy Stock Photo **283b** Michel Sima/Archive Photos/Getty Images **288** GlobalVision Communication/GlobalFlyCam/Moment/Getty Images **289tl** Travel Library Limited/Superstock **289tr** Panther Media GmbH/Alamy Stock Photo **289b** Senior Airman Christophe/age fotostock/SuperstockWW

First published in the United Kingdom in 2018 by
Thames & Hudson Ltd, 181A High Holborn,
London WC1V 7QX

www.thamesandhudson.com

© 2018 Quarto Publishing plc

This book was designed and produced by
Quintessence Editions, an imprint of The Quarto Group
The Old Brewery
6 Blundell Street
London N7 9BH

Senior Editor	Elspeth Beidas
Editors	Carol King, Juliet Lecouffe
Senior Designer	Isabel Eeles
Design Assistance	Josse Pickard
Production Manager	Anna Pauletti
Editorial Director	Ruth Patrick
Publisher	Philip Cooper

British Library Cataloguing-in-Publication Data
A catalogue record for this book is available from the British Library

ISBN 978-0-500-34337-1

Printed in China

To find out about all our publications, please visit **www.thamesandhudson.com**.
There you can subscribe to our e-newsletter, browse or download our current
catalogue, and buy any titles that are in print.